God and Violence

The Christian Experience of God in Dialogue with Myths and Other Religions

Georg Baudler

Translated from the German
by
Fabian C. Lochner

Templegate Publishers
Springfield, Illinois

This book was originally published in German under the title
ERLÖSUNG VOM STIERGOTT

© 1989 Kösel Verlag, München und Calwer Verlag, Stuttgart

English translation © 1992 by Templegate Publishers

ISBN 0-87243-193-2

Library of Congress Catalog Card Number
91-68344

Templegate Publishers
302 East Adams Street
P.O. Box 5152
Springfield, Illinois 62705

*To my granddaughter
Lisa Lea*

It is only in the perspective of a world history of religions that the significance of any single religion, as well as the state of its evolution, can come into full focus.

Wolfhart Pannenberg,
Wissenschaftstheorie und Theologie,
Frankfurt 1977, 364.

Our senses and passions speak and understand nothing but images. In images lies the whole treasure of human experience and bliss.

Johann Georg Hamann,
Complete Works (critical edition by J. Nadler),
Vienna 1949-1953, vol. II, 197.

Translator's note: Throughout the text the author follows the usage of the Martin Buber/Franz Rosenzweig translation of the Hebrew Bible into German in which Yahweh's answer to Moses' question about his name as given in Exod. 3:14 ("What is his name? What shall I tell them?") is "Tell them: I-will-be-there sends me to you." Readers are referred to "Now These Are the Names: A New English Rendition of the Book of Exodus" by Everett Fox (Schocken Books; New York) in which he says that the Buber/Rosenzweig translation has served as a close model for his work. In his commentary on these passages from Exodus Fox says: "In our text, Moshe refuses the commission (that he should go to Pharaoh) five times, and five times God counters. In four of these cases the assurance is given that God will 'be there' with him (3;12,14;4:12,15), and the use of that verb carries in its essence one of the most significant motifs of the Bush Narrative: the interpretation of God's name."

F.C.L.

Georg Baudler, born in 1936, is professor of theology on the philosophical faculty of the Rhineland-Westphalia Technical College at Aachen.

Table of Contents

Preface

The incentives which led me to undertake the present book can be traced to the beginning of my scholarly work. On the one hand, I learned from my dissertation on the linguistic philosophy of Johann Georg Hamann (Immanuel Kant's contemporary and fellow-countryman at Königsberg), directed by Karl Rahner, that "the whole treasure of human knowledge and happiness" is hidden neither in theoretical nor in practical reason, but—preceding both—in language, in its images and metaphors. Ultimately, the history of the redemption and salvation of mankind is to be sought in a history of those *images and symbols*. On the other hand, I began my theological research and pedagogy at a time when religious educators realized that the crisis in the transmission of Christian faith—which had become acutely manifest for the first time in a widespread withdrawal from religious education in schools—could only be overcome if the content of that faith were to be successfully read and articulated as a symbolic and metaphorical expression of experience that was plausible and relevant to everyone. It was clear from the beginning that this task could not be confined to religious education and pastoral care alone. All the disciplines of theology were challenged, particularly theology's dialogue with the Humanities. In conversations with Hermann Seifermann (at that time a scholar of the Old Testament) whose colleague I was when I worked at the Institut für Katechik und Homiletik in Munich in 1971, as well as in his lectures, I first encountered an experiential dimension of the God of the Old Testament that was rooted in the histories of culture and religion, and, at the same time, had existential relevance.

From that point, it was a long, meandering way to the present book. The fact that the two impulses mentioned above were fused into the idea of this book is due to my friend and collaborator, Dr. Egon Spiegel. Widely acclaimed in the theological field of peace studies for his works on non-violence and deeply engaged in the Christian peace movement, he opened my eyes to the significance of René Girard's interpretations of myths. This approach, in conjunction with the works of Walter Burkert, provided the focal point around which the present dialogue between the Christian experience of God and mythologies and religions crystallized and could be developed. Egon Spiegel has critically reviewed the book in all of its phases and enriched it considerably with his stimulating suggestions.

This book stands at the crossroads of theology and cultural anthropology, and thus takes up the principle of correlation formulated by recent religious pedagogy. Questions of cultural anthropology have preoccupied me ever since I began my research. In this area, my brother Rudi Baudler has been a source of great stimulation. Of course, the questions, methods, and insights of this area of knowledge are numerous. Accordingly, one can be a specialist in only one field. Any attempt to view this field, so devoid of empirical boundaries, in its entirety can only be of an interdisciplinary (both philosophical and theological) nature. And yet this approach is fully legitimate since man pursues the meaning of the whole even in times of the greatest scientific specialization. This book does not venture into specific research in the history of civilization or cultural anthropology. Rather, it develops a possible Christian answer to the question of the meaning and goal of mankind's cultural and religious history.

I am grateful to the two publishers who, from the very beginning, have shown a keen interest in the idea of the book and have thus encouraged me. In long talks with me and with Egon Spiegel, Winfrid Nonhoff of Kösel Verlag has seen the manuscript develop and offered his kind help with many difficult editorial problems.

Finally, the efficient staff of our seminar — from Angelika Weingärtner to the many student assistants — lent their support to the project and were instrumental in delivering the manuscript on time. I would also like to thank Dr. Friedrich Trzaskalik, my colleague at the seminar for many years, for his great help in proofreading.

Aachen, June 1989   Georg Baudler

Introduction:

The symbolic experience of reality as the foundation for a dialogue between Christians and the cultural and religious history of mankind

1 The Intention and the method

On the Intention:

Our world has grown small. This holds true especially for the encounter between different religions. At school, for example, we often find Christian children sitting next to very fervent young Muslims, who courageously renounce the tempting grilled sausage on the school trip — much to the amazement of our children. Only a few hours of flight separate the cathedral of Cologne and the Jaina temple in Calcutta, on which is written in big letters: "Not to kill is the highest religion"; or those temples of Shiva where, instead of the consecrated bread, the representation of a vulva and phallus are kept in the innermost sanctuary. In the valley of the Dordogne in France and in the Pyrenees of Northern Spain, huge crowds of tourists pour daily into the "cathedrals of the Stone Age," into those large caves of Lascaux and Altamira which were decorated with colorful pictures of beasts and humans by prehistoric people more than 20,000 years ago, obviously for cultic use and for the performance of their religious rites (Fig. 30). An affordable charter flight takes us to Crete in two and a half hours, where more or less knowledgeable guides lead us through the maze of the Minoan palace of Knossos and tell us about Cretan mother-goddesses who were worshipped several thousand years before Christ.

What does it mean when we speak of "God" in this context? What "God" do we mean? Or don't the expressive cultic bulls of Lascaux, and the potent Hindu god Shiva, and the serpent goddess of Crete (Fig. 46) have anything to do with that Being whom we Christians invoke for our personal needs, and whom we address in our liturgical ceremonies as "God"? Is it an abuse of language to use for all of those different phenomena the words "God," "religion," "prayer," "cult"? Does not the Second Vatican Council recognize explicitly that "from the oldest times until our day there is among different peoples a certain perception of that hidden power which is present in the affairs of the world and in the events of human life"?[1] The Council even emphasizes that it is necessary in our time, "in which the human race draws closer together every day and the relations between the people multiply," to rethink and to re-evaluate the relation between the Church and non-Christian religions (of both the past and the present).[2]

But nowadays such a reevaluation is not only a task for the church and for theologians. Indeed, a certain recognition has begun to dawn, especially in the Western industrialized nations, and now also in countries with communist governments. That is that natural science, technology, and a purely rational structuring of social and political life are missing an essential dimension of human existence and therefore, in the long run, cannot respond adequately to its needs.[3] An important event in this respect was the disaster at Chernobyl. In the New-Age movement and related spiritual movements of our time, people strive to recover the trans-empirical reality that had for years been disregarded and try to enter into contact with it—although they very often capsize into anti-rationalism. Hence there arises from all sides a new appreciation of myths, of fairy tales, and of religions: They always were, and still are, an expression of man's communication with that trans-empirical reality.

Whoever turns his attention toward these phenomena runs the risk of drowning in an ocean of irritating images, symbols, and paradoxes. Everything appears similar and related, but yet very different, sometimes contradictory, and it is very difficult to define this field, or to gain an overview of it. For some, this fact is precisely what makes man happy and leads him towards his true destination. But history has taught us that surrendering to an ocean of dreams and feelings has often led to a sobering awakening. We must take seriously everything that speaks to us in images, myths, and divine symbols, accepting them as reality, but we must not overreact against the former blind faith in science and make the opposite mistake of renouncing the search for solid structure and rationally responsible orientation within the apparent overflow of trans-empirical reality.

On the Method:

The path towards such an orientation, structured in a Christian way, is to be found in a historical approach to religious phenomena in the form of a dialogue. On the one hand, this approach is rational. It looks for plausible structures in the flow of events and tries to show the direction which certain developments have taken, and whether, from their results, they should be viewed as good and purposeful, or as harmful to human life. On the other hand, we cannot achieve our goal if we make an exclusive use of rational, analytic, or empirical, descriptive approaches to the historical phenomena. We have to let them act upon us in a holistic way, and try to empathize with them in an existential way. However, given the boundless riches of these trans-empirical (religious) phenomena, the method just described is not yet sufficient to provide us with an actual orientation. It is true that the scientific phenomenology of religions has provided valuable insights that have opened up our understanding of the world of religion in a new way. But precisely the sheer wealth of the materials made available in this manner seems to call for a broader orientation that would help place the individual phenomena within a whole.

We may see a first attempt in this direction in C.G. Jung's interpretation of myths, fairy tales and religious phenomena as an expression of archetypal structures located in a collective human unconscious. Here, the structure of the human psyche, as Jung, a physician and therapist, encountered it through the conversations and dreams of his patients, provides a referential framework that allows us to put the multiplicity of phenomena into a certain order. Jung was also able to identify a goal for the path that took his patients through the years of the process of healing their psychological illnesses. He described it as "individuation," or the "process of becoming oneself." Thus he could give a certain evaluation of the different forms of the unconscious. A man who meets women in his dreams more in the guise of a Mona Lisa, of the Greek goddess Athena, or of the Holy Virgin seems more advanced in his process of individuation, of becoming himself, than one who thinks and dreams of women predominantly in images of devouring witches, terrifying Gorgons, or sirens of merely sexual attraction.[4]

This concept is useful in the context in which it was developed by Jung, namely the intimate relationship between a human being and a therapist. But it is doomed to fail if applied to the understanding and ordering of the entire religious and cultural history.[5] Many aspects of such an endeavor could be criticized.[6] If we want to concede a proper value, a proper existence and life to those religious and trans-empirical phenomena — which we will develop later — then the following point seems of particular relevance: The ground of reality of these phenomena is, according to Jung, the human psyche, as it is described empirically, within the categories of natural science. They live and act according to the laws of the psyche and of psychic development that are to be delineated empirically.[7] Thus Jung remains in fact within the framework of *Religionskritik* that originated with Feuerbach and Freud, in which religious phenomena are explained as mere projections of the psyche. Jung goes further than Freud insofar as he attributes those phenomena not only to the individual unconscious, but introduces the notion of a "collective unconscious." But in doing so, he defines the psyche itself as a trans-empirical, quasi-religious phenomenon, building a sort of meta-religion above the individual religious phenomena, without, however, rooting that notion in a genuine historical tradition of religious thought and feeling. The dangerous effect of such non-historical religious images and categories, created from nothing, can be seen when we realize that this central Jungian category of the "collective unconscious," was eventually sucked into Nazi ideology. In 1934, Jung published an article on "The Present State of Psychotherapy" in which he distinguished between an "Aryan unconscious" and a "Jewish unconscious," depicting the latter as decadent and parasitical.[8]

This example shows that an orientation in the consuming multiplicity of religious images and phenomena cannot be gained by building a "meta-religion," a sort of religious Esperanto. For insofar as a religion has not grown genuinely and historically from basic religious experiences, it will remain an intellectual construct and cannot provide strength and solidity to individuals or societies in times of crisis, as can a religion that has grown historically. Not by raising ourselves above each of the historically grown myths or religions, but rather by searching for a *dialogue* with different (often strange) phenomena from *within* a particular religious tradition — normally the one into which we ourselves are placed by birth or by conviction — can we hope to achieve clarity and orientation. The word "dialogue" in this context presupposes that we will not establish our own religion beforehand as a "meta-religion" that surpasses all others in ethos and truth, and therefore has the right to judge all the others by a critical evaluation "from on high."

In history, and to the present day, there have always been religions which viewed their relation towards other religions in these terms, and which did not hesitate to implement their claims of truth by resorting to violence (whether gross violence or a more subtle form). This attitude weighs with special heaviness on the history of Christianity.[9] The question of the relation between the Christian faith and other religions has a long history which unfortunately, like religious history in general, has not only been written in ink, but also in blood and tears. This is not the place to recapitulate this history, neither on a factual nor on a speculative level. In principle, the Second Vatican Council has paved the way within the Catholic church for a relation of dialogue and understanding with other religions. Many theologians and missionaries have reformulated their formerly exclusive claims, reexamining them from a new perspective of Christian dogma and religious history.[10]

The formula "orientation through dialogue" marks a position that characterizes the exchange between religions today that is increasingly adopted within Christianity itself.[11] The present project fits into that context but specifically emphasizes the dimension of historic experience within that dialogue. We will not be concerned with different concepts and representations of God, with expectations of afterlife or with ethical attitudes, but solely with the question of how man experiences transempirical reality, and how he has reacted to it historically, as we find it spelled out in the rites, symbols, myths and fairy tales of religious history.

Such an experiential and historical approach will bring to the forefront certain phenomena that, traditionally, seemed to have nothing or little to do with religion, or, indeed, with the Christian faith. Thus, the transition of man from gatherer to game hunter, the cave-art of the prehistoric hunters, their use of fire, the progression to a sedentary lifestyle, the earliest foundings of states, insights from ethnology and behavioral science, the Minoan civilization of Crete, the world of fairy tales, and other topics that were hitherto described and discussed most often under the rubric "cultural anthropology" will reveal themselves as essential for the course of our present endeavor. All of those phenomena will disclose a rarely acknowledged but genuinely religious significance. In this way, the Christian understanding of man, his history and present state, may gain some essential insights. The possibility of a unity between "being human" and "being Christian" will appear, and both will be mutually corrected through a historical dialogue. In these dialogues between phenomena of cultural and religious history, the Christian faith will eventually lose its character as "superstructure," which is suspect in the critical investigation of religions. It will appear as a particular form of human life that is founded upon a specific revelation, that is, upon a specific experience of the divine. This experience of the divine does not refer to a religious message that is preached to man, but to an experience in the sense of a perception that is accessible to all humans, and thus comprehensible in its own terms. Thus, this project may be defined as an experience-oriented Christian cultural anthropology.

But since there is no "point zero" in the history of religious and cultural experience, we cannot venture to write a "linear" history of religious experience. This is the point where our own religion, in which we are historically rooted, comes in: Insofar as we try to understand our own religion consistently through its fundamental experiences, a new path is broken for the understanding of other religious and cultural experiences. Moreover, to the degree that we open ourselves to the signification of different religious and cultural experiences—and that is the secret of dialogue—we grow better able to understand our own religion and culture, and thereby ourselves as human beings. That is the essential issue. The aim of this book is to initiate this orienting dialogue, and to aquire through the Christian interpretation of religious and cultural history, and within a religious dialogue, a new Christian understanding of man and his situation.

This orienting dialogue between the Christian experience of God and the experiences of the divine that are expressed in myths, fairy tales and religions shall be made in two steps. First, the experience of the divine will be treated in a way that is yet relatively undifferentiated, namely, as the experience of the overpowering and of the frightful. The biblical experience of this phenomenon will prompt the question of how man has dealt with these experiences since the beginning of his history, and the question of how the specifically biblical tradition is to be seen within that context of cultural and religious history. On the second level, the dialogue will become more differentiated. I shall base my discussion upon the insight commonly accepted in today's Christian theology, that the revelation of God in Jesus consists in the fact that within himself and in his fate, he makes God perceptible as the relational event between the Son, the Father, and the healing Breath of Life that unifies them both (the Holy Spirit).[12] I will try to fathom the experiential content of these divine symbols that are unfolded in and through Jesus — child (son, daughter), wind and breath, father and mother — in their biblical context. I will then try to bring each of these experiences into a dialogue with similar experiences in myths, fairy tales, religions and cultural phenomena.

2 Experience and Symbolic Discourse

On the Perception of Symbols:

If we want our religious and cultural dialogue to remain on the level of experience, we have to move within a symbolic discourse.[13] For the experience of a trans-empirical, religious phenomenon itself has a symbolical structure: As a living being who has awakened to the knowledge of his own finitude, man becomes sensitive to a dimension within the things and events of his life that surpasses the concrete given. An earthquake, for example, that destroys his home and kills people who are close to him, is not merely a natural phenomenon to be perceived with regret and sadness. In the fury of its assault, it has something frightful that stirs up his innermost being and makes him live his finitude and vulnerability in a radically new way. It is (e.g. in Crete) the "divine" bull of the underworld who eludes any human control, who tears up the earth with his horns, and tramples people to death. The sun, which rises every morning, chasing the darkness of night, sending light and warmth to man, and making everything grow and prosper, is not only a gigantic fireball, but in it and through it a kindly power reaches down to man, and grants him life.

There is no reason why we, as enlightened people of the 20th century, should be forced to qualify such an experience, undergone by primeval people and even today by children (and by the "child-ego" of the grown-ups), as deception and as illusion. Of course our seismographic instruments and solar observatories cannot register any data other than movements subject to certain laws of the earth's crust or a huge mass of helium atoms. But by what authority should we be bound to see only that which is revealed by our technical instruments? Just as during Galileo Galilei's trial the cardinals of the Inquisition refused to look through the telescope in order to see proof of the earth's orbital motion around the sun, so do we refuse today to perceive the world around us *without* telescopes, in a spontaneous, holistic encounter. In a full human life both parts belong together. If we want to see only the trans-empirical world and refuse to deal with the empirical, then we are trapped in an ideology. If, on the contrary, we wish to perceive the world exclusively in the empirical way, and push away everything else as "projection" and unfounded emotion, then we renounce and repress a sensitivity for the perception of the world that is particular to us as human beings, and that has grown within us during our evolution.[14] We would then be nothing but intelligent monkeys who surpass similar animals only through their higher intelligence and their ability to see through their emotions, and to distance themselves from these emotions.

Today, man is at the end of his blind faith in science and he is beginning to set aside the armor that he had to wear in his fight against rigid ideologies. Once again, he begins to perceive the world in a holistic way—both its empirical *and* trans-empirical dimensions. Galileo's legacy to science was the observation of reality without the blurred glasses of ideology, as a given of nature. In the same way, a text from the yoga tradition like the Amitabha meditation from 424 AD, which Jung has brought to our attention, can teach us to see in the setting sun not only a gigantic mass of helium atoms but, in and beyond this physical reality, the "Buddha-Amitabha," the land of immense dissolving light, and the "Lord of Sukhavati," the Lord of the land of bliss.[15] He is the meaning of the setting sun, its symbolic message to man, to that being who in the course of his evolution has developed a sensitivity towards messages of this kind.

Preliminary stages of such sensitivity for symbols are found in animal behavior, wherever we encounter acts of ritualization. For in this case a certain pattern of behavior is separated from its functional context and used in a new function. Feeding, for example, has its original function in the care of the offspring. In many species of birds and in chimpanzees (which are the closest relatives of man in evolution) it appears not only in that function, but also in the courting for sexual partners. Eibl-Eibesfeldt speaks of "nose-nuzzling" and "caressing feeding."[16] Obviously these animals have discovered in the behavioral pattern of feeding a *significance,* a deeper message, a "surplus value," that goes beyond its original function of nourishing the breed. They have realized that feeding can also overcome relational barriers and the defense of territory, which might stand in the way of mating, and thus they use the same pattern for this new function. They transform the act of feeding into a courting ceremony—into a ritual.[17]

Indeed it is likely that in man, too, rituals are more ancient than myths. The message perceived in the surrounding reality is expressed first in a non-verbal way, in dances, in rhythmic shouting, drumming, in cave painting, ritual killings etc., and only on a second level as verbal narration and communication.[18] Thus man is first and foremost an *animal meditans,* a "praying animal"[19]—in A. Hardy's vivid formulation—a being who perceives the symbolic messages of things, a "listener to the Word."[20] When this message speaks to him and makes him think,[21] when it motivates him to speculate upon nature and the essence of those things that talk to him, he becomes—on a second level—the "animal rationale," according to the definition of man that was first developed by Greek philosophers. The Western scholar of religions who explains the symbolic message of things as illusion and wishful projection, a mirage, as it were, is rooted in that predominantly rational tradition. As a Western scientist he has lost himself so much in the exploration of things themselves that he has become blind and deaf to the symbolic message of these things. He has forgotten that it was this message that made things "stimulating" and "interesting" in the first place, and had motivated the investigation. For him, as opposed to the Eastern person, it is not so much the things apprehended by the senses that seem to disintegrate, to become "Maya," the Unspecified. It is rather the symbolic message of these things that he sees as dream and illusion.

But would it not be strange if evolution had positively selected the formation of a nervous system that believes it perceives something where there is nothing to be perceived? The neck of the giraffe extended during evolution only because in the savannah there actually were trees with leaves that could be reached more easily with a longer neck.[22] Had those leaves not existed, the long neck of the giraffe would not have either. Mutations of this kind would have been selected negatively as monster-births, and an animal of such a kind would have died out quickly. In the same way, man could not have populated the earth for over a million years and multiplied profusely, if the qualitative improvement of his perceptive abilities were to aim at the void and fool him with a mirage.

In symbolic perception, however, subject and object are not as clearly divided as in scientific experiments. More than in abstractions or everyday perception, different horizons tend to "amalgamate" in symbolic perception.[23] The subject is involved existentially in the perception, and the perceived reality "affects" the perceiving subject in a formative way.[24] But whatever the particular nature of this relation, it is definitely a dialogue, not a monologuing phantasy (which would prove pathological). It is from this holistic dialogue between man and his universe that religious symbols arise.

The Perception of Symbols and Empirical Reality

According to this view, a symbol is a reality that consists of two indivisible parts.[25] The first half is given empirically in the object: the earthquake as a motion of the earth's surface, the sun as a fireball of helium atoms. Within these empirical phenomena, a specific kind of perception (which we call "holistic") has access to another, trans-empirical reality, which eludes pure functionalism and goes beyond the given object: the second half of the symbol. Potentially, everything which man encounters in his universe — an event, a breeze he feels, physiological processes (like eating, drinking, or sexuality), or visual objects — may become a symbol for him.[26]

22

The decisive factor is only the nature of the perception: We perceive the symbolical quality of the universe only when we cease relying on technical devices that merely *record* reality—albeit with higher precision—without an emotional involvement with the world they encounter. But whenever we open ourselves to the claim of the encountered universe for "affecting" us, it may happen (it may, of course, not always happen) that a transcendent dimension arises from this encounter: a message that affects our existential feeling. Whenever this happens and whenever we react towards this encountered claim in thought, word, or deed, a communication takes place which is necessarily first articulated on a symbolic level. An act of imagination occurs (which can already be understood as a prayer in the broader sense), or an exclamation, or a dance-like motion, a chant, a narration, a confession, or the decision to take action. All these responses, in so far as they are an immediate response to the symbolic claim of reality, have, themselves, a symbolic quality. In this way, the religious utterings of man come into being.

Now, this view is in no way pantheistic. For we retain the distinction between that which is given as object, and that which surpasses this object and opens into a new dimension.[27] Not everything is divine, but in everything that we encounter, a divine message can be revealed to us. Traditionally one describes the transmission of such divine messages as the apparition of an angel. The author of the Letter to the Hebrews tells the Christians that through their conversion they have "come to Mount Zion and the city of the living God, the heavenly Jerusalem where the millions of angels have gathered for the festival..." (Hebr 12, 22). He thus indicates the many ways the symbolical message of the early Christian community affects the Christian. He says that "millions of angels" talk to him from within the (empirical) reality of the Christian festival gathering. Shintoism speaks in very similar terms about the "kami." This is translated mostly as "higher being, godhead," but not in an absolute and omnipotent sense; more as spiritual reality that surpasses the given object. And the Shintoist also acknowledges the existence of eighty billion such "kamis" and their formative role within the human world.[28]

To be able to perceive the symbolic quality of the encountered world we do *not* need a "third eye,"[29] or an "eye in the belly."[30] Indeed, such a supplementary eye would induce the risk of seeing this "third eye" separate from the two normal eyes, and of judging those two bodily eyes as "profane" or unimportant for our religious lives. But this would bring us back to the ideological blindness of those cardinals who refused to look through Galileo's telescope. For while contemplating the moons of Jupiter through the telescope, they could very well have seen angels, if they only had looked *with their whole heart* into that part of the firmament which was opened to them. There is no need for new organs in order to see the symbolical message of the surrounding world—only a specifically human usage of those existing organs: a seeing in which not only the eyes see, but the whole of man through the eyes. When Pascal and Saint-Exupéry said that we only see well with our hearts, they did not mean by "heart" a third instrument of visual perception. They meant the participation of the heart in the very normal vision of our two eyes. This is the only way for us to avoid repeatedly splitting the symbol's two halves.

The English mathematician, philosopher, and bishop, I.T. Ramsey[31] (whose work has been acknowledged nowadays by almost all theological disciplines)[32] has come to very similar conclusions through his analysis of religious discourse although he does not use the term "symbol." According to Ramsey, a genuine religious language arises when man responds to a "disclosure," to a revelatory experience. "Disclosure" means that in the midst of any routine activity, in court, at a boring party, during a fishing trip, a dimension breaks open that enhances the commonplace and allows the objects of a given situation to be newly perceived.

This may happen, as Ramsey explains, when, for example, a certain "Judge Brown" notices in the middle of his weekly court routine that the defendant who is facing him, is none other than "Sammy," his old friend from college. Although nothing has happened that would be relevant for the evidence in court, this perception changes the whole situation. The red garment and fur collar, traditional in the English court, seem suddenly out of place. The defendant has ceased to be just a "case" in the judicial system. He has become a person in a way that is unusual for court procedures. The personality of the accused, expressed by the familiar nickname "Sammy," has transcended the phenomenon of Mr. Smith who has been apprehended as a thief. Mr. Smith's angel has made a visible and audible appearance in the courtroom.

In a similar way, the encounter with a child, the contemplation of a sunset at the ocean, or the sight of a snow-covered mountain peak, may suddenly "come alive" and open its trans-empirical reality to us. Ramsey speaks in this context of a "cosmic disclosure."[33] We wonder why it happens and we do not know. Although we may love the mountains, they may not "talk to us" on certain days, and appear to us as just a pile of granite rock (which indeed they are). The occurrence of a "disclosure" does not depend solely on the weather, or on our personal mood. For a certain mood of depression can be changed very rapidly even with overcast skies—for example, during the winter sport season by the sight of a peak covered with fresh snow. And, on the other hand, we might be in the best of moods, open to every prospect, and yet the mountain, wrapped in sizzling summerheat, or shrouded by heavy clouds, may not appeal to us at all. So whether the mountain angel will talk to us or not depends on our openness and readiness to listen to him as well as on the ways in which the mountain offers itself to us on a particular day. A "disclosure," an angelic apparition, is an event that depends upon both the sender and the recipient. Of course it might happen that the transcendent dimension reveals itself with such intensity that it breaks through all the receiver's defenses, so that one may feel literally "overwhelmed" by an angel.

Symbolic Worldview and Monotheism

In the science of religion the apparition of a sacred or divine reality is called "hierophany." Mircea Eliade stresses that "all that man does, lives or loves" may become such a hierophany.[34] From a single hierophany or from a group of related hierophanies (such as develop around the deeds of a powerful warrior or king) a saga or myth can arise. But a concrete religion that reaches out to many people and is transmitted through history emerges only when people experience a certain hierophany with such intensity and power that all other hierophanies are now evaluated by their closeness or remoteness to that central hierophany. From this perspective, some apparitions may lose their hierophantic (sacred) character altogether, and begin to appear as negative hierophanies, as manifestations of the demonic and evil.

Mohammed, for example, focused on Allah as the highest ruling power to such a degree that angels were reduced to a role of mere transmitters and executors. In such a context many hierophantic experiences are perceived as abominable idolatry. On the contrary, the eighty billion Shinto kami-divinities show little signs of structural hierarchy. The only kami-godhead invested with a superior quality is the one that shines forth through the emperor, the *Tenno,* who was first venerated as an ancestral godhead, and later as the sun-god Amaterasu. In Hindu religion a highly structured hierophany of divinities emerged, the central hierophany being Vishnu for some traditions, and Shiva for others. In the religions of ancient Greece we can observe how the principal godhead of the invading Arian shepherds, Zeus, the god of thunder and lightning, came to dominate the hierophantic experience of man and how the other divinities of the land yielded to the conqueror—not without certain struggles which were reflected in mythic tales.

Like Judaism and Islam, Christianity is an Abrahamitic, that is, a monotheistic religion, and it carefully distinguishes the one God who is uncreated from eternity, from the angels who are spiritual beings, created by God. In the ancient church, Pseudo-Dionysius divided the millions of angels of Scripture (Heb. 12, 22) into nine choirs or orders of angels.

These orders are built up from below and, step by step, come closer and closer to God, every three choirs forming another hierarchy. They lead from the Angels, Archangels and Principalities, the Powers, Virtues and Dominations, the Thrones, Cherubim and Seraphim to the almighty God.[35] This division was very influential during the middle ages, especially in popular belief, and shaped, for example, the structure of Dante's "Divine Comedy."

However, these divisions prove inadequate on the level of experience. For angels have the "rudeness" not to introduce themselves when they appear, and not to indicate by their rank and name their respective distance or closeness to the triune God. Indeed, they do not even say whether they are good or fallen angels. I am convinced that even as in the Middle Ages certain angels are venerated today in the Christian church whom revelation would identify as fallen angels. In fact, the revelation to Elijah at Mount Horeb (1 Kings 19, 11-13) says that the great and frightening angels that cause trembling and submission do not reveal the God Yahweh: The strong and violent storm that "tore the mountain and shattered the rocks," the destructive earthquake and consuming fire did not make him manifest. Only after the fire, when "the sound of a gentle breeze" passed Elijah's cave, did he know that this was not just an angel, but Yahweh himself who had come to him, and he left the cave and stood at the entrance to listen to the voice of God.

At times the suspicion is aroused that such an experiential and thus symbolic discourse on God and the divine might be a threat to biblical monotheism.[36] But if we really wish to promote a free and unbiased dialogue between religions, and an understanding of man based upon universal history, we cannot look down with more or less contempt upon the multiple hierophanies in religious history from the superior position of "biblical monotheism." Rather, through an open dialogue with myths, tales, religions, and cultural phenomena, we have to relive patiently the path of experience that has led, and still can lead, to the biblical faith in the one God of the New Testament who manifested his Trinity in Jesus Christ. Our dialogue may be structured in its methodical approach by our Christian belief that God manifests himself in Jesus Christ as Three in One. But the meaning and the hierophantic potential of this belief can emerge only at the end of the dialogue between biblical and other religious experiences. Only a discourse that takes seriously different religious experiences and their symbols — and thus necessarily casts its own experience in symbolic language — can be called a "truth-seeking" discourse.[37] From this point of view, the traditional discourse of systematic theology seems to be more of a "truth-affirming," rather than a "truth-seeking," nature.

Contemporary missionary studies acknowledge this problem. In a joint meeting of the Asian bishops with the Christian conference of Asia in Singapore in July 1987, the Indian theologian and priest Felix Wilfred pointed out that interreligious dialogue must use a symbolic discourse, and that this was the only chance for a serious encounter between Christianity and the Asian religions.[38] Only in such a discourse can Christians make manifest their respect and appreciation for the symbolic universe of other religious beliefs. This much needed dialogue between religions on a symbolic level is still in its very early stages.[39] Christianity is still dominated "in its life and teaching by logic, systems, formulas etc."[40] According to Wilfred, this is the reason why Christianity is an alien presence on the Asian continent. It has become intolerable that "this language that lives in monolithic uniformity, keeps on ruling over the spirit which wishes to express itself in a discourse that is rich in meanings, differentiated, and pluralistic."[41] An encounter between religions and different cultures is possible only on the level of symbols. Only a symbolic discourse can articulate the actual anthropological dimension of experience in theological beliefs and insights. Both interreligious dialogue and Christian cultural anthropology are in need of symbolic discourse.

From our discussion of the genesis and inner structure of religious discourse it becomes obvious that the distinction between monotheism and polytheism is quite complex. That which seems so obvious on the level of abstract speculation loses its unequivocal quality very rapidly when used to order the multiplicity of life and experience. In religious practice and experience the follower of a polytheistic religion does not always keep in mind a whole crowd of "gods and goddesses," trying through his ritual and prayers to satisfy, so to speak, each of them by rank and order. Comparative religious studies have opened our eyes to the fact that many, mostly locally confined, divinities are in fact variations of a certain type of godhead. They are localized differently or receive different accentuations and can in turn relate to other archetypes. For example, the Ugaritic Baal, the Sumerian-Babylonian Tammuz, and the Egyptian Osiris are nothing other than local variations and accentuations of the basic human experiences of fertility, the growth of vegetation, and the overcoming of destructive natural forces. The innumerable mother-godheads and love-goddesses of historic religions — Annat, Ishtar, Inanna, Schams, Isis, Hera, Gaia, Demeter, Artemis, and Lakshmi — are different models of the same existential experience of maternal and feminine love, while the divine bulls and dragons and different godheads of thunder and lightning reflect the experience of a thrusting ferocity, of the wildness and blind elemental violence of fate.

Furthermore, we have to take into account that man, as a finite being, is often consumed and absorbed by the existential situation of the moment. Therefore the transcendence that shines through such a situation becomes for him, for his subjective experience, the "One and All" besides which there is no other God. When a woman invoked Eileithyia in the hour of parturition—a relatively minor goddess of the Greek pantheon, a daughter of Zeus and Hera who protected childbirth—then all the experiences of the transcendent that were ever accessible to that woman—Hera and Artemis, Demeter and Gaia, even Persephone, and the almighty power of Zeus and the male gods—were all fused into that one godhead. In the encounter with her, the woman in labor encountered the one God who operates in all. Indeed, an old text relates that Eileithyia is older than Chronos, from whom heaven and earth proceeded.[42] Similar situations occur in the invocation of all other godheads in the various situations of life that are specific to them.

We can recognize monotheism, even in a biblical sense, to the degree that those very different hierophanies all appear in one single "countenance" in the concrete devotion of a human being, converging into a comforting, strengthening power, redeeming even beyond death. The Benedictine abbot and systematic theologian Christian Schütz writes: "The aim of monotheism is to recognize God in various manifestations and situations in life and history as the same. The acknowledgment of monotheism reflects the belief in an identity that runs through all difference and change."[43] In this sense, Christianity will remain monotheistic, even within the symbolic discourse of the dialogue with cultural and religious history.

3 Jesus—A "Symbol" of God?

On the Origin of the Divine Symbol of Jesus in the Old Testament

Is Christianity, in its particularity and its basic structure, able to articulate itself in a symbolic language? This would, for example, certainly prove very difficult, if not impossible, for the main branches of Islam (except, perhaps, for certain mystical movements). On the other hand, Judaism is able to express its central divine revelation, the manifestation of God as Yahweh, as "I-am-here," in genuinely symbolic narrations, as can be seen in the narrative texts of the Hebrew Bible, in the parables of the New Testament by the Jewish poet Jesus, and even in the 19th century in the tales of the Hassidim. Christianity, as a daughter of Judaism, shares in this quality of the Jewish religion as well. In these religious traditions, the transcendent dimension of reality is manifested not so much in visual phenomena that are to be contemplated, like a sunset, but rather in a series of occurences in historical events.

Yet events can have a very deep symbolic nature. What is symbolized in them is a deeper meaning, a "statement." If we listen and look carefully, such a condensed statement may even arise from the event as a "countenance" that turns towards us. Thus the liberation of Moses' people at the Red Sea manifests its transcendent dimension as "Yahweh;" as "I-am-here." In the facts of Jesus' life, death and life beyond death, this God "I-am-here" reveals himself as "Abba," as the "Mama/Papa" of all mankind. Plots and events that are similar to these two basic events in their structure and meaning are able, then, to express this experience of the divine as "angelic apparitions," each time with different accents and gradations.

Thus, there is indeed a multitude of symbols in the biblical context. In the different salvations that Israel has experienced in the course of its history, the countenance of the God "I-am-here" is revealed in quite different ways. In Jesus' parables, in the narration of his healing and saving of the sick and rejected, and in similar tales of care and healing in the early Christian community, the essence of the Abba is experienced in multiple ways.

Quite often a narrative symbol and a natural symbol are combined. This fact has all too often escaped the attention of theological exegetes. On the sacred Mount Horeb God appears to Elijah in a soft, whispering wind; Adam and Eve encountered Him in "the cool of the day" (Gen. 3, 8); He appeared to Abraham "during the hottest part of the day" (Gen. 18, 1) while he was sitting under the giant oaks of Mamre, looking up into

29

the leaves; and during his vocation at his baptism Jesus experienced the breath of Yahweh descending upon him, blowing into him when he rose from the waters of Jordan and looked up into the opening sky. None of these symbols is fully explored in exegetical literature. But it is precisely at this point that many convergences with hierophanies from other (e.g. Asian) religions could be discovered. Buddha himself has his "'highest and most perfect illumination" (annuttarasamyaksambodhi), which is able to free man from the cycle of birth and death, while meditating at the Nairanjana River, under the sacred Pipal-tree.[44] From the earliest times, sacred ablutions and submersions in river water play an important role in ancient Hindu traditions.[45]

In contrast to Judaism, Christianity has placed the symbolism of natural, visible phenomena at the very center of divine revelation. This development will be part of our subsequent discussions. It has made Christianity into the historic religion that is best disposed, from its internal structure, to enter into a dialogue with Asian and archaic religions in which the experience of the Divine is shaped more by visual phenomena. In that respect, Christianity might become a mediator between Abrahamite and Asian religions.

The nature of Yahweh could only be grapsed in his liberation of Moses' people from Egypt, that is, as a series of events, as history. The creed of Israel, as recited for example during harvest festivals, is therefore the *narration* of this event (Deut. 26, 5-9). This God's apparitions in the whispering wind, in the cool of the day of Paradise, or in the hottest part of the day under the oaks of Mamre are quite revealing of his nature and character. But they are only a sort of backdrop for what Yahweh says in this situation to the man to whom he appears. Yahweh himself does not have a visual symbol. This is the sense of the prohibition of images in the Old Testament.[46] It is true that cultic images of bulls were built in Dan and Bethel after the splitting of the empire, as an expression of the might and omnipotence of the God of Israel. But the prophetic tradition and the later history of Israel have condemned these efforts. The God "I-am-here" who was experienced in the historic event of Israel's liberation from Egypt could not be adequately expressed in that way.

If he could be visualized at all, this God could be visualized in man, for only man is his single image, made "in the likeness" of himself (Gen. 1, 26). Thus the outstanding man, especially the king, was sometimes called "Son of God," that is, an expression of God's nature. In the so-called King's Psalm (Ps. 2, 7) we read: "You are my son, I have today become your father." In other words, by becoming king this man has become the image of God in a special way, as "son" of God. His function as son and image is established not by the fact that he is placed *between* God and his people, representing God's power to them (as was traditionally the case in the theocratic kingdoms of the East) but that he keeps *facing* God. He is the chosen one for the dialogue with God that includes the whole of the people. Thus Yahweh speaks in the ancient prophecy of Nathan to David: "I will be a father to him and he a son to me" (2 Sam. 7, 14). The king, as human being, can only be the son of God in the dialogue of a living relation, not a static one.

Here again, the same basic structure is preserved which first appeared in the events revealing the God "I-am-here" — the redeeming and healing dialogue between the one who is in need and the one who turns towards him: "...Yahweh heard our voice and saw our misery, our toil and our oppression; and Yahweh brought us out of Egypt with mighty hand and an outstretched arm, with great terror, and with signs and wonders. He brought us here and gave us this land, a land where milk and honey flow" (Deut. 26, 7-9). Accordingly, the people of Israel are called "sons of God" much more frequently than the king — he is called "son of God" only three times in the Old Testament. Israel is his "first-born son" (Exod. 4, 22; Jer. 31, 9), his favoured child (Jer. 31, 20). The Israelites are the sons and daughters of Yahweh (Deut. 14, 1; 32, 5.19; Isa. 43, 6 etc.). The same breath unites the child calling in distress with the caring father.

But again and again, both the king and the people of Israel abandoned these traditions, wishing to *be* God, instead of facing God. By building military defenses, by providing their armies with chariots and horses, they tried to usurp the power over life and to free themselves from facing God.[47] That way they fell under foreign domination and became irreverent.[48] Only when Israel suffered exile, oppression and humiliation, did this toiling servant of God become, once again, Yahweh's child and the expression of his nature.

This Son Israel has found an unsurpassable expression in the figure of Jesus Christ. He alone has lived through the existence of the indigent, creaturely and finite counterpart to the loving and saving God, and shown its redeeming truth through his death. He has permanently and seamlessly closed the circle between the helpless son and the caring God "I-am-here." When Jesus says in the Gospel of John, "the Father and I are one" (John 10, 30) and, "to have seen me is to have seen the Father" (John 14, 9), he does not describe a static, but a dynamic identity, the identity of an equal. The identification of Jesus as the beloved son through the God "I-am-here" which began with the baptism in the river Jordan, was sometimes obscured during his life, and was eventually given an irrevocable confirmation in his death.

In this way, Jesus emerges as a new symbol of God from the history of Israel. A man has become the symbol of God, precisely because he did not want to "be like God" — which is the original sin of man according to the narrative of the Fall (Gen. 3, 1-24), but remained in his humanity, in his creatureliness, in his helplessness, and was accepted as such by the God "I-am-here," by the infinitely loving Father, into that divine life that was his dwelling place from all eternity.

It was not the will of Yahweh that this human existence of helplessness be manifested in Jesus' fate on the cross. Instead it was the will and the work of the Roman emperor-god, the work of one who had claimed for himself the *vis vitae necisque,* the absolute power over life and death within the whole known world, and had thus set himself up as God. But the Crucifixion opens the eyes of the blind man who compromised his humanity through original sin, and wanted to be like God. It shows how, in himself, through the dynamics of freeing and redeeming love, man can experience not only hosts of angels, but even the one and eternal God.

Thus, Christians have been granted a very distinct symbol of God. This will become clear through a comparison with other important symbols of the divine from the history of religions which will only be outlined here. A more thorough discussion will follow in the main section of the book.

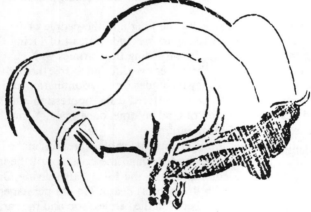

Fig. 1: The figure of a bison (from the cave of Font-de-Gaume, France); note the exaggerated size of the animal's neck.

On the Distinctiveness of Jesus as Symbol, in the Context of Other Divine Symbols

Those Paleolithic caves, which were painted by our ancestors 20,000 or 30,000 years ago with mostly animal motifs, are to be seen as cultic

Fig. 2: The Matterhorn.

spaces, as shall be further developed in the following chapters. The most frequent representations are wild bulls, bison and buffalo. As can be seen from the illustration (Fig. 1), these pictures are strongly expressive. The exaggerated neck and oversized front (with an enormous breast and short sturdy legs) express the awesome vitality, force and strength of this animal. It embodies, as it were, the universal power of nature — a power that is fearful to man, but which he also feels within himself. For the primeval man this bull was a sort of "incarnation," a symbol for the transcendent dimension of reality which he experienced. He tried to appropriate this power, to "communicate" with it by hunting, killing and devouring it.

A symbol of God that is closer to us is the mountain peak (Fig. 2). In all religions, as well as in the Bible, there are sacred mountains — such as, for example, Mount Horeb in the Old Testament, with the cave where Yahweh appeared to Elijah in a whispering breeze. Mountains exert a powerful fascination even today. Every year some forty people lose their lives in the attempt to climb the Matterhorn. What is it that drives these people to such dangerous excursions? Is it more than, strictly speaking, some millions of tons of granite rock? Is the mountain not in reality simply a pile of stones? But man sees more than meets the physical eye. He sees the outreaching gesture, the closeness to heaven, the strong and eternal quality that is manifested in its physical reality. He responds to this "cosmic disclosure" (I.T. Ramsey), to the apparition of the mountain

33

angel, by trying to "conquer" it, to put his foot on its very peak, and thus to communicate with it.

Apart from animal pictures we find mainly representations of women and mothers in the ancient Stone Age caves. More than 20,000 years ago men chiselled the female figure (Fig. 3) in the stone walls of Laussel cave.

Fig. 3: The "Venus of Laussel" (cave of Laussel, France).

It is a human symbol of fertility and life. The woman holds her hand on her pregnant belly and will soon give birth to new human life. The other hand holds the horn of plenty in which she gathers food that will soon be shared with her offspring and siblings. The breasts which will nourish the new-born are heavy. To the primeval people, who perhaps ignored the relation between procreation and parturition, such a being must have seemed liked a divine miracle. It is this fullness, warmth and fertility that man strove to acquire when he adopted a settled lifestyle.

Within nomadic, pastoral tribes it was the male who became the divine symbol. Zeus sits on his throne imperially, gazing into the distance (Fig. 4). He determines what is just and what is unjust. He shows men the way. He rules over the gods and mankind with thunder and lightning. Man's response to this divine apparition is submission on the one side, and — as a necessary counterweight — the bloody sacrifice, in which he himself exerts the power to kill, and thus places himself on the level of the godhead, as a counterpart.

Of course, when this divine and imperial power appears concretely as God-king or Emperor-God like the Roman emperor Augustus, who ruled over the entire world, as it was known then, the majority of people had no other option but slavish submission (Fig. 5). His arm stretches out to rule the whole universe, with his armor and sceptre. Even the muse, the gift for philosophy and art, clings to him. He is the perfect man, the "Augustus divinus," the venerable Divine. Like the Eastern God-king, he has no transcendent counterpart. In him man has become "like gods" (Gen. 3, 5).

In the artwork of painter Roland Peter Litzenburger (Fig. 6) Jesus stands before Pilate. The power of the Roman emperor is embodied in the stocky, bull-neck features and the grave expression of his procurator Pilate. He, Pilate, has the power to set free or to crucify. Jesus stands before him as the one who is handed over to a man-become-God. Having been accused of competing with the emperor's divine power, Jesus was made into a mock king. His shattered shoulders are cloaked with the scarlet robe of kings, his hands hold a weak reed as a sceptre, and a crown of thorns "adorns" his head. The viewer experiences a curious transformation while examining this picture. The holder of real power, the emperor's representative, is suddenly no longer god-like; there is no longer any symbolic transparence. The symbolic power shines forth from the mocked and powerless king. He communicates a dignity and majesty in strange contradiction to the apparent helplessness and powerlessness of this laughingstock. We are drawn towards him, wanting to help and to save him.

In the following picture by the same artist, entitled "Death on the Cross" (Fig. 7), we can see how the power structures of the state finished

Fig. 4: Zeus, the highest god of the Greek pantheon.

Fig. 5: The Roman Emperor Augustus.

off the alleged rebel. Above this ruined body "King of the Jews" is written in four languages to deride any possible identification with the emperor's divine power. The limbs hang limply. The head is a burst of lines, as if a bomb had exploded from within and destroyed everything. This "death on the cross" is the imperial response to a challenge to its power.

But the artist does not yet turn his eyes from this scene of horror. He looks for that "minimal ground" that, according to Karl Jaspers, remains and becomes visible in the destruction of any human being, but especially in the death of that "archetypal human being, Jesus Christ."[49] What the painter finds is expressed in his picture "Christ of the Shielding Robe," (Fig. 8). It is still the figure of the Crucified, with the same limp limbs, the same empty countenance. And yet, the character of the picture has changed dramatically. The arms of the Crucified are stretched out in a protective gesture. Under them there is a gathering of people. The Crucified bows down towards them in maternal affection. Blood pours from the wound in his side as a comforting and strengthening nourishment. It seems to be the emanation and symbol of his love. The arms of the Crucified do not hold the people gathered at his feet. They stretch out freely and protectively over them. The people's faces look forward; they gather for a departure. The Crucified gives them the mission of going out into the world and bringing this new symbol of God to all men—the symbol of a God who leans down towards them in powerless love and in so doing, shields and saves them even beyond death and their own powerlessness. Jesus the Crucified who lives on beyond death, who bends down to his people to comfort and nourish them, reveals the Father, the saving Other who dwells now in perfect unity with his "beloved son" (Mark 1, 11).

If we look back now to the preceding pictures, an important difference strikes us. With all other symbols of God we had to distinguish between the substance proper to the empirical phenomenon as symbol, and the symbolized itself, that which is designated by the phenomenon. We had to *abstract* from the huge muscular mass of the bison, from the millions of tons of granite, from the figure of the woman, from the thunder and lightning as scientific phenomena, and also—albeit with some difficulty—from the power of the Roman emperor, based on military force, in order to experience the God or the angel through each of those symbols. Had we omitted that abstraction, we would have committed idolatry.[50]

Here, with Jesus the Crucified who lives beyond death, the situation is different. Not because we postulate this in a speculative way, but because the nature of the symbol involved, the phenomenon itself, prompts this very experience. The brutal enforcement of the Roman im-

Fig. 6: R. P. Litzenburger: Christ before Pilate.

Fig. 7: R. P. Litzenburger: Death on the Cross.

perial power has already accomplished the necessary "abstraction." It has utterly destroyed everything that had any kind of force or impact in a human being—and this was the point of this method of execution, which was reserved for insurgents. There is nothing left in the Crucified from which we would have to abstract. Whenever and wherever we will find life, love, warmth, care, protection and comfort in Jesus the Crucified, we will know that what we experience is the very last foundation of being that continues beyond death (and is thus God himself), unveiled, in absolute transparency. It is not because Jesus is more powerful, more "divine" than other symbols of God, but rather because he offers to the empirical eye the image of radical powerlessness, even of nothingness, that we do not need to preserve the separation between the symbol and its abstraction, when, in the light of the accounts of his life and deeds, something shines forth from this very nothingness. We may then, without committing idolatry, do what Thomas did in the Gospel according to John when he saw the deadly wounds of the living Crucified: fall down before him and say "My Lord and my God!" (John 20, 28).

Anyone who is able to relive this experience of Thomas, in at least a rudimentary way, may be called a Christian. Even if we might not see with such clarity "and yet believe" (John 20, 29), the essential aspect of our faith in the religious pluralism and indifference of our times is that the "light" may shine in the heart of the Christian, and that "God's glory" dawns upon him "on the face of Christ" (2 Cor. 4, 6). A believer's life and character are then immediately shaped by this experience. The Protestant educator Dietrich Zilleßen speaks, somewhat exaggeratedly, but still correctly enough, of the fundamental "brokenness" of the Christian experience of symbols.[51] Indeed for the Christian schooled in the symbol of the living Crucified, the abstraction from an empirical foreground, the partial desecration of the symbol, becomes an inner attitude within the symbolic experience. When gigantic muscles, masses of stone, a whirling fire, sexual infatuation and political power become hierophanies, that is when they speak to me existentially. They still are nothing but angels that may prepare me and guide me towards the manifestation of God in Jesus.

In a world less fascinated by the power to kill this Jesus might not have been crucified. In fact, the image of the infant alone, which is also by its nature radically dependent upon others, might have been sufficient to bring forth the redeeming Christian hierophany of the divine. But in this world of ours, our eyes, struck with blindness—as it is said of the apostles who did not recognize Jesus on the road to Emmaus (Luke 24, 16)—could not be opened unless we saw this child, this "beloved son," in direct confrontation with murderous power and its claims of divinity. In this confrontation, this power was ultimately revealed as nothing but the brutal and profane machinery of death.

41

Fig. 8: R. P. Litzenburger: Christ as "protective cloak."

Thus Jesus the Crucified is nothing other than the image of the child in a world that is shaped by cycles of violence. In him, man can contemplate a dynamic process which, for the Christian, encompasses and contains innumerable possible hierophanies: the helpless being, the one who is handed over, who cries for his mother, for his father. And the father, aroused by the breath of life expressed in the cry, moves to save the child. In this sense, Jesus is *the* symbol of God for the Christian. And it is the Christian's task, in the present world, to take this symbol as a starting point and to search for a dialogue with other divine symbols and experiences of God in cultural and religious history.

Exposition:

The experience of the frightful in myths, fairy tales and religions, and the biblical way to liberation

1 God as bull and dragon and his "fall"

Religion and the Experience of Evil

In the final report on the ecumenical efforts of the *Oratio Domenica* from 1965 to 1986, Walter Stolz remarked that human inquiry "is baffled and dismayed when confronted with the unsolvable problem of evil, even from an atheist perspective."[1] In general though, this topic is approached only from the standpoint of the major religions,[2] where the question has been raised to a philosophical level.

In Judaism, Christianity and Islam this became the question of how the experience of evil and suffering is compatible with the belief in a good and venerable God.[3] Among the most sophisticated traditions of Hinduism evil is identical with ignorance (avidya). It is a blind fascination with powers and forces that are hostile to life and enmesh mankind into a cycle of killing and violence. "Ahimsa," "to-not-kill" is therefore the unshakable principle of Jainism—the first movement of Indian monasticism that, in our century, influenced Mahatma Gandhi—the principle needed to break the cycle of violence and to achieve illumination, and liberation from ignorance. This ignorance is the result of *karma,* the negative, harmful energy that man has accumulated during his former life through evil deeds.[4] For Buddhism as well, man's basic experience is that of suffering caused by "avidya." Buddhism's central principle says: Life is suffering; and clinging to life obscures man's vision and causes ignorance and thus more suffering. Rather pragmatically and rationally, it looks for a way that leads away from the tendency to cling to life and to the world, and thus leads away from suffering. The very essence of Buddhism is a philosophy of overcoming suffering.[5]

In the face of helplessness and dismay, in the face of the oppressive quality that the experience of evil has taken in recent European history, the question arises whether the phenomenon of evil has not been overrationalized within the major religions, and whether this rationalization really can help the individual human being in his affliction.

Perhaps the relative helplessness of the major religions in the face of the phenomenon of evil is one of the causes of the rise of atheism today. Indeed, for someone who is struck by tangible suffering—and who is not, at least at some point of his life?—the reasonings offered by traditional religions may even seem cynical. This is especially true for the doctrine of *karma,* but also for some very similar teachings in Judaism, Christianity and Islam, in which illness and suffering are the result of wrongdoing, whether by ourselves in this life, or by our ancestors or, as in *karma,* in a former life. What assistance can such reasoning give to a person with a stroke who is paralyzed and bound to a wheelchair for the rest of his life? Even if it were obvious in a concrete situation that an illness was at least partially caused by wrong living habits, the perception of one's own guilt, and the idea of doing penance for it in this way, does not help much to cope with the suffering. Such thoughts become truly cynical if they are applied, for example, to the situation of children harmed by the drug "Contergan."[6]

At this point, even the Christian idea of vicarious penance proves flawed. Should these many children, who have to live with deformed limbs, "do penance" in substitution for the Grünental Company managers (who, of course, never intended any harm, but acted negligently) or perhaps for the entire chemical and medical industry? The question seems trivial. The impressive analyses of the French cultural anthropologist René Girard have opened our eyes to the fact that wherever suffering and death are combined with the idea of penance, albeit in an indirect or hidden way, the profound violence of human nature comes to the surface.[7] According to Girard, the idea and the cult of sacrifice follows the brutal mechanism of the scapegoat whose purpose is to channel this destructive human violence in such a way that human culture and community is made possible—at least for a certain period of time, after which the "offering" has to be renewed. Many theologians have already accepted this view of the essence of sacrifice and, like Girard, advocate a "non-sacrificial interpretation of the Gospel" (that is, the suffering and death of Jesus should not be viewed as a "sacrifice").[8]

The idea of penance and sacrifice does not make the suffering that is visited upon man easier to deal with. Penance is good and necessary if it is done voluntarily as reparation in a situation of clear causal relations. But when, as in the previous examples, such evident relations and voluntariness are absent, it becomes a myth as defined by Girard, a masking of human violence and brutality. For it is brutal and violent to tell a man who has suffered a stroke that he may now do penance for himself, or for others, or for God. No one asked him beforehand whether he would accept that. Such a reaction reveals the belief in a blind and ruthless God.

When religion is not able to be of any assistance to man in coming to terms with the experience of evil, it has perhaps missed its most important anthropological purpose. The consequences of this failure can be seen today in the widespread acceptance of atheism and a reversion to occultism. As I have tried to show, this is a weakness of all major contemporary religions. The weakness is due to the fact that concrete pain, the shock of evil, is far too vital and immediate to be remedied by relatively abstract philosophical reasoning. A rational teaching of any nature will be unmasked as merely an intellectual exercise in the face of the concrete experience of evil.

47

In this situation the question arises whether the major religions have not abandoned something in the course of their history, which is still present in archaic religions and might be helpful in coping with the experience of evil in a more human way. In recent religious education, concerned with being "oriented towards experience and issues,"[9] the genuine insight has emerged that concrete human experiences cannot be met with thoughts and doctrines. In the immediate experience of evil, they ultimately seem artificial. On the other hand, concrete experience can enter into a productive and creative dialogue with religious tradition when this tradition is brought in not as an abstract doctrine, but as a network of symbols. For religious symbols — divine and angelic figures, inspiring tales of lives shaped by religious attitudes, parables, even myths and fairy tales — contain human *experience* in a condensed form and make it present. Such religious experiences, actualized by symbols, may then initiate a creative and productive exchange with the present experiences of man. The didactics of religion has thus evolved in recent times towards a didactics of symbols.[10] The questions, therefore, arise whether the symbolic element has not receded too much in favor of discursive teaching, and whether the major religions are still able to respond adequately to the very basic and vital experience of evil in human life.

Now what was the primeval situation? In what way could the original quality of the symbols that occurred in ancient religions be preserved and refocused within a major historical religion — in our case Christianity? These questions will be examined presently if only in a brief way, because of the wealth of material from the history of religions.

God and Evil as Bull-power in Archaic Religions

Archaic religion can be approached only with great care and with a considerable latitude of interpretation. It cannot simply be equated with the religions of so-called primitive cultures, as they are discovered and described by ethnologists in painstaking fieldwork. It is impossible to postulate or, indeed, to reconstruct some sort of primeval religion from the beliefs of these tribes because, despite the fact that they reflect, to a certain extent, the ways of Stone Age cultures, they have been influenced by many outside forces over the course of their history. In his handbook on prehistory, Müller-Karpe is certainly right to point out that the concept of a personified godhead, as is often encountered in primitive ethnic cultures, involves a degree of abstract thought that "can in no way be considered primeval."[11] Müller-Karpe's argument is convincing: "In this early period, transcendence was probably not abstracted from the sensible forces of nature, but rather experienced within naturally perceptible

48

things, as a dimension beyond the objective. In the same way the personalities of fellow-men and one's own self were not experienced as detached from the body, but in a close relationship to it, although transcending it."[12] These "naturally perceptible things," and "sensible forces of nature" including their "dimension beyond the objective" can be encountered in the impressive wealth of primeval paintings, engravings, sculptures and clay-models that have been uncovered by archeologists, especially in recent decades. We may assume that primeval peoples were particularly drawn to represent on bones, cave walls, in ivory or clay those objects in which they experienced this transcendent dimension most intensely. Artistic response is prompted by whatever has most significance and, in the manner of his representation, the artist will try to render this transcendent significance.

If we look at the findings from this perspective, the following basic categories emerge: animals, people (mostly female figures), human hands, and hunting tools. The animal motif outnumbers the rest by far. Among them, the greatest number are those animals that are potentially dangerous to man: bison, mammoths, wild horses, rhinoceroses, bears, panthers. Deer and reindeer are also found frequently. All these animals were hunted and eaten by primeval men. However, they are not depicted under a "culinary" aspect, as potential food. We never find a separated joint, and the animals that are eaten most commonly are not represented most frequently. Rather, it is clear from the representations, that primeval people were most fascinated with the vitality and wild, forceful aspects of the animal world. Many representations of bison express the elemental power of nature that is embodied in the animal by overemphasizing the bull-neck and the stocky features of the body in an almost expressionist way, similar to Picasso's bull paintings (Fig. 9, see also Fig. 1).

Bison and other large and dangerous wild animals certainly belong to those "naturally perceptible things" and "sensible forces of nature" in which the primeval man recognized "a dimension beyond the objective" and thus experienced transcendence.[13] This corresponds to the insight that in early religions the divine and the demonic were still thoroughly fused. In one of the pits of the Lascaux cave there is a representation of a bull knocking down a hunter. So, even in its deadly and demonic aspect, the elemental power of nature maintains its fascination and inspires illustration (Fig. 30).

In symbology the bull is most commonly regarded as a symbol of fertility.[14] But originally its demonic and destructive aspects must have been dominant. This becomes very clear from a fresco in a portico of the palace at Knossos in Crete, flanking the north entrance (Fig. 10). It shows a raging bull, charging with lowered horns towards an olive tree. The lower part of the picture is filled with a wave-shaped pattern. Obviously, this bull does not represent fertility, but quite the opposite: a power that attacks, jeopardizes and threatens fertility—as expressed in the olive tree. The waves probably represent the sea that threatens culture, civilization, and fertility by floods and tidal waves. In a similar way, the sea-god Jamm of Ugarit battles with Baal, the god of fertility—and Jamm is closely related to "thr il", the "bull El".[15] Not unlike the foaming horses of Poseidon that symbolized the wildness of the sea in later times, the raging bull can also come to express the destructive power of the water. In Germanic and Scandinavian as well as Celtic and Frankish sagas, the bull very often comes from the sea. The "Elbstier" is seen on the shores of rivers and lakes.[16] In the Cretan myth of king Minos of Knossos, the bull who begets the man-eating Minotaur comes out of the sea. The sea-bull that runs against the olive tree is a symbol that corresponds to the hunting scene at Lascaux within the context of an agricultural society. In both instances, the bull is not a symbol of power and fertility,[17] but of a destructive—and nonetheless fascinating—savage force.

Thus the bull is probably the oldest symbol of the divine. It expresses how primeval man experienced destruction, suffering, and death: as an overpowering fate, as the rage of some divinity. Werner Daum has reconstructed a "primeval semitic myth" through close examination of

Fig. 9: The bull as an expression of the primeval force of nature (wall-painting from the cave of Font-de-Gaume, France).

Fig. 10: The bull as an expression of destructive power charges with lowered horns at an olive tree (fresco in the portico flanking the north entrance of the Knossos palace in Crete).

old Yemeni fairy tales, of near-Eastern myths and rites, hunting customs and wedding ceremonials, and of Islamic and Jewish feasts.[18] This ancient myth survives in later Judaism and Islam as a basic pattern for religious feasts, rites and customs despite all subsequent layers of Ugarit and Mesopotamian myths and of later Judaic and Islamic monotheism, and its influence extends to the whole Eastern Mediterranean region (even in Greece, Crete, Africa and Egypt). Its clearest articulation is preserved in the religious traditions of ancient Sheba, a remote southern Arabic empire from which the legendary queen came to Solomon to see his glory and to hear his wisdom (1 Kings 10, 1-13).

The pantheon of ancient Sheba was organized around the three divinities Almaqah-Athtar-Schams. Athtar and Schams are benevolent godheads. Athtar is the name for the supernatural and divine quality of the tranquil water that grants fertility and fills irrigation systems, wells and cisterns. Schams alternate name is "Giving-from-abundance" and signifies all that man experiences when he contemplates the sun as light, warmth and growth. Almaqah, on the other hand, is called the "Enraged," the "Destroyer." He carries a club in his hand, and his symbol is the charging goat and the bull. He expresses what man experiences holistically when black clouds pile up in the sky, when the raging storm rumbles down the mountains, flooding the wadis and shattering the irrigation systems built with such painstaking effort. In later times Athtar and Schams are wed and fight together against Almaqah in order to expel him, although they never really achieve their goal.

Originally Almaqah is the old, powerful god of the wilderness. People tried to appease his fury by sacrificing young girls, exposing them in the wilderness or burying them alive at the upper course of the wadi. In later Yemeni fairy tales he appears, therefore, as "Il Afrit" the ogre.[19] Because the semitic language is written without vowels, the basic form for "God," — 'L — is vocalized "Il," "Al," or "El" at different times. According to Werner Daum, Al-maqah is the God of the rainstorm,[20] and Il-Afrit is the water-demon in ancient Arabic fairy tales. He has "neither sons, nor daughters. He had always existed and was not begotten. Everything belongs to him. He owns the land. His dwelling place is in the wilderness far from the homes of man. He uses his great power at his pleasure for good and for evil. Although he is sometimes kind and helpful, his wild and destructive character prevails."[21]

El later becomes the principal divinity of Ugarit, the father of all gods. His "beloved sons," that is, his most important and striking features, are Jamm — the god of the furious and destructive sea, and Mot — the god of the deadly drought. The symbolic animal for El is the bull. Baal, the god of fertility, is often represented in his iconography as standing on a bull (Fig. 11). But this does not mean, as has so often been contended, that the bull is the symbol of Baal, a sign of his power and fertility. Rather, this representation shows how Baal, a new version of the old Athtar, has overcome the "bull El," and put his foot on the head of the defeated enemy. In some pictures Baal even stands in front of the bull and strikes him down.[22]

God as Bull-power in the Old Testament

In a relatively old version of the Old Testament, the name Yahweh is replaced by the name El (the plural form being Elohim). And indeed, in many texts Yahweh reveals very El-like bull-like features. In the night, he comes to meet Moses and tries to kill him (Exod. 4, 24). As a nocturnal river-demon he wrestles with Jacob at the ford (Gen. 32, 25). He demands from a father his only son as a sacrifice for burning (Gen. 22, 2). Only by blood is he appeased (Exod. 4, 25; 12, 23). Wherever the fury and anger of Yahweh is leveled against the enemies of Israel, the "bull El" appears, capricious, unpredictable, and wild. He howls, he slashes

Fig. 11: Victory over the wilderness-power: The Syrian god of fertility sets his foot on the back and neck of the bull.

with a blade, he walks in flames, he strikes, hunts down, grabs and strangles. He stalks like a panther; he assaults like a bear; he lacerates like a lion. He splits the earth, makes it tremble, frightens the sun and the moon who hide from him. He pelts with hail, shatters people like earthenware, and casts the fleeing kings of Sodom and Gomorrha into pits of pitch. He is a maiming rock, he demands banishment and impalement, he appears as one who has trodden in the winepress and his garments are red from the blood of the people he has trampled in his wrath (Isa. 63, 2ff).

This "bull-like" aspect of Yahweh also appears in ceremonies. At least in Dan and Bethel, the power of Yahweh was represented and venerated in the image of a bull (1 Kings 12, 28ff).[23] And even the famous golden calf which Aaron built at Mount Sinai and for which he ordered a feast was not intended to show an alien idol, but Yahweh (Exod. 32). When later prophetic tradition condemns this as an apostasy (e.g. Hos. 8, 4-6), it argues against violating the prohibition of images: The immense power of Yahweh cannot be pictured by man, it is too great and powerful.[24] Nonetheless, the temple of Solomon housed a sculpture of the sea, supported by twelve oxen (1 King 7, 23 ff) that recalls the sea-bull from Knossos. The ferocity of the bull is best shown by his lowered horns, ready for attack. And so the prophet Balaam says of the God of Israel: "God...is like the wild ox's horns to him. He feeds on the carcasses of his enemies, and he breaks their bones in pieces" (Num. 24, 8; Num. 23, 22). Accordingly, not only the palaces of Crete, but also the altars of Israel are adorned with bull's horns, mentioned in many places in the Scriptures (e.g. Amos 3, 14; Ps. 118, 27).[25]

In Islam, the ancient semitic form Il, El, Al for God becomes "Allah." Like El-Yahweh, the protective and paternal/maternal God "I-am-here," Allah is kind and merciful.[26] All suras of the Koran (except for Sura 9) begin "In the name of Allah, the merciful, the compassionate". His mercifulness includes everything, it "knows no limit" (Sura 7, 156). His original character as bull has metamorphosed into grandeur, majesty, and omnipotence. And yet, he has not lost his temperamental tendencies. In contrast to Yahweh, and even more so to the Abba Jesus, who "is love" (John 1, 14-16), his mercy does not include meekness and charity. "He is above such emotions. His "rahma" (mercy) is only a "in'am" (gift), and "ifdal" and "ihsam" (favor and blessing).[27] Love, in the sense of an emotional bond, does not occur in the Koran.[28] In this sense, Allah has adopted little of the features of Baal and the mothergoddess and even less of Yahweh and the Abba Jesus. He remains much more an Al, Il, El: the original bull, pushing forward with power and might.

Perhaps religion could help to master the experience of evil in human life more efficiently if this bull-like aspect of God, which crystalizes a concrete experience, were not pushed aside too quickly in favor of an abstract teaching in which God *cannot* be anything but good.

God and Evil as Serpent-Dragon (for a Sedentary Culture)

The divine trinity of Sheba, Werner Daum's "primeval semitic myth," contains a potential dualism: Athtar, the god of the fresh and life giving waters, and Schams, the goddess of warmth and sunlight, make an alliance against the old Almaqah who represents the elemental force of nature in rainstorms and gushing floods. The precondition of such dualism is that some tribes became settled. Those tribes and groups which are nomadic always move to those places where nature offers the largest food supply in a given season, and make an "arrangement" with the god of the wilderness: they adapt. They leave barren places in search of the land of "milk and honey." They appeal to the kindly aspects of the godhead, and through prayer and sacrifice they ask for his guidance and blessing. They do not have and do not need a god for irrigation or a goddess of warmth and light. They need a leader of their tribe who knows how to communicate with the god of the wilderness and how to make an alliance with him, so that the elemental force of the bull might not bring raging destruction but shed mercy and blessings upon them. The divine protection that the nomads hope and pray for is expressed symbolically in the events of their travels. The god of the wilderness thus becomes a god of protection in their travels, a god of history. He appears as the transcendent dimension of historic events, as their "countenance," perceived in a holistic way.

The situation is different for a sedentary people. Here, their attention is turned towards that which makes life possible and strengthens it within the space of their culture and civilization: towards irrigation systems, wells, cisterns and water; towards the potential for growth, symbolized by trees, towards granaries and the central organization — the "king" who rules the commonwealth, and above all, towards the sun which makes this abundance of life possible through its warmth and light. In those realities a transcendent dimension upon which their lives depend and by which they are protected appears to them. The god of the wilderness is excluded, although he retains his transcendent character, for his might is experienced in every new calamity and natural disaster. But his former more kindly aspects, his powerful mercy, are now rarely experienced. The bull loses his magnificence and fascination and turns into a man-eating

Fig. 12: Two interlaced serpents, each with two heads, one serpent with horns (ceramic from the Nazca culture, ancient Peru).

monster, a Minotaur. He is experienced now as a power that devours. One of the prominent features of this power is that it is ever changing and unfathomable: It raises its deadly head with an ever renewed form. Thus the bull is transformed into serpent and dragon. The horned snake[29] and the horned dragon[30] are amalgamations and mergers between bull and serpent, or dragon (Fig. 12). In Chinese legends dragons are transformed into bulls, and they fight with each other, one for man and one against him.[31] When snake and bull coexist, the snake often represents, in a separate form, the evil aspect of the wilderness god. Thus the El-god Yahweh curses the serpent in Paradise. In Germanic sagas the bull fights against the dragon; the dragon-killer appears in the form of a bull; the heavenly bull from ancient Norseland gives a sword to the young warrior on his way to free the maiden captured by a two-headed dragon.[32]

The expression of evil is often the most dominant characteristic of the serpent and the dragon. The dragon might have several heads that devour and spit fire, and two heads grow back when one is cut off. However, in some mythologies and cultures there is a persistent memory of the positive aspects of this elemental force, now symbolized by the dragon and the serpent. Poison can be used for healing. Whoever looks upon the bronze serpent erected by Moses is safe and healed from the bite of the

56

poisonous snake (Num. 21, 8 f). In China and Japan the dragon can become a bringer of good luck in certain circumstances and is celebrated in joyous festivals.[33] The wisdom and knowledge of the snake are well-known and sometimes used in oracles.[34] But in general, the dragon represents a force that must be banned from a settled culture and civilization. Athtar, the hero of civilization, and Schams, the wife and mother who provides food and grants fertility, must enter into an alliance; the creative power of heaven, the masterful skill of Daedalus, and the fertility of the earth must unite in order to eliminate the powers of evil from the community: the rainstorm, the flood, the drought, chaos, and destruction.

An ample supply of fresh and life-giving water is the most basic precondition of a young civilization that tries to survive in the face of the wilderness. The struggle of the hero of civilization with the serpent or the dragon is therefore very often a struggle for water. The heroic achievement of the Vedic god Indra is his victory over the serpent Vtra which is eventually forced to release the waters that it had been withholding. Krishna, too, fights a serpent-king at the upper river so that water may flow again. Even the Christian dragon fighter St. George controls waters and currents. Churches that are dedicated to him are often situated on hills near a creek or river.[35] In the valleys of the Bündnerland the streams that run down the mountain sides are called "Dröck," a word etymologically related to dragon.[36] In Ugarit the god of vegetation Baal, and the goddess of love and maternity Anat, enter into an alliance in order to conquer the river god Jamm, who is helped by dragons and serpents like Lothan and Tannin. In India, the Nagas, serpentlike divinities, are able to change into clouds. And in China, the dragon was always considered a cloud-creature that, in this case, must not be killed, but has to be implored in prayers, processions, games, and sacrifices to pour forth its rain as a blessing on the land.

It is in this very real situation of neolithic, settled life that fantastic fairy tales originate—not from some inherent archetypes of the soul.[37] Of course, these "situations" are examined with the "eyes of the heart" (Saint-Exupéry), for their "surplus value," and thus their transcendent dimension takes root deep in the soul. Later, these elements are separated from the rites and myths of a given society, and are reshaped into fairy tales. The imagination often delves far into the past, when the gods of the wilderness had to be appeased by the sacrifice of children. In such a way, Hansel and Gretel are abandoned in the wilderness. But, in their fight against the evil witch, they become descendants of the god of fertility Baal and the maternal goddess Anat. When they kill the witch, a large stream of water erupts, which they cross with the help of a duck and eventually find their way back home.[38] Similarly, the forester finds the "Foundling Bird" exposed in the woods. After it had grown up with little Lenchen, the old witch Sanne plans to thrown it into boiling water and to eat it. But the children manage to escape and to drown the witch in a duckpond. The "Two Brothers" are also abandoned in a wild forest where they are found and raised by a ranger. One of them will eventually kill a dragon, the other an evil witch.

As devouring monsters the dragon and the witch are interchangeable with the wolf.[39] Thus "Little Red Riding Hood" is swallowed together with her grandmother by a wolf in the woods, but is rescued from the monster's belly by the intervention of a courageous hunter, the descendant of Athtar-Baal, who kills the wolf. In the story of "The Wolf and the Seven Little Goats," it is the mother goddess who saves her children. With the help of the only child spared, she frees them from the wolf's belly and drowns the wolf in a well. The common theme of these fairy tales is the casting out of evil from the circle of life, and the creation of a situation in which people can live happily in peace as man and wife, as Baal and Anat, "til the end of their days."

Serpent-dragon and Bird, Darkness and Light (Dualistic Symbols)

The counterpart of the dragon and the serpent is the bird. In the hymn of the Siberian Jakutes the eagle is venerated as the sun-bird who "slowly gazes up towards the white world and beats down the mist with his wings," so that the "light mist" of the wooded lowlands rises, followed eventually by the "clear sun, large as a barn."[40] The bird disperses the dark waters and the wilderness. It brings light, brightness and clarity. According to the story of creation in the Old Testament, in the beginning "God's spirit hovered over the waters" (Gen. 1, 2). The Talmud comments: "Like a dove above her young, so did the breath of Yahweh hover over the darkness of the ancient waters, and by his word he divided light from darkness."[41] In the symbolic identification with that light and brightly colored creature which makes its way from the earth up to the sun, man can raise himself above chaos and wilderness to overcome them. That Stone Age hunter, whom we encountered in the caves of Lascaux, fighting against the raging bull, already wears a bird-shaped mask, and from his hands falls a stick with a bird on top. A bird also sits on the head of the serpent goddess of Crete, who holds two snakes in her two hands with an iron grip (Fig. 30 and Fig. 46). A divine bird from India, the wild duck Garuda, a symbol for Vishnu, is also called "snake-killer."[42] In many cultures we find representations of flying eagles that carry snakes in their talons.

This symbolism expresses a dualistic view of the world. Good and evil are strictly separated. The god of the wilderness no longer has the kindly aspects of the semitic bull-god El or the dragon-god in China or even the serpent-goddess in India, to whom one could pray and make sacrifices for abundant blessings. No mediation between good and evil is possible when the masculine force of procreation and invention and the feminine source of fertility (Athtar and Schams, Baal and Anat) unite in order to destroy the god of the wilderness. God and the world are divided in two.

Even the symbolism of historic human actions is drawn into this duality. Historic events are subjected to the symbolism of nature. The enemies that threaten the country belong to the same realm of evil as do the rainstorm, the flood, and the drought. They are all manifestations of evil, a breed of the serpent that has to be annihilated without mercy.

There are small nuances, however. Besides its traditional enemies, the Philistines and the Assyrians, Israel knew other tribes that were not part of the people of Yahweh, but with whom they maintained friendly relations, like the Kenites and the Medianites. Later Islam did not stop at the simple distinction between the faithful and the unfaithful, but saw a separate category in the Jews and Christians, the "People of the Book" who were treated more indulgently than the idolaters. On the other hand, Zarathustra in ancient Persia distinguished only between the followers of the good god Ahura Mazda, and the followers of "Daeva," a word that in the Indian language signifies manifold divinities, but has only retained the meaning of "evil spirit," "demon" in modern Iran. This dualistic rupture extends through the whole cosmos. It even results in duality of language. The Indian language has two words for "son": "puthra" and "sunu." But today, in the Iranian-Avestan language, the words are sharply distinct in meaning: "puthra" is only the son of a follower of Ahura Mazda, whereas "sunu" is the son of a man from the realm of Daeva, the realm of evil.[43]

To a degree, this dualism has also penetrated the religious thought of Israel. For Israel, too, had to defend its culture against external threats of destruction when it became sedentary. Thus Yahweh sometimes takes on the characteristics of Baal: He "smashes the heads of monsters on the waters" and he "crushes Leviathan's head." Like Athtar, he opens springs and creeks of fresh water (Ps. 74, 13-15). He "pierced" and "split" the sea-monster Rehab "in two like a carcass" (Ps. 89, 10; Isa. 59, 9). "With his power he calmed the sea...His breath made the heavens luminous, his hand pierced the fleeing serpent" (Job 26, 12 f). And again, the symbolism of nature is transposed upon historic events: Rehab, the dragon, the coiled viper, becomes the symbol of Egypt and of the Pharaoh (Isa. 30, 7), who must be crushed in the same way.

In the monastery of Qumran in the desert around the time of Jesus, monks distinguished clearly between the sons of light and the sons of darkness, doomed to rejection and annihilation. In the New Testament this dualism is particularly evident in the Apocalypse of John. Here a huge, flaming, red dragon with seven heads and ten horns fights with the woman whose garment is the sun, and tries to devour her child (Rev. 12, 1 f). The angel Michael takes over the role of Athtar-Baal and fights as a hero of light for the woman and mother against the dragon. In the end, the great dragon, the old serpent named "devil" and "Satan" is thrown in the lake of fire and sulfur (Rev. 20, 10).

Coping with Existence and Suffering through Symbols

At a conference of pyschotherapists in 1978, Victor E. Frankl, the founder of logotherapy,[44] gave a paper in which he distinguished between two kinds of pain. On the one hand, he said, there is a kind of pain that man has to fight with the utmost dedication. That in this abundant world children starve every day is a revolting injustice that must be fought. That there are still many diseases caused by inadequate hygiene, poor diet, contaminated water and unsanitary living conditions is a scandal that must be corrected. But on the other hand, there is suffering that cannot be overcome in the same way. We may try to lengthen the span of a human life, and to ease the process of aging and dying, but it would be hubris to hope for a total abolition of the natural limits of human life. For example, even if we would prefer to remain awake, we must accept the fact that we become tired after a number of hours without sleep.

Often the line between the suffering that has to be accepted and that which has to be fought against is a fine one. A man who has suffered a stroke must be given all possible options, and he himself must do everything possible to exercise and to enhance his remaining abilities. It is remarkable how much can be accomplished through steadfast exercising and use of the remaining brain cells. A certain disability will remain. Medical tests should determine precisely the nature of this impairment. But when it is determined with certainty, acceptance is the only remaining response. It will be necessary to accept this new status and to integrate it into the rest of one's life. Frankl says that the eventual success of a human life depends to a great extent on one's ability to discriminate between these two forms of suffering and to respond to them appropriately.

The help that he as a therapist could offer, he said, was above all to enable people to come to such a discernment, and to apply their decision within the context of their lives. But where can one find the criteria that offer guidance in these difficult but vital decisions, and that help him make the right judgment? A truly human and liberating effect of such a decision of conscience cannot be achieved by mere submission to religious authority, or by accepting traditional religious teachings or ethical precepts as "true" and relevant to one's own life. If religion is experienced only under this aspect, it will remain superficial to man.[45]

Only when religion provides symbols for the human heart and eyes, symbols in which he can recognize himself and his existential experience in a deep and focused way, can it help man to "lead a successful human life."[46] The successful encounter with a symbol results in a "disclosure,"[47] an opening of the eyes, a flash of insight in which the "scales fall from his eyes," so that man sees his situation clearly, and finds the means to cope with it. The symbol of the resurrection, for example, is the transcendent dimension of an everyday experience: the waking from sleep, seen in a holistic way. From this symbol, the angels come forth on Easter morning in shining garments, leaving the darkness of the grave and telling the desperate women, "Why do you look for the living among the dead?" (Luke 24, 4 f). Thus, the darkness is lifted from them, and they see the road they must follow, the way that leads them first to the apostles in Galilee.

The ravenous hunger for esoteric teaching especially among our young people is nothing other than a search for symbols that give light and a direction to our lives. But the question is how efficient these symbols are, symbols which mirror my life and to which I look for direction. The symbolism of many esoteric writings that circulate in great numbers nowadays seems indeed to respond to certain unclear although forceful longings and hopes of modern man, but only because they parrot and imitate those feelings. The space from which these symbols come is shallow, has no depth, and is not born from a living tradition. After a while these symbols dissolve into the very mist and darkness which they had promised to enlighten in the first place. A similar thing happens when the searching modern man is confronted with ancient but alien symbols from other traditions. For a short time he might imagine he recognizes his life and gains orientation. But he soon gets lost in the network of foreign symbols. Individual symbols lose their context, and are swept away by the rising flood of the problems of life.

The symbols of the bull and of the dragon—and of the bird as its counterpart—are probably the oldest symbols in religious history. As we have tried to show, they lead us from the darkness of the Stone Age caves all the way to Judeo-Christian religion. On the one hand they seem far away, and therefore have a certain esoteric flavor that makes them attractive. On the other hand, they are encountered in the Bible, in the basic texts of the Jews and Christians, and are therefore rooted in historic and social traditions. In concrete situations of suffering, these symbols can help much more than a clever discourse, even though it may be a heartfelt one. The charging bull with his lowered horns is a powerful symbol for the experience of a man who has suffered a stroke or who has lost a person he loves. It does not provide him with any kind of "concept" that might help him raise himself above the pain. But can conceptual statements really have that effect anyway? Can existential pain be coped with by the intellect alone? Is it not the case that too much life and vitality are lost in such an attempt?

The suffering man recognizes his own situation in the charging bull. This symbol helps him grasp what has happened to him. At the same time, he knows that in experiencing that symbol he is in communication with hundreds of thousands of years of people who have experienced similar things. And if he then goes on living with that symbol and learns from the biblical tradition that the same "El Shaddai," the terrible transcendent power of the bull, changed—in certain situations also related to human suffering—into the paternal/maternal God "I-am-here," or even into the Abba, as "Mama/Papa" (Exod. 6, 2 f: Jesus' name for the Father), then his vitality may be refreshed and renewed. He will have experienced a close, existential encounter with the dark side of this God, of whom it is also said that his deepest nature is pure love. How both of these aspects are possible remains incomprehensible—and even the Bible does not resolve this paradox with any sort of theory—but there is the credible account of the darkness of the tomb turning into the brightest day. Suffering man will then be on the lookout for experiences in which the night brightens. The most important experience of this nature that makes possible the real encounter with the biblical symbol of God, is the caring of other people who believe in God. Insofar as these people symbolize the "I-am-here," and maybe even the Abba, in their concrete being and actions, the symbol can "catch on" and give strength and support to the grief-stricken man.

The same holds true for the symbols of the serpent and the dragon. In certain situations man is not struck down by some exterior event, but the trouble may rise from within; satiety and boredom may afflict him. Life may become filled with a mass of small but tiring frustrations; depression may follow. These situations are most adequately expressed by the symbol of the creeping serpent and dragon. These symbols show more of the slow rise of evil, while the bull incarnates the sudden blow of a tragic fate. When man starts to ponder his situation in this symbolic perspective, he will also find the images that bring him salvation. Above the dragon, which threatens to swallow him up in the slimy darkness of its bottomless gullet, will appear the image of the brightly feathered bird, which beats the mist with his wings until the dry land appears, until the sun rises, large as a barn. A man should be on the look-out for these symbols. He will discover the dove, hovering over the chaos, in some hitherto neglected dimension of his life, and when he lets the bird into his life, it will divide light and darkness for him. Coping with life is coping with suffering, and that is possible only through symbols.

Evil as Sin (and Satan) in the Bible

The power of evil works against man's projects throughout his life. Like a prosecutor in court, it turns all actions, words, and intentions into evil. Eventually, man is confronted with the shattered pieces of his life, and, often enough, has himself to blame for the disaster. The Bible calls this power "sin" and "Satan." The liberally minded man takes these terms as belonging in the realm of mythology. It is said that they are "ideas limited to their time" that have to be abandoned by modern people.[48]

Indeed, it is not a scientific concept, pointing at a circumscribed, well-defined empirical reality. In the perspective of scientific empiricism, sin and Satan "do not exist." But did the Bible ever use these words in this context? Are they not rather symbols in which the universal human experience of evil and destruction is expressed in a single figure that, although not scientifically and empirically tangible, can be perceived through experience? And does this figure not thus grant man the possibility of dealing with these experiences in a historical way, within a dialogue?

Of course, if Satan and sin are treated as quasi-empirical reality, evil becomes frozen, so to speak, and man's abilities to cope with it are paralyzed. But by doing away with the *symbol* together with the concepts do we not deprive ourselves of the potential of a meditative approach through dialogue to the negative experiences in our lives? For by doing so we will lose the ability to discern the evil angels in our lives and will fall prey to them.[49]

"Sin" is a biblical symbol. It expresses the fall, an event that is recounted in Genesis. Often pride and presumption were considered the root of sin. "You will be like gods, knowing good and evil" (Gen. 3, 5) is the serpent's bait, which entices the woman and her husband to eat from the forbidden tree. For centuries, the catechism taught that humility and obedience, the acceptance of any given condition, of the social "class" into which one was born, submission to the Church and lay authorities, were the basic virtues which protected one from evil. The biblical text, of course, says nothing of the kind. The serpent's temptation does not consist in an elevation from vassal to free citizen and free Christian believer, but in becoming like God and knowing good and evil. Man may and should use and develop all his potential in life. Adam and Eve may eat from all trees of the garden but the tree that stands in the middle of the garden they may not touch lest they be doomed to perish. This means that the "tree in the middle of the garden" embodies divine power itself. The Old Testament relates several times that he who comes in close contact with it must die: "For man cannot see me and live" (Exod. 33, 20; see also the divine apparition in Isa. 6, 1-7). Therefore, the root of evil is not rebellion against men and against circumstances created by men—on the contrary, the rebellion against the Egyptian Pharaoh and his enslaving is at the very root of Judeo-Christian faith, it was ordered by the Godhead itself—but only in the exceeding of man's limits as human being, the violent attempt at usurping divine power and knowledge.

Man sins when he chooses not to be human. Sin is the violent appropriation of an existence and a life that is not fit for man, but harms and destroys him. When the epistle to the Hebrews and subsequently the Council of Chalcedon describe Jesus Christ as in all ways similar to man, "though he is without sin" (Heb. 4, 15), they do not mean that Jesus was not actually like man, since sinfulness is part of human reality. Rather, the phrase means that Jesus was the first man in world history who did not succumb to the temptation of escaping from the rich possibilities of his humanity and of seizing that divine power which does not belong to man, but destroys him whenever he usurps it. Jesus was the first man who remained human and lived out the fullness of human potentiality: the first perfect man. Sin, on the other hand, is the usurpation of God by man, the attempt to seize and appropriate divine authority: The bull is slaughtered and eaten in a sacred meal.[50]

This usurpation of the divine also underlies the Cain and Abel story of a fall through sin. Cain murders his brother because he sees that Abel's offering is accepted, while his is not. It is the situation of two rival brothers who imitate each other, where the one becomes both a model and an obstacle for the other.[51] In the murder of his brother, Cain tries by means of violence to gain the divine attention that was expressed through the acceptance of Abel's sacrifice. His brother's murder is thus an attempted usurpation of God.

This symbolism is pursued very obviously in the story of the tower of Babel: "Come, they said, let us build ourselves a town and a tower with its top reaching heaven" (Gen. 11, 4). Man no longer wanted to depend on God to give him rain and to make his fields fertile—he wanted to create an "artificial paradise" for himself. The idea of ruling everything and everyone by a centralized power (the "tree in the middle of the garden") is, as we shall see in more detail, the form divine usurpation takes during the founding of early states, in which entire classes of the population were forced into slavery.[52]

64

Slaves are property. They are counted like cattle and corn. King David, by taking a census of the free Israelites, declared the people of Yahweh his property, seizing for himself what belonged to Yahweh. In 1 Chron. 21, Satan is said to have induced David to commit this sin. The punishment shows the gravity of his wrongdoing: After acknowledging his guilt, David is given by Yahweh the choice between three very severe punishments — famine, plague, or invasion and destruction by enemies. David chooses the plague. Thus it is mainly the people who have to suffer for David's wrongdoing. Because of his presumption in counting Yahweh's people, as if he were an "alter deus," 70,000 Israelites, we are told, died.

The same symbolism of sin is found throughout the New Testament as well. Like our first parents, Jesus is led into the temptation of sin (Matt. 4, 1-11 and Luke 4, 1-13). His seducer suggests that he "tell these stones to turn into loaves" (Matt. 4, 3). This is an invitation to violence, to the usurpation of a power which would not let be what is, which does not yield to the given, but wishes to raise itself above it. The second temptation also suggests an act of violence. Yahweh should be forced to interfere in order to save his beloved son. Man wants to avail himself of divine power. In the last temptation the political dimension of sin as usurpation becomes visible. The "empires of the worlds and their glory" refer quite clearly to the Roman empire that was built on military force and conquests. The Roman emperor has usurped the world, the creation and property of Yahweh. These plundered goods are offered to Jesus if he would fall on his knees and worship the power of the conquerer (and thereby become a conquerer himself).

In contrast to our first parents, Jesus withstands the temptation. He does not want to be like God, he wants to remain a man who accepts the limits of his humanity, fully confident of the Abba and his love, and who accepts as a gift all the things that he needs to live and to be happy. In this attitude, the healing breath of God is active in him and enables him to comfort men and to heal them. But the divinity that becomes manifest in him provokes others to usurpation. Jesus makes this very clear in the parable of the murder at the vineyard (Mark 12, 1-8).[53] Yahweh has entrusted the people which he has planted (his "vineyard") to the care of the religious leaders of Israel. These leaders do not behave like leaseholders, but like owners of the vineyard. They beat the servants sent by the Lord to collect the rent. When the owner patiently continues sending servants, the tenants finally put them to death. And when, in the end, he sends his "beloved son" to them, hoping they would respect him at last, the wine-growers say to each other: "This is the heir. Come, let us kill him, and the inheritance will be ours. So they seized him and killed him and threw him out of the vineyard." (Mark 12, 7).

The usurpation is complete. Wherever the divine shines through in this world, it is sucked into a whirlpool of violence. Just as Cain became the murderer of Abel on whom God's favor rested in order to usurp this divine blessing, so the beloved son on whom "my favor rests" (Mark 1, 11) is tried for blasphemy by his brothers, the people of Israel, and put to death. Therefore the gospel of John says of them: "The devil is your father, and you prefer to do what your father wants. He was a murderer from the start" (John 8, 44). He has murdered and incited to murder in order to seize the divine by force.[54]

Even the last and dearest of Jesus' remaining friends fall prey to this usurpation. In a crisis, abandoned by most of his followers, Jesus asks his faithful friends about his identity (Mark 8, 29-33): " 'But you,' he asked 'who do you say I am?' Peter spoke up and said to him, 'You are the Christ'." We mostly remember Jesus' answer from Matt. 16, 16 ff., in which Simon is blessed for this answer and named the "rock" of the church. But this passage has been recognized by historical-critical exegesis as a later interpolation. Jesus cared about his mission in Israel; he was not thinking of the later church at that moment. In the oldest Gospel text, namely Mark 8, 29, Jesus gives Peter a different answer. He tells him to keep silent and points to the suffering that he is about to endure in Jerusalem. When Peter tries to dissuade him, Jesus addresses him in the same way as he did when he pushed away (Matt. 4, 10) the temptation of aggressive messianism: "Get behind me, Satan! Because the way you think is not God's way but man's" (Mark 4, 8-10). Peter is still captivated by violence. He is the first to draw his sword and to assault the servant of the high priest at Jesus' arrest in Gethsemane (Matt. 4, 8-10). When Peter calls Jesus the Christ, the Messiah, he does so in expectation of a political messiah who will drive the Romans out of the country and free Israel. Even in the conversation of the disciples at Emmaus this hope shines through: "Our own hope had been that he would be the one to set Israel free" (Luke 24, 21). When Peter, in the courtyard of the palace where Jesus is being questioned, finally comes to recognize that Jesus is not willing to play the role that he expected, he begins to curse and to swear that he does not know "the man" (Mark 14, 71), and Judas commits suicide.[55]

Thus Jesus died on the gallows "for the sake of sin" — that is, because of that cycle of violence and killing that tries to usurp and to seize the divine whenever it appears. A later tradition transformed this into the theory of "sacrifice of penance" by which Jesus "atones" for the sins of man. Girard, who uncovers primeval human violence hidden in the rites of sacrifice in all cultures and religions, comments: "Nothing in the gospels points to the fact that Jesus' death was a sacrifice of any nature: sacrifice of penance, of substitution etc... . The passages that are

66

generally quoted to confirm the sacrificial view of the Passion cannot be and do not need to be interpreted as sacrifice".[56]Important theologians have subscribed to this opinion of Girard,[57] or have, themselves, come to similar conclusions.[58] Girard's theses seem to be confirmed by the Old Testament as well.[59] Girard does not make a distinction between offerings—whether of first fruits and gifts or of slaughtered animals or humans.[60] But this much is clear: Jesus is not a sacrifice slaughtered for the reconciliation of a vengeful, and therefore violent God. Rather, it is our own sinfulness rooted in the usurpation of the divine since the beginning of mankind that drove Jesus to his death. We did not leave him with any choice other than the betrayal of himself and his innermost mission, or death. He died for the sake of our sins, because we did not let him live.[61]

The Profanation of Evil in the History of Biblical Thought: the "Fall" of Satan

In the oldest biblical texts, evil is a dimension of God. For example, it is told in Exod. 4, 24 that Yahweh orders Moses to go to Egypt and to lead the people of Israel out of captivity. Moses is hesitant and refuses for a long time. Eventually he gives in. With the help of his brother Aaron he will fulfill the command and be obedient to Yahweh. He sets off for Egypt with his wife and his little son to take up his difficult task. While they rest on their journey—fulfilling Yahweh's commands—the text says, "When Moses had halted for the night, Yahweh came to meet him and tried to kill him." Obviously, Yahweh has a demonic character here. This is emphasized by the action of Zipporah, Moses' wife. She takes a flint,[62] cuts off her son's foreskin and touches Moses' legs with it to mark him a "bridegroom of blood," a hero who has fought against the power of chaos, shedding his blood and thus earning a place at the sacred wedding. Only when he sees this blood does the demon let go of Moses. Similarly, Yahweh spares the men and beasts of those houses whose doorposts are marked with blood when, on the night of the Passover, he goes through Egypt to "strike down all the first-born in the land of Egypt, man and beast alike" (Exod. 12, 12).[63]

The "Jabbok fight" is another impressive example of evil, of the wild and demonic as a dimension of God. At a ford of the river Jabbok, Jacob is attacked by a male being, a sort of nocturnal water demon. Jacob wrestles with him until dawn. He withstands the assailant, but his hip is seriously injured. When the sun rises, the demon wants to go. His time is over. But Jacob says: "I will not let you go unless you bless me" (Gen. 32, 27). Thereupon the god of the wilderness gives Jacob the name

67

"Israel" and blesses him. He explains the name by saying: "You have been strong against God (El), you shall prevail against man" (Gen. 32, 29). This etymology might not correspond to the accepted one—according to W. Beltz, Israel means "El rules" or "El is bright"[64]—but it shows that there were tribes[65] who thought of themselves as "fighters with El," as people who wrested the blessing and the fertility of their land with great effort from the old bull and wilderness god El,[66] and therefore projected this name onto their mythical ancestor.

At any rate, in this old story Yahweh-El is still intimately linked to the experience of the demonic, including its benevolent and blessing aspects, as is customary in the history of religions. These aspects—that is, the aspects of Yahweh, of "I-am-here"—Jacob wrestled from him.[67] This attitude is a general characteristic of the relation between Israel and its God.

This demonic aspect of God is also evident in the ancient version of the story of David's census (2 Sam. 24, 1 ff.) in which it is said bluntly that *Yahweh himself* induced David to commit this usurpation of the people of Yahweh.

In all these passages we perceive those ancient layers of the Old Testament in which the demonic is still a dimension of God. In these stories Yahweh clearly has the features of the wilderness god. Like the "mountain spirits" and other personifications of the wild and frightening forces in ancient folk tales, he can wantonly exercise a benevolent or a destructive power.[68] He embodies the universal power that causes everything, both good and evil. The prophet Amos asks: "Does misfortune come to a city if Yahweh has not sent it?" (Amos 3, 6) and even in the prophet of the exile (Deutero-) Isaiah, Yahweh says about himself: "I am Yahweh, unrivalled, I form the light and create the dark. I make good fortune and create calamity, it is I, Yahweh, who do all this" (Isa. 45, 7 f.).

In later texts evil is separated from the identification with God. The prologue to the book of Job 1, 6 ff. is characteristic in this respect: "...One day the Sons of God came to attend on Yahweh, and among them was Satan...". Thus Satan is one of the "Sons of God." El and the demon are still closely related; they are linked as father and son, but are no longer identical. Now this "Son of God" Satan provokes Yahweh into testing Job. He makes a bet with Yahweh that Job is not the good obedient servant that Yahweh thinks. Evil is still an element of Yahweh, but separated from him to a certain degree.

In even later texts Yahweh and Satan are seen as separate and opposing powers.[69] This evolution can be followed very clearly by comparing the older and the more recent versions of the story of David's census. In the oldest version (2 Sam. 24), it is "Yahweh" who induces David to commit sin; in the later version (1 Chron. 21, 1 ff.) the name "Yahweh" is replaced by "Satan." The "wrath of Yahweh," his negative wilderness aspect, has become an independent figure that is related to him at first (the "Son of God" in Job), but is progressively detached from him and becomes his opponent.[70] In later texts this tendency is noticeable: In Zech. 3, 1 ff., Satan appears as a plaintiff against the just and devout Joshua—but without being summoned to do so by God, rather as a free opponent of Yahweh. In an apocryphal tale about the "fight of the Sons of God," which was formerly much used in catechesis, the rebellious angel "Lucifer" who wanted to be like God—and thus prefigures the original sin of usurping the divine—is cast down into hell by the Archangel Michael.

In this myth of the angel's fall the ancient history of religion shines through.[71] The opponent is called "Lucifer," that is: bearer of light. Like the ancient god Athtar from Sheba and his successor Baal in Ugarit, he is a divinity of light, related to Venus and the moon.[72] Athtar marries the sun-goddess Schams and both try—as in the Yemeni tale "The Darkness" and in the Grimm fairy tale "Hänsel and Gretel"—to kill the dark god of the wilderness, the witch, the dragon of chaos. In other Arabic tales the hero of light steals the sword of lightning from "Il Afrit," the monster of the wilderness, and puts him to death with his own weapon. He beheads him with a single stroke.[73] But in the apocryphal myth El is the stronger. He casts the rebellious hero of light ("Lucifer"), who by his usurpation has become Satan, the opponent, into the abyss of hell.

The symbolism of the Fall from Paradise belongs in this cultural and historic context. In many tales and myths from the Mediterranean, the goddess of love or maternity chooses her lover by offering him a piece of fruit, most often an apple. In the Yemeni story of "The Donkey's Skin"[74] the daughter of the sultan stands on the roof of her palace while noble warriors circle the castle. She throws an apple to the chosen one. The Greeks who thought in terms of patriarchy, reversed this scenario: Paris gives the apple to Aphrodite (not Hera or Athena) and thus wins Helen. But even this myth still expresses what man can win from woman: Hera offers him a kingdom, Athena promises victory over his enemies, and Aphrodite offers sensual love. Paris will accept only this last gift from a woman.

In the ancient Arabic tales, on the other hand, man receives everything from woman. She gives the hero a "donkey's skin"—a name that expresses virile potency and fertility[75]—the powerful horse and the sword of lightning with which he will overcome the god of the wilderness and become king. So the chosen one is originally the hero of light and culture who, together with the wife and mother, takes complete possession of the realm of civilization, the garden of Eden, and reigns therein as king. He usurps the central authority, the "tree in the middle of the garden," the force of growth and vegetation in nature. He no longer lives according to the rhythms of nature, but determines himself what is good and what is evil. Man and woman have been seduced by the fascination of the unfathomable, ever renewing, elemental might of nature and its deadly power, the serpent, and later the dragon.

But, as in the celestial events of the apocryphal myth, the usurpation fails. Of course, the woman and her hero of light in Genesis do not become transcendent opponents of God, as in non-biblical myths. They are not cast into the abyss, but merely driven out of paradise. Their world becomes profane. Adam no longer works in the garden, but on stony and thorny soil, making and eating his bread "by the sweat of his brow." Eve is no longer the strong woman who rules the commonwealth as wife and mother, but the submissive companion of man, who gives birth to their children in pain, and yet yearns for her husband (Gen. 3, 16). Those who wanted to usurp the elemental power of nature, the "tree in the middle of the garden," El-Yahweh, the force of the wilderness, must now wrest their life from him who once gave in superabundance. Of course the god of the wilderness still shows his kindness: In a feminine, motherly gesture, he makes garments from animal pelts for them and clothes them. But the decisive point is that he curses and separates himself from the seducing force, depriving it of the power over life and death, condemning the serpent to absolute un-sacredness: "…be accursed beyond all cattle, all wild beasts. You shall crawl on your belly and eat dust every day of your life" (Gen. 3, 14).

This progression of the separation of evil from El-Yahweh continues all the way to the story of Jesus. Jesus, a Jew of late Judaism, says to the seventy-two disciples whom he had sent out to announce the coming of the kingdom of God, and who have returned full of joy, telling him that even the demons submitted to them (Luke 10, 18): "I watched Satan fall like lightning from heaven." Here again, the fall of Satan is not into hell, as in the apocryphal myth, but onto the earth. Henceforth, he becomes neither a super-terrestrial nor a sub-terrestrial power, but a terrestrial one. The fascination with the power of death is denounced as profane brutality and evil. He no longer has any divine or angelic power. Through the power of the coming rule of the Abba-god, Jesus, it is eventually reduced to nothing (although it still can make man die): "I have given you the power to trample serpents and scorpions and all the power of the enemy" (Luke 10, 19).

Jesus senses that through his influence the power of evil is broken, and that there is nothing evil left in heaven with Yahweh. However, he did not "fight a war" against Satan and his adherents, or strike the pagans with a "sharp sword," like an "apocalyptic rider" on a white horse, "his cloak soaked in blood" (Rev. 19, 11-16). Jesus is not a hero. To be sure, he has wrestled with God and men. "He offered up prayer and entreaty, aloud and in silent tears, to the one who had the power to save him out of death" (Heb. 5, 7), and in other parables he struggled to open his adversaries to the message of the new divine kingdom that had begun with his coming. But he never fought a war, neither against gods and demons, nor against men. He is, therefore, neither victor nor victim. Nor did he conquer Satan and banish him from heaven. Rather he clung faithfully to his experience at the river Jordan, to the experience of being the beloved son of the heavenly father. By the power of that love Satan, the serpent, the dragon, was separated from El-Yahweh and fell to the earth as a profane and eventually harmless being. The power to kill thereby lost its transcendent, divine character: "Do not be afraid of those who kill the body and after that can do no more" (Luke 12, 4).

For Jesus, Yahweh is the pure Abba from whom comes a "ruach," a wind and breath that are no longer symbolized in the bull, the powerful animals or the eagle, but in the dove, the symbol of reconciliation between man and God (Gen. 8, 18 ff. and 8, 21 f.), the sacred animal of the goddesses of love, Ishtar and Aphrodite. This breath of love without violence had filled him at the river Jordan and had made him into what he is: the "Son," the manifestation of God as Love. We see here a fundamental, historic turn in the history of man's symbolic values. Originally, Yahweh was closely associated with the bull god El, the El-Shaddai, the Almighty, and as such he was the enemy and opponent of the hero of light, Athtar-Baal and his female ally. But the more men explore the mystery of Yahweh's explanation of his name during the Exodus—"I-am-here"—the more Yahweh begins to resemble both Baal, the giver of life and fertility, and the caring wife and mother. In the psalms, he struggles against the sea monster Rehab, like Baal in Ugarit (Ps. 89, 11). And in Job, "his hand pierces the fugitive dragon" (Job 26, 12 f.), which he had cursed in Paradise. His "beloved son" Jesus is therefore the redeemer without violence, who no longer fights wars against the god of the wilderness presuming to kill him in the course of usurpation. Rather, he wrestles with his God—as a second Jacob, a new Isra-El, a fighter not *against,* but *with* God—in the night of his passage over the river of death. He holds on to his God like Jacob (Gen. 32, 27: "I will not release you unless you bless me"), until the sun rises on Easter morning and shines brightly into the empty grave, showing that death and the fascination of the power to kill are nothing but a projection of man's fear that has been eliminated by love, wrestled out of God by Jesus Christ and unmasked as *pro-fanum,* as not belonging to God.

The Book of Revelation has transformed the actions of Jesus into the old images of the war against chaos that is fought by the hero of light and the woman against the god of the wilderness. Here Jesus, the conquerer on the white horse (Rev. 6, 2), and Michael, the conquerer of Satan, fight together for the "woman, clothed with the sun, standing on the moon, and with the twelve stars on her head for a crown" (Rev. 12, 1) and against the red dragon with his seven heads and ten horns. The trumpet is blown for the final war of annihilation against the god of the wilderness. The God "I-am-here" and the Abba Jesus are unrecognizable. In the end, "the devil, the seducer, will be flung into the lake of fire and sulphur, where the beast and the false prophet are, and they will be tormented day and night, for ever." (Rev. 20, 10). Here the symbolism of separation freezes into a picture of horror that can hardly be balanced by the subsequent image of the heavenly Jerusalem. The image of horror is in contradiction with what Jesus had announced and lived as the coming of a new kingdom of the God "I-am-here" (especially in his parables).[76] Insofar as the sacred city is founded on the violent expulsion of the dragon and the false prophet, it is not the symbol of that new life in the kingdom of God which Jesus has experienced and to which he testified in his death and resurrection.

In contrast to these pictures of a militant, violent separation of evil from the divine, the idea of universal restoration appears in Peter's speech at the temple-square (Acts 3, 21), an idea that gives hope for a final rehabilitation of the separated, of a *metamorphosis* of evil and a reconciliation. "Jesus must remain in heaven until the universal restoration comes which God proclaimed, speaking through his holy prophets." There are theologians who took this sentence to mean that hell is not eternal, but that through Jesus *everything* will eventually be reconciled.[77] In the form of a revealed doctrine, this would of course challenge the idea of human freedom: man must open himself to the Abba-God, whether he wants to or not. Man would be God's puppet, pulled into His kingdom by inescapable strings. Finally, even in this perspective, God would be nothing but the almighty El-Shaddai, the bull. Therefore, the dogma of universal reconciliation has been rightfully rejected by the magisterium as a formal statement.[78] But nothing keeps the Christian from *hoping* that, although the *possibility* exists of a separation of free spirits from God, not only temporarily in the earthly realm, but permanently in transcendence (thus in the realm of the divine) and *has* to exist for the sake of human freedom, no free spirit would choose the "impossible" option, so that in the end God will be "all in all" (1 Col. 15, 28).

It is characteristic of the biblical history of salvation and its structure that there is another line of tradition parallel to the line of severance of evil, which emphasizes the maternal, protective aspects of God's nature. It is grounded in the original symbolism of the name Yahweh: The oldest texts already interpret this God who frees his people from Egypt, and thus founds the religion of Yahweh, as "I-am-here." This presence corresponds to the desire of the infant for permanent closeness to its mother or its father, a desire that no earthly mother or father can ever fulfill. But Israel experiences the "God from Egypt" as a caring and protective force that is always "present." Thus Yahweh is a sort of divine mother and father. Only a divine mother or father can always be present.

In the context of biblical language, names reveal the nature of things. The revelation of "Yahweh" as the worthy name for God therefore opens a new chapter in religious history: Until then God was called "El" (the Old Testament uses the plural form — "Elohim"). That name designates the highest, indeed the only, God, who asks submission and devotion (in Arabic "Islam") from all human beings. The name "Yahweh" reveals a different nature. To his people, with whom he has entered into a covenant through Moses, God is not the bull "El" or "Elohim" any more, but the "I-am-here." In the burning thornbush the voice of God speaks to Moses: "This is what you must say to the sons of Israel: I-am has sent me to you," and continues, "To Abraham and Isaac and Jacob I appeared as El Shaddai — as the frightening, mighty El (compare Jacob's oath by "the fear of his father Isaac" in Gen. 31, 53); I did not make myself known to them by my name Yahweh" (Exod. 6, 3). This happens only after the freeing of the Israelites from slavery in Egypt. Throughout the sorrowful history of Yahweh and his people of Israel, this revelation of God unfolds and is developed until it finds new dimension in Jesus.

In the Old Testament, there is no parental relation between Yahweh and the gentiles. To the enemies of Israel Yahweh is still the frightening El: He throws the army of Egypt into confusion (Exod. 14, 24). And later, he spreads terror among the enemies of Israel and throws them into confusion (Exod. 23, 27). Indeed, he is the terrifying one who treads the winepress, whose garment is red with the blood of the people (Isa. 63, 2 ff.). The extension of God's revelation as Yahweh to other peoples begins only fifty days after Jesus' death at the feast of Pentecost in Jerusalem, in Peter's speech. Only the breath of the crucified and resurrected Jesus generates a speech about the God "I-am-here" that "every nation under heaven" ("Parthians, Medes and Elamites; people from

Mesopotamia, Judaea and Cappadocia, Pontus and Asia, Phrygia and Pamphylia"...and even Romans) understands in its "mother tongue" (Acts 2, 5 ff.), because it promises the fulfilment of the child's elemental desire for the presence of its mother and father to them as well. In the Old Testament, only Israel is the beloved son of Yahweh for whom he is present.

Yahweh's relation with Israel is characterized by his mercy.[79] In Hebrew "mercy" is "rahamim." This term has a common root with the Hebrew "reheb," mother's womb. Thus, when Yahweh's mercy is mentioned, his motherliness, his maternal affection is implied. This line of tradition can be traced in many passages. It is most clear in the prophet Hosea through whom Yahweh speaks in Hos. 11, 3 f.: "I also taught Ephraim[80] to walk, I took them in my arms...I led them with the reins of kindness, with bonds of love. I was like someone lifting a child close against his cheek; bending down to him I gave him his food." This is characteristic of the prophetic tradition as a whole, e.g. the Deutero-Isaiah who proclaimed the figure of the suffering servant of God which Jesus later took to refer to him. Through Isaiah Yahweh says: "Like a son comforted by his mother I will comfort you" (Isa. 66, 13); and he gives the promise of unfailing maternal faithfulness: "Can a woman forget her infant at the breast, or fail to love the son of her womb? Yet even if these forget, I will never forget you" (Isa. 49, 15).

Yahweh's motherliness also comes through in a narrative text, in the symbolism of the story of Jonah. Jonah is swallowed by a sea monster, which would, in other mythological contexts, signify a dragon of chaos who, like the black bull, embodies untameable violence, and would normally be fought and conquered by the dragon fighter.[81] By contrast, Jonah is swallowed by the monster, not to be eaten, but instead, to be protected. It swims towards the shores of Nineveh, the destination that was given to Jonah and which he had tried to escape. There, it "vomits him onto the shore," that is, it releases him from its belly like a mother her offspring—exactly at the place where he was to fulfill his destiny.

That is why in this story the dragon of chaos, the serpent, is transformed into a fish. And this is probably the solution of the mystery why in early Christianity the fish was a symbol of Jesus.[82] Through his life, actions, and death he changed the serpent into a fish, the poisonous into edible, evil into good. How much Jesus' own imagination was filled with Yahweh's motherliness can be seen in the grandest and most beautiful of his parables: the parable of the prodigal son, or of the merciful father, as it is called by modern exegetes (Luke 15, 11-32). It is a representation of the mercy, of the "rahamim," of that maternal love which reaches out to the beloved son in his estrangement even to the farthest foreign land, a love that catches up with him and makes the dead come alive: "Because your brother here was dead and has come to life" (Luke 15, 32).

This line of tradition of Yahweh's maternal care corresponds to the separation of evil from him: To the degree that evil is separated from him, he unveils his kindly maternal nature. To be sure, he is and remains a mother who does not restrain her son when he leaves for distant countries to squander his inheritance with prostitutes. She allows him his freedom. Only her love, a love without violence, accompanies him, unseen and unrecognized, building the foundation for a possible reconciliation: "I will leave this place and go to my father" (Luke 15, 18). It prevents man from establishing himself forever in usurpation, the root of sin, and from burning eternally in the sulphurous lake of the Apocalypse.

Whenever there is talk of sin and the violence of evil that strikes man—in sermons, catechism, religious education or pastoral counseling—the symbolism of religious history and the Bible as we have analyzed it here should be used in a decisive way. The elemental power with which evil strikes us may be articulated and mirrored in the ancient images of the bull-like god of the wilderness, and in the biblical images of the demonic features of Yahweh—the Yahweh who comes in the night to kill Moses (Exod. 4, 24 ff.), the angel of death who passes through Egypt, and the nocturnal river demon who assaults Jacob at the ford. One can meditate upon guilt, one's own or that of others, using the images of the dragon and the serpent from religious history, and using the Old and New Testament stories of sin as usurpation of the Divine. Finally, by reliving the historic path of the experience of God from the Old to the New Testament, a path of hope can be discovered: After Jesus, evil is no longer part of God. It has fallen from God as some earthly attribute that man had projected into God. It lives on in our readiness, when stirred up by fear, to commit acts of violence and usurpation, which we sorrowfully experience within and outside of ourselves and which obscure our perception of nature and of history. But in the image of God cleansed of evil as was revealed by the prophets and by Jesus Christ, in the image of the child and its Abba, and the breath of the dove that unites them both, we have been given symbols that can heal us from evil. He who internalizes this image feels new forces streaming toward him, forces that dissolve the fear and the clenching grip of evil, just as the strength of the nocturnal river demon who fought with Jacob at the ford dissolved with the first light of morning.

2 Liberation from the Spell of the Power to Kill: The Path of Christian Salvation

Violence and Terror (Lynching) as the Foundation of Human Community (R. Girard)

Paul's reference to Christ being sacrificed as our Passover lamb (1 Cor. 5, 7) serves in his letter to justify an act of violence. Through the blood of Christ, the sacrificial lamb, the old leaven is discarded. The Christian community is purified and sanctified. But one member of the community, who lives "with his father's wife," jeopardizes this purity. Now the cleansing of the community must be renewed. This occurs in such a way that the sinful member is excluded from the community and "killed" (in a magical-spiritual way): "When you are assembled together in the name of the Lord Jesus he is to be handed over to Satan for the destruction of his corrupt nature so that his spirit may find salvation on the day of the Lord" (1 Cor. 5, 4-5). That we are really dealing with a magical-spiritual mechanism of execution becomes clear in the last sentence of the pericope in which Paul, the critic of the Old Law—the law of sinfulness, as he puts it (Rom. 8, 2)—takes up this same law and quotes, in a vigorous conclusion to this section of his letter, the very passage that demands the merciless stoning of erring fellow beings: "You must expel this evil-doer from among you" (1 Cor. 5, 13; Deut. 17, 7, with the addition in 19, 21: "...You are to show no pity..."). This statement—his physical body may be destroyed so that his spirit be saved—was the formula according to which heretics and witches were mercilessly executed and burnt at the stake.

In this reading from Paul, a mechanism is at work upon which, according to René Girard, human society is founded both as a whole and in its parts:[1] This is the mechanism of violence, the conspiracy of all against one who will be cast out and killed as a scapegoat, so that through this horror of witnessing death the others might be brought closer together and might stabilize their community upon the victim's grave. "Others will hear of it and be afraid and never again do such an evil thing" (Deut. 19, 20). Girard, familiar with the texts of world literature, has discovered that the scapegoat mechanism underlies most ancient myths and most great literary texts, from the plays of Sophocles, through Shakespeare's plays and up to the novels of Camus. The significance of a text, its special atmosphere that inspires both dread and fascination, always comes from the distant memory of that violence upon which human society is founded. Girard talks about the "founding murder,"[2] which nourishes those texts. They play with it, try to veil it, or attempt to show its tragic necessity in order to legitimize (that is, to consecrate) the power that stands behind it.

The founding myth of the Ojibwa Indians tells that the five clans of the tribe go back to six supersensual beings who came from the ocean. They were all kind to humans, but one of them had such an intense look in his eyes that everyone who looked at him immediately dropped dead. So his five companions begged him to return to the bottom of the sea. They then founded the five clans and thus the whole tribe. The community of the five is founded on the exclusion of the one (who had, just as the witches in the middle ages, the "evil eye").[3] Romulus "had to" kill his brother Remus, even if the latter, out of playful bravado, merely crossed the imaginary "city wall" of Rome, sketched as a furrow in the sand. Only thus could he impose his new law, establishing it with his brother's blood and the horror of death, so that Rome and its empire could be founded and rise to prosperity.

Cadmus founded the city of Thebes by killing a terrifying dragon and sowing its teeth into the earth with a plough. From the dragon seeds fierce warriors sprang up, fighting and killing each other until there were only five left. These five entered into an alliance with Cadmus and built the city of Thebes. In numerous fairy tales, sagas, and legends, (also, for example, in the legend of St. George) the killing of a dragon is the deed upon which a city or a kingdom is founded. Even the Holy City in the Apocalypse of John, the New Jerusalem, descends from heaven only after the devil, the dragon, the false prophet, all evil powers and all those who were not signed into the book of life, are cast into the lake of sulphur. There they are being tortured "day and night, for ever and ever" (Rev. 20, 10). Only against the backdrop of a horrifying transcendent power can the sacred order of the city and of the commonwealth arise.

In the symbolism of these texts we see the conditions of life in the Neolithic Period, as it was described above in the context of the ancient symbols of the divine, the bull and the dragon. The old bull-like god of the wilderness is seen from his dreadful noctural side, forcefully separated from the realm of human civilization, and killed as dragon or serpent. In this way, the transcendent power of the god of the wilderness is transferred to the dragon killer, who can now establish and rule over a human community with his strength. The king is the bearer of the El-like, elemental power of the divine.

But memories fade. Therefore the divine power that founds a human community and makes its continuing existence possible, has to be renewed from time to time, at regular intervals, after a year, or after a cycle of harvesting, and especially in times of hardship. Originally this was per-

77

formed by human sacrifices. They were much more widespread in ancient cultures than is generally assumed.[4] Even a careful and conservative scholar such as Müller-Karpe interprets the buried skulls from the Middle Palaeolithic Period in this way. The skulls that were found in an oval-shaped stone circle at the Guattari cave of Monte Circeo, south of Rome, are particularly noteworthy (Fig. 13). The skull is clearly damaged by a blow and the hole between skull and spine has been widened artificially, an indication that the brain might have been removed. This is characteristic of many skulls found in such excavations. Müller-Karpe writes: "Expert anthropologists exclude the possiblility of accidental or subsequent damage to the skulls. We have therefore to assume that these individuals met a violent death, probably within a cultic ritual—as the findings of Monte Circeo should have proved."[5]

The Aztec human sacrifices are well known. They were described by Padre Bernardino de Sahagún, a Spanish missionary (Fig. 14). The prisoners are led up the steps of the temple-pyramids. "After they have been brought up before the countenance of Uitzilopóchtli, they are laid, one by one, on the sacrificial stone, and handed over to six priests. They turn them face up and cut open their breasts with thick flint knives. The prisoner's heart is called the fruit of the eagle, or the precious stone. They lift it up and consecrate it to the sun, to the prince of turquoise, to the rising eagle, give it to him, and feed him with it. After the offering, the

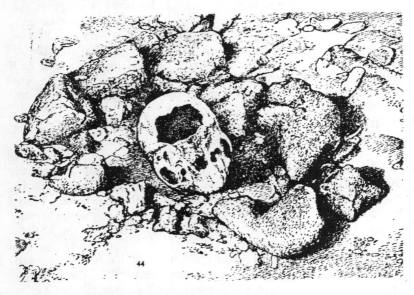

Fig. 13: Buried skull in the Guattari cave near Monte Circeo.

78

Fig. 14: Mayan scene of human sacrifice; from the Temple of the Jaguars, Chichen Itza, Yucatan.

hearts are dropped in the eagle's bowl. The prisoners that were sacrificed are called 'the ones from the eagle's land.' Afterwards, they are rolled down the steps of the temple. They bounce and roll like pumpkins, hit the steps, turn over and over until they reach the Apétlac (the patio at the bottom of the pyramid)."[6] The god Uitzilopóchtli was at the same time the god of war and the god of spring. The gruesome ritual killing shows his terrible power to kill his enemies, a power that is expressed to his followers in a new growth and blossoming of the fields and meadows. Life and prosperity are possible only against the backdrop of this terrible power.

Later, these human sacrifices are replaced by animal sacrifices.[7] Very often the cultic tales of ancient ritual places still give indications of original human sacrifices. In many rituals the sacrificial animals are separated from the herd and put into a certain special relation with the human world (e.g. in Indonesia where small piglets are nursed by women before being sacrificed). The favored animals for sacrifices are those that express strength and vitality: bulls, horses, goats and bucks. While tying up and killing the animal, man becomes shudderingly aware that it is in fact he himself who should have been the victim. In the gushing blood of the slaughtered animal the royal/priestly power to kill rises to a degree of gravity and ceremony that consecrates and validates the bonds and laws of the community. Important contracts were always concluded by a sacrifice. The sacrificial blood expressed the importance and the existential seriousness of the event, and sealed the contract for all participants. Sacrifice was required for reconciliation and community accord. Even the letter to the Hebrews says: "if no blood is shed, there is no remission" (Heb. 9, 22). The interpretation of Jesus' execution as sacred, sacrificial death is probably rooted in this tradition of thought from the Old Testament.[8]

However, when a community confronted a major crisis the blood of animals was no longer sufficient. The blood of humans, even of whole groups of people, had to be shed. When in the middle ages the human community was threatened by the plague the Jews were held responsible for the disaster and were killed by the thousands. In a similar way the Nazis looked for scapegoats in the chaotic situation following World War I to "cleanse" their own people through the extermination of another people. Of course the victim can also be an exterior enemy on whom the accumulated inner aggressions of a society are focused. That means war. Initially, every war is a "holy" war, a "sacrifice," namely the sacrifice of the enemy to the god and for the welfare of one's own people.

Girard traces this mechanism of killing and violence back to the very beginnings of mankind. He explains the rise of aggression and violence from the urge to imitate that can be observed in higher mammals: an object or a piece of food appears even more desirable because the other, the rival, longs for it.[9] This "mimetic urge" causes an increase in aggression within the community that threatens to paralyze its vital functions. Eventually this paralysis is overcome by channelling the aggressions towards the killing of an arbitrary victim from within the community. From time to time this procedure has to be renewed.

The Origins of Violence in Man's Transition to Game Hunter

Girard's analyses become even more plausible when seen in the light of Walter Burkert's research in prehistory.[10] Independently of Girard, he too comes to the interpretation of religious sacrifice as a "consecration of violence."[11] He sees the original situation which urgently needed such a consecration of human killing power in order to build and maintain communities in the passage of prehistorical and protohistorical man from being a gatherer and scavenger to being a game hunter. The behavioral change from gatherer and scavenger to game hunter consists in a violent self-exaltation of man. And this occurs at the cradle of humanity. "From the predatory behavior that he developed during his emerging humanity we may get some perspective to help us understand human violence."[12]

80

The relation to Girard's theories can be demonstrated in this way: Human nature is not inherently equipped with an apparatus of instincts that makes man fit for predatory behavior.[13] The killing of a large animal is not programmed in his network of instincts. He has to *learn* to kill as a "cultural" act. There are many accounts of hunting cultures in which the men seek several days of isolation from their wives and children before a hunt, practice sexual abstinence, and work themselves into an artificial, aggressive trance—similar to that of war dances.[14] Because man does not have the instinct to distinguish fellow man from prey, the transition to game hunting entails the beginning of the ability to kill his fellow man. Indeed, it is this very ability that shows most clearly whether someone has achieved the status of game hunter, of "homo necans." Accordingly, in many primitive races, the initiation, i.e. the introduction of the young man into adulthood, consists of an instruction in the art of killing and of being killed. In his isolation from the community, through fasting and inflicted pain, he suffers a cultic death from which he is born again—now in possession of the power to kill. Among the headhunters of New Guinea, the person responsible for the education of the young man, namely the brother of the mother (not the father), is obliged to provide a prisoner whom the nephew can kill. Killing is the characteristic of the strong man: "The strong man shatters all that comes into his hand; he takes pleasure in killing."[15]

This example is frightening—but it might make us aware that in our own allegedly civilized world, the duties of every young man include learning the art of killing in the name of the state. The inhibition to kill is weakened by the fact that humans do not kill with their own teeth or claws, but with weapons. That allows even the prehistoric man to kill from a distance. In our evolved civilization, we have become fully distanced from the act of killing, which is done by pressing a button. Thus man is a sort of unnatural or supernatural predator (lifting himself above his own nature). He may see any of his fellow men as potential prey: *homo homini lupus.*

It is only this background that makes Girard's analyses truly convincing. In a group of men in which everyone confronts the other as a potentially deadly adversary, as a predator ready to kill, it is plausible that no one dares to move and to follow his instinctive desires. As soon as a man approaches a woman of the community, he runs the risk of provoking anger and jealousy and being pierced by his fellow man's spear. The result is a paralysis that can only be overcome by that which has become possible through man's transition to predatory behavior: the killing of man by man. When one of the group provokes the aggression of most or all of the others, each individual realizes the obvious danger that faces everyone. For anyone could have been the victim. The

81

blood that is shed is the blood of one's own species. All are deeply marked by the realization that the situation which led to the bloody act must never occur again—because one might himself be the next victim. That which triggered the murder is henceforth taboo. This is the origin of the oldest laws and commands that focus, characteristically, on the interdiction of approaching a woman from one's own community. Exogamy, the obligation to mate with a woman from a different clan, is a widespread practice in almost all ethnic cultures even to this day. From time to time this "founding murder" has to be repeated in order to keep alive the horror of the power to kill and to ensure the observance of community rules.

According to Girard's book "Violence and the Sacred," this is the origin of religion. Violence, the human power to kill, imposes itself as a force that both fascinates and makes one shudder. The sacred is encountered, according to Rudolf Otto's well known formulation, as the *"fascinosum et tremendum."* But Girard overlooks the fact that even before this transition of human nature to the *homo necans,* man was surrounded by a fascinating world of objects. Very early in the transitional phase between beast and human being, man developed the faculty to "experience within the naturally preceptible things a dimension that transcends the objective," which is where Müller-Karpe sees the origin of religion.[17]

In his often quoted work testing the intelligence of anthropoid apes,[18] Manfred Köhler relates how objects with a particular shape can provoke an inexplicable fear or a superstitious attraction in chimpanzees. The female chimp Tschego for example always carried a stone, made round and smooth by water. She would not let anyone touch it and took it into her nest at night. It was for her a sort of fetish—the step that immediately precedes the perception and experience of the absolute, of "something of absolute concern" (P. Tillich), that is, a divine symbol. While digging up bones of Australopithecus in Makapansgat, the palaeontologist Dart found a dark, perforated stone that looked as if it had been polished by generations who had handled it[19]—very early evidence of how "within naturally perceptible things a dimension that transcends the objective" (Müller-Karpe) was experienced and how certain early forms of religion were already practiced on the threshold of humanity.

Certainly the bull and the wild horse, the tiger and the panther, the vitality of large and strong animals, had fascinated man even before the transition to game hunting—as it still does today in many symbols used in advertising. Consider, for example, the well-known commercial for "Esso" brand gasoline with the tiger, or numerous images of predators and powerful animals in advertisements for cars or cigarettes (Fig. 15).

82

Fig. 15: Advertisement for Varta batteries. The panther, as domesticated predator, symbolizes strength and superiority.

Other things must have fascinated the early man as well, like the stones mentioned earlier, trees, and, to a great extent, human sexuality as is documented in the numerous representations of phalluses and vulvas in Stone Age caves. Through his sexual organs and their functions, man again experienced a dimension that transcends the objective, the merely biological—thus: religion. Up to this day, the images of the phallus and the vulva are at the center of the innermost sanctuary of many Hindu temples.

However, this particular symbol is linked to the power to kill at the very moment of the transition to game hunting, that is, in the attempt to appropriate the spell-binding, divine symbol of the animal by piercing and eating it. As Walter Burkert rightly observes, the symbol of sexuality thus undergoes a considerable accretion in power. The sacredness that henceforth would be the foundation of human companionship is reenforced by a violent usurpation of life—in bloodshed, in the sacrificial killing of man and beast.

But the faculty of symbolic perception preceded all this. This perception is, according to S. K. Langer, the root of language and therefore of humanity.[20] To express it in an even more fundamental way (insofar as the faculty of perception develops by adapting itself to that which is perceived) we should look at St. John's gospel—"In the beginning was the Word." Here is the claim of events in a dimension that surpasses the empirical level of reality. Here is their inner transcendence, their angel, their symbolic message. This Word was "God." To perceive him and to live with him was simultaneously the beginning of language, of religion and of humanity: The Word which is God has created man and his "world." "Through him all things came to be, and apart from him nothing came to be" (John 1, 3).[21]

We do not know what moved the ancient people to engage in predatory behavior. It was not necessarily a lack of food or starvation. For even prehuman species, like the Australopithecus and the *Homo habilis*, who did not hunt, prospered and certainly could have preserved their species without resorting to hunting. It is generally thought that only twenty percent of prehistoric man's diet consisted of hunted game, as it does in contemporary tribes of hunters and gatherers such as the Pygmies. For meat supply, carrion and small animals would have sufficed.

It was probably this fascination, the experience of a dimension beyond the objective, that led man to this primeval deed, to the original sin that defined the very core of his life and experience. Size, strength and vitality—the giant deer or the bison, stalked and attacked by dangerous predators and surrounded by buzzards; the "central power" (later the "tree in the middle of the garden")—these fascinated prehistoric man more than anything else. These were all the more seductive since he himself was also a contentious scavenger, although he excelled them all by his superior intelligence. He did not resist the temptation to appropriate this size, strength and vitality by directly attacking and consuming it. The power of this fascination is evidenced by the wealth of images on the walls of Stone Age caves, especially by those images that depict man in animal costumes. Just as little girls like to put on their mother's clothes and shoes because they want to be like her, so prehistoric man put on the skins of animals and danced around in playful rhythms—independently of any specific religious meaning attached to that behavior (Fig. 16).

Fig. 16: A hunter clothed in a deerskin; the ''sorcerer'' (shaman) from the cave of Trois-Frères, later Paleolithic period.

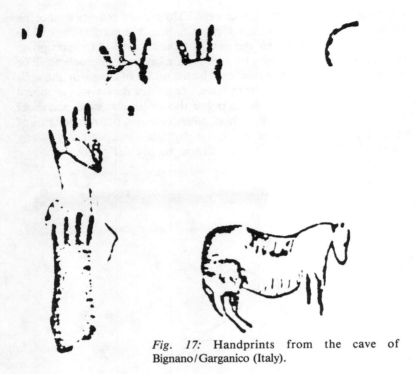

Fig. 17: Handprints from the cave of Bignano/Garganico (Italy).

God as Killing-power and the Other "Gods"

Thus, the "founding murder" was not the origin of religion. Rather, it was the expression of religion. It was the murder of God, the usurpation of the divine, as it is mirrored, in a different cultural milieu, in the biblical story of the Fall: the reaching for the tree in the middle of the garden in order to be "like gods" (Gen. 3, 4 ff.); the slaying of the brother Abel to force God to accept the offering of the murderer (Gen. 4, 1-16); the tower at Babel "with its top reaching heaven" (Gen. 11, 1-9).

Man was surely human before he began to indulge in this usurping behavior. He walked upright and his hands were free. Mothers could easily hold their newborns in their hands and in their arms. They did not need to cling to her as baby apes fearfully cling to their mothers' fur—a situation that, with anthropoid apes, often leads to deadly accidents when the baby slips off during a jump. Man could embrace, caress and fondle his partner as well as his child. With his free hands he could make mallets, scrapers, and sticks to dig out roots and plants. He could gather food in liana bags and carry it to the common resting place. There, the

Fig. 18: The "Red woman from Mauern." A red-colored figurine with female buttocks and a phallus-shaped upper body, a powerful sexual symbol (from the caves in the vineyards of Mauern, Landkreis Neuburg-Schrobenhausen (Germany), ca. 30,000-15,000 BC).

mothers and wives could hand out the food to the members of the group.[22] So the hand was yet another thing that continued to fascinate man. The hand-prints found on the walls of Stone Age caves still bear witness to that fascination (Fig. 17). Through original sin, however, the gathering stick became a spear, and the hand that clenched it with an iron grip fused with the spear and became a brutal instrument of slaughter, stabbing the large and mighty animal to death.

We have already mentioned the strong fascination of sexuality. In prehistoric art, the representation of naked women with pronounced, often exaggerated sexual characteristics is, after animals, the most frequent motif (Fig. 3). Some pictures of parturition can be seen, although not very distinctly. Nude female figures, shaped from ivory, wood or clay, are found in the later Paleolithic Period on sites from Siberia to Spain (see Fig. 18). Certain variations and transformations in these representations can be traced (see in chap. 3.3 of "Development," the section on Crete) up to the civilization of the Neolithic Period and the Bronze Age.[23]

Using different perspectives we will show how even the realm of sexuality has come under the influence of violence and killing, of original sin. In all cultures, the lance, the spear and the arrow, even guns and pistols, are phallic symbols, symbols of male potency as a deadly force. This potency is provided by woman. The connection is made very clear in a drawing in Algeria from the later Paleolithic Period (Fig. 19). The hunter's arrow is as thick and strong as a lance and points in the same

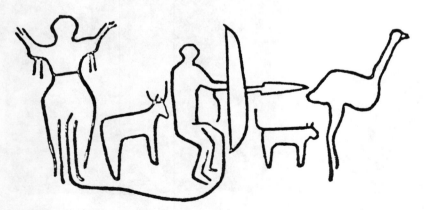

Fig. 19: Sexuality and hunting: The power of the hunter arises from the connection between the woman's vagina and the man's penis (note the connecting line); the penis points in the same direction as the arrow (rock-drawing from Tiout, Algeria; late Paleolithic period).

88

direction as his erect penis, that is, towards his prey. Behind the hunter stands a woman, lifting her arms in a gesture of surrender. A sort of "electrical wire" joins her vagina and the hunter's penis. This "cable" provides him with the energy that brings the penis to erection and thus makes him a successful (potent) hunter. This is confirmed by many hunting scenes in Paleolithic art in which the hunter has an erect penis (Fig. 20 and 21, as well as Fig. 30). Burkert has gathered an impressive amount of ethnological and mythological materials on the connection between hunting, killing and sexuality.[24] It is the woman who, sexually, provides man with potency and the power to kill. In later cultures, she therefore hands over to him the magic sword, or the apple from the "tree in the middle of the garden," the "central authority," and makes him king, the ruler over good and evil.

Of course, we do not intend to renew old incriminations here. Such an incrimination, whether it is aimed at man or at woman, would itself be part of a circle of violence and slaying. It is the expression of the mechanism of the scapegoat which Girard places at the beginning of human history. Even if certain passages from the Bible seem to establish the roles of the sexes in favor of the male (1 Tim. 2, 14), today we acknowledge the validity of the statement issued by Pope John Paul II in his encyclical "Mulieris dignitatem," on the occasion of the Marian Year, 1988: "There is no doubt that, apart from this 'distribution of roles,' the original sin in the account of the Bible is the sin of the human being who was created by God as man and woman."[25] To be sure, it is the male who

Fig. 20: A hunter in a deerskin stalking two stags; the erect penis is conspicuous (cave of Trois-Frères, Magdalénien period).

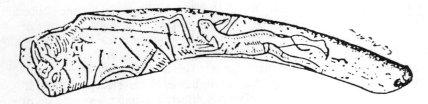

Fig. 21: A hunter creeps up on a bison. His right hand (not visible in the upper margin of the picture) probably holds a spear sling, which he aims at the animal; the penis is erect as well (discovered under the cliffs of Laugerie-basse in the Dordogne; late Paleolithic period).

pierces the beast with his phallic spear, and thus becomes a hunter. But if woman had not been his accomplice, if she had not shared in the perverted sexual excitement of the slaying, if she had not rewarded the great hunter with her love and sexual surrender, this sinful change of behavior, the transition from the gatherer and scavenger to game hunter and unnatural predator could never have taken place. The phallus could never have turned into a spear, and later into cannons and missiles — at least not permanently. Sexuality binds man and woman together. Its perversion into an act of killing is therefore a deed in which both are indivisibly coupled.

The potential transformation of sexuality to aggression can be observed to a certain degree in animal behavior. In many mammals, the male's erection is also a demonstration of rank, and in certain species of apes, the males defend their terrritory by taking threatening postures with erect penises.[26] But only in humans is this behavior transformed into stabbing large animals to death with spears as artificial phalluses, inducing a radical change in thought and feeling. A specifically sinful mentality evolves that infuses preying, hunting and killing with libidinous associations — the so-called hunting instinct in humans is a perverted sexual instinct — and confuses a sense of property, of mutual appropriation and of grandeur, power, and tragedy with love and sexuality, spoiling both in the process.

Of course, human sexuality existed even before this transition to game hunting, even before male potency was perverted into the power to kill. Indeed, it was very highly developed in man, compared to other species of his kind, for it existed independently of mating periods. It served not only for procreation, but also helped the human female whose child is born relatively early and still undeveloped (demanding a long period of care and upbringing), to tie the male to her through a common, ecstatic experience. Thus she could turn him into a faithful assistant in the difficult task of feeding and caring for the child. Before any perversion, human sexuality is an expression of joy and the superabundance of life, and as such it serves to strengthen human relations. The meaning of excitement and penetration is not death, but the ecstasy of life.

The birth of a child, the entrance of a new human being into the world, also belongs to this "ec-stasis," this "going outside of oneself." The use of the child as a divine symbol will be the topic of a separate chapter (Chap. 1 of the "Development" section). But for the time being, consider this quotation from a handbook of prehistory: "From that time on, in which material conditions allowed the preservation of burial places, namely from the Middle Paleolithic Period, the graves of children stand out, in number as well as in the wealth of the burial gifts."[27] Personhood has been recognized since very early times as the transcendent aspect of the child and indeed of all human beings. Perhaps it is this perception, above all, that signifies the beginning of humanity.[28] Of course, even this perception eventually comes under the spell of the power to kill. In the slaying of a fellowman, in human sacrifice, and especially in the sacrifice of children, the fascination of the power to kill is based on the usurpation of that most precious thing—the personality of one's fellowman and of the child, their transcendent dimension. But even here, the usurpation implies a preceding good. Man must have experienced the personal element, the divine quality within the child and within his fellowman before he could usurp it and draw it into the cycle of violence and killing.

So ancient man was not completely dominated by his fascination with the strong animal and the power to kill. With the help of this power, which is so unnatural to his species, he raised himself to a level of greater strength and vitality than even that of the strong animal. And yet, it did not engulf everything in his life. The violent mechanism of the scapegoat could work only because man loved his life—women, children, his own creativity, the search for and consuming of food, social gatherings and sexuality—and because he saw that his life was threatened by his uncontrolled power. If primeval man had experienced the "dimension beyond the objective within naturally perceivable things"[29] only in mighty animals and in his own even mightier power to kill, his transition to game hunting would have ended with the extinction of humankind in an orgy of horror and bloodshed.

Today, such an orgy of horror appears again on the horizon of human history in the form of a possible nuclear holocaust. In the past, man controlled the situation paradoxically by using the same power that he encountered in animals as a transcendent dimension and that he tried to confer upon himself in the act of killing and eating, as a shield for his own life. In his killing (sacrificing) he activated the transcendent power in such a way that people bowed to the rules of communal life, making their survival possible.

Until this very day, fear and terror, "global deterrence," ensure civilization's survival. "Deterrence" is not meant only in its strategic military sense. Wherever people live together in great numbers they need a superior authority, a high and mighty power that prevents the possible terror, checks the aggression within our species, and summons the members of the community to abide by the given rules and laws. Every executive office has something of a temple about it. The building in which the laws of the United States are defined is called the Supreme Court Building. The judges themselves wear black robes. Even in modern times there have been public executions in which the state authority manifested its power to kill. A relatively harmless variant of the fascination with force and violence can be observed in the athletic world; and yet the violent incidents at soccer games are alarming. The bold headlines of the sports pages such as "Boris Becker Destroys Ivan Lendl," or "Steffi Graf Murdered by Newcomer" are worthy of examination and may say more than they intend.

The fascination of violence as the power to kill still dwells in us and man can live in a community only insofar as he yields to an ascending hierarchy of power, leading eventually to "El Shaddai" of the Old Testament (Exod. 6, 3), to the transcendent being, symbolized in the bull, to the god of terror. But he chooses to yield because (and as long as) he loves peace and life, security and happiness more than death and terror. The fascination of life always exceeded and still exceeds the fascination of the killing power.

The Offering of the First Fruits and the Sacrificial Killing

Thus, religion must not be interpreted one-sidedly in terms of slaying in hunt and sacrifice as suggested by Burkert and Girard. Both are preceded by the fascination of life. Even the animal world knows purposeless games, playful motions, the song of birds, all of which express a superabundance of life. In humans this superabundance is experienced as a transcendent dimension beyond the objective, venerated in cultic acts. Music and dance, the luxury of artistic works, the exuberant paintings in caves, the ornamentation of tools, the modelling and carving of figures from clay, bone and ivory, as well as the wanton wasting of food and drink during harvest festivals, are all expressions of this excess of life and of the fascination that primeval man experienced in this life.

The fascination of life finds its religious expression in the offering of the first fruits which mostly consists of food and drink, and during which people joyously and gratefully spread out and "offer" the first harvested sheaves, the first fermented wine, fresh milk, or the firstborn calf, to that transcendent dimension that manifests itself in those elemental rhythms of life. As Josef Blank puts it,[30] the offering of the first fruits is the expression of an enthusiastic joy of life and thanksgiving for the gift of life. As such, this form of religious expression is fundamentally different from the sacrificial killing described above, which sacralizes violence and the power to kill in order to protect life.[31] In all religions and cultures we can distinguish between these two forms of offering. Could the life of Jesus be interpreted as an overflow of his vitality, offered in the gesture of the Last Supper,[32] as an offering of the first fruits, as an expression of thanksgiving and of superabundance of life—rather than a sacrificial killing for reconciliation with a wrathful godhead?

Of course, the origin of offering the first fruits does not exclude later transitions to sacrificial killing. Wherever the overflow of life is celebrated, cake and sweets are set out, milk and wine are poured into fires. An enthusiastic joy of life is the unmistakable origin of these religious forms of expression. But when the first-born lamb, or indeed the first-born human child is put to death and offered up, the offering of the first fruits can turn into a sacrificial killing. Therefore the criticism of cults by the prophets in the Old Testament which specifically bans the sacrificing of children, rejects both "burnt and slaughtered offerings" and "offerings of food and gifts" as hateful to Yahweh.

God as the Power to Kill and as "I-am-Here" in the Old Testament

In all religions there is a cult of life and a cult of death. Paradoxically, even the cult of death is in the service of life. But the great, grave and ceremonial literary traditions of human culture have all been written from the perspective of those who perform sacrifices for the protection of life and the community. Girard's great discovery, however, consists in his having found, among all these texts (whose origins are religious) *one* that has very different roots. This is the tradition of biblical texts. Their origin is not in the building of a community or a state, nor in the elevation of the killing power (as in the founding of cities). On the contrary, it is the flight, the liberation from this power, the liberation of a people from the great centralized state of Egypt. It is from the house of slavery that is Egypt, from "Egypt" as an expression of a community in which people rule over others by oppressing them with the power to kill, that biblical man sought liberation.[33] The primeval experience of biblical man included the unmasking as profane and mortal things those animals, objects, and people that inspired him with the fascination of strength, force and violence—horses, chariots, and armed warriors. Helpless, they stuck fast in the bog and drowned. The terror which they inspired was an illusion. They no longer are the symbols of divine power, but the expression of the presumption of man in enslaving his fellow beings. The God of Moses, whom the tribe experiences in this liberation, is different. Indeed, for the rulers of the Egyptian state he is the old frightful "El Shaddai," the primeval god of the wilderness, not visible in things made and done by men, but whose transcendent symbols are dark thunder clouds and raging flames. Towards his own people, however, he shows a new and different face: "I am who I am. This...is what you must say to the sons of Israel: I AM has sent me to you...This is my name for all time; by this name I shall be invoked for all generations to come" (Exod. 3, 14 f.). Even before he revealed himself to Moses as the God "I-am-here" for his people, he was there and cared for them like a mother: "I have visited you and seen all that the Egyptians are doing to you. And so I have resolved to bring you up out of Egypt where you are oppressed..to a land where milk and honey flow" (Exod. 3, 17). The old "El Shaddai," the primeval god of terror to whom nomadic ancestors had yielded and whom they had worshipped as their protector on the road, has now revealed himself to Moses as Yahweh, as the God "I-am-here" (Exod. 6, 3).

Although this event is a turning point in history, it should not be viewed in isolation. Several centuries later, when the biblical prophets strove to revitalize the old Mosaic tradition of Yahweh within Israel—while the world was being governed by god-like kings, by the power to kill held by the state and legitimized by divine law—there were people on other continents who tried to break away from the fascination of the god of terror, thus founding new religious traditions. In the fifth century BC, Lao-tzu indicated in his obscure aphorisms that wherever life was ruled by a code of ethical norms, people had already fallen away from the "Tao," the primeval womb of all being. Legend tells how he left the political structure of his homeland, and departed like Abraham for alien lands, riding on a black ox. Around the same time, Jain and Buddha distance themselves from the spirituality of the Vedic sacrificial tradition in India, searching for a human existence that can unfold without terror and violence. By renouncing everything that men might desire and that might turn them into rivals (possessions, power, sexuality), those who followed such a way of life would no longer need a threatening god in order to live in community. In Persia, Zarathustra declared the whole of the traditional pantheon to be a world of evil and violent demons and countered it with his only true and holy god, Ahura

Mazda. Karl Jaspers refers to this time, in which people all over the world were groping for a way to be freed from the fascination of god as the terrifying power to kill, as the religious "axis" of human history.[34]

Reversion to the Fascination of the Killing-power in the Old Testament

Even within the biblical tradition, the liberation from millions of years of fascination with the god of terror is by no means achieved overnight. Not only does Yahweh remain the god of terror to Egypt and other foreign peoples, but Israel's own laws and religious rules are enforced through fear, terror, and the threat of authority. When God gave the Ten Commandments, "all the people shook with fear at the rumbling thunder and the flashing lightning, the sound of the trumpet, and the smoking mountain; and they kept their distance" (Exod. 20, 18). And Moses comments: "God would have you possessed with the fear of him, to preserve you from sin" (Exod. 20, 20). In the "Law of Holiness" (Lev. 17, 1-16) almost every interdiction is ended with the words: Whosoever does not do what is ordered "shall be outlawed from his people." According to the collection of laws in Deuteronomy the function of this "outlawing" is that "others will hear of it and shall fear and never again do a thing so evil among you" (Deut. 19, 20). The method of execution was public stoning, as in the story of Stephen from the Acts of the Apostles (Acts 7, 54-60). Everyone must participate in the execution: all against one. Repeatedly it is said: "You are to show no pity" (Deut. 19, 13, 21). And although sacrifices of children, widespread in Israel at the time, were replaced in the official rituals by animal sacrifices, the readiness of Abraham to sacrifice his only son "whom he loves" shows that, for the people of that time, even the God of Israel expected readiness to offer human sacrifices (Gen. 22, 1-19).

Just as Girard describes the mechanism of violence within the human community, the power to kill is sanctioned here as a divine power to ensure stability within the community. The building of a state is not yet possible without a threatening and terrorizing authority with the power to kill. In Israel, after the founding of the state, an official priest shed the blood of the bulls on major feast days to consecrate the state's power to kill. In the post-exile period the feast of the Great Reconciliation (Yom Kippur) takes on particular significance. It forms, together with the feast of New Year, the "great (or frightful) days" on which the god of terror is appeased in an impressive penitential ritual and his claim of sanctity is recognized.[35] The high priest lays his hands first on a young bull, then on a buck and utters a confession of sins by which he loads his own sins and the sins of his people on the sacrificial animal, so that the animal visibly takes the place of the sinful human. He then kills first the bull then the buck, takes some blood from each, and enters the shrine of the temple behind the curtain. He sprinkles the *kapporet,* the tile of reconciliation in which Yahweh is thought to be present, with the sacrificial blood. The holy god is reconciled through blood—in fact through the blood of sinners: "...if there is no shedding of blood, there is no forgiveness" (Heb. 9, 22). After that, he lays his hands upon a second buck to load it with the sins of the Israelites. Then one man drives the animal, loaded with the sins of the whole people, out into the desert, where it is handed over to "Asasel," the evil demon of the wilderness, and will die a slow, miserable death from heat, hunger and thirst.[36] This double rite expresses very clearly how Yahweh is both the frightful, holy god of the state and the primeval god of the wilderness who lives in the desert. This bloody ritual was "in full bloom"[37] in the time of Jesus, and even in the time of the early Christians. The changes in tradition that Jesus brought about have to be seen against this background.

In fact, Jesus' criticism of cultic practices is nothing but a revival and development of the original Jewish tradition. For the caring God "I-am-here" is in fact no longer "El Shaddai," the god of the wilderness (at least not to his people), and thus he does not require sacrifices. During the period of kings, when the cult of sacrifices in the temple flourished, the prophet Jeremiah reminded the people of Israel of their origins: "When I brought your ancestors out of the land of Egypt, I said nothing to them, gave them no orders about offerings and burnt sacrifices" (Jer. 7, 22). In a very similar way, the prophet Amos justifies his rejection of sacrifices by pointing to Israel's origins: "Did you bring me sacrifices and offerings in the wilderness for all those forty years, O House of Israel?" (Amos 5, 25). The cult of sacrifices is a regression to the cult of "El-Shaddai." The caring God "I-am-here" of Egypt wants his people to open their hearts and minds to his life-giving impulses and precepts. He does not want them to be fascinated and terrorized at the same time by a transcendent power to kill and to observe customs publicly out of fear.

Thus there is a consistent parallel to the emphasis on the motherly and caring aspects of Yahweh in the prophetic tradition, one that criticizes the cult of sacrifices.

It begins with the prophet Samuel in the time of Saul (1 Sam. 15, 22 f.: "...Yes, obedience is better than sacrifice, submission better than the fat of rams"), and is followed:

by Amos (Amos 5, 21-27: "I hate and despise your feasts, I take no pleasure in your solemnities. When you offer me holocausts...I reject your oblations, and refuse to look at your sacrifices of fattened cattle");

by Hosea, the prophet of Yahweh's motherliness (Hos. 8, 13: "appointed sacrifice they still offer, flesh of the sacrifice still eat, but the Lord will have none of it");

by the first Isaiah (Isa. 1, 10-17: "...What care I for your sacrifices says Yahweh. I am sick of holocausts and rams and the fat of calves. The blood of bulls and of goats gives me no pleasure...");

by the prophet Micah (Mic. 6, 6-8: "...Will he be pleased with thousands of rams with libations of oil in torrents? Shall I give my firstborn for what I have done wrong, the fruit of my body for the sin of my soul? What is good has been explained to you, man; this is what Yahweh requires of you: only this, to act justly, to love goodness and to walk humbly with your God");

by the sermon of Jeremiah (Jer. 6, 16-21: "Yahweh says this: ...ask about the ancient paths: which was the good way?...What do I care about incense that comes from Sheba, or fragrant cane from a distant country? Your holocausts find no favor, your sacrifices do not please me.");

and it reaches the period of exile[38] with Deutero-Isaiah (Isa. 43, 22-28: "Little burden have my offerings been to you, nor have I troubled you for incense....you have not filled me with the fat of your sacrifices"), and certain psalms (Ps. 40, 7-9: "You wanted no sacrifice or oblation, you asked no holocaust or sacrifice for sin;" see also Ps. 9, Ps. 50, Ps. 51, 18-19).

Finally, in Deutero-Isaiah's songs about the servant of God, a figure appears that expresses what the God "I-am-here" wants his people to be. He will become the "light for all people" not by building a great empire as a threat to neighboring people, but by destroying the murderous mechanism that makes these empires work. In his own life and being, he prefers to allow himself to be beaten rather than to beat others: "I made no resistance...I offered my back to those who struck me..." (Isa. 50, 5 f.). A strength shines through this powerlessness and non-violence that is fascinating indeed, for it bears witness to confidence—confidence in the God "I-am-here" who, from the beginning, is a God for the enslaved, the suffering and the beaten.[39]

The Abba Jesus and the God of Terror in the New Testament

According to the gospel of Luke, the mission of John the Baptist was "to give his people knowledge of salvation through the forgiveness of their sins" (Luke 1, 77). The forgiving of sins, purity in the face of God, no longer having to fear him, was the salvation for which man was longing.

97

This salvation was mediated by the cultic sacrifices in the temple of Jerusalem. There were certain groups who questioned whether this cult could really forgive people their sins, for example the Essenes at Qumran. But the doubts of those Essenes were not aimed at the sacrificial actions as such, but rather at the fact that the high priests were no longer of the lineage of Zadok. Indeed, the highest religious office was filled first by Hasmoneans and then arbitrarily by king Herod and by Roman procurators, according to political considerations. For them, the cult of the temple was therefore invalid and they retired into the desert to lead ascetic lives and practice daily ablutions that would purify them before God and prepare them for his promised coming to the people of Israel. John the Baptist did away with the esotericism of this elitist community, which excluded all other Israelites from salvation. He went to the river Jordan and prophesied to all people—including the soldiers of Herod and the publicans—the purification and the remission of all their sins through repentance, manifested by their submersion in the water of the river. He announced Yahweh's impending day of judgment, which would mark his active presence among the people of Israel. And he admonished everyone to participate in this baptism of repentance to ensure their entry into the kingdom of God. Thus John entered into direct competition with the cult of the temple, questioning its exclusive privilege to pardon sins.

Jesus followed the call for penitence of John the Baptist. His name Jeshua ("Yahweh is salvation") indicates that his mission will also be the remission of sins: "...you must name him Jesus, because he is the one who is to save his people from their sins" (Matt. 1, 21). But at first, he himself seeks forgiveness and purification—outside the official cult of the temple, through baptism by John. In this event he "saw the heavens rent in two" (Mark 1, 10): Yahweh, signified by the word "heaven," opened up to him. In this event he did not encounter the fuming breath of the god of wrath prophesied by John as universal judge, but he experienced the breath of the dove entering him, the breath of the maternal God "I-am-here." Jesus had reached back through all the obscurities of the history of Israel, to the very origins of its religious tradition, and had given a new dimension to this fount of divine revelation. For him, the God "I-am-here" became the "Abba" (his usual way of addressing God), the Mama/Papa who never cast out their child, to whom it can return for protection in any situation or need. This Abba does not come as a judge who separates the good from the evil and inflicts terrible punishments upon the wicked. No, his love and kindness is offered to all without distinction and he invites them to the heavenly wedding feast. He lets his sun rise above the just and the unjust and rains upon the good and the evil (Matt. 5, 45). He demands neither sprinkling with sacrificial blood nor ablution with water. He cleanses all by the unconditional love with which he turns toward them to be their God. When people open themselves to this love and forgive each other's trespasses (as expressed in the Lord's Prayer), they become pure before God and do not need to fear him any more.

Jesus thus follows the tradition of the prophetic criticism of cult and sacrifice. With Samuel (1 Sam. 15, 22: "Submissiveness is better than the fat of rams") and Hosea (Hos. 6, 6: "what I want is love, not sacrifice") he says that the love of God and of one's neighbor is "far more important than any holocaust and sacrifice" (Mark 12, 33). The temple as a "cultic institution of penance is superfluous."[40] Making a business of sacrifice and penance turns this house, which should be a simple "house of prayer" according to Isaiah (Isa. 56, 7), into a "robber's den" (Mark 11, 15-19; Matt. 21, 12-13; Luke 19, 45-46; John 2, 13-17). It is made by human hands and can be torn down and built up again (Mark 14, 58, Acts 6, 14, John 2, 19). The God who reveals himself in Jesus as Abba does not need such "institutions" in order to heal and to save man. That is why Jesus no longer baptizes with water, as his teacher John did, but "with the Holy Spirit" (Acts 1, 5; Matt. 3, 11). He immerses men in Abba's breath of love, in the fire of his love. Thus they are purified and the kingdom of God begins to operate in them. In this process a holistic healing is accomplished: "The blind see again, and the lame walk, lepers are cleansed, the deaf hear, the dead are raised to life and the Good News is proclaimed to the poor" (Matt. 11, 2-6; Luke 7, 18-23; Isa. 35, 5 f.). The miracle happens, and those who thought they were lost, those who were abandoned, the "sinners and publicans," open themselves to the Good News and identify themselves, like Jesus, as sons and daughters of the heavenly father.

The God who has manifested himself to Abraham, Isaac and Jacob as "El Shaddai" and protected them, and who appeared to Moses as the caring God "I-am-here," unveils his true countenance at last: He is Abba, pure love incarnate in humanity. To Moses and his people even the God "I-am-here" still appeared "like a devouring fire" (Exod. 24, 17): in the burning thornbush, in thunder and lightning, and in the "dense cloud" over Mount Sinai (Exod. 19, 16). There is still terror in him; no one can see him and live (Exod. 33, 20). Moses walks up to him alone to communicate with him. Their communion is limited in time, and the glory of God is merely reflected as a radiance on Moses' face which he veils so that the people will not be afraid (Exod. 34, 29 ff.). The revelation of God through Jesus is quite different: The voice of God does not speak to him in a dark cloud, but from the opened heaven (Mark 1, 11). He does not give Jesus any laws etched in stone, but acknowledges him as his "beloved son." And God does not remain apart, but enters into Jesus as the breath of love and reconciliation (Mark 1, 10: "like a dove"). His vital breath is the divine breath of Abba. In it Jesus is "conceived" (Matt. 1, 20); he is one with the Father (John 10, 30). To have seen him is to have seen the Father (John 14, 9). To see him does not mean one will die of terror, but that one will be free to become the beloved son or daughter of the Abba. "I personally am free...I have seen Jesus our Lord" (1 Cor. 9, 1). To see Jesus, to see "the glory on the face of Christ," leads us to faith and to eternal life (John 1, 45 ff.; 20, 29). Jesus is not alone like Moses when he ascends to God, but God descends upon Jesus, and Jesus descends to mankind, "living among us" (John 1, 14); he "addresses them and their associates as friends, in overflowing love" (the Constitution on Divine Revelation; Vatican Council II).

In parables and miracles Jesus continually reminds people of his experience. He accepts the attacks of those faithful to the Torah who anxiously cling to the stern God of justice, and he talks to them in parables,[41] hoping to ready them too for the greater love of the Abba. And indeed, when he incurs the deadly enmity of those who profit from the cult of the god of terror, he pursues his path which began with the revelation of God as Abba, as love without violence during the baptism in the river Jordan. He continues with stunning consistency and faithfulness to the very end, despite repeated temptations and fears. It was probably in the spring of the year 30 that, "as the time drew near for him to be taken up to heaven, he resolutely took the road for Jerusalem" to face the conflict (Luke 9, 51).[42] Even when many of his followers misunderstand, leave or betray him as at Caesarea Philippi (Mark 8, 27-30, John 6, 67: "Do you want to go away too?"), he does not depart from his path. Finally, when he realizes that it will take his life to stand up for his gospel and his friends, he celebrates a farewell supper with them in which he expresses with stunning clarity what brought him to this life and his approaching death. Just as ancient man, fascinated by life's superabundance, lays out food and drink in the offering of the first fruits as a gift to God, so Jesus offers up his life in the gesture with which he gives bread and wine to his friends—"Take it, this is my body...this is my blood"—moved by a dynamism of life that cannot consider death an end: "From now on, I tell you, I shall not drink wine until the day I drink the new wine with you in the kingdom of my father" (Matt. 26, 29; Mark 14, 25).

That which had been anticipated in gestures, thoughts, and feelings comes true: In Gethsemane he gives himself up without resistance to the power of the state, because he does not want to be the cause of an insurrection nor to manifest any kind of killing-power. He falls into the hands of the Roman God-king who renews and demonstrates his own "divine" power in every rebel whom he executes. But the execution of Jesus unmasks the fear of death, built up by men, as the idle threat, the rattling mechanism it had always been. Ultimately, it is not the imperial power of Rome, standing behind this cruel execution trying to reaffirm its transcendent power to kill, but the Crucified who is praised as divine by the same Roman officer who exerted divine imperial power in the execution. And shortly thereafter his friends experience the dead Jesus as living among them, eating and drinking with them once more.

A more radical change in the historical development of divine symbolism that occurs in these narrations from the gospel about Jesus could hardly be imagined. Hitherto, the sacred and the divine have been experienced in the *fascinosum et tremendum,* as Rudolf Otto describes it: as a power and authority that fascinates because it proves through sacrificial slayings that it has life at its disposal—"Surely you know I have power to release you and I have power to crucify you?" (John 19, 10)—and that everyone must fear it, knowing that anyone could have been the victim. But this power aimed too high in its attempt to take Jesus of Nazareth as a victim and to assert the divinity of its power in *his* execution. At the river Jordan Jesus had experienced a quite different God—a loving Abba—and himself as his "beloved son (Mark 1, 11). The state's mechanism of terror that now faced him—his arrest and trial, his flogging, his exposure to mockery and ultimate crucifixion—could not overcome this consciousness of God and of himself. This experience was related by his few faithful friends, probably mostly women, who went with him to his execution. The others had fled when on the night of the arrest the god of terror had risen against Jesus and his followers. But they had already absorbed the consciousness of God as Abba so thoroughly that they were able to withstand the fear, and to witness the unmasking of the divine terror by Jesus' demeanor as merely profane cruelty and a miserable political intrigue. In this execution, the God of the *fascinosum et tremendum* has died for them—and thus for all Christians. Indeed, they realized that this divine terror had never really existed, that it was only an artificial construction that had served to support an equally artificial unity among men, a unity born of fear.

When this construction collapsed at Jesus' execution, their experience of the Abba remained unchanged and was even purified. They had seen how the Abba freed his beloved son from the sorrow of death and gave him new and everlasting life. Thus Jesus brought full circle that which had begun with the liberation of Moses' people from the slavery of Egypt. An image of God that had been erected millions of years ago at the beginning of humankind had dissolved like mist. The image of God as the bull and the dragon, as flashing fire and dark storm clouds, had disappeared in the clear sky that opened over Jesus in his baptism at the river Jordan.

Deterioration in the Historical Reception of Jesus' Divine Revelation

Both the revelation of God to Moses' people during the liberation from Egypt and the divine revelation of Jesus counteract a human experience that goes back millions of years. For immeasurable periods of time men have experienced God as the bull-like force of the wilderness, and as a frightful deadly power that had to be appeased by submission and obedience. This experience is deeply rooted in the early childhood of mankind. Because man is a historic being (as understood by the Judeo-Christian tradition), neither Peter, John, Mary Magdalen, Mary the mother of Jesus, Paul, nor Luke could immediately grasp what had happened in Jesus. They could comprehend and interpret the new and different only within the terms offered by the tradition of the Judaic Old Testament, or later by the tradition of Greek philosophy. But they also could not go all the way back to the historical beginning of humanity. They had no notion of a universal religious history. Of course, they knew intuitively that they themselves and the people of all times and cultures had been redeemed through Jesus and that mankind did not need to wait for another Savior. But in their groping attempts to describe this redemption, they clung to the relatively limited repertoire of ideas, images and words that was provided to them by their religious tradition.

Great changes in religious history do not occur in the form of violent revolutions, but slowly from within. Thus, the early Christians felt themselves to be Jews and went to the temple for prayer (Acts 2, 46; 3, 1). There they witnessed the daily sacrifices. On Yom Kippur the bloody ritual of reconciliation was celebrated in their presence. But more and more those on whose minds Jesus had stamped the message of the Abba felt that the sacrifice was an idle motion, and that God, as they had come to experience him through Jesus, was not brought any closer to them. They experienced this God much more in the company of other friends of Jesus, in breaking bread and in praising the God who had been disclosed to them by Jesus (Acts 2, 46). Their fundamental insight, which was of enormous consequence and accompanied by visions of fear (Acts 10, 9-23: Peter's vision in Jaffa), was that this God-Abba, who had been disclosed to them by Jesus, was no longer just a God of the Jews. "Parthians, Medes and Elamites; people from Mesopotamia, Judaea and Cappadocia, Pontus and Asia, Phrygia and Pamphylia, Egypt and the parts of Libya around Cyrene, as well as visitors from Rome—Jews and proselytes alike—Cretans and Arabs"—all could understand this gospel of God as the loving Abba from within their own traditions, "in their own language." They did not need first to become Jews in order to be the beloved daughters and sons of this Abba (Pentecost—Acts 2, 5-11).

Of course, the first Christians lived within the traditions of the Old Testament and had to try to understand the events in that language. Thus it seemed obvious to argue that the bloody ritual of reconciliation at Yom Kippur was superfluous, because Jesus had reconciled them with God and all their sins were forgiven. Jesus in his life and his death replaced the scapegoat upon whom they formerly had loaded their sins and driven into the wilderness. He, the crucified and risen, took the place of the tile of reconciliation in the temple sprinkled with sacrificial blood (Rom. 3, 23-25). Their eyes had been opened by the faithfulness even to the death with which he ended the path that had begun for him at the river Jordan. They were thus freed from the fascination of the old "El Shaddai," the god of terror. Jesus redeemed them through his blood, and offered hismelf as a "ransom," as a "sacrifice of penance" for his people.

The transposition of these images to Jesus is a metaphorical process in which the meanings of the transposed words are changed. "Achilles is a lion," in a metaphorical example Paul Ricoeur frequently uses, but we understand that Achilles is not a lion in a zoological sense. In the same way the life, death and resurrection of Jesus are not a "ransom" or a "sacrifice of penance" in traditional Old Testament usage. These images are an initial orientation, the bridge which leads from the old to the new understanding. E. Schillebeeckx is certainly correct when he says that as the faithful of today we are not bound to the first articulations of the events connected to Jesus, but to that which "finds expression" in them.[43] By saying so, he is not "caught in a hermeneutic booby trap" as J. Blank claimed.[44] For Schillebeeckx used the present tense ("What *finds* expression in Jesus"), not the perfect tense (as quoted by Blank: "...what *has found* expression in Jesus"). For, since Jesus is and remains alive, he finds a new expression in every period of history. Therefore, every age must find its way back to what Jesus means for humanity, starting from its own ideas, categories and images—under the necessary *guidance* of the first articulation of the faith, of course. Because man and the world evolve and because today man can understand his history and his environment more thoroughly than men of biblical times, it may very well be that today's images and ideas allow for a better "hermeneutics of Jesus"[45] than the images and categories of the rituals of reconciliation in the Old Testament. If their interpretation of the Jesus-event would be considered final, then these bloody rituals would not have been fully superceded by the divine revelation of Jesus.

103

More disturbing than the somewhat limited understanding of Jesus within the ancient church, but equally understandable, is the fact that even the first witnesses of the revelation of Abba reveal traces of the spirituality of violence in their thoughts, feelings and actions. Once again we have to realize that certain patterns of behavior have been impressed upon man and developed within him over the course of a million years and cannot be changed overnight. What are the mere thirty-five hundred years of the history of Yahweh's and of the Abba's revelation compared to the one and a half million years during which the behavior of man was shaped in his experience of the god of terror! If we draw a line on a chalkboard and indicate first the one and a half million and then the thirty-five hundred years, the part corresponding to the latter would be so small in relation to the former (which fills the board), that we could not see it with the naked eye. Thus we ourselves are at only the very beginning of an effective reception of the message of Yahweh and Jesus.

Therefore it is not surprising that the passage from Paul quoted earlier imitates and repeats in an almost classical manner the "founding murder" which, according to Girard, is the basis of human community. We also noticed how, in the Book of Revelation, the world had to be cleansed by frightful and gruesome acts of violence before the heavenly Jerusalem could descend upon the purified earth.[46] The letter to the Hebrews tries painstakingly to explain to the Jewish-Christian community why there is no longer any need for sacrifices: The blood of bulls and goats is useless for taking away sins" (Heb. 10, 4). Christ abolishes the burnt offerings and sacrifices which, in fact, had never pleased Yahweh. In accordance with the prophets' criticism of the cults, Jesus replaces these sacrifices by opening himself to the love of Yahweh and fulfilling his will (Heb. 10, 8 f.). But a sacrifice must still take place: Jesus' death is interpreted as the one great sacrifice by which he consecrates and brings to perfection those who follow him in such a way that henceforth they no longer need any sacrifices (Heb. 10, 14 f.).

Even in the innermost core of the Gospel, in the corpus of narrations that go back directly to Jesus, in that world of parables, the foundation of Jesus' message, where we hear his own voice, his own thought and feelings, more strongly than anywhere else,[47] even there, certain attitudes that belong to the God of terror have permeated the tradition. Even the early Christian narrator upon whom Mark relies, could not end the parable of the "murder in the vineyard" (Mark 12, 1-8) as Jesus had told it. He could not bear the tension that generates the story: the immense contrast between the murderous brutality of the tenants — who usurp the vineyard, mistreat and kill the owner's servants, and finally even murder his beloved son — and the boundless kindness of the owner who sends his son, instead of a retaliatory expedition, to the tenants. The early Christian narrator relates that in the end the kind owner resorts to violence nonetheless and punishes and destroys the wicked tenants of the vineyard. But this manipulation destroys the structure of Jesus' story, and, in fact, makes it pointless. Why did the owner hand over his son to the brutality of the tenants, when he had the means of violence at hand?[48]

A similar phenomenon can be observed in the parable of the unforgiving debtor (Matt. 18, 23-30). Here the immeasurable kindness of the king, who forgives his servant the formidable debt of ten thousand talents, is contrasted with the brutality of the same servant who seizes a fellow servant who owes him one hundred denarii by the throat, throttles him and has him thrown into prison. This story was intended to show those faithful to the Torah that their insistence on a prescribed reparation by sinners and publicans was impossible once Yahweh had shown himself as Abba to his people. Here too the parable deteriorates when in the end the king withdraws his kindness and hands the unforgiving debtor "over to the torturers" (Matt. 18, 34 f.). There are other passages in Matthew where a punishment of the wicked by the angels of God is mentioned in a stereotypical manner: "The son of man will send his angels and they will gather out of his kingdom all those who provoke offences and all who do evil, and throw them into the blazing furnace, where there will be weeping and gnashing of teeth" (Matt. 13, 41 f.). This terrible threat is added to the parable of the tares (Matt. 13, 24-30; 34 ff.), the parable of the conscientious (and the dishonest) steward (Matt. 24, 45-47; 51), and to the parable of the talents (Matt. 25, 14-28; 30).

In the parable of the Last Judgment in Matthew (25, 31-46), which exegetes believe not to be authentic in its present textual form, the terror of the highest judge is finally unveiled. He separates certain men from others, curses them, and sentences them to eternal torture (Greek *kolasis:* Matt. 25, 41), while the "good" enjoy a heavenly community against this gruesome backdrop. Here we find authentic motifs that recur in the stories of Jesus — like the king who dwells unrecognized among men, or the good shepherd who carefully separates the sheep from the goats at the drinking place before they spoil and muddy the waters (Ezek. 34, 17 f.) — mixed with the old picture of the god of terror which Jesus had overcome in his experience at the river Jordan, and for the truth of which he accepted death. Certainly Jesus experienced in the opposition, indeed in the deadly enmity that he met with, a fact that remained almost incomprehensible: namely, that people are free to refuse the unconditional love of God as Abba and to cling to the fascination of the god of terror. But Jesus never made any statement about whether people actually chose this total refusal even beyond death, and beyond himself, in an eschatological, irrevocable way—in other words, whether there are people "in hell". Thus we too can only hope that it is not so. But neither the Abba nor his son Jesus will ever on his own initiative hand over any man to "endless torture." Rather, in this image the old god of the wilderness raises himself to a pitch of absolute transcendent horror, and thereby shows his own absurdity.

The revelation of God as Abba through Jesus suffered a severe setback when, in the beginning of the fourth century, the emperor Constantine painted the cross, the sign of love without violence, on the helmets and shields of his soldiers and sent them out to kill on the battlefield. The image of the state's authority had been weakened by inner dissent and this was an attempt to strengthen and consecrate the state's power to kill by means of the young and vigorous religion of Christianity. Thus, in the following centuries a "Holy Roman Empire of the German Nation" could come into being. This empire gained great political significance insofar as it was able to achieve a partial unity of Europe and thus promote commercial and economic prosperity and a flourishing of the arts and sciences. But in terrible wars, in crusades and in pogroms against the Jews, in persecutions of witches and heretics (where alleged enemies of the faith were "weeded out" according to the Levitic law of holiness and publicly burnt) a terrible tribute was paid to the god of terror who held this empire together. Eventually it perished in the inferno of the Thirty Years' War and left the country torn and shattered.

The interpretation of the life and death of Jesus by Anselm of Canterbury, which perceives redemption as reparation and still influences many faithful today, had indeed a liberating and emancipating effect in its time.[49] It was, however, a product of its time and was never raised to the status of doctrine by the Church. According to this theory, God became man in Jesus Christ because man by himself is incapable of "giving satisfaction" to the eternal God. Only when God's son who shares in God's nature accepts the fate of mankind and offers himself as human can people be freed from their sins and integrated into the community of God's kingdom. As Rome was founded on the murder of Remus, so the kingdom of God would be founded on the death of Jesus. It is true that according to Christian belief salvation comes from God; yet it does not come to man in the form of a human or divine sacrifice, but in the unconditional and faithful love of the Abba towards all men.

Excursus: The Path of Christian Salvation and Theology

Only an interpretation of the gospel that is no longer based on the idea of sacrifice can release the liberating and saving power contained in it. Apparently the Christian theologians themselves remained so much under the spell of the god of terror that a non-theologian, a historian of literature, had to come and open the Christians' eyes to the character of their writings and their tradition. In the German speaking world the theological significance of Girard's writings were first recognized and championed by Raymund Schwager.[50] He has traced the history of the ecclesiastical teaching on salvation from Athanasius to Anselm of Canterbury, and from Martin Luther to Karl Barth and Hans Urs von Balthasar. He shows to what kinds of dead-ends the sacrificial theory leads and how nevertheless, beside and beyond those dead-ends, traces of an authentic, non-sacrificial understanding of salvation are ubiquitous.[51] In addition to R. Schwager, N. Lohfink, H. U. von Balthasar, A. Schenker, B. Häring, and O. Keel in particular have followed Girard's direction.[52]

To accuse these attempts of "sociologism" seems a dismissive judgment.[53] "Sociologism" — as well as the reproach of "psychologism" from a different camp[54] — are catchwords that aim at devaluating, a priori and without differentiation, the legitimate and necessary desire to communicate the gospel in the terms of contemporary thought. Today, our insights are different from those of the people in biblical times concerning religious history, the sociology of religion and the human psyche. If we confine the gospel to the terms of the thought of those times, it will be fit for nothing but a museum. Instead, we must find our way back to the origins of the revelation of Yahweh and of Jesus—albeit at times closer to biblical categories than Drewermann and Girard—in order to disclose God as the source of a free and redeemed life in our own time. We can achieve this only if we break through the theological word games.

The present study on the character and the history of Christian salvation, for example, tries consciously to keep a balance between a discourse on God, who discloses himself to man through grace, and a discourse on man, who is captivated by his environment, by the "dimension beyond the objective that is experienced in naturally perceivable things" (Müller-Karpe), and who tries presumptuously to usurp this *fascinosum*. The second discourse is neither "sociologism" nor "psychologism" but an attempt to translate the biblical tradition of original sin and of salvation through the biblical God into the language and the ideas of the contemporary world.

The problem of sin and guilt will not be discussed "mainly on a mere psychological, socio-psychological, or sociological level," as is often alleged.[55] On the level of social and evolutionary history, sin, as the killing and eating of the mighty bison whose vitality and force fascinated primeval people, is the transition of mankind from gatherers and scavengers to hunters, the transition to predatory behavior. But for one who observes the world and history not only empirically but in a holistic way, this same event is the presumptuous attempt of man to usurp the divine which is expressed in the living forces of nature. It is, in biblical language, the attempt to be like gods, and to eat the fruit from the tree in the middle of the garden.

On a psychological-sociological level, man's transition to being a predator, without the checks of corresponding instincts, provokes aggression, fear and eventually the paralysis of life within a group. This paralysis is overcome by a mob murder and thus opens the way for generations of human communities based on fear and terror. Interpreting the symbols expressed in these events, we can say that for man the experience of God (as transcendent force and vitality) is obscured in the encounter with a frightful transcendent power to kill from which he must hide and retreat into a profane and burdensome existence, full of thorns and thistles. Thus Cain will come upon his brother again and again at regular intervals and slay him like a beast in the field, in order to found a city or a community (Gen. 4, 17: "He became builder of a town and he gave the town the name of his son Enoch").

In no way is this view of life a superficial one; it rather penetrates deeply "to the roots of the problem of guilt which is, ultimately, of a religious nature."[56] However, in this view we do not simply ignore the level on which man lives and thinks today and jump towards an abstract discourse of a God who has no place in people's experience of reality. Seen from the point of view of religious history, sociology, and psychology, the history of the salvation of mankind by Christ is a process of overcoming the symbol of the bull and of the dragon as the oldest divine symbols of man—putting an end to the fascination of violence which erects itself as terrifying killing power and rules over human life. Viewed from within, these events mean that God breaks through the wall of terror, erected by original sin, in two stages: in the experience of Moses and in the experience of Jesus (and additionally, in different ways, in the religious experience of a Lao-tzu, Buddha, or Zarathustra), making himself known first as the God "I-am-here," and eventually through Jesus as Abba. By means of such interweaving of empirical and religious perspectives, the practical relevance of theological statements becomes immediately obvious. There is no longer any need for special elaboration on the practical, the political-sociological, or the individual-psychological implications of the theological statement. Such a correlative theological discourse contains, as it were, inherent political and psychological systems of hermeneutics. It makes immediately obvious what the implications of the Judeo-Christian revelation of God are in social and individual life.

This correlative theology is impossible to harmonize with attempts to transpose Christian biblical meaning into an argumentative, doctrinal discourse. The construction of a system of Christian teachings that would contain and preserve the whole of the tradition without contradictions, and the adoption of such an authoritative system by the individual Christian, are justifiable and necessary within a homogeneous religious society, as was exemplified by the Holy Roman Empire of the German Nation. Inasmuch as this society was founded on a Christian God of terror, on a politically motivated Christian consecration of the state's power to kill that obscured its true origins, this Christian dogmatic system itself had the effect of darkening the authentic gospel, and of consecrating the great and the mighty. Such a construction has the character of original sin and usurpation, because it attempted to bind the revelation of God that came to man through Moses and Jesus into a system and thus to possess it. Thus it seems quite plausible when we read the life of Thomas Aquinas who in his "summae" defined the Christian dogma with stunning clarity, eventually turned away from his scientific work and ended his life in a childlike, mystical intimacy with God.[57]

The Judeo-Christian revelation of God as the salvation of mankind is necessarily rooted in history. To be sure, man, in the course of his evolution, and through a deeper understanding of himself, of his history, and of the world, will be able to come to an ever deeper penetration of the truth and meaning of Moses and Jesus. But because of the original sin of unnatural killing, forces which man cannot reverse — helplessness, weakness, aging, dying — have taken on the character of abandonment and death. Therefore they are permanently linked with terror and dread. Thus man will know what God as Abba is only through the final experience of death. It is in that experience — and not in doctrines preached — that this end will become manifest as a more plentiful life.

Development:

The Christian experience of the Trinity in the context of myth, fairy tale and religion

Language and the Trinity

The Christian God is a threefold God. He exists (in the conventional order) as "Father," "Son," and "Holy Spirit." This last expression has its origin in a mistranslation by Irish-Scottish monks, as we shall see later on.[1] An English translation that would reflect the symbolic content of the Greek word "pneuma" from the New Testament and "paraklet" from the gospel of John, would read: "healing, comforting wind and breath."

Tradition stresses the "absolute mystery"[2] of all statements about the Trinity. Common sense may infer the existence of God as first cause of all created things and thereby form a sort of idea about God's nature. But in that sense God is only understood as a unity, for the divine nature is common to all three persons. According to tradition, the fact that three separate relations — the father (mother), the child (son/daughter), and the healing breath of life which emanates from both — exist within the one God, must be revealed to man by holy writ and especially by the New Testament. By reason alone he cannot come to the Trinity. And, according to this teaching, even after its revelation man's understanding is unable to penetrate the dogma of the Trinity. It remains "shrouded with the veil of faith."[3]

Modern theology, inspired by the Second Vatican council and its theological godfather Karl Rahner, makes a distinction between the "immanent" and the "economic" Trinity. Although we must admit that this latter term is indeed "a terrible word, truly theological jargon,"[4] the distinction itself is very useful for religious pedagogy, pastoral care, and the dialogue between religions. Traditional speculation about the Trinity, which has become so incomprehensible to us, was almost exclusively confined to the immanent Trinity, the Trinity within God (and not to the "economic" Trinity which Rahner defines as the Trinity as it relates to the economy of man's salvation). This speculation consists, as it were, of paraphrases of the Trinity's absolute mystery. The talk of "economic" Trinity, on the other hand, assumes that the Trinity is not merely a concept that is simply put forward by the New Testament and must be accepted blindly. Rather, the passages from the New Testament that form the basis of the doctrine of the Holy Spirit are held to be the expression of the first Christians' specific experience of the divine, in and through their encounter with the Messiah Jesus. Thus, to believe in the Trinity does not mean that one accepts it as true and repeats incomprehensible doctrines, but that one relives those *experiences* that have led to the formulations suggesting the Trinity in the New Testament.

Because these statements do not have a doctrinal character, but are poetic-metaphorical expressions of experience, the reenactment of this experience requires more than cognitive abilities. It calls for an existential empathy for the meaning of those sentences. For example: for proof of the divine procession within the Trinity, Gal. 4, 6 is often quoted. "The proof that you are sons is that God has sent the spirit of his Son into our hearts: the Spirit that cries, 'Abba, Father'." In this sentence Paul does not intend to make the metaphysical claim that the Holy Spirit is sent by the Father. This is revealed by the entire context of the passage in question. Rather, the point is that Christ in his relation to God is no longer a slave, but a son. This filial relationship is expressed by addressing God in the babbling form of the infant: Abba/Mama/Papa. The passage is also an expression of a unique immediacy in the relationship with God. As the infant and its nurturer form a unity and develop an absolutely immediate affinity, so the Christian experiences himself in and through Christ in his relation to God. To believe in the triune God means trying to relive and participate in that experience.

However one may describe the relation between economic and immanent Trinity — Karl Rahner merely speaks of the "identity of both forms of Trinity,"[5] others look for differentiations,[6] and J. Wohlmuth defends the thesis that the immanent Trinity is the truth of the economic Trinity[7] — it is clear that access to the Christian-Trinitarian God (a necessarily holistic access, emotional as well as intellectual[8]) is provided by the economic Trinity, and thus by the way in which man experiences the divine in and through Jesus.[9]

This pedagogical and pastoral perspective also makes possible and encourages a dialogue with other experiences of the divine as they are revealed through the religions of the world and through the history of religion. For the Christian, the crucified and living Jesus is *the* symbol of God,[10] and the goal must be to bring this experience and this symbol of God into a dialogue with other experiences of the divine and their symbols. The tradition of the Trinity is in that respect the first and most basic interpretation of the symbol Jesus.[11] Just as Christology employs a majestic language in its discipline, Trinitarian symbolism tries to articulate that dimension which is encountered in Jesus by human perception, but experienced and evaluated as transcending the objective given.[12] This transcendent dimension of Jesus of Nazareth can only be articulated in the words of human languages, and these words, again, by being applied to that transcendent dimension, take on a metaphorical character: "father," "son," "(healing) breath of life." Thus, through this work of interpretation, the divinity that is made manifest through Jesus is re-translated into an earthly experience through metaphors. The words "father", "son" (and, analogously, "mother," "daughter"), and "breath" begin to sound different, even in daily use, insofar as they have proven useful as metaphorical expressions of the divine apparition of Jesus. The original, historic meanings of these words enters into a relationship with that which is encountered in Jesus as "Father," "Son," and "Healing Breath of Life," and their nature is enlarged and opened toward this reality experienced in Jesus.

Of course, this effect can take place only if the words taken from everyday language to signify the divine revealed in Jesus retain their metaphoric-symbolic character, that is, retain their common meaning. When "Father" as the name for the first divine person of the Trinity has nothing to do with experience of the father in one's daily life; when "Son" has nothing to do with one's son or daughter; when the healing, comforting, strengthening and liberating "pneuma" (breath), which descended upon Jesus during his baptism in the river Jordan and which poured forth upon the early Christians from the living Crucified, helping them, comforting them, and shaping their Christianity, is absolutely not comparable to a mother's breath when she blows on her child's scraped knee to comfort it and to relieve its pain (almost always successfully) — then this reciprocal, metaphorical action obviously cannot take place. Then Trinity has become an independent, intellectual abstraction, hovering above the world of human experience. A theological magician is required to bring this balloon of detached words back into the sight of people and to make it reflect at least some element of their life and everyday experiences. The rediscovery of the "economic Trinity" is the belated attempt to return to the Trinitarian statements of the New Testament, and to fill them with new life and meaning.

As E. Drewermann correctly pointed out,[13] in this original function the tradition of the Trinity has a linguistic character and an effect that are similar to the myth. If we interpret the transcendent dimension of the sun as Indra or Pharaoh, namely as the victorious force of the warrior hero, the experience of the heroic itself receives a sun-like glamour. The bloody business of war is transformed by the metaphorical meaning of the word "hero," and covered with sun-like radiance. The blood-soaked warrior becomes the brilliant victor, the "Sol invictus" who, as king, grants security, protection, and prosperity to the country. He becomes the Sun King. In a similar way, new insights — of a different nature, of course — should arise from the metaphorical meaning of "father" (analogously "mother"), "son" (analogously "daughter"), and "breath of life," if the relation between everyday language and its metaphorical transposition into the experience of the divine continues. Christian salvation would then have a healing effect on human language.

114

Our example sets forth the criteria that must be considered if the tradition of the Trinity is to be translated back into its original symbolic, metaphorical language and thereby put into contact with other experiences of the divine. On the one hand, the intended dialogue presupposes a common linguistic basis. Mythical language and the symbolism of the Trinity have a common logical structure, a common "grammar." Only thus can the Christian understanding of God enter into a dialogue with other religions and with the history of religion. On the other hand, a common grammar does not imply similar content. Within the grammatical structure of the English language we can express many different and contradictory things. But the language for the dialogue must be the same. We cannot engage in a conversation in English with someone who speaks only Chinese.

Both aspects, the community of language and the difference in contents, must be taken into account when we re-symbolize the Trinity. While emphasizing the common linguistic basis, we should not fail to elaborate on the differences, in specific aspects of Christianity. The claim that the Christian Trinitarian symbolism simply derives from and is understandable through the myth of Aesculapius and the divine procreation of the Egyptian Pharaohs,[14] would obscure distinctly Christian aspects from a mythologic perspective in the same way as an imperialistic Christianity would obscure the truths contained in myths. A dialogue is possible only when everyone maintains his own identity and brings it into the conversation.

With those two criteria in mind, we will try to interpret the Trinity by means of the symbolism in the words "child" (son/daughter), "wind and breath," and "father" ("mother"), and to open a dialogue with other experiences in religious history.

1 The Child as Symbol of God

1.1 Jesus and Pharaoh as "Sons of God"—On the Character of the Son of God in Christian Symbolism

Unique History—Recurring Phenomenon

According to the well-known scholar of religious history Mircea Eliade "everything that man does, experiences or loves—an object, an action, a physiological phenomenon, a historical event, reality or illusion—can become a 'hierophany,' that is, an apparition of the divine."[1] It should be added that each individual religion, its rites and imagery, is largely defined by the specific nature of its central hierophany.If the central hierophany is a historical event (as, for example, it was in Judaism), it will generate a different kind of spirituality than would the experience of an "object" (the sun, for example); or a physiological phenomenon (like birth or fertility); or an action (like killing). To be sure, every religion recognizes a great number of symbols (hierophanies), but they are centered differently, they are focused on different central symbols, and therefore evaluated differently.

The fundamental hierophany of the Christian faith is the totality of events surrounding Jesus of Nazareth. That which Christians call "God" appears in him. In the gospels, Jesus is called "Son." This name is found frequently without further qualification. "In the past and in different ways, God spoke to our fathers...but in our own times, he has spoken to us through his Son" (Heb. 1, 1 f.). "Whoever sees the Son and believes in him shall have eternal life" (John 6, 40). "The Father may be glorified in the Son" (John 14, 13). "To have seen me is to have seen the Father" (John 14, 9). Therefore, a genuine interpretation of the economic Trinity must not begin with the Father, as do most speculations about the immanent Trinity, but must begin with the experience of the Son. Whoever perceives the Son in a holistic way, whoever sees him with the eyes of the heart, is overcome by a wind and breath that makes him cry out, "Abba" (Gal. 4, 6). In the encounter with the Son Jesus, the healing, divine Breath of Life and the Father are disclosed to man.

As a historic religion, Christianity remains a daughter of Judaism. The Son Jesus is not—at least not primarily—a given natural phenomenon like the sun, whose transcendent dimension we may contemplate through a holistic vision. The Son Jesus is essentially an event, a historic event, similar to the liberation of Moses' people from Egypt. His divinity is disclosed when we meditate upon his life, death, and life beyond death, as it is told in the gospels. The necessity of this process of understanding is very clear from the oldest gospel, that of Mark, in the "Messianic mystery" that surrounds Jesus during his life and ministry.[2] Only during his agony on Calvary, and only to him who has followed or relived his path, is the curtain of the temple, the veil of the innermost sanctuary, "torn in two from top to bottom." Only at the very end of his life does the centurion "who stood guard over him and saw how he had died" proclaim to the whole world that this man Jesus was in truth the Son of God (Mark 15, 38 f.).

It is therefore not true to the historic origin of the Christian religion to attempt a symbolic interpretation of the Trinity on the premise of an archetypal character of the child or the Son.[3] If, like C. G. Jung,[4] we see Christ as an archetypal hero, and identify in him the attributes of a hero's life — "improbable origins, divine father, endangered birth, narrow escape, early maturity (heroic growth), overcoming the bondage of mother and death, postmortal activity (apparitions, miracles etc.)"[5] — then we have buried the true character of what Jesus means for the Christian under a heap of materials from religious history and psychoanalysis. Thus a dialogue between the Christian experience of God and a possibly *different* "heroic" experience of God would be made impossible. The theory of archetypes would be the standard reality within which Jesus would be only one possible realization of the heroic archetype. The same dead-end is reached when a phenomenological description of the "form of the child" — the still unfinished, beginning, maturing character — is used to derive the transcendent dimension of the object.[6] What the "Son" means to the Christian cannot be deduced from the individual dreams of Jung's patients, nor from Greek or Egyptian mythologies. It can only be known by paying attention to the narrative about Jesus in the gospels in an exegetical and critical way, as well as in a sensitive and compassionate way. It is only after that process that we may and must bring the Christian symbol of the "Son" into a dialogue with similar forms of divine manifestation in religious history.

The outline of the life in which Jesus is revealed as God's son is most visible in the oldest gospel, the one according to Mark.[7] At the river Jordan John the Baptist preaches about the imminent universal judgment, calling for repentance through the symbolic action of immersion in the river. "Jesus...from Nazareth in Galilee" (Mark 1, 9) comes to him and is baptized by him in the river Jordan. "No sooner had he come up out of the water than he saw the heavens torn apart and the Breath, like a dove, descending on him. And a voice came from heaven, 'You are my Son, the beloved, my favor rests on you' " (Mark 1, 10 f.). Jesus interprets this event as the activation of the power of the God "I-am-here" among his people—beginning then, rather than after some universal judgement. It is the "malkût Yahweh" (the messianic rule of God) which had been announced for centuries by the prophets. Jesus begins to travel, first to Capernaum, then through the entire land of the Jews (in seven stages, according to the reconstruction of the original gospel of Mark by Schmithals),[8] trying through his parables, healings, and prophetic common meals to open people to his experience, to awaken this experience in themselves. But some Jews, especially the more orthodox, see in Jesus' message of a coming kingdom of God that is accessible to all without distinction (even to "publicans and sinners") a desecration of Israel's most sacred promises, and they try to kill him. When Jesus is in Jerusalem for Passover he is handed over to his enemies and eventually to the Roman occupiers who execute him as an insurgent. Dying on the cross, his divinity and messianic character are revealed to the few faithful followers who experience him even beyond death as the living mediator of divine salvation.

The other gospels add more stories to this basic plot, trying especially to elaborate on the divinity of Jesus as it is experienced in his death and in his life beyond death. Matthew and especially Luke adopt stories that circulated about Jesus' nativity and childhood, integrating them into the outline as we have described it.

There is no other means than the use of the gospel itself to understand who that Jesus is who is called the "Son" and who discloses God as Pneuma (Breath) and Abba. Only on the basis of this insight can we enter into a dialogue with similar symbols of the divine. Before discussing individual symbols, it is important to emphasize again the different linguistic character of the gospels on the one hand and of mythology on the other. Whatever specific definition of myth one chooses to adopt,[9] on *one* point we do agree with Mircea Eliade, namely that in the myth there is no imitation or recollection of a single "sacred" phenomenon or event which transcends the objective in a divine dimension, but instead an *identical* repetition of the experience of God.[10] Eliade applies the characteristic of repetition to the Christian ritual which constantly repeats the life, death and resurrection of Christ. But Christians do not consider their ritual to be an identical repetition of the divine experience mediated by Christ, nor, in particular, do the gospels contain any such repetition. They are narrative recollections of the event which disclosed God as Abba. "The Son" *is* that event. It happened *once,* and man may come close to it by meditating upon and reliving the narration emotionally, so that the divine rises within him as "Son" as well. The mention of place, time,

118

and witnesses that are woven into the narrative clearly mark the uniqueness of the event (not its historicity in the modern sense). It would be unthinkable to name a "witness" of the dismembering of Osiris by Seth or of the events surrounding the Holy Grail in the Celtic Arthurian tradition.[11] Thus, the myth is a different type of narration. It does not describe events that happen *once,* but events that recur time and again. It focuses on the phenomenon.

However, Christianity takes a special place, in contrast to the historic religion of Judaism (and also of Islam). The fundamental hierophany of the Jewish religion is the historic event of the liberation of Moses' people from Egypt. For those who experienced it, this event had a transcendent dimension that went beyond the "objective," in this case beyond "history" in the modern sense: a divine protector who manifested himself as Yahweh, as God "I-am-here." This experience of God has happened in an event that cannot be contemplated as a "phenomenon," but has to be recounted as a story. Consequently, in the "pronouncement of salvation" (Deut. 26, 5-9) this story of the liberation of Israel from Egypt is told in very concise words. Yahweh cannot be seen, but he must be heard in the narration of a unique event. This is why it is not possible to represent him pictorially. Wherever such attempts at representation were made, as in the shrines of Dan and Bethel, they caused a shift towards natural religions: Yahweh was represented by a bull. But Christianity is different. The event that forms its fundamental hierophany is called Jesus. He becomes a living, perceivable human being. In his death and life beyond death that divine dimension which transcends the objective-historical aspect of his being is revealed. Therefore, the living Crucified is also a visible symbol of that which Christians call "God."[12]

The God-king— Crucified and Reigning

Like the Egyptians and like the Romans during the imperial period, Christians use a man as a symbol for God. But what a difference! In the first instance, an officiating king radiant in the splendor of his power and rule, enthralling his subjects with his vitality and strength. In the other, a crucified man, miserably destroyed, hanging powerless and lifeless on the cross. In fact, Jesus is a counter-symbol. But he can become a symbol when we recall the events that led to his crucifixion. Then the basis, the personal foundation that embraces and supports this belief, becomes visible and the Crucified appears alive in a new way. The counter-symbol then is changed into the divine symbol which makes God manifest without any veils, in total transparence. "To have seen me is to have seen the Father" (John 14, 9). To prostrate oneself before him—the Crucified, recognizable by his wounds—as in the cult of the God-king, and to say together with the converted apostle Thomas, "My Lord and my God" (John 20, 28) is not idolatry. For in him who lives beyond death, but who is encountered as the Crucified—"Look at my hands and feet" (Luke 24, 39)—we do not adore the transcendent dimension of an empirical phenomenon, but we acknowledge the history, the historical forces that made him, for all eternity, what his followers perceived in him when he died.

Neither the ruling Pharaoh nor the Roman emperor has need for such a history. No one needs to tell us about them. We need only to look at either and a bright "sun" will rise (and to say of the sun that it is only a lump of fiery matter, as did Tantalus according to Greek myth,[13] is a sacrilege that must be expiated with hellish tortures). This Pharaoh does not need a history. From the moment of his enthronement he becomes the divine brightness, the son of the sun-god. He rises as a "sun." We need only to look at it to experience it. From now on his mother will be the virgin bride of the wind-god Amon who was led by the divine messenger (angel) Thot to the elected queen, lived with her in the palace and she conceived by him.

Both Jesus and the Pharaoh are "sons," "sons of God." The list of identical or similar themes that Drewermann has drawn up from the childhood tales in Luke and the Egyptian myth is long and impressive. It goes from the annunciation by the messenger, Thot, to the procreation of the child from a virgin by God (although the Egyptian text describes it as a sexual act, unlike the gospel); the enunciation of a genealogy unexpectedly naming the earthly ancestors of the Pharaoh along with an account of his divine generation (as in Matthew and Luke); the theme of persecution (in the gospel the persecution by King Herod; in the Egyptian text the persecution of the divine child Horus by the evil Seth), up to the account in which the twelve-year-old Si-Osire amazes all the scriptural scholars in the temple by his wisdom and his prophecies, and the acceptance of the child by God as "child of my flesh," (as "beloved son" in the baptism at the river Jordan).[14]

The interpretations of these motifs by Drewermann are equally impressive: "We are children of the light and of the wind, beings without boundaries, born free, filled with spirit, enlightened with consciousness, close to the invisible secret of heaven, the most sublime matter that could come to the earth...Every man is called to take a place on the throne of the golden Horus, and certainly such a feast of enthronement would be identical with the second birth of the spirit and the truth, as John says (John 3, 8; 1 John 3, 9), the moment in which it is revealed whose children we really are."[15]

120

But in what sense is the Pharaoh a "son," and in what sense is Jesus? What is it that makes the son into a symbol? Which element of "being a son" reveals the transcendent dimension which goes beyond the objective and the historical, and makes the "son" into a son of God? This is the central point on which the religions disagree.

We can say that the fundamental hierophany of ancient Egyptian religion is the sun. In this tradition, in its brightness, its light, its warmth, the divine breaks through. Even a happy, healthy child has something of that radiance. The sight of such a child makes the heart rejoice and expand. The young, newly enthroned king has this sun-like radiance in a special way. When he takes his place on the golden throne of Horus, clothed in rich garments, surrounded by servants and soldiers, the "sun" rises over Egypt. It is obvious and cannot be otherwise: the Pharaoh is a son of the sun-god. "You are a son of my flesh," Amon says to him when he first sees him.[16] He is the sun and the wind in human form. The sun-god is incarnate in him and acts through him among the people.

It cannot be denied that these ideas come close to what is later said about Jesus: "He is...God from God, Light from Light, true God from true God...of one being with the Father. Through him all things were made. For us men and for our salvation he came down from heaven..." are the terms of the creed of the Council of Nicea (325 AD), and later of the Council of Constantinople.[17] But Drewermann overlooks the fact that these are merely formal similarities. There is a statement on the *relation* between the divine and the human Jesus (analogously to the ruling Pharaoh). But nothing has been said as yet about the *content* of that which is experienced and understood as divine. To be sure, the motifs of light ("Light from Light") and of heaven ("came down from heaven") point to the symbolism of the sun. But that in itself does not mean very much. For in every religion God has sun-like features. Even the Jew Jesus talks of the God who "causes the sun to rise on bad men as well as good" (Matt. 5, 45), and in the experience of the beginning kingdom of God he sees "the heavens torn apart" (Mark 1, 10). Furthermore, if we take into consideration that the Council of Nicaea was summoned by the Roman emperor-god, who was not yet baptized and who was venerated in the state cult as "Sol invictus," as son of the unconquered sun, and that, according to Eusebius of Nicodemia's account of that council, this godly and sun-like emperor paced through the conference rooms "like a messenger from heaven, radiant with the brightness of purple and gold,"[18] then we do not need to marvel at the references to symbols of light and sun in the Christian creed. They are secondary additions. The mainstream of the Judeo-Christian tradition has a different symbolism. Jesus is "Son of God" in a much different, indeed in an opposite, sense.

For the Judeo-Christian tradition we can say that the fundamental hierophany of the Jewish religion is the liberation of the people of Moses from the slavery of Egypt. When at the harvest-festival the Israeli laid down his basket full of gifts on the altar, he pronounced this formula:

"My father was a wandering Aramaean. He went down into Egypt to find refuge there, with a small household; but there he became a nation, great, numerous and strong. The Egyptians ill-treated us, they gave us no peace and inflicted harsh slavery on us. But we cried to the Lord, the God of our fathers. Yahweh heard our cry and saw our misery, our toil and our oppression; and he brought us out of Egypt with mighty hand and outstretched arm, with terrifying power, and with signs and wonders. Yahweh brought us here and gave us this land, a land flowing with milk and honey" (Deut. 26, 5-9).

Through this event Yahweh called his people of Israel to life. He is its procreator and its creator. Israel is his Son: "I called my son out of Egypt" (Hos. 11, 1). But it is not the bright splendor of the child that establishes the relation. On the contrary, it is the misery, the deprivation of rights, the harsh slavery, the helplessness that calls forth the divine: "But we cried to the Lord, the God of our fathers. Yahweh heard our cry and saw our misery, our toil and our oppression." In his helpless cry the child, the abandoned son, has found an answer. The old, protective god of the nomadic tribe has manifested himself as the God "I-am-here" of the abandoned son and has made an alliance with him for all generations. He has seen his misery and heard his appeal (Exod. 3, 7); he has bent down to him and "was like someone who lifts an infant close against his cheek; stooping down to him I gave him his food" (Hos. 11, 4). As in that ancient Roman custom in which an infant became the son or the daughter of the father only after the "pater familias" took it from the bare ground, where it was lying exposed and totally helpless, and lifted it up—thus Israel became the child of Yahweh: "This is what Yahweh says: Israel is my first-born son" (Exod. 4, 22).

In this tradition the child, the son, is not understood in a sun-like, radiant sense but, more basically, in a sense of the child's, the son's helplessness, his misery and his dependence upon the divine protector. In the four songs of the servant of Yahweh in Deutero-Isaiah (Isa. 42, 1-9; 49, 1-9; 50, 4-9; 52, 13; 53, 12), which some theologians view as the key texts of the entire Old Testament,[19] the abandoned Son, Israel, is raised into an impressive figure. He is characterized by an absolute refusal to use violence that makes him powerless: "For my part, I made no resistance, neither did I turn away. I offered my back to those who struck me" (Isa. 50, 5 f.). There is no splendor here. "Without beauty, without majesty, with nothing to attract our eyes" (Isa. 53, 2). But it is his childlike abandonment that calls forth the God "I-am-here" of Egypt. He is well pleased in the wretched one and redeems him: "He shall see his heirs, he shall have a long life...he shall be bathed in light and shall be content. By his sufferings shall my servant justify many" (Isa. 53, 10 f.).

The earliest Christian tradition has seen in these songs of the servant of Yahweh the basis for the understanding of what they encountered in Jesus. The fate of the child, the fate of the son as the one who has been handed over is fulfilled in Jesus. The Greek word "paradidonai" with its basic meaning "to hand over," "to hand down," is a key word for the understanding of the person and the life of Jesus. It appears in many places of the Greek text in which modern vernacular translations prefer other terms. Thus, for example, the term used in Greek to describe Judas' action is consistently "paradidonai": not "to betray," but "to hand over."[20]

Thus the earliest interpretational framework of the early Christians for what they encountered in Jesus' fate was given in the song of the servant of Yahweh: "...surrendering himself to death" (Isa. 53, 12). In Walter Schmithals' reconstruction of the original version of the gospel according to Mark, the motif of the handing over of Jesus is developed three times in a threefold way within the story of the passion (which itself is the center and goal of all four gospels).[21] Jesus is handed over step by step, as it were: first to men (Gethsemani), then to Pilate (Mark 15, 1-14), then to death (in the threefold form: "crucified"-"dead"-"buried").

Jesus is essentially the one who is handed over. As such, he calls forth the God "I-am-here," like the son Israel who was abandoned in Egypt, and he reveals himself to him as Abba/Mama/Papa. So the old, protective god of the semitic nomadic tribes has heard the call of the crucified from the Roman slavery of Judaea, as he had in Egypt in olden times. He has looked upon his son and has seen all that was done to him (Exod. 3, 16). In his son's utmost distress, at the peak of the crisis (in the biblical term: "on the third day"[22]), at the extreme of his abandonment, when Jesus was nothing but the one who is handed over, the child in the biblical sense, the God "I-am-here" stooped down to him and became the Abba/Mama/Papa to the child. "The world's breakthrough to God was accomplished on the cross, in Jesus' last agony."[23] Since then we "know" that all who die have a Mama/Papa who rescues them from the darkness of death and breathes new life into them.

The stories of Jesus' childhood that became known and were recorded especially by Luke have to be interpreted in the light of Jesus' life as the central event and not according to Egyptian mythology. As exegetical research has shown,[24] the oldest layer of the Christmas story is "the revelation to the shepherds of the birth of the Messiah."[25] The story is centered around the helpless child, found in a manger[26] by the shepherds. The sign of the divine infant is not stunning beauty and vital force,[27] but "here is a sign for you: you will find a baby wrapped in swaddling clothes and lying in a manger" (Luke 2, 12). According to G. Schneider, the background of this story is David's election as king by the prophet Samuel which also happens at Bethlehem (1 Sam. 16, 1-13).[28] It is to be noted that among the sons of Jesse, from which Samuel chooses, appearance and height do not matter. It is rather the youngest son who is chosen and anointed king by Samuel, the one whom Jesse did not present, and whom Samuel did not see because he was out looking after the sheep. "God does not see as man sees" (1 Sam. 16, 7). He is fond of the small, the unappealing, the powerless. The brightness from above and the joyous annunciation of the heavenly messengers that recall the Egyptian myth and other myths of birth, have a different meaning in this story.

In the representation of the annunciation and virgin birth of the god-king on a relief at the funeral temple of Queen Hatshepsut at Deir el Bahari (Fig. 22) we can see that the newborn king stands erect like an adult (although in smaller proportion) on the palm of the hand of the goddess of love Hathor, and, in this posture, faces his father Amon who acknowledges him as his own flesh. Even in those representations where Isis, as Hathor-Aphrodite, holds the Horus-child in her lap and nurses him, the boy sits straight, in a royal posture (Fig. 22a). Similarly, in most representations of the virgin, little Jesus is enthroned as the Christ on the lap of his mother.

As we will show in the following examples from the history of religions, this is the figure of the light-hero: The strong, wise, and radiant child comes forth like the sun from his mother's womb, spreading his brightness over all the earth, and is praised by gods and men. Weakness, powerlessness and abandonment have no luster. They belong to the realm of darkness and of evil. Locked up in a box and drifting out into the sea, the bright god-king Osiris is in the hands of his evil brother Seth. Only in the new son, the Horus-child, does the sun rise again. This Horus-child is sometimes represented as a paralytic, or with two crippled legs, sitting on the lap of Isis or on a lotus. This image expresses the nostalgic insight that beauty, truth, and life are always somehow ex-

124

Fig. 22: Divine conception and birth of the Pharaoh (relief series in the birth-hall of Queen Hatshepsut in Deir-el-Bahari, 15th century BC).

perienced in a weakened, "crippled" state, in spite of all the healing love of Isis.[29] This weakness and disability diminishes the brilliance of the sun. After his sister and wife, Isis, brings him back to life, Osiris, the original sun-god is left only with an artificial phallus.[30] Evil and darkness have taken away the power of procreation from the bright and good.

Jews and Christians, however, experience the world differently. The weak and powerless, the helpless, the abandoned child, the deprived exiles in Egypt, the innocent, suffering servant of Yahweh, and Jesus the crucified—these do not belong to the realm of night and death, despite outer appearances. Whoever looks at them with the eyes of the heart, mindful of their history, will see that they are embraced by love, indeed that theirs is the very condition that calls forth the Abba, the divine love, thus creating true light and true life. In the face of the innocently

Fig. 22a: The Horus-child on the lap of the goddess of love, Hathor (Bronze sculpture, Louvre, Paris)

crucified, in the face of the infant, abandoned in a manger and wrapped in swaddling clothes, the heavens open in their brightness, and peace is announced to mankind.

It is important to see that the situation of abandonment, which calls forth the God "I-am-here" and the love of Abba, is not the machination of some god or demon, but is a result of *man's* criminal frenzy of power. In the tradition of the Old Testament, the Pharaoh who enslaved the nomadic tribes is not a god, but a man who arrogantly claimed divinity. To be sure, people thought of the servant of Yahweh "as someone punished, struck by God, and brought low. Yet he was pierced through for our offenses, crushed for our sins" (Isa. 53, 4-5).[31] And the Son Jesus is handed over to his adversaries and mortal enemies among the people of Israel by his own friends, in an act of insidious treachery. At night and with false witnesses they hand over the son of their people to the brutal power of the Roman occupation forces. Eventually, during a trial which turns into a farce marked by cynicism and cruelty, Pilate aquits him of any obvious wrongdoing, but nevertheless hands him over to death on the cross, fearing for his own political position. The son, the helpless abandoned child crying for the Abba has fallen into the hands of *men,* not into the hands of God.

This genuinely Christian symbolism of the child can and must be the basis for a dialogue with similar symbols in other religions. We have already to some extent examined the features of the Egyptian religion when we showed its contrast with Christian symbolism. In the following pages we will make certain observations about the rest of religious history. Of course, we cannot present a complete survey of religious history for that would require a separate book. But we will single out certain examples in order to show the possibility and the nature of a dialogue born from an understanding of the symbols of faith.

1.2 The Human Child — A Fascinating Sacrifice

Traces from the Paleolithic Period

As we can see from the pictures found in the caves and campsites of the Paleolithic period, that which most fascinated the ancient people besides animals was the human being.[1] Particularly women, but also men, hunters, and human hands are represented. There are no pictures of children. However, we find several scenes of parturition.[2] Obviously, even the ancient people were fascinated by the miracle of the birth of a new human being.

The burial rites for that time for which we have evidence show that the people of the first Stone Age already perceived a transcendent dimension in their fellow-beings. The burial of skulls, separated from the body, seems to date from the very beginning of humanity.[3] The burial of a lifeless body shows that men saw more in their fellow-beings than merely their bodies. The body—and especially the head with its facial expression—was the manifestation of a reality that was not identical with the physically given, but went beyond it. The body and the head of a human being were treated with reverence even after his death because this transcendent dimension had been revealed through them. The body, the head, and the face are the symbols of a human personality and, because this personality seemed to be more than the sum of the physical body, it was thought of and experienced as real even beyond death.

This also holds true for man's encounter with the child. A surprising number of children's tombs dating from the Paleolithic period have been found laden with particularly rich and beautiful burial gifts.[4] The children's graves were richly ornamented with perforated shells and teeth, finished flint-tools that often seem to have been made exclusively for this purpose. The child's personality was obviously perceived as lasting beyond death. Red ocher powder, the color of feasting and of life, was strewn all over the deceased, and their bodies were stained with it. Müller-Karpe assumes that primeval men used these colors at great festivals to color their bodies and faces, and thus interprets the red tinting of the dead as an expression of festivity.[5]

The deceased were often placed on a layer of colored soil, as if on a red carpet, or they were covered with such a layer. They were put into a trench, often in a sleeping posture, with the right hand under the head. The head particularly was protected from wild animals with stone plates or huge shoulder blades of mammoths. The head was most often positioned facing westward, towards the setting sun. Müller-Karpe says that "these interments of children are impressive testimony to the fact that the communal life of Paleolithic men was not limited to the practical matters of shaping and securing their physical lives, but that the family formed a bond of mutual care and love, embracing all members down to the infants and the newborn."[6]

But these findings are qualified by a disturbing observation. Many of the skeletons show signs of severe injuries, especially those from the sites of skull burials. Sometimes the upper jaw has been chopped off by a strong blow to the region of the nose.[7] These severe injuries are also found in children's skulls. In the Ofnet cave near Nördlingen in Bavaria two adjacent graves were excavated in which skulls were buried carefully in ocher powder and ashes, twenty-seven in the larger trench, six in the smaller one (Fig. 23). Because all the lower jaws and in most cases the first vertebrae of the spine were still attached, archaeologists believe that the heads were severed from the bodies with flint-knives. The skulls were those of four men, nine women and twenty children. The women and children had been richly adorned with ornaments: some two hundred perforated deer's teeth, and four thousand perforated snailshells. The faces had been turned westward. Many of these skulls, even those of the children, bore traces of cuts or blows. Obviously, the men, women, and a great number of children had been killed and then entombed in this place. Faced with such evidence, archaeologists speak of the "well-established fact of ritual killings."[8] This, of course, is only a very general term which says nothing about the religious content of those actions. When, at the beginning of this century, Obermaier first described this site, he used the phrase "religious human sacrifice" to emphasize the connection between violent deaths and careful ritual burials.[9]

We are presented with a paradox: On the one hand, there is the fascination with the personality of one's fellow-being, with the radiance of his body and countenance—especially noticeable in children—a radiance that transforms the body, particularly the head, into the symbol of a dimension of being that transcends the objective. On the other hand, there is the violent killing of that fellow-being, of that child, the beheading, perhaps even the eating of his brain, the separation of flesh from bone, the embellishment of the skull with an ocher color and perforated teeth, shells, and snailshells. But both aspects are actually related through the logic of sin. If sin is the usurpation, the violent appropriation, of the divine as prefigured in the biblical account of the fall; if man, who has become a sinner during the transition from gatherer and scavenger to game-hunter, seizes the transcendent dimension which he encounters in and through natural reality by violent killing, and forces it under his own power[10]—then the logic of this behavior demands that he kill his fellow-being in a ritual in order to brutally appropriate his *mana,* his emanation, and thus to increase his own mana. The helpless child, having a particularly strong emanation, especially within its own family, is handed over to its siblings and becomes the favorite victim of this terrifying mechanism of sin and violence. Thus from primeval times the child has been the one who is handed over for sacrifice.

Drewermann has made a convincing case that the psychological origin of the killing sacrifice, of the cycle of death and violence, is fear.[11] It arises from the justifiable dread that this transcendent dimension en-

Fig. 23: Burial of heads in the Ofnet cave (ca. 12,000 BC): four men, nine women, twenty children.

countered in things—that angelic experience—might be lost again. Primeval man clung to this experience, for example in the experience of the vitality and power he observed in huge animals; or, as just mentioned, in his encounter with the personality of the human being, its "character," as it emerged from his physical movement and especially his facial expression. He experienced the light and warmth emanating from the sun and saw the blistering heat of summer relieved by life-giving rain. He observed the water as it nourished the earth. He saw that life itself depended on these experiences and perhaps looked upon the dawn as a presentiment of eternal life. But he also saw that all of this was beyond human control. Herds came and went. A man was born, one came to cherish him and feel happy and secure in his presence—and suddenly, after an illness or a disaster, he just lay down, stiff and motionless. He had lost all his emanation, and his body decomposed. Rain came with fair regularity in certain seasons, but not with perfect regularity—sometimes the rainy season came too late, sometimes it did not come at all, or the rain came storming through the land with such violence that it flooded and swept away the fruit of man's hard labor, his dams and irrigation works, his huts and storage-houses, handing man over to death.

The Aztecs, whose human sacrifices were the most cruel that have been recorded, were panic-stricken by the constant fear that the sun could be swallowed up by the earth, once it disappeared below the horizon, and that there would be no more dawn. They imagined that during the night the sun, having colored the sea and the sky in scarlet while setting, had to fight for its life against many warriors, so that men had to offer their own life-force as nourishment, so that the sun could triumph. "The dominant religious background was a fear of monstrous intensity that the sun's energy would be exhausted, spelling disaster for all life."[12]

From the moment that it was perceived (as a transcendent dimension of the objective given), the divine was experienced as something beyond control and therefore as something unpredictable. All of man's misery stems from the primeval decision not to accept the perception of the divine as a gift and a grace, but to capture and possess it by killing and devouring it. In the Paleolithic period this violent appropriation was done directly by slaying a great animal and by slaying a man. At the same time, these killings had the social function of establishing divine authority through the power to kill, and thus of causing men to respect the basic rules of communal life. The slain man or beast was a sacrifice that had to die so that the community, freed from paralyzing fear, could breathe, live, and act again.

Estimates vary but man has lived according to this pattern of behavior for between ninety-five and ninety-nine per cent of his history. His development as a human being has followed this pattern: "The 10,000 years, at the most, since the beginning of agriculture are almost negligible in comparison."[13] When, some 8,000 or 10,000 years ago, man adopted the settled lifestyle of an agricultural civilization, this behavioral pattern was already deeply rooted in him. When communal life was threatened, when droughts, floods, earthquakes, epidemics, or enemies threatened the stability of life, bloodshed was inevitable. Through the sacrifice of human beings or of symbolic animals, the religious dimension of peoples' lives had to be strengthened and activated so that man could establish a communion with the divine, and thus have a better grasp of his universe and on the shaping of a livable human existence.

Sacrifices of Children in the Old Testament

According to the testimony of the ancient historian Diodorus, testimony which has been confirmed by archaeological findings, in the year 310 BC the Carthaginians sacrificed a great number of children to the God

Cronos. They were laid on the arms of the idol and then cast into a fire.[14] This sacrificial practice is the basic pattern of child sacrifice as was denounced by the prophets and by the Hebrew Law of Holiness: "You must not allow any of your children to be passed through the fire to Molech" (Lev. 18, 21). "Say to the sons of Israel: Any son of Israel or any stranger living in Israel must die if he gives any children to Molech. The people of the country must stone him" (Lev. 20, 2). When the Israelites settled in Canaan, they were not allowed to adopt the religious customs of the local inhabitants: "For Yahweh detests all this and hates what they have done unto their gods, even their sons and daughters they have burnt in the fire for their gods" (Deut. 12, 31).

Even in Israel, however, there were recurrences of such sacrifices. Of King Ahaz of Judah, who was open to foreign cultic influences, it is said: "He walked in the way of the kings of Israel, even causing his son to pass through fire, according to the shameful practices of the nations which Yahweh had cast out for the sons of Israel" (2 Kings 16, 3). "To cause his son to pass through fire" was a standard euphemism for the sacrificial burning of a son. It is reported, for example, that King Manasseh "caused his son to pass through fire. He practiced soothsaying and wizardry..." (2 Kings 21, 6). During his religious reformation, King Josiah "desecrated the furnace in the Valley of Ben-hinnom, so that no one could make his son or daughter pass through fire in honor of Molech" (2 Kings 23, 10). This cultic place is also mentioned by Jeremiah, when he enumerates the misdeeds of the sons of Judah. "They have built the high place of Topheth in the Valley of Ben-hinnom, to burn their sons and their daughters; something I never commanded, something that never entered my thoughts" (Jer. 7, 31; 19, 5). When, in the days of King Ahab who was also criticized for adopting foreign rites, a certain Hiel from Beth-El rebuilt Jericho, he laid its foundations "at the price of Abiram, his first born; its gates he erected at the price of his youngest son Segub" (1 Kings 16, 34).

Without any reproof, the book of Judges relates the theme of the ancient story about the commander Jephthah's vow to offer to Yahweh as a holocaust the first person to greet him from the door of his house on his return from battle if the Lord would grant him victory of the Ammonites. Jephthah defeated the Ammonites and when he returned to his house in Mizpah, "his daughter came out from it to meet him; she was dancing to the sound of tambourines. She was his only child" (Judg. 11, 34). Although he tears his clothes in sorrow and lets her go free for two months to "wander in the mountains, and with my companions bewail my virginity" (11, 37). Jephthah eventually "treated her as the vow that he had uttered bound him" (11, 39) and he continued to be a judge in

132

Israel for another six years. It is a characteristic feature of child sacrifice none but the dearest and most precious child that is offered, for such a sacrifice makes the strongest appeal to the transcendental mystery. Thus, in the popular story of Abraham's sacrifice, God says to Abraham: "Take your son...your only child Isaac, whom you love...you shall bring him as a burnt offering" (Gen. 22, 2). But according to the story, God only wanted to test Abraham's obedience, and in the end he is satisfied with an animal as a burnt offering in place of the son.[15]

These customs from the Old Testament show that even in matters of human sacrifice the revelation of Yahweh could not maintain a continous influence, and that there were frequent relapses into former practices. For it is clear from the beginning that the God "I-am-here" does not want human sacrifices. Indeed, he is the God of those who in Egypt became the victims of Pharoh's assumption of divine authority. He is the God of those who were handed over to death, the God of sacrificed children. In the revelation of his name — "I am the I-am-here" — he expresses his fundamental freedom from man's attempts at manipulation, and forbids any pictorial representation and even the utterance of his name (which is also a way of putting him at one's disposal).[16] The desire to move the absolutely unmanipulable God "I-am-here" to some specific action with offerings (either of animals or of humans) shows that man has not yet opened himself to the real nature of God; it is ultimately a sign of faithlessness.

The Dismembered Body of the Child as a Source of Life

But it is the Near East in particular that has an especially long tradition of child sacrifices. In his sensitive interpretation of Yemeni fairytales and popular customs, Werner Daum has attempted to reconstruct the offering of young girls as the basic feature of Semitic religion.[17] Having lived in Yemen for many years, Werner Daum is thoroughly familiar with these tales and customs (perhaps more so than with the Islamic and Judaic rites which he tries to explain from this perspective).[18] His basic assumption, confirmed by recent archaeological studies, is that the transition to sedentary life was quite independent of the transition to agriculture. The high plains on the fringes and on the lower regions of the mountains of the Near East were particularly favorable to such a development. There was so much wild grain (especially red wheat and barley) and so much game, that man no longer needed to quit his dwelling place, and in time learned to grow the grain himself and to domesticate the wild pigs, sheep, goats, and cattle.

Of course, those settlements were only small clearings, tiny islands in the ocean of the surrounding wilderness. In this wilderness, the almighty power of the divine was experienced, especially in the tropical storms and rains that would fill the wadis, fed by mountain streams to overflowing, and devastate the settlements. Black clouds, storms, thunder, and lightning, the attributes of the highest godhead in many religions (Wotan, Zeus, and Indra; and in the Old Testament, Yahweh's appearance in a storm, on Mount Sinai, in a cloud, and in a pillar of fire) are the symbols in which the manifestation of the divine was expressed after man's transition to a settled lifestyle. For these people they expressed the same power which was experienced by the ancient hunter in the raging bull.

When the rhythm of the seasons brought the threat of thunderstorms and torrential rains, paralyzing the community with fear, a human being had to be sacrificed according to the old pattern, to ensure the stability and survival of the community. The new way of life called only for a new interpretation. The gruesome slaying of man's most beloved and precious possession would make the terrifying old wilderness god aware of the community and, they hoped, spare their settlements. In the slaying one acknowledged him and anticipated his action. This is the reason why girls were usually chosen to be brought into the wilderness, abandoned at the well of the wadi, or buried alive in the riverbed. The girl was offered to the lord of the wadi as a bride.[19] Later, or after climatic changes, when heat and drought were the main threats to human life, children were made to "go through the fire," in order to give an offering to the god of the burning heat and to establish contact with him. The same rule applied when enemies threatened the settlements. It is told that the king of Moab, when he could no longer resist the assault of the Israelites on his city, Kirhareseth, took his eldest son "who was to succeed him" and offered him as a sacrifice on the city wall. Thereupon, the Israelites withdrew "with bitter indignation," terrified by this appearance of the god of terror on the city walls (2 Kings 3, 26 f.).

In numerous myths we learn how the life and prosperity of man, the functioning of his world, depends upon the violent killing of a human child. In the myth of the Wemale from the Moluccan island of Ceram, the girl Hainuwele is pushed towards and into a pit during a spiral dance which moves in slow and ever narrowing circular motions. Afterwards, the dancers fill the pit with earth and stamp it down, still dancing. Later her body is exhumed, dismembered, and the pieces buried in different places. From the fragments of her body new and hitherto unknown things arose, such as tuberous plants, and became a source of nutrition for the tribe. Thus the girl had to die so that the others could live. Similar stories are told of the divine child Dionysos Zagreus, a Greek divinity of ancient, pre-Greek origins. Later mythology turned him into the fruit of the love between Zeus and Persephone, the goddess of the underworld. After the jealous Hera discovered him at play she sent the Titans to capture and dismember him. But this dismembering is the origin of new life: "When the Titans had cut his limbs with iron knives, his death became the beginning of new growth."[20] He appears now in many different forms—as old man, as infant, as young man, as raging lion, as proud steed, as dragon, tiger and bull. His death created the universe of the divine and fascinating.

The Rig-Veda, the central text of ancient Hinduism and perhaps the most ancient sacred scripture of mankind, relates the myth of the primeval man Purusha.[21] When he was born "he stretched out to the East and to the West and over the whole earth." He towers over everything and he contains all that is precious in the world. "With him the gods and all Sadhyas (ancient celestial beings) and Rishis (the primeval seers) made their offering." His body was dismembered, and from this "great and complete sacrifice" arose the divine and the human cosmos. "From his eyes came the sun, from his mouth came the gods Indra and Agni and the caste of the Brahmans, from his breath came the wind, from his navel came the air, from his head the sky, from his feet the earth...all that is came from him: The sacrifice of the first human offspring and its dismemberment is the basis for all being and life." This is Francis X. D'Sa's interpretation of the myth. In it is reflected the "wholeness, the inner sense of belonging and the dependence of all beings on each other."[22] In the light of Girard's insights we might ask ourselves if such an interpretation (in this uncritical form) might not itself still be under the spell of primeval sacrifice.

This pattern of thought and behavior is broken in the gospels—at least in their fundamental structure. Jesus was put to death not by "gods, celestial beings and primeval seers," but by fanatic and narrow-minded people driven by fear. The curtain that divided man from God since the primeval times of original sin was not torn down by the dismembered body nor the blood of the Crucified, but only by the cry of Christ's agony, in which he gathered all his strength, all his being from the innermost core of his personality, in one last effort to make it universally audible and recognizable. He *alone* has called forth divine salvation for the universe and liberated man from the cycle of violence and sacrifice. His body as such had no significance as is proven by the story of the empty tomb (Luke 24, 1-12, esp. 5).[23]

It now becomes clear why it ever was possible to interpret the life and death of Jesus as a sacrifice organized by God for cosmic salvation. This pattern of feeling and thought is so old and so deeply ingrained in the origins of humanity that it is difficult to avoid.[24] Wherever a new manifestation of the divine appears in the world, man's first attempt is to interpret the new within old and pre-existing categories. But in the long run, the fate of the son Jesus does not fit into such a category because of its unique nature. In his experience of the Abba Jesus has revealed the source of all being to be quite unlike that which those practicing human sacrifice had sought to placate. Because he lives and dies in unfailing truthfulness, despite all temptations, this experience of the sinless basis of his life, becomes a symbol, a parable, a place of revelation for a God who appears to the abandoned as a motherly, protective God, carrying him beyond death, and who thus unmasks the sinfulness of the ideology of sacrifice.

1.3 The Divine Maiden (Daughter)

On the Character of Sacrifices of Young Girls

Even though one might have certain reservations concerning Werner Daum's quite detailed reconstructions—insofar as they are based on uncertain linguistic derivations—Daum, who has a sound knowledge of the tales and customs of ancient Yemen, accurately describes the characteristics of religious sensibilities that accompany the transition to a settled life. They seem more plausible given the fact that, at the dawn of the Neolithic period, man had already lived for millions of years under the spell of that power to kill, a power which he had appropriated through usurpation when he became a hunter against his natural disposition. The fascination with this power held him spellbound. The raging bull, the charging wild horse, the trampling herd of the mammoths, with which he had lived in deadly rivalry, and in which this fascination of the power to kill was symbolized, were encountered anew. They appeared again perhaps even more powerfully to those who had dared to found a homestead and to live their lives on small pieces of land, in the form of raging winds, earthquakes, thunder and lightning, floods and the merciless heat of droughts, which threatened again and again to wash away, to burn down, or to dry out these new homes of theirs, these little pieces of land wrested from the wilderness.

In the face of these powers the spear proved useless. On the other hand, man had only his own killing power to fight these forces. This is the moment of what Girard described as the "crisis of a lack of differen-

136

tiation"—the disappearance in times of crisis of the rules and differences that define cultural divisions.[1] This crisis, whenever it comes about, calls for a scapegoat, whose death allows the disintegrating human world to be grounded once again in the divine, in the awe of the power to kill, and gives man his last reserve of energy to rebel against his fate.

What happens here cannot be adequately described as an attempt to "appease" the god of the wilderness, or as a magic ritual intended to bring rain or sunshine. The cave paintings of a "rain-sacrifice" in Rhodesia, as well as the ancient Mexican representations of human offerings that were dedicated to the sun, express something quite different

Fig. 24: Rain sacrifice (rock-drawing, Rhodesia).

(Fig. 24). The immense bolt of lightning rises steeply from the victim, linking the human world to the great goddess. It builds a powerful "ladder into heaven" (Gen. 28, 12 f.), by which men ascend to the divinity. From the upper end, a meandering stream pours forth from the lightning, bringing the needed water, the basis of human life.

The second image shows the same basic features (Fig. 25). The ejaculating penis of the sacrificial priest is pointed towards the victim, a girl whose dismembered limbs have been laid before him. In this piercing, killing, and dismembering of the victim the performer of the sacrifice assumes superhuman proportions. He is almost as large as the great goddess who stoops down to him from above and gives the welcome rain. A tree on the right is the symbol of the new life that has been gained through the establishment of the power to kill.

A similar story is told by the pictures of an ancient Mexican sacrifice (Fig. 26). There is no feeling of humble surrender to God ("to appease the godhead") or of magic and incantation. These images (see also Fig. 14) express aggression, like their Rhodesian counterparts, although with Indian characteristics. They correspond to the descriptions given by the Spanish conquistadors who witnessed these ceremonies. The victim is stretched over a stone, his breast is opened wide, and the heart, still throbbing, is cut out and lifted up, while the dead body is thrown down the pyramid.[2] The picture shows how the tree of life grows from the brutally maimed victim, with an attentive and satisfied divinity enthroned on top.

Neither appeasement nor magic is the issue here. When Homer tells us that Iphigenia was to be offered in appeasement of the goddess Artemis before the Greeks set out against Troy, or when in fairy tales the whole city is in mourning because the king's daughter had to be given to the dragon as ransom, or when some magic is linked to the slaying in such tales, we have to take into account the fact that these versions are relatively recent revisions. At the time of their revisions the light-hero had risen to rescue the woman from the god of the wilderness; and therefore the killings began to be regarded as ruthless and inhumane. In the revised plot the human sacrifice is either replaced by an animal offering (as with Iphigenia and Abraham), or the light-hero might kill the dragon, the wilderness-force. Therefore, the original gesture of human sacrifice can no longer be found in these stories. In human sacrifice, the point is to establish the human power to kill and with it the awe of the divine in order to prevent the dissolution of the human world — Girard speaks of a "lack of differentiation" — by drought, flood, or eternal darkness. The basic ideology of sin becomes visible. By aggressively usurping the power to kill, man himself becomes "like gods" (Gen. 3, 5). He raises himself as

Fig. 25: Rain sacrifice (rock-drawing, Rhodesia).

a partner of the godhead who can no longer ignore him, but must acknowledge him, just as Cain tried to force God's attention by slaying his brother Abel. Whenever the divine authority communicates with the human community — with its priest or with its priest-king — dissolution, drought and flood no longer threaten human life. For the human world depends upon that transcendent dimension revitalized by the offerings.

Of course, in the early stages of man's change from hunter to settler he feared the destruction of his newly constituted world and the practice

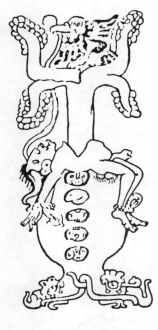

Fig. 26: The tree of fertility grows from a human sacrifice, with a satisfied god enthroned on top (relief drawing from ancient Mexico; Mayan culture).

of human sacrifice probably increased when crises arose. This is shown very clearly from the situation in ancient Mexico, where this period of human evolution happened later than in other places and is therefore more accessible to us.

To the degree that the role of the woman and mother (at home, at the hearth, as keeper of stored goods) and her symbolic importance became more prominent in settled life—especially in the Near East—the daughter, the young girl became the focus of an ominous attention. For the terror of human killing-power could be most effective when it struck the most precious and beloved creature (by piercing it through, by dismembering it, or by pushing it into its grave). In a culture exalting marriage and motherhood, a young girl who had just reached marriageable age was the embodiment of supreme value, holding all the promises of maternity, a being from whom the transcendent dimension of life radiated in the most powerful way. Therefore, as Werner Daum has pointed out, it is most often the marriageable daughter of the sultan who in ancient Arabic tales is brought into the wilderness to be killed. Even in familiar German fairy tales the dragon demands the life of the king's daughter, and Sleeping Beauty and Snow White sleep the sleep of death in the wilderness until they are found and saved by the light-hero.

140

The Maiden Sacrificed (Persecuted) and Deified: Hainuwele-Cora (Persephone)-Ishtar-Artemis (Britomartis, Iphigenia)-Athena

It is a characteristic feature of this kind of spirituality that the victim takes part in the deification process. For as we have seen in the images previously discussed, the victims establish communciation with the divine. This is especially obvious in the myth of Hainuwele, which appears as a genre all over the world, and which has been described many times from a psycho-analytical point of view.[3] Hainuwele is the divine maiden, the daughter of god who comes to men in supernatural circumstances to bring them precious gifts. Through her sacrificial death and dismemberment she grants them their basic food (tuberous plants). She is the link with the great goddess and she has the vital influence on the life of man. All that is was given by her and through her. She is the figure of a divine redeemer. Her type is found in numerous goddesses who originated from these early times of settled life and from the ritual sacrificing of maidens. Youthful beauty is the characteristic making them particularly eligible as sacrifices.

The pre-Hellenic goddess Cora-Persephone belongs to this group, a virgin of unusual beauty, a daughter of the pre-Hellenic Great Mother (Demeter). She is coveted by Hades, the god of the underworld, who abducted her in his chariot drawn by wild horses when she was picking flowers in a meadow. Her mother's sorrow dries out the land, bringing the threat of famine. But Hades and Demeter come to an agreement, according to which Persephone may stay one part of the year with Hades in the underworld and the other with her mother on earth. Only this reconciliation brings full fertility to the land: Demeter had given grain and taught man the art of agriculture. In secret rites, which were perpetuated in the Eleusinian mysteries, she grants humans the gift of fertility. But the sacrificial mediator of this gift of fertility and of the cycle of life is Persephone, the heavenly maiden, the daughter of the goddess, who continuously offers herself to the god of the underworld.

In the old Sumerian tale of Ishtar's descent into hell, written in cuneiform characters, Ishtar (Inanna) becomes a victim of the goddess of the underworld. But because Ishtar enters the underworld as the goddess of fertility (she might have become the goddess of fertility through a previous sacrifice), this (second) persecution makes life and fertility wither on earth. In order to save the cosmos, the watergod Ea sends a "young lover" to the goddess of the underworld—in another version this is Tammuz, the lover of Ishtar before her descent into the underworld. Thanks to this "ransom" Ishtar is freed and earthly life begins to flourish once again. Tammuz's sister relieves her brother by taking his place in the underworld for six months of every year.

It is likely that not only Persephone but also other virgins of the Greek pantheon have their origins in this type of sacrificial maiden. Even Artemis, who is linked with the fertility of animals—a pre-Hellenic figure as well—has similar symbolic features.[4] When her mother, the Titan Leto, was pregnant with her she wandered through all the lands of the earth—like the Christian mother of God searching for an inn—but none would receive her and let her give birth to her child. This was later explained by the fact that her child was a daughter of Zeus and that she was being persecuted by the jealous Hera. At no place upon which the sun shone was she to give birth to her child. Even the Delphian dragon threatened to swallow both her and her child. Eventually, Ortygia, later identified as the island of Delos, offers her shelter. According to one version of the myth, Poseidon flooded the island with his waves when Leto gave birth to the twins Artemis and Apollo, so that the sun could not shine upon it. But precisely because of this, Artemis, born in persecution and ill-fortune, becomes the great and helpful goddess and, just as her twin brother becomes the god of light, she brings good luck to hunters, and protects the offspring of all creatures, especially of man. Thus she is venerated by males as the goddess of hunting, while women view her as the goddess of parturition and call upon her when in labor. Born from misery and from persecution, she has, as do almost all ancient godheads, an ambivalent character as well: When a woman died of a sudden, unexpected death, it was said that she was struck by the arrow of Artemis.

The type of the divine maiden who serves as a sacrifice and thereby has a healing effect on mankind is found in many mythical figures who resemble Artemis and sometimes even merge with her. One of these figures is the nymph Britomartis, whose name, according to Solinus, is the Cretan name for Artemis and means "sweet girl."[5] Coveted and pursued by King Minos, she jumps off a cliff into the sea. According to another version, she dives into the sacred cave of Artemis at Aegina and thus becomes the goddess Aphaia, venerated by the Aeginatens. Iphigenia, who is chosen by her father Agamemnon for a sacrifice, is also closely related to Artemis. On the one hand, Artemis herself demands the offering as an expiation of Agamemnon's offense. On the other hand, she feels so strongly for the girl that she snatches her at the moment of the sacrifice and brings her to her temple among the Tauri to serve as a priestess. Depending on the different versions of the myth, at the moment of the slaying a hind, a bear, or a bull suddenly appears on the altar—all symbols of Artemis, so that one even suspected that Iphigenia was no other than Artemis herself.[6]

Athena, Zeus' favorite daughter, fair, with virginal gravity, clad in armor with a richly adorned helmet, a long spear, and the terrifying head of a Gorgon on her shield, belongs to this type of divine maiden as well. Originally, she was probably the protector of the fortresses of Mycenae, from which she derives her martial character.[7] The story of her birth from the head of Zeus, first related by Pindar, probably has historical roots and may be regarded as "an interesting piece of early religious policy-making," as Rose puts it.[8] Indeed, the invading tribes had somehow to clarify the relation between their principal godhead and the protector-goddess of Mycenae, who enjoyed universal recognition. She could not be Zeus' wife, because goddesses of her kind usually were virgins. Her high rank in the country made it impossible to provide her with a Greek mother, not even Hera. So the god had to bring her forth from himself, in a sort of virgin birth: By dividing his nature — his head was split in two with an axe during the birth — he freed Athena as an independent aspect of himself. An older recurring theme, which belongs to the authentic type of the divine virgin maiden, is the ancient and wild motive of devouring that is also linked to the story of Athena's birth. According to the later version, it was Zeus who, as in the story of Artemis, persecuted the mother of Athena even during her pregnancy, and swallowed both mother and child. Originally Zeus was certainly a wilderness-god. The fair but terrifying goddess, strong and full of blessings, came forth from this sacrificial slaying.

The Sacrifice of Young Girls as a Universal Structure in Mythologies and the Reality of Jesus

Given the wide diffusion of the mythologic structure of the divine sacrificial maiden who grants fertility through her death, Drewermann with A. E. Jensen[9] asks whether the multiple variants of this single, universal theme can in fact be adequately explained by some archetypal structure of the human soul. His own answer is: "Even as a faithful disciple of Jung one cannot believe such a thing."[10] He openly admits that in this case "the psychological explanation, based on the hypothesis of the collective unconscious, is a failure," and that "only a cultural and historical explanation" could account for the widespread tradition and the unified/diversified variations of the myth, namely "that it was created once, in a particular place by a single invention, and that it was handed down and elaborated by cultural tradition."[11]

But "single invention" and "collective unconscious" are not the only alternatives for the explanation of this or, for that matter, of any myth. Rather, mythology and rituals develop as direct expressions of the ongoing dialogue between the human being who has awakened to a sensitivity to symbol and the transcendent dimension which he experiences. The sacrificial slaying of a blossoming young girl and the veneration of her as a divine redeemer consistently follow from the history of human religious experience as we have presented it — a history that is shaped at its very origins by a freely chosen, violent usurpation of the transcendent dimension.[12]

It is understandable that Christians, who themselves are formed in their perceptions, thoughts, and feelings by millions of years of this history, tend to interpret the transcendent dimension of reality that is encountered in Jesus of Nazareth through this myth. Jesus becomes the victim who, through his bloody sacrificial death, gives "satisfaction" to an offended and furious God by facing him on the same level, reestablishing the dialogue with his people, thus redeeming and healing humanity, saving it from inner and outer destruction.[13] But once we have become sensitive to this mythological antecedent, we need only to read the gospel without prejudice to realize that Jesus has never played this role. He has not offered his life as a sacrifice to appease a raging godhead. Rather, he has died for the truth of his experience at the river Jordan, which showed that the fuming, punishing God is nothing but a projection of human fear, and that in reality God is pure Love, Abba/Mama/Papa.

However, a definite similarity between Jesus and the "divine maiden" arises wherever people renounce this way of treating the transcendent dimension of their lives and become open to compassion for the victimized maiden. In the myths and fairy tales that have come down to us, this is almost always the case. The great goddess Saténe from the myth of Hainuwele, abandons humanity because of the killing of Hainuwele. In the ancient Babylonian myth Ea feels compassion for Ishtar, who is being tortured in the underworld, and Tammuz's sister feels compassion for her brother who freed Ishtar. Artemis is compassionate toward Iphigenia. Demeter desperately searches the whole cosmos for her daughter who had been abducted by the god of the underworld. The Arabic and the European storytellers (and the father of the children in the story) are saddened because the children — e.g. Hänsel and Gretel — must be abandoned in the wilderness. Similar accounts are found in "Snow White," "Red Riding Hood," "Cinderella," and in many other fairy tales.

At those moments of the myths and fairy tales, a genuinely Christian sensitivity breaks through in compassion, in being existentially touched by the helpless child, the abandoned being. This mentality, this wind and breath of compassion and of care for the helplessly abandoned one, is the wind, the *ruach* and the *pneuma hagion* that has already called forth the God "I-am-here" of the Old Testament (Deut. 26, 5-9: "...Yahweh

heard our voice and saw our misery, our toil and our oppression...").
This is why, in the New Testament, the Son who had been handed over
to death, was freed "from the pangs of Hades" (Acts 2, 24) by the
transcendent love of the Abba, and was revealed as the Messiah to all
people. Therefore, to foster this feeling and this thinking in man and to
expect salvation and healing from it, is not only authentic Christian
teaching, but also authentic Christian revelation: the opening of man to
the specifically Christian experience of the triune God.

This mentality first sprang up in the transitional period to a settled life
but did not then have a decisive impact on the human community. As
will be shown in the following chapters about the wind and the breath
and about father/mother as symbols of God, the sinful fascination with
violence and killing was still firmly rooted in man. Thus, the burgeoning
feeling of compassion was overcome, as it were, and people again were
led to violence and killing, to the merciless fight between the light-hero
and the wilderness-god, who had now become the dragon of chaos, the
devouring beast. In religious history, this struggle is the mission of the
"Son of God."

1.4 The Divine Son

*From the Divine Maiden to the Divine Son: The Failed Liberation from
the Fascination of the Power to Kill*

In many myths and fairy tales we encounter the theme in which the
maiden and her brother are to be handed over to the powers of evil,
which, together, they overcome — sometimes with more activity on the
part of the girl, sometimes more on the part of the boy. A prototype of
this theme can perhaps be found in the story of Ishtar's descent into hell
in which Ishtar, who has been chained and tortured by the goddess of the
underworld, is brought back in exchange for a youthful lover and can
return to earth endowed with rich gifts. The theme is reminiscent of
"Hänsel and Gretel," in which Hänsel, the chosen victim of the witch,
must stick his index finger (probably a phallic symbol) out of his cage
every day so that the witch can check on his fattening. In this case, of
course, brother and sister cooperate: Gretel takes the initiative, kills the
witch and sets her brother free. In the Yemeni fairy tale "The Darkness"

145

it is also the girl who takes the initiative and overcomes the powers of darkness, the old witch. Apollo, whom we shall have to discuss in more detail, is the twin brother of Artemis. He escaped together with his sister and fought as a light-hero against the powers of darkness. The theme also appears in numerous Grimm fairy tales (besides *Hänsel and Gretel* see *The Brother and Sister, The Bird-foundling, The Juniper Tree* etc.).

In ancient Egypt Isis fights together with her brother and husband Osiris against their dark, evil brother Seth, the incarnation of the powers of death. Osiris is killed by Seth, but his procreating power can be awakened a last time by Isis, who thus conceives and gives birth to the falcon god Horus. As a god of light — his eyes are like the sun and the moon, and he hovers in the skies in the form of a falcon — Horus continues to fight Seth. Eventually, he shares the ruling power with Seth and is incarnated as Horus-Seth in the Pharaoh who brings "mercy and punishment, blessing and misery, upon the people."[1] Although Horus marries his mother Isis, he is known as "Horus the child."[2] He is represented as a child, nursing on his mother's lap (Fig. 22a). The hero of light, who fights against the powers of darkness, is in his essence a son and a lover.

Of course, this god of light, who is sent out by his mother to kill the god of the wilderness and to free the community from the obligation of human sacrifice, can not actually break the cycle of violence. He is able to overcome the god of the wilderness only with his own weapons. He must seize his sword of lightning and behead him with a single stroke.[3] Thus, both he and the woman who sent him into the fight now hold the power of terror. Baal competes with El for the attributes of storm, thunder and lightning — the symbols of terror. Thus the great woman and mother has ambivalent features in all religions. She is not only the godess of love and fertility, but also — as, for example, is the Sumerian Inanna — the goddess of war and death. In her hands also lies the fate of the hero, who, as her brother or son, is also primarily her lover, and who may not grow old in this role which embodies life and fertility. If he slays the god of the wilderness, and the community prospers and flourishes, he may live. But when the wilderness god returns either as flood or drought, and vegetation dies, the hero must go into the underworld. In the context of an actual historical rite, this means that the lover who had been enthroned by the priestly queen in a sacred marriage, must die after a fixed period of time.

To be sure, the queen will choose a new son and lover at the beginning of every cycle of fertility. She will install him in his office through a sacred marriage and tell her people that the old hero of light, who had been killed in a sacrifice at the time of harvest, is come to new life in this new king. But everyone is uneasily aware that this is ideology and that the young man who was killed at harvest-time is rotting in his grave. The human sacrifice could not be abolished; it was just provided with a new character, a new ideology. Even as a hero of light, the child remains the abandoned being. Indeed, when exceptional hardship and misery that surpassed the expected seasonal destructions came upon the community, the new ideology often broke down completely, and people returned — as we will see in the example of Crete (Chap. 3.3) — to the old idea of anticipating the fury of the raging god by offering their dearest and most beloved possession, in the hope of appeasing his wrath.

By this regression into the cycle of violence the symbolism of the woman loses its redemptive power. In the myth of Isis and Osiris it is said that in the end Horus snatches the crown from his mother's head. In another version, he tears off her head.[4] The fatal attraction of violence has caught up with the symbolism of the woman and the hero of light.

The Divine Son as Light-hero, (Independent of Women)

The symbolism of the hero of light has penetrated the Old Testament in a more patriarchal form, namely in the figure of Jacob (Gen. 25, 19-36.43).[5] Rebekah, Isaac's wife, gives birth to twin sons, of which the first-born Esau, with his dark skin and wild character, is the father's favorite, while the other son, Jacob, fair skinned and without fault, is the beloved of his mother. The bright son, Jacob, buys the birthright from his dark brother for a bowl of lentil stew, and together with his mother he tricks his old father and Esau, the dark brother and obtains Isaac's blessing: "Yes the smell of my son is like the smell of a fertile field blessed by Yahweh" (Gen. 27, 27). Jacob takes refuge in Canaan from his dark brother Esau, and he acquires wives and great property. Upon his return, as we have seen previously, Jacob fights with a nocturnal demon who reveals himself at dawn as "El," the primeval Semitic god of terror who, overcome by the light-hero, blesses him and gives him the name "Isra-el" ("fighter of God"). But even the blessed son and hero of light, Jacob, does not leave the battle without scars: "The sun rose when he left Peniel, limping because of his hip" (Gen. 32, 32). Light and happiness, where they exist, are bought from darkness through compromise. These heroes limp; they have crippled legs like Horus, the bright, divine son. As Horus was reconciled to Seth, so does the limping Jacob seek reconciliation with his dark brother Esau.

In Indian religion the principal god of light and vegetation is Indra, called "Indra sahasramuska" (Indra with one thousand testicles), who drinks the intoxicating Soma and fights against the dragon Vrtra who holds back the waters in the canyons of the mountains. Indra wins, frees the water, and thus makes human life possible. "You are famous because you have overcome Vrtra. You have unleashed the waters that were bound" (Rig-Veda IV, 42, 7).[6] In the much later texts of the Upanishads, from the fourth century AD, Vishnu, who in the Veda was an insignificant, non-Aryan divinity, takes the place of Indra. In his incarnation as the divine child Krishna he kills his evil brother Agha, in the guise of the giant serpent and he overcomes the serpent-demon, Kaliya, dancing on the head of the monster. Yet, he does not kill Kaliya, but sends him into the far ocean, where he retires with his company of dragons and serpents.[7]

Vishnu is always represented as a child. The great ascetic Markandeya was allowed to see him lying in peaceful slumber under a fig tree, in the midst of the dark and silent ocean; or as a lonely little boy who plays without taking notice of the blackness of the abyss surrounding him.[8] Although Kansa, the son of a demon, tries brutally to prevent his birth as Krishna, Vishnu comes forth from the heart of his earthly mother Devaki in the deep darkness of the night, unrecognized by Kansa but surrounded by signs of light and blessing in the whole world "as the full moon which rises on the Eastern horizon." He is born with the fully developed features of an adult, clad in yellow garments, adorned with jewels, and holding his weapons in his hands. Only later does he take on the features of a common child.[9]

The symbolism of Vishnu-Krishna is related to the Greek god of light, Apollo. He embodies the bright aspect of Zeus, the king of the gods, and is born on the island Delos of the Titan, Leto, a pre-Aryan mother goddess. He is born of his dark mother in festive brightness as the healing conquerer of all darkness and evil, as the "god of solemn measure, of harmony, and of equality and justice."[10] The earth rejoices, the goddesses of heaven hasten to greet him with joy. The newborn, erect in his brilliant glory, grasps the bow, the arrow, and the golden lyre which Zeus has placed in his hands. As a light-hero he overcomes the dark powers of the earth, the giant Tithyos, and the serpent Python, which lived in a fissure of a rock at the temple of Delphi, where it inspired the oracular utterances of the priestess Pythia by strong vapors. Now the god of light controls the messages of the priestess and becomes the lord and owner of the Delphic oracle. But in contrast to Hercules, the son of Zeus and the mortal woman Alcmene, who, even as an infant, strangled with his bare hands those snakes that crawled into his cradle to kill him, the martial aspects subside in Apollo, as they do in Vishnu-Krishna. The predominant impression is one of light, healing, of the peace and harmony that

148

belong to the symbolism of the child. When Apollo as a boy plays the flute while watching the sheep, the whole of nature glows peacefully, and even the wild animals listen to the glorious sounds.

But the god of light, Apollo, is and remains an Olympian. The harmony which he symbolizes entails the destruction of the earthly. The flutist Apollo competes with the earthly satyr Pan. He wins and skins the satyr alive—themes that would be unthinkable with Jesus.

The healing god Aesculapius, the son of Apollo and Coronis, a bright and mysterious mortal woman who is related to the moon and to the underworld, is closer to the world of men and their needs and miseries. This symbol of a caring and healing attitude towards men is indeed related to the figure of Jesus as the "redeemer of the world."[11] Just as Jesus is found by shepherds in the familiar Christmas story, so Aesculapius is found by shepherds as an abandoned child among the wild beasts. A bright, divine apparition and a heavenly voice announce that the newborn will bring healing to all the sick and will raise the dead. In many statues he is represented bending over an invalid, bandaging wounds, and laying his hands on the sick. In his temple at Epidaurus man experiences the protection of and acceptance by divine forces. Stretched out on the floor of the sanctuary, he surrenders to a sleep that will heal and grant him inner renewal. The god who was himself abandoned as a child and experienced the protection of good forces, can now, in his turn, give comfort and healing to man.

But unlike Jesus, Aesculapius remains integrated in the divine world which is still ruled by the god of terror eager to affirm his power. The highest god, Zeus, resents the beneficent activity of Aesulapius, who seems likely to win his battle against sickness and death, thereby narrowing the difference between men and gods. Zeus kills the healer with his lightning. Unlike the narrators of the gospels, the narrators of the myth of Aesulapius abandoned hope of overcoming death and entering the realm of the divine.[12]

According to the experience of this myth, the divine power of terror that manifests itself in violent killing has the last word. The myth thus remains within the cycle of violence that started with the "founding murder," as described by René Girard.[13] But this is precisely the redeeming significance of the healer Jesus. Through his own death, in the cry of his agony, he has torn the veil of the temple "from top to bottom" (Mark 15, 38): that veil which shrouded the "innermost sanctuary," a religious sensibility grounded in the power to kill which hid the true nature of God. The Abba who was disclosed by Jesus to the sick and suffering, under whose protection they could gain new strength and be healed, is love without violence that survives beyond death. Through him, death has lost its power: "Death where is your victory?" (1 Cor. 15, 55).

Buddha

Buddha is also a light-hero. To be sure, he does not conquer darkness and demons with the killing power of violent weapons. The concentrated force of his mind alone breaks through the darkness that enshrouds human life, and he achieves the illumination that frees him from the cycle of death and darkness, from the limits of samsara, of the human life dominated by the killing power. Relatively soon after the historical Gautama Siddharta, men venerated the man Buddha as the child of light who descends from the divine realm onto the earth to enlighten it with his example and his teaching. Thus his birth is not the birth of a common man. His mother conceives him without his father's participation. While she is asleep on the roof of her house, a white elephant[14] impregnates her. She carries the child for ten months and during the birth she stands upright and Buddha steps forth from her right side. The whole world fills with brightness, and gods and men rejoice in the birth. Like the Pharaoh, Krishna and Apollo—but unlike Jesus—he comes forth from his mother's womb as a perfectly shaped little adult. He stands on his feet, facing North, takes seven great steps forward, looks in all directions and utters these powerful words: "I am the most noble in this world! I am the first of this universe! I am the highest of this world! This is the last incarnation! There will be no reincarnation!"[15]

According to one legend, the mother, Queen Maya, when she feels the hour of the birth of the "Bodhisattva," of the human being predestined to future illumination, is close, goes to the meadows of Lumbini, sprinkled with fragrant water and covered with heavenly flowers, taking with her an immense retinue—80,000 adorned horse-drawn chariots, 80,000 elephant carriages, 80,000 soldiers, "all handsome and courageous heroes," 60,000 Sakya-girls, 60,000 singing women from the king's harem—to give birth to her child.[16]

In these stories, the illuminations of the historic Gautama Siddharta are fused with the symbolism of light and of the sun-child that floods the whole world with its radiance. Evil and darkness are powerless in the face of this child. Later, when Buddha is sitting under the Pipal-tree—shortly before his illumination—the thousand-armed prince of demons, Mara, gathers his terrible army with frightful weapons around the tree in a huge circle, about 70 kilometers in width, in order to intercept Buddha's illumination. The gods and good spirits who had gathered around Buddha

150

flee at this terrifying sight. But Buddha calmly reveals his ten virtues and thereby forces the armies of terror to retreat. Mara's last weapon, one with which he can split mountains, is a circular disk, the Cakkavudha. He hurls this at Buddha but it hovers over the head of the enlightened one like a garland of flowers.[17] These images indicate that the illumination of Buddha and the resulting redemption of man are not conceived as an historical event, but as a quasi-natural phenomenon similar to the unpreventable rising of the sun which dispels the darkness of the night. There is hardly any connection with the symbol of the child abandoned in the crib, or, for that matter, of the beloved son who dies in faithfulness to his mission and thus kindles a "light" that is beyond the polarities of bright sunlight and dark night, of life and death—a light which comprehends them both and causes them to be seen in a different way.

In Buddha and Jesus a spirituality of natural symbols meets a spirituality of historical symbols in the way a line and a circle touch without one penetrating the other. On the one hand there is Buddha born and raised (even as an historical figure), in the power and glory of a far-eastern royalty, who then renounces the world, finds illumination in an ascetic life, and finally, as an octogenarian, dies peacefully in the arms of his favorite disciple, Ananda, at the riverside under the blooming trees. On the other hand there is Jesus, born as the son of a Jewish craftsman in Palestine, a land occupied and exploited by the Romans. For a short time he is under the influence of the penitential preacher John, but then, following his experience of the unconditional love of the God Abba during his baptism in the river Jordan, Jesus turns away from the ascetic life. Sharing this experience of love with all people at banquets and in many healings, he is accused by his detractors of being a "glutton and drunkard, a friend of tax collectors and sinners" (Matt. 11, 19).[18] Despite growing enmity he pursues his path until the end, until with an anguished cry he dies on the cross.

The symbolism of these two figures could not be in sharper contrast. And yet, they meet at a crucial point, in the symbolism of the child. The redemption which they bring is completely without violence. In the one case it is achieved through illumination, by concentrated meditation, by a profound submersion which leaves behind all exterior things, and by the dawning of a light that shows the origin of human suffering and the way to break its chains. In the other case, it is accomplished through Jesus' experience that must be relived through faith—the experience that God is the Abba who loves every human being and carries him beyond death—man is called to the active shaping of life in all its dimensions from within that faith and that experience, and to faithfulness to that experience in spite of enmities, persecution, and violent death. Both ways can lead away from the cycle of violent rivalry that drags man down and weakens him.

Buddha finds the way back into that world which existed before original sin by sitting motionlessly under the tree and looking into himself and beyond himself. Jesus reaches the same goal dynamically, by listening attentively to what is revealed to him in the transcendent dimension of the events of his life, and by following faithfully and without violence—"obediently"—to the end of the path which he finds indicated in those experiences. Of course the goal is colored by the different ways that lead towards it. For Buddha, it is characterized by the renouncement of the violent world and its life, and by the entrance into the realm of the "fading away." For Jesus, it is marked by the acceptance of the few, yet real, experiences of this life and world that are not (or not totally) structured by the mechanism of violence, but emanate love without violence as a transcendent dimension of objective reality. Thus Buddha reaches Nirvana (that is, the fading away), and Jesus reaches the Abba, the living abode of love without violence. But everything seems to indicate that these two words designate nothing less than parallel lines that meet in infinity.

Jesus

On the whole, Jesus is not a light-hero in the sense religious history understands such a figure. This type of divine hero arose from the contrast between the ordered human settlement, the small clearing, and the unending, almighty dark wilderness that surrounded it. The light-hero goes out to conquer the terrible god of the wilderness and thereby to free and to redeem the human sacrifice that was supposed to appease him. But Jesus does not have a god of terror and wilderness as an enemy. The judging God who is ruthless to the evil and merciful to the pure, as he was described by John the Baptist, was revealed to Jesus in the baptism at the river Jordan as the healing and reconciling breath of the dove that came into him and as the Abba who addressed him from the opened sky as beloved son and who wants to be the Abba of all men, good and evil.

Of course, Jesus sees around him the forces that drive man into the cycle of violence, that degrade him, and he tries to drive those forces, those "demons" out of the human world by handing on his experience at the river Jordan. But, unlike the divine light-hero, or George the dragon-killer, he does not lead any campaigns of extermination against the dark powers. Even the demons are creatures of the heavenly father. As such they have their place in creation. To be sure, their dull, unspiritual force

152

does not belong in the human soul. But it rightfully belongs in the beasts, in the desert, and in the storm which stirs up the waters. Indeed, it is crucial that the demon, when he has left the soul of man, should find a place in which he belongs and in which he can come to rest. Only then can man be safe from him (see the parable of the return of the unclean spirit in Luke 11, 24-26; Matt. 12, 43-45).

In his experience at the river Jordan, when the heavens were opened to him, Jesus learned that this "heaven," the realm of the divine, is free from demonic elements. The demonic forces fell "like lightning from heaven" (Luke 10, 18).[19] There is nothing divine, no longer anything heavenly about "Satan." He has been unmasked as the violence of man, born out of fear, suspicion, and insecurity. This violence may grow into a power that is capable of destroying the whole earth. Yet, even so, it would have no transcendence. It would be nothing other than human stupidity, blindness, and coldness of heart. Power and terror, fright and unfathomable chaos—the reality of the cruel procurator of the emperor-god, as well as the symbol of the serpent and the dragon, thunder and lightning—no longer impress Jesus and the apostles. The transcendent dimension that was hitherto experienced in these has been unmasked as a projection of man's own violence and fear. For Jesus, thunder and lightning, the old attributes of the highest godhead—Wotan, Zeus, Indra, the Iranian light-god Mithras, as well as, in a sense, Yahweh as perceived in the apparition of God on Mount Sinai with thunder and lightning, (Exod. 19, 14 ff.; Ps. 18, 14)—no longer possess divine fascination. They are not compatible with the loving hands of the Abba.

It is true that the Abba's countenance is temporarily obscured when Jesus is wrestling with his fate—at such moments fear and the demons arise again as transcendent powers. In his utmost distress, when the dark clouds pile up on the horizon and Jesus is surrounded by his deadly enemies, the Abba appears strangely unconcerned. He is like the man in the parable who at first refuses to get up when his importunate friend comes and wakes him in the middle of the night to ask for bread to offer a guest: "Do not bother me. The door is bolted now, and my children and I are in bed; I cannot get up to give it to you" (Luke 11, 7). He can be moved only by persistence. He is also like the deaf and ruthless judge who does not give the widow her just rights when she calls for his help until he is worn down by her persistence: "...she will persist in coming and worry me to death" (Luke 18, 5).[20] Indeed, as the crisis intensifies, it seems as if Yahweh, the protector of Israel and of Jesus, would open his ear to those detractors who denounce the activity of the son as a squander of entrusted property, namely of the sacred prophecies of Israel: "Draw me up an account of your stewardship...you are to be my steward no longer" (Luke 16, 2). But even in this misery, Jesus does not use the same means as his enemies. He follows his path, which is being denounced as squander and larceny with even more resolution: "...'How much do you owe my master?' 'One hundred measures of oil'...'Here, take your bond; sit down quickly and write fifty'." He hopes that this will ensure that "there will be some to welcome me into their homes" even if fate works against him.[21]

Then, in the agony of death, he quotes the Psalm of Lamentation (Ps. 22), which is not addressed to the Abba, but to El, to the dark, divine power of the forefathers: "Eloi, Eloi, lama sabachthani?" (Mark 15, 34) "My God, my God, why have you forsaken me?" But in the cry of his agony, as interpreted by Luke, he is back in touch with the child-experience, commending his life to the hands of the Abba (Luke 23, 46). At no place does Jesus engage in a heroic fight against divine-demonic forces. At the risk of his life, he withstands the temptation to worship the power to which "all the kingdoms of the world and their splendor" belong, as is said in the narration of the temptation (Matt. 4, 1-11), and to take up arms against the Roman emperor who embodies this power.[22] The world that he has entered through the baptism in the river Jordan is of a different nature than the world that has been conquered by Rome. Handed over for persecution, he tells the procurator of the Roman emperor, his highest judge, that "if my kingdom were of this world, my men would have fought to save me from arrest" (John 18, 36). But he had forbidden them to fight, and when they were anticipating the strug-gle and had already drawn their swords, he said: "Put your sword back, for all who draw the sword will die by the sword" (Matt. 26, 52). This is not the talk of a light-hero when he is pressed by the powers of chaos which threaten to devour him and his followers. In the very moment that he is handed over to death, Jesus is placed beyond the light and darkness of our divided world, in the different world of the Abba, the original world that existed before the "homo necans."

Jesus is not a light-hero who defeats the dark powers of chaos. But he is a child of men who, by his entrance into the world, has brought light into life. This child does not need to be supernatural—no hero who, like Hercules, as an infant kills snakes in his cradle, no Apollo, no Krishna, Buddha, nor pharaoh, coming from the mother's womb fully grown and with all the insignia of power. No, life becomes a little brighter and precisely because of the helpless child, abandoned, "wrapped in swad-dling clothes," found by shepherds in a manger. All too often this light which comes into the world with a newborn child is quickly veiled and soon becomes part of the cycle of violence—either by the people sur-rounding it, or by the child itself, or by both. Only the child Jesus, the beloved son, has kept alive the light of being a child, and has made it shine even brighter throughout the world by his life and death. Little older than thirty years, but mature and "grown-up" as no man before him, he died—crying out in a loud voice—as a child. And whoever becomes a child like him (be it only in the abandonment of old age and of death), will enter into that eternal life which was disclosed by him (Luke 18, 17; Matt. 18, 3).

2 Wind and Breath as Symbols of God

According to our interpretation of the "economic Trinity" God is first encountered in the abandoned son, the child, the daughter exposed at the wild wadi. From the encounter with this child arises the "spirit" who makes us cry out: "Abba, Father" (Rom. 8, 15; Gal. 4, 6). And in this cry, the Abba leans down to us, issuing the same wind and breath. Thus, in the symbolic interpretation of Trinitarian theology, the divine symbol of the child is followed by the symbol of the "Holy Spirit." But is the "Holy Spirit" a symbol? In Manfred Lurker's "Dictionary of Biblical Images and Symbols" we find an entry for "Son (Sons) of God" but none for "(Holy) Spirit." It seems almost as if the "Holy Spirit" were an objective entity that, unlike the Father and the Son, has no analogous symbol in the history of religions. But this is a misconception. It is based on the Irish-Scottish monks' mistranslation as I hope to demonstrate.

In the following I will develop this theme and clarify the terms that underlie the concept of "Holy Spirit," namely the Hebrew "ruach" and the Greek "pneuma." Through a dialogue with religious history I will then elaborate on the specifically Christian content of this symbol.

2.1 "Spirit" as Wind and Breath—A Mistranslation by Irish-Scottish Monks [1]

Spirituality and devotion are kindled by symbols. The richer a given religious tradition is in symbols, the more it resonates in ritual and personal devotion. Thus we can understand why in the later history of Christianity, the birthday of the divine child became the Christian feast during which everyone tries to recall his Christian heritage albeit sometimes dimly. In the first growth and spread of Christianity the feast of Christ's birth had virtually no significance. In the early church, the festivals of his death and resurrection and the events of Pentecost were of much greater importance. Today, however, Pentecost has paled as a Christian feast. Professors of religion and catechists, as well as preachers, are likely to groan when it comes time to present the tradition of the Holy Spirit. In contrast to the tradition of the divine child, the pentecostal tradition offers few accessible symbolic associations. When they try to explain the symbolism, they are likely to cause bizarre misunderstandings. Thus a child from elementary school once came up with the following: "God is a ghost. He is nothing but bones."

God as Wind and Breath in the Old Testament

The Christian tradition is founded on the biblical scriptures which were originally written in Hebrew and Greek. The English word "Spirit" corresponds to the Hebrew "ruach." This word has the basic meaning of "wind" and "breath." Both meanings were originally associated: The wind is the breath of the earth or the fuming and raging of Yahweh. Exodus 14, 21 tells how Moses stretched out his hand over the sea, and how the sea was driven back by a strong easterly wind so that it dried out and the sons of Israel could cross it. In the song of Moses (Exod. 15, 8) this easterly wind is praised as the "blast of (Yahweh's) nostrils" which piled the waters up and made the waves stand upright like a wall.

Here we see the process of generating symbols that lies at the very origin of religions. In a specific historic circumstance, the objective given, the sensual perception of the east wind, the sirocco, which comes in from the desert and whose heat is so intense that it immediately withers all vegetation, is experienced and celebrated in song as a transcendent dimension, in this case as the breath of Yahweh. Wherever the natural event of the wind coincides with an historical event important to the people of Israel, the natural phenomenon becomes a divine symbol. It can punish and destroy, or fertilize and vivify. For example, the prophet Hosea announces to the unfaithful "Ephraim" — that is to the people of Israel — who are turning away from Yahweh:

"Ephraim may flourish among the reeds,
but the East wind will come,
the breath of Yahweh will rise from the desert
to dry his fountains, to parch his springs,
to strip his lands of every precious thing."

(Hos. 13, 15)

On the other hand, the "ruach Yahweh" hovers over the floods of chaos in the primeval ocean and fills it with seeds of life and order (Gen. 1, 2). Here the breath of God is no longer a storm, a raging cyclone, but a vivifying breeze. Elijah encountered Yahweh on the sacred Mount Horeb not in the form of the raging storm which "tore the mountains and shattered the rocks" (1 Kings 19, 11), but in the gentle breeze that came once the storm had receded. This pleasant, comforting, and soothing wind was the breath of Yahweh. It was the "cool of the day" in which Yahweh walked in the garden (Gen. 3, 8).

The invisible reality of the wind and of the protecting breath of God becomes visible in the bird that spreads its wings and seems to move weightlessly through the skies. It is therefore a symbol of this divine reality. Yahweh protects and guides his people "like an eagle guarding its nest, hovering over its young, he spreads out his wings to hold them, he supports them on his pinions" (Deut. 32, 11 f.).

Unlike the Hebrew word "neschama," the term "ruach" does not describe the involuntary process of breathing, but "the special breathing in which man's dynamic vitality is expressed."[2] "Ruach" is breath as expression of life and emotion. The queen of Sheba is left breathless — without "ruach" — when she sees the incredible riches of Solomon (1 Kings 10, 5; 2 Chron. 9, 4). When Samson is about to die of thirst and cries to Yahweh who offers him water, "his 'ruach' returned, and he revived" (Judg. 15, 18 f.). This dynamic "ruach" itself has features of Yahweh. Only in later times was the windy, dynamic character of "ruach" trivialized[3] into the common meaning "breath of life," and only then could it be used synonymously with "neschama": God breathed into man's nostrils the breath of life (Gen. 2, 7).

As the wind can both destroy, in a storm, and envigorate and revitalize, in the "cool of the day," so does "ruach" have an ambivalent meaning. It can signify force, vitality and fertility, as well as anger and raging destruction. In that sense "ruach" can be included in the sphere of the demonic. The old Saul is seized by an "evil 'ruach' from Yahweh" (1 Sam. 16, 14; 18, 10; 19, 9) and attempts to pin David to a wall with his spear. Here we find the often mentioned ambivalence of the divine as it is reflected in the Bible (see chap. 2 of our "Exposition").

Only in the latest period of the Old Testament does "ruach" turn into a "fully-fledged theological concept which does not signify any specific (wind-like) action of God."[4] Sometimes the word simply stands for "God." Only at this point does the combination "ruach kadosh" (holy breath) spring up:

"He lifted them up, carried them,
all the days of old.
But they rebelled, they grieved
His holy spirit."

(Isa. 63, 9 f.)

The renowned scholar of the Old Testament, Claus Westermann, thinks that, in fact, the combination of "kadosh" and "ruach" is a contradiction in terms "if one takes into account the original, dynamic meaning of 'ruach' and the static character of 'kadosh,' 'sacred'."[5] This contradiction becomes even more obvious when we translate the word "ruach" as "spirit" which, in its contemporary meaning, has scarcely anything to do with wind and breath.

God as Wind and Breath in the New Testament

In the New Testament the reality of "ruach" is rendered by the Greek word "pneuma." The basic meaning is again wind and breath. In demotic Greek it can mean any kind of wind, a powerful storm, a fresh wind, propitious or unpropitious to sailors, a breeze, a mild gust, as well as the steam that rises from the earth at certain places.[6] Moreover, "pneuma" signifies the air that is breathed in and out by humans and animals. Insofar as words and sounds are formed by exhaled breath, "pneuma" can also take on the meaning of living, audible voice. Derived from the meaning "breath of life," "pneuma" can also signify "life." We can owe our "pneuma," our life, to someone and when we die, our "pneuma" leaves us. In the last exhalation this breath of life departs into the region from whence it came, into the air or the ether in order to fulfill its higher destiny.[7]

In the Greek language, "pneuma" refers to animals, humans, and gods. The divine "pneuma" can be experienced in the excited voice and breath of the seer and of the priestess who are inspired by the divine wind, often stammering unintelligible words which call for interpretation, not unlike the speaking in tongues of the Pauline community at Corinth. In its universal power of generation, "pneuma" is associated with the divine even in its original meaning. The Hellenes, particularly sensitive to symbolism, experienced in each wind and in each breath a dimension that transcends the objective. Even the Boreas, the ancient Greek personification of the harsh North wind — and known as Bora in today's Yugoslavia — who comes in the morning, descending from a clear sky, was a son of Eos, the goddess of dawn. According to the myth, Boreas attacked the Athenian princess Orithyia while she was playing, and abducted her to Thrace where she bore him two sons, Calais and Zetes. As "ruach", "pneuma" is also ambivalent: There is a divine, healing, and revitalizing "pneuma", and a demonic, destructive one.

The Greek word "pneuma" is used in several ways in the New Testament. Traditional exegesis has emphasized the "different character of its

159

essence and content of truth" that separates the demotic Greek "pneuma" from the "pneuma" of the New Testament.[8] (We will have to come back to this question.) But, in an examination of religious discourse that is focused on experience the first significance of a word has to be the meaning that it has in common usage. When Jesus is begotten from the "pneuma hagion," and this "pneuma" comes down on him in the baptism at the river Jordan — when he drives out demons and heals people with its force, and hands it over to his Father in the moment of his death — then nothing else is understood in this discourse than what people at that time meant by the word "pneuma," even if it is given a more specific meaning by the qualifier "hagion" (holy). Even as "pneuma hagion," "pneuma" remains "pneuma." It retains the basic connotation of "wind" and "breath," and its specific symbolism can only be fully grasped on the basis of this meaning.

The influence of Hellenic thought is particularly evident in passages in which (as in Mark and Matthew) "pneuma akatharton" or "daimonion" are mentioned, that is, "unclean 'pneuma' " or demons. Through the "pneuma hagion" which is active in him Jesus can drive out the unclean "pneuma." Wherever this is done, the reign of God, the "malkût Yahweh," the new power of Yahweh among his people has begun. The prophecy that Yahweh will endow his servant with his breath has come true (Isa. 42, 1).

However, it is no longer the eagle's pinions which make Yahweh's breath visible, but the figure of the dove. This bird was the bird of the goddess of love in the ancient Orient. Among the symbols of the Babylonian Ishtar, the west-Semitic Astarte and the Greek goddess Aphrodite was a dove. Even in the Old Testament the dove symbolizes love, reconciliation, and peace. Noah sent a dove out three times to see if the great flood had receded. The second time it came back with a fresh olive twig in its beak (Gen. 8, 11). When the dove sent out for the third time did not return, Noah left the ark and offered God a sacrifice of thanksgiving. Yahweh then resolved never again to "strike down every living thing as I have done." Rather:

"So long as the earth lasts,
seedtime and harvest,
cold and heat,
summer and winter,
day and night
shall not cease."

(Gen. 8, 21 f.)

The cycle of fertility would not be disrupted again. The symbol of the dove stands for this breath of fertility and peace. Accordingly, the Song of Songs compares the beauty of the bride to a dove. "Your eyes are doves" (Cant. 1, 15). "My dove, hiding in the clefts of the rock...show me your face" (Cant. 2, 14). "But my dove is unique, mine, unique and perfect" (Cant. 6, 9).[9]

This dove-breath, the breath of life and of fertility, of love and beauty, is what descends upon Jesus from the opening heavens (that is, from the new disclosure of the God Yahweh) to dwell within him at the baptism in the river Jordan. It is articulated in the words: "You are my Son, the Beloved; my favor rests on you" (Mark 1, 10). This divine dove-breath will henceforth shape his whole life and activity. It speaks through his parables, it operates through his healings and miraculous deeds, which are signified by the Greek "dynameis." They are deeds that come forth from the "dynamics," from the power of this breath. It resembles the breath of the mother when she blows on the wound of her frightened child, who having fallen, comes running to her, and then goes on playing, comforted and undisturbed. The few friends who followed Jesus to his death, experience how the healing breath of the Abba, to whom he had returned it (Luke 23, 46), carries the Crucified even across the gateway of death, and gives him life beyond death. So imbued with this wind of God is the living and crucified Jesus that Luke and Matthew declare in their gospels that he was begotten by it. The death-defying dove's breath of the Crucified, grown into the storm of Pentecost, reaches and seizes the apostles who are confused after Jesus' execution, and transforms them into Christians acknowledging Jesus the Crucified as the living Messiah throughout the world. Only through the Yahweh-breath of Jesus is this possible: "No one can say, 'Jesus is Lord' unless he is under the influence of the 'pneuma hagion' " (1 Cor. 12, 3).

When man is bathed in this wind and breath of Jesus he becomes a Christian. This is the essence of baptism. The water ritual is only of a secondary nature. Alive and sitting at the table with them, the Crucified tells his frightened followers to wait for what the Father had promised: "John baptized with water but you, not many days from now, will be baptized with the 'pneuma hagion' " (Acts 1, 4-5). In the Gospel of John, Jesus is also described as the one who does not baptize with water (as did John the Baptist), but with the healing and comforting breath of the Abba. What counts is to be steeped in that breath. Enveloped by this breath, our experience of Yahweh loses all the features of the god of terror, and the dove's breath that has been infused in us can utter the redeeming word of prayer: "Abba," Mama/Papa (Gal. 4, 6; Rom. 8, 15).

161

Only in this sort of imagery can religious discourse be comprehensible; otherwise, it becomes hieratic, theological jargon, more apt to choke one's faith than to build and to foster it. In the traditional discourse on the "pneuma hagion," the "spiritus sanctus," and on the "Holy Spirit," such a rigid formalization has taken place. The reason for this strong tendency is that this particular strand of tradition has been under the special influence of Platonic thought that tried to keep anything material or corporeal separate from God. Although "pneuma" as wind and breath is a material, physical phenomenon, it is of a particularly rarefied, weightless, incorporeal kind. For the Platonist it is therefore the point where "matter" and "spirit" meet ("spirit" in the sense of an immaterial essence — in Greek "nous").

Clement of Alexandria, for example, tries to detach completely the concept of pneuma from all of its material connotations. Wherever the New Testament mentions "pneuma," Clement understands it is as an "incorporeal" (asomatos) and imperceptible (aperiograntos, literally "not circumscribable") essence. But because the word "pneuma" still carries its basic material meaning, he purposefully avoids relating it to Christ, which he does successfully, with one exception.[10] The Platonist thinker Celsus, a critic of the Christian faith, points out that the Christian God has material features because of his "pneumatic" character. He therefore cannot be immortal. Origen responds to this argument by saying that the description of God as "pneuma" can only have a symbolic meaning, hinting at the totally spiritual, and incorporeal nature of God.

Kleinknecht, in his article on "pneuma" in the *Theologisches Wörterbuch zum Neuen Testament,* founded by G. Kittel, follows the same argument when he distinguishes the Greek concept of "pneuma" from its usage in the New Testament. The difference, he says, is that the concept of "pneuma" in the New Testament signifies something "purely spiritual"[11] in the sense of something incorporeal, "supersensual,"[12] "supernatural,"[13] and "otherworldly,"[14] while the Greek word "pneuma" always suggests corporeality and materiality, however refined — that is: wind and breath. According to Kleinknecht, in the New Testament the "physical mediation of the spirit has nothing to do with the nature of the spirit as the spirit of truth which reacts upon sin and is able to kindle faith in Jesus Christ."[15]

This distinction is fatal for the language of theology as well as for pastoral and religious pedagogy. It completely separates the symbol and the symbolized in religious discourse. Language is always bound to the sensual world, and since religious discourse is essentially a symbolical discourse, distinctions of this kind make theological and religious statements meaningless. We cannot talk meaningfully about realities that have nothing to do with concrete, material being. For them the famous statement of Wittgenstein holds true: "Whatever can be said at all, can be said clearly. Whereof one cannot speak thereof one must be silent.[16] It is a Platonic (that is, un-Christian) error to think that one can have a symbolized reality without a symbol. As in the beginning of mankind, religious reality will always remain a reality that is mediated through symbols: a dimension which is experienced as transcending concrete, material reality, but without ever being completely detached or independently perceptible. The "pneuma hagion" will always remain a sacred "wind" and "breath," with all the concrete, material associations that make up the content of the words "wind" and "breath." The qualification "holy" acts as a "functor" in the terms of I. T. Ramsey's linguistic theory,[17] making us aware that in our thoughts and ideas we have to focus on the *transcendent* dimension of the physical phenomenon of wind and breath, that is, to take wind and breath as symbols. Wherever the link between the symbolized in its transcendent dimension and the symbol as a concrete, material, sensual basis of reality is lost, the symbolized will evaporate as well. It then becomes something unreal, something ghostly.

The translation of "pneuma hagion" as "Heiliger Geist" (German for "Holy Spirit") has hastened this process of dissolution and evaporation of the Christian tradition of divine wind and breath with serious consequences for pastoral care in German speaking countries. The translation was made indirectly from the Latin. The Latin language has developed a rather dry character, shaped by legal thought, and deals rather clumsily with enthusiastic religious phenomena such as the one originally referred to as "ruach" and "pneuma." Nonetheless, the Latin word "spiritus" (sometimes also "afflatus") which was chosen by Christian translators adequately renders the symbolic content of "ruach" and "pneuma." "Spiritus" also has the basic meanings of "breeze," "wind," "action of breathing," and "breath." In derived words such as the French "esprit" and the English "spirit," this element of "airiness," of windy motion, of "inspiration" can still be sensed.

In order to distinguish the word from the Stoics' metaphysical/cosmological concept of pneuma, the Greek Christians did not choose the expression "pneuma theou" or "pneuma hieron" (divine breath), but "pneuma hagion" (sacred breath). Accordingly, Latin-speaking Christians did not translate a new linguistic construction like "pneuma hagion" as "spiritus sacer" or "spiritus divinus," but as "spiritus sanctus." However, just as "pneuma hagion" is still a "pneuma," so "spiritus sanctus" remains "spiritus," that is wind and breath. At the time when the Irish-Scottish monks began studying the Christian tradition in Latin, this language had become a dead, formal tongue, used for official purposes in the church. The basic meaning of "spiritus" ("wind" and "breath") had largely evaporated. "Spiritus sanctus" had already become a technical term within the official church language, signifying a purely supernatural reality, not a reality to be grasped through sensual association.

Thus when the monks began to translate this tradition into their own language, they did not choose the most obvious West Germanic words "athom" (old Saxon for breath) and "wind" (old Saxon, old Frisian, Anglo-saxon and English for wind), but the West Germanic word "ghost" (old Frisian and Anglo-saxon: gàst). According to the *Etymologisches Wörterbuch der deutschen Sprache* edited by Friedrich Kluge (Berlin 1957), this word has the basic meaning of "supernatural be-ing." Even if, according to the German dictionary published in 1897 by the Grimm brothers (mentioned by Kleinknecht),[18] there are indeed some ancient linguistic connections between "ghost" and the words "wind" and "breath." However, this earlier, literal meaning had vanished by the time of the Irish-Scottish monks, while the meaning "supernatural being" in the sense of "giant," "specter" had come to the foreground. Related words that reflect this meaning are the Anglo-Saxon "gaestan," "to terrorize," and English "aghast" and "ghastly." The "Holy Ghost," which was to become the German "Heiliger Geist" in the Irish and Anglo-Saxon missions in Germany, implied at that time the notion of a terrifying supernatural being. As such, the term becomes detached from normal sensual demotic language and is therefore no longer an ap-propriate description of the reality which the Old Testament called "ruach Yahweh" and the New Testament "pneuma hagion."

So the ultimate reason why children (and not only children) form the most incomprehensible associations — they hear that Mary had conceived by the "Holy Ghost" and that the "Holy Ghost" descended on Jesus at the river Jordan — is rooted in the history of linguistics and translations. But this pastoral problem is not helped by discussions of linguistic history. Words have their own life and cannot be re-defined capriciously. A reasonable religious discourse on the "pneuma hagion" is only possible with a translation as "holy (in fact: healing) wind and breath." Everyone is familiar with the experience of a refreshing wind, a wind that drives us forward and the experience of a healing, comforting breath; and therefore everyone can also experience the dimension that transcends this concrete, sensual phenomenon.

The *personality* of the Christian "pneuma hagion" does not contradict this interpretation.[19] Kittel even suggests that the whole question of the pneuma's personality is "out of place, because the word simply does not exist either in Hebrew or in Greek."[20] However, we have to admit that although the modern concept of person did not exist at that time (in the sense of a human center of will and action), people did have the experience that someone could speak out of an inner conviction, and out of an existential identity — for example when Jesus "taught with authority" (Matt. 7, 29). To be a person means (at least potentially) to exist and to speak authentically from within oneself. But if we want to emphasize this aspect of the "pneuma hagion," it does not make much sense to call it a "supersensual being" which is suggestive of giants. We might describe this aspect in a much more biblical way by referring to the breath as a joining of sound and *voice*. There is but little distance between divine breath and divine voice. Thus, the healing breath that descends on Jesus and dwells in him during the baptism at the river Jordan articulates itself in the affirmation: "You are my beloved son..." Therefore, if we want to emphasize the personality of the "pneuma" in our translation, we may speak about the "holy and healing voice (of God)."

The difficulties of a discourse on God as "pneuma hagion" reveal that the crisis of continuity in handing on the faith that affects Christianity today is not only a matter of religious pedagogy or of pastoral care. What we need is a consistent re-translation of the content of faith into a comprehensible and meaningful symbolic language. This is especially true for the realm in which most people encounter the Christian heritage of faith — the liturgy. It is not enough to attempt liturgical reform by translating the official Latin language into an equally stiff and unsymbolic vernacular language. For the tradition of the "pneuma hagion" this means specifically: the discourse on the "Holy Spirit" would be appropriately replaced in catechesis, religious education, sermons, and *also* in the liturgy with a discourse on the holy, healing wind and breath of Jesus and of his Abba.[21]

As the following dialogue with religious history will show, the recollection of the symbolic meaning of "pneuma hagion" and "ruach Yahweh" is not an attempt of syncretic conformism. It is rather the *precondition* for a meaningful description of the specifically Christian character of the divine symbols of wind and breath. If we say — as did Clement of Alexandria and Origen — that the specific difference is that pneuma is not actually wind and breath, then we cannot enter into a religious dialogue. In fact, we would be able to speak about the content of our faith only as children do who sometimes surprise their parents by uttering incomprehensible sounds, claiming that they invented their own language which none but themselves and their friends can understand, and which cannot be translated. Thus Christian faith could only be articulated in an incommunicable ghetto-language.

But the Bible does not speak in a ghetto-language. The Bible speaks about "ruach" and "pneuma," and these words mean wind and breath. These words have a religious meaning in other religious traditions as well. The difference between Egyptian and Christian religions is *not* that Pharaoh is conceived by the wind-god Amun and that, while Christianity also mentions the Messiah Jesus as being born from the "pneuma," from the wind and breath, these things are in fact not wind and breath, but rather radically "supernatural" and "otherworldly" realities which cannot be described in words.[22] This is not the difference between Christian and Egyptian religion. Rather, the "total difference," which is claimed for the Christian religion by dialectic theologians, can only mean that Christian faith speaks of a completely different kind of *wind and breath.* Like the symbols of the son, the daughter, and the child, wind and breath are the necessary linguistic basis for a dialogue with other myths and religions.

As we previously examined the symbol of the child, we will now examine the history of culture and of religions under the aspect of the "wind" and "breath," and relate it to the Christian tradition of ruach/pneuma.

2.2 From the Ice Age to the Industrial Era: The Breath of the Hunter

Wind and breath are realities that cannot be seen by the eyes but are perceived through the senses of touch and hearing. The breath of God blows upon us especially through music. It is, as Beethoven put it, "a higher revelation than all wisdom and philosophy."[1] But even in the visual arts, in painting and sculpture, the artist's own "wind and breath," his "inspiration" and outlook are expressed. In impressionist paintings, reality becomes translucent; things seem weightless. In expressionist paintings, on the other hand, things appear in an unusual, alien character, which expresses the direct impact of reality upon the artist. Art is always and everywhere the expression of an inner motion, of being seized by a wind and breath, which discloses the transcendent dimension of material objects and tries to express this dimension. There is no art without "inspiration."

166

Art already existed by the early Paleolithic Period. The oldest human drawings, carvings found on an ox's rib at Pech de l'Azé in the Dordogne valley, are approximately 200,000 years old (Fig. 27). Unfortunately, this finding is utterly unique and therefore difficult to interpret. We can, however, in the light of our hypothesis of man's transition to hunting as the foundation of the original sin, say that it would seem that the drawing represents a bull's horns. This god of terror obviously dominated the consciousness of primeval people.

In contrast to this single finding, the wall-paintings of the later Paleolithic Period in the caves of Lascaux, Altamira, and many others, especially those of the Franco-cantabrian region, form a homogenous group with characteristic features. On the whole, they all have pronounced expressionistic qualities. The observer immediately understands the exaggerated dome of the bull's neck (Fig. 1), the horns pointed forward, the forceful bodies of the wild horses, the flying manes and lifted heads, and the huge, erect antlers as embodiments of the primeval man's fascination with the vitality and strength of the beasts. In the "bull room" of the Lascaux cave the observer feels surrounded by living beings, emanating vitality and force (Fig. 28). In another part of the cave there is a frieze representing a herd of deer with powerful antlers, swimming across the wall (Fig. 29). Another picture shows wild horses tumbling down a cliff. There is no notion here of a magic spell that would capture the animals on the cave wall to make them available to the hunter; in that case, the animals would have been represented in a static manner. Rather, man tries to immerse himself in the wind and breath of life surrounding himself with the forms of the fascinating animal world. What is being held by a spell is not the animal, but man's own fear of the wildness and force which he encounters in the animal. By painting, and by contemplating his pictures, he feels his way into this world and thus gathers courage to encounter the animal during the hunt.

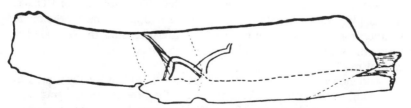

Fig. 27: The oldest extant drawing by human hands (engraved ox rib from Pech de L'Azé/Dordogne—ca. 200,000 years old); it may represent the horns of a bull.

Fig. 28: A part of the frieze in the "Hall of the Bulls."

It is especially the maturing young man who has to be initiated into that atmosphere in order to become a hunter. Therefore it is a widely held opinion that these wall-paintings were mainly used for the purpose of initiations. This is particularly true of the deep pit of the Lascaux cave which has, at its lowest end, the picture we have already mentioned—the wounded bull overpowering a man.

This chamber is difficult to enter. It is reached from the great oval "chamber of the bulls" by way of a fifteen-meter-long corridor which gives into a smaller room, at the side of which is located a sort of apse. From there, through a small hole, one can enter the pit which has a depth of seven meters. During the first excavations by H. Breuil a small piece of cord was discovered which prompted the conclusion that the primeval observer of these pictures was let down into the pit by means of a rope. Here, deep in the earth, he found himself in front of the black drawing, illuminated by a flickering oil-lamp (Fig. 30).

The interpretations of this picture differ widely. It has been suggested that it represents a "ritual sorcery of fertility,"[2] a representation of stars for orientation,[3] a "hunting accident," as well as a fight between the bison and the rhinoceros, retreating to the left side of the picture.[4] This is not the place for a critical review of all the attempts that have been made to interpret this picture. In most of the interpretations the struggle between the wounded bison and the man who faces him is viewed as the central motif.[5]

And indeed, this is its prominent feature: The bison's belly is pierced by a long spear with a barbed hook and the bowels are hanging out. Close to the man lies a second barbed spear (or is it a sling for a spear?). The bison points its horns towards the man, who spreads his arms while falling backwards. The difficulties of interpretation concern the man's

Fig. 29: The "frieze of the swimming stags" in the Lascaux cave.

erect penis, his bird-mask, the vertical staff with a bird on top, and the rhinoceros, visible in the left part of the picture. Very often this rhinoceros has been excluded altogether from the interpretation, as if it did not belong in the picture. But Müller-Karpe points out that the figures represented in this pit have to be regarded as a unity: "The exclusive use of black paint (in contrast to the multicolored pictures in the other caverns), the spatial alignment, and the fact that this pit has no other pictures, all speak rather *in favor* of a unified composition."[6]

It is precisely these difficult motifs that are crucial in this context. A great number of observations confirm the fact that the hunter is always in some sort of erotic relation to the hunted animal.[7] Because human sexuality is experienced as a strong motivating power, it is often associated with the element of moving air and of the birds. We may recall the famous motif of the phallic bird on Attic vases. From this we may gain insight into the bird motifs of the picture. The bird head and the hunter's erect phallus express the man's erotic hunting motions. This man, a relatively small and frail being—as is clear from the proportions of the picture—"rises" through the force of this motion to an encounter with the powerful animal. The motif is repeated with the bird on the staff, a motif which is often interpreted as a shamanist element.[8] Such staffs are metamorphosed into birds during the ecstasy of the shaman, allowing

Fig. 30: Picture from the pit of the Lascaux cave (ca. 20,000 BC): The bison, pierced by the hunter (note the hanging entrails and the erect penis as expression of the hunter's potency), thrusts at the hunter but the hunter's spirit (note the bird on the staff) is already searching for new prey, the departing rhinoceros. Might this have been a picture used for the initiation of hunters?

him the magical flight into the heavens and the underworld.[9] In the picture of the Lascaux cave, the bird looks from the very top of the staff in the direction of the rhinoceros. This bird, sitting freely on the top of the staff, is a powerful symbol of the hunter's erotic transport. Even if the man is thrown down and killed by the wounded bison, the wind and breath of the hunter, his ecstatic enthusiasm, his "soul" perseveres. Even if the hunter dies, his "pneuma," which arises out of death,[10] already searches for new prey. The wind and breath of the hunt lives on beyond the death of any individual human being. It surpasses the individual and may claim the sacrifice of his life. This is the hunter's mentality which has to be acquired through initiation.

This interpretation becomes even more plausible if we take into account the fact that the most inaccessibly located pictures were used especially for initiation rites. A young man is about to be accepted into the group of hunters. Now, since human beings are not predators by nature, they need an intensive psychological preparation in order to overcome fear and inhibitions when facing large animals. The young man is lowered seven meters into the pit. By the light of a little oil-lamp, alone in the pit day and night, he meditates on the picture, perhaps for a long period. He sees and internalizes what he will be confronted with as a hunter. The picture helps him feel his way into the future situation of hunting, and to prepare for it mentally. He begins to feel the intoxication of the hunt which animates the men of his tribe. He strengthens his will to

170

confront the animals, to be seized by the wind and breath of the hunt, to be immersed in it, even at the risk of his life. What counts is not his individual fate, but the bird, the breath and wind, which give wings to frail humans for the hunt. In the pit of the Lascaux cave the young man was baptized in the baptism of the hunter, just as the Christian was immersed in the baptistery into the *totally different* wind and breath of Jesus and of his Abba, also in a subterranean chamber, in a crypt under the church nave.

The Hunter's Religion

The sharply pointed beak of the bird mask worn by the falling man, as well as the Lascaux scene as a whole, indicate that the wind and breath of the hunter is not symbolized by a dove, like the baptismal "pneuma" of the river Jordan, but by a predator, sometimes a vulture or a falcon, most often an eagle. For the Jakun people, the eagle is the "maternal predator" who initiates the shaman. The eagle abducts the soul of the initiate and leaves it to ripen in the branches of a big pine tree. He dismembers the initiate in his trance and puts him together again as a new human being. Through the initiation rite the shaman becomes a new man, created by the eagle. Buryat people believed that the first shaman was procreated by an eagle. He descended upon a sleeping woman and made her pregnant.[11] When the shaman undertakes his magical flight, in order to lure prey from the depth of the earth and from the height of the heavens, he is borne upon an eagle's pinions. "The people of the eagle" is the name the Aztecs gave to those humans whose hearts were cut still throbbing, from their breasts and sacrificed, so that the eagle could carry them up as an offering to the sun.

Thus the eagle symbolizes the wind and breath of an attitude of hunting and killing, a communal focus on prey that includes the readiness of each individual to sacrifice his own life for the life of the community, under any circumstances. To this very day, this breath animates human communities in many ways. It is not a coincidence that the eagle is the most frequently used heraldic animal. On the emblems and seals of many countries the eagle symbolizes the wind and breath of a nation. To be immersed in *that* breath means to be ready to kill and be killed. That is what the young man in a society of game hunters must learn and internalize. Compared to this baptism of hunting and killing, the Christian baptism has unfortunately remained rather ineffective throughout history.

The wind and breath of the hunter, of the "homo necans," (Burkert) emanate from the wall paintings of the later Paleolithic Period and fill the

171

primeval caves. They blow through those "cathedrals" and "sanctuaries" of the Ice Age[12] — as those caves are rightly called with our recent understanding of the religious significance of prehistoric art.[13] Of course, we are no longer talking about the simple theories of hunting magic, such as those developed by Spencer and Gillen around the end of the previous century, according to which animals were bound in spells through representations and hunting luck was assured by "wounding" these representations. As Herbig points out,[14] such primitive magical beliefs would contradict the fact that the animals represented in the caves were not primarily those that were actually hunted. In the Dordogne valley with the Lascaux site and other caves, this would be essentially the reindeer. Rather, the cave paintings of the later Paleolithic Period express a complex world-view which encompasses the whole of life and is dominated by the relation between man and beast.

Leroi-Gourhan's thorough investigations have shown that the decorations in numerous caves scattered over southern France and northern Spain which were painted over the course of thousands of years reveal a striking consistency in the choice and the ordering of motifs.[15] The caves consist of an intricate system of caverns linked by a number of long corridors. A large central cavern served as a "hall" and was usually decorated with pictures of wild oxen, bison and horses, as well as representations of women or feminine symbols such as the stylized representation of a vulva. The entrance to the cave and the adjacent caverns, on the other hand, abound with paintings of deer, wild goats, and mammoths, often in relation to a phallic symbol. The majority of predators such as bears, lions, and other felines, as well as the dangerous rhinoceros, are represented in the most remote chambers of the caves.

We are not able to interpret the whole of the evidence (as Leroi-Gourhan attempted to do), because we lack any knowledge of the rites and myths of its creators. But the religious character of this art is undeniable. Following Durkheim's analyses,[16] this religion is interpreted only in sociological terms: as a system of rites and mythical ideas which form a framework enabling larger groups of humans, divided into tribes and clans, to communicate in an efficient way, to develop common rules of behavior and to overcome times of individual or general crisis. This was viewed as the functional advantage of religion and art in primeval man's struggle for survival.

But the question of how such a development of religious and mythical thought ever came to be remains open. With Durkheim and Herbig one sometimes gets the impression that religion had been thought up by some clever chief, in order to create a "sacred aura" with which they would "consecrate" themselves and the rules of behavior they believed in, which "protected their authority from being challenged by individuals."[17]

However, such a view is completely unsatisfactory. How could it be possible for an individual human being to create a "sacred aura" if, in reality, nothing is sacred? Although we know that shamans and other primeval religious leaders may have abused their power at times and worked with trickery and deceit — as can be observed to this day among certain ethnic peoples — their authority is based in principle on their particular sensitivity to that transcendent dimension which emanates from objective phenomena. Through fasting, sexual abstinence, vigils, self-inflicted injuries, and sometimes drugs, the leader tries to enhance his supersensual perception. To the degree that this is achieved, he tunes into the ecstasy of this dimension beyond the objective, and takes part in it. All people experience this dimension as an atmosphere, as something in inner and outer motion, as a wind and breath.[18] All religious ideas and codes of behavior which define the common life of large groups of humans originate in this perception, notwithstanding possible manipulations by the focus on hunting for prey. A larger human community emerges not because chiefs and leaders can profit from it but because the perceived transcendent dimension of things itself (ultimately "God") is felt to be calling for such a community. Man's most ancient cultural community is the cultic community.

The most important factor shaping the community and the religious question is the *nature* of this sacredness which is perceived in things and phenomena as a transcendent dimension. Without attempting any specific interpretation of primeval religious thought as expressed in ancient art, we can say this: The aura of this art and of the cultic spaces which it created, is the "pneuma," the wind and breath of the hunt and of the hunter. The transcendent dimension appears to man above all in animals, in their size, their strength, and their wild vitality. And man's relation to this sacredness is characterized by his attempt, from the beginning, to incorporate it by killing and eating the animal. His ability and readiness to confront huge and dangerous animals (and, as a consequence, his fellow men) with the intention of killing them is not the inheritance of man's natural evolution. It is the behavioral pattern (of original sin) with which man responded to the experience of the sacred in the animal. From the beginning, therefore, his readiness to kill and to be killed is linked to the sacred aura. This is why it is *this* specific sacredness and not, as Rudolf Otto thought, *any* sacredness for which the description of "fascinosum et tremendum," as at once fascinating and frightful, is adequate. For primeval man this fascination is expressed directly as an

173

erotic, sexual attraction which explains the intertwining of sexual motifs with animal paintings. The frightfulness lies in the expressionistic "bullness" and force of the huge animal man is ready to confront in a deadly struggle. The god of these hunters is the equally fascinating and frightful transcendent dimension of the beast: the mistress or master of the animals.

The Breath of the Hunter Today

The mentality and spirituality of the primeval hunter which found its artistic expression in the later Paleolithic Period was the expression of a view of life that had shaped humanity for hundreds of thousands of years. From a Christian point of view, it is at the beginning of our contemporary humanity, shaped by original sin. The wind and breath of killing, the attitude and mentality of the hunter who hunts down his prey, kills and eats whatever holds a fascination for him, is that which has poisoned humanity at its roots. Through education and initiation society tries to enhance and strengthen the readiness of people to live with this attitude. It is the condition for entry into the adult world and independent responsibility. In all cultures the process of initiation is a painful process that tests and improves the young person's physical and mental endurance. The initiate must always endure painful procedures that put him under considerable physical and mental pressure. Additionally, the males have to learn how to kill and how to face death themselves.

Those anthropological studies which attempt to show how even contemporary humanity is still shaped by the mentality of the hunter are mainly inspired by the biology of behavior.[19] Very often these studies ignore the fact that modern man did not develop the mentality of the hunter as a result of natural evolution. Rather he adopted predatory behavior "artificially," without possessing the necessary apparatus of instincts. The transition to game-hunting did not follow from his nature. It sprang from the ability of homo erectus to perceive in the animal a dimension transcending the objective (becoming therefore religiously fascinating) and from his decision to appropriate the object of this fascinating encounter by killing and eating it. The hunting behavior of man is not inherited. But it stands as a major event at the very beginning of his cultural evolution and has established itself as a pattern of human behavior over many hundreds of thousands of years.

Thus when Lionel Tiger and Robin Fox chose the subtitle "Stone Age Hunters in Late Capitalism" for their book, the catchy phrase held a kernel of truth.[20] The fraternal community of men which accepts women

174

only insofar as they adopt masculine behavior; the search for profit and prey; the trapping, lurking, and back-stabbing; the absolute submission of the individual to the hierarchy of the group; the thorough division of labor according to gender which excludes women from the center of power, the sacred domain of the hunter; the competition for leading positions within the group in which personal strength and superiority can be displayed; the distribution of the "prey" according to differences in rank and status, and especially the jockeying for higher position which is no longer the playful test establishing who is the stronger, as among primates, but behavior which reveals itself as a deadly power, ready to destroy the competitor's very existence. All of these behavior patterns are cloaked in the aura of the hunter.

They are evident especially in the world of politics and business, but also in individual human relations. In earlier chapters we have shown how this mentality shapes religions dominated by sacrificial practices. Even the world of leisure and entertainment is at least in part influenced by this aura. Recently we have become aware of how intensely competitive sports can resemble the ancient rituals of sacrifice in their merciless competition. Indeed, athletic activity has its historical origins in such rituals.[21] And this is also the root of war—"the big killing-show."

The Breath of the Hunter and the Breath of Jesus

There have been many attempts to escape this wind and breath of killing and of being killed, and to live from within a different breath. Insofar as these attempts were not irrational programs of world improvement which are often doomed to failure because of faulty premises, they were always concerned with viewing the transcendent dimension from a different perspective and within a different phenomenon, in order to develop a new way of life and a new world view. One of these attempts is the Christian faith. Its path consists in seeing the transcendent dimension not in the powerful and strong, but in the humble and weak, in the symbol of the (abandoned) "child." This new means of perceiving the sacred was given to man when Jesus the Crucified, the abandoned, revealed himself in his transcendent dimension as Messiah, as "Son of God." The new wind and breath which emanated from him spread all over the world of antiquity with amazing speed.

To be sure, there were "regressive" interpretations of Jesus' coming even at the very beginning, as we have shown in earlier chapters.[22] When the Emperor Constantine had the sign of the cross painted on the shields and helmets of his soldiers before the battle at the Milvian Bridge in the

175

year 325 AD, and when henceforth people killed in the name of this sign, it became especially difficult to perceive the authentic breath of Jesus and to be immersed in it. The fact that since the Middle Ages almost every European received Christian baptism (and confirmation) was of little help. As we have mentioned, it is important for the Christian to be baptized not only with water—like the disciples of John—but to be immersed in the "pneuma hagion," the breath of Jesus and the Abba. When in Samaria many came to be baptized, but were not filled with the "pneuma hagion," the ancient community sent Peter and John so that the breath of Jesus could come into them by the laying on of their hands (Acts 8, 14-17).

But at least since the time of the Emperor Constantine, the breath of the hunter, symbolized by the figures of the eagle and the falcon, overpowered the breath of universal reconciliation and of universal peace which had come into the world with Jesus. Fortunately, some traces of it survived. And now, in our own century, after the insanity of the Second World War revealed the barbarism of the breath of hunting and warfare (which now threatens the whole globe with nuclear extermination), many people are inspired not by the hunter's breath but by the dove's breath of Jesus and are looking for new and different ways of human life and community.

At this point of our investigation, we must become clearly aware that the "pneuma" of the hunter, the wind and breath of killing, was present at the cradle of humanity and has shaped man and his communal life for about one and a half million years. The two thousand years that have elapsed since the breath of the Abba descended upon Jesus from the open skies during the baptism at the river Jordan are almost nothing compared to these immense lengths of time. On a graphic time chart these two thousand years would hardly be visible. However, in the fact that within this very short period the *public* killing of children, prisoners and animals has virtually ceased all over the world, and in international organizations like Amnesty International and Greenpeace, which are backed by the consciences of a multitude of men and women, we have a powerful witness to a breath and wind in our world that is radically different from the aura of the hunter.

But that which has been shaped and built in hundreds of thousands of years cannot be dismantled and replaced within a few millenia. The way of life of the hunter was not thought up by some clever chiefs and carried out according to a master plan. Instead, it grew out of the perception of the transcendent dimension of force and vitality, visible in large animals—a perception that was perverted through violent appropriation. Similarly, the new way of life which is grounded in the breath of peace and reconciliation cannot be plotted in advance and then carried out in struggles and confrontations. Such an attempt would be a regression to the hunter's mentality. The new way of being must also grow out of the perception of a transcendent dimension, out of the perception of that sacredness which surrounds the "child"; the abandoned, helpless being; the powerless; the one who is handed over. More important than political manifestos is the training of the eye, so that it may learn to see "God" in the abandoned human being.[23]

When the breath of the Abba, the "pneuma hagion," eventually shapes all aspects of humanity, as it shaped Jesus, then the kingdom of God will have come. Then Jesus will have returned in every single human being. Even the experience of death will be radically altered and the dead, those eminently abandoned beings, will come to life in a new way. We cannot foresee the path that will lead to that goal — and therefore we cannot map it out. Instead of creeping forward like the hunter, to focus on the goal as on prey, we as Christians should focus with the utmost concentration on that place where the heavens are opened and the dove's breath comes forth: on the child, on the old person, on the person who is abandoned and needs help. Then the "kingdom of God" will grow in the sense of its original meaning, as "malkût Yahweh," as a new action of Yahweh among men. The God "I-am-here," the Abba of Jesus, will rise among men and will reign.

2.3 A Failed Neolithic Experiment: the "Solar Wind," or the Search for a Permanent Homeland.

Where Does the New Behavioral Pattern (the Transformation Within the Soul) Come From?

In a lecture on the "concept of the collective unconscious" C. G. Jung tries to prove the existence of archetypes using the following example.[1] He describes the fantasy of a paranoid patient who stood at the window, looked into the sun, moved his head back and forth and described what he saw as the "solar penis," as the origin of the wind. In a text from the liturgy of Mithras and in medieval paintings where the annunciation is represented by a tube-shaped link between the throne of God and Mary's womb, letting in the dove as the "Holy-wind-spirit," Jung recognized this same symbolism. Because it was proved that his patient was unaware of any such representations, Jung deduced the presence of a collective unconscious from the paranoid man's narration. However, it is well known that in almost all cultures there is a recognized link between the mentally ill and the religious ecstatic. As with drugs or other shamanistic techniques of ecstasy in which the sensitivity to the transcendent is enhanced, many forms of mental illness entail a sharpened sensitivity for this type of perception. An important element of that which is symbolized by the sun, of that which transcends its physical perception, is the expression of an emanation of a calm, steady and powerful force. This force makes vegetal life grow and ripen and can be felt in an immediate way. As a static potency it is symbolized by the "solar penis," and as an active force, it is symbolized by wind. The similarity of images therefore does not derive from a mythical "collective unconscious," as it were, but from a similar symbolic, holistic perception of reality.

This perception is expressed clearly on the relief of an ancient Egyptian altar piece (Fig. 31). Ikhnaton, the son of the sun-god Aton, and his wife Nefertiti sit facing each other, with their three daughters on their laps. In the upper margin of the picture, between the two persons (somewhat closer to Ikhnaton) is a representation of Aton, the radiant sun. Its beams which end with a series of little hands, are swinging, as it were, between Ikhnaton and Nefertiti. A strong wind blows from those beams, fluttering the ribbons of their crowns like flags. This picture (apparently unknown to Jung) shows strikingly that one does not need to be paranoid to experience the force and wind of the sun in this way, nor that some mythical archetypes need to surface. Indeed, the early Christians had a similar experience when, fifty days after Jesus' execution, at the feast of Pentecost in Jerusalem, the awesome significance of Jesus dawned upon them in a sun-like fashion. They too saw "tongues of fire" which spread among them, and they heard "what sounded like a powerful wind from heaven" which filled the entire house (Acts 2, 2 f.).

Besides this fulfilling and mobile/immobile force, the celestial body of the sun also projects an image of a quiet and universal order. This element is also perceived as a transcendent dimension. According to Kant, "the sphere of the stars above me and the moral law within me" are the two things "that fill the soul with ever new admiration and awe" and convince the practical reason (if not the theoretical one) of the existence of God.[2] Both the fulfilling, enlivening force and the universal order, which rests in itself, are an experience of the divine fundamentally different from the one experienced in the wild animal. The animal is an element of the fascinating, all-pervasive wilderness in which primeval humans lived. The god who arises from the animals of this wilderness is the wilderness-god, the master or the mistress of animals, living in a dark

178

Fig. 31: Echnaton and Nefertiti in the radiance of the solar wind. Note the ribbons fluttering from their crowns (relief from a private altar in a home dating from the Armana period).

maze of caves, and later in the squall, in the thunderstorm and in dark clouds. The divinity arising from the stars and the sun is of a different nature. The force which emanates from it is calm and consistent. It is associated not with the sudden spring of the prowling animal, but with the steady, rooted plant, with the nest, with the house, or with the bird hovering calmly in the skies. The light and warmth of the sun cause plants to grow and fruits to ripen. Even in hunting cultures, man depended primarily on these plants for his food. Since the transition from being mere gatherers to becoming hunters as well, men and women have been assigned different labors. The women remain principally gatherers and hunting expeditions are carried out by groups of men. In this context, it is women in particular who relate to the vegetal growth caused by the sun and who gather the fruits. Earth, growth, and vegetal life are therefore associated with women. Indeed it is women who bear new life in their womb, and bring forth this fruit—this life—into the world.

We cannot be sure what caused this evolution to a settled life and later to a life of agriculture, cattle raising and the foundation of states in different places and at different times during the Neolithic Period. (The English archaeologist Gordon Child described the process as "the Neolithic revolution" but it is now viewed as more of an evolution.) This, however, we can say for sure: Such a fundamental change in human behavior could never have taken place if man had not been seized by a new awareness, by a new attitude towards himself, towards life, and towards the world—in short, by a new "wind" and "breath" of life during the few millenia in which this change occurred. This precondition is necessary because the transformation in question is not a biological evolution but a cultural one. Genetic mutations can spring up randomly and are selected as "positive" if they turn out to be better adapted to the new environment than the old genetic mass. In other words, the carrier of the new genome will multiply with more abundant success than the others. But the inner attitude of man alone is not subject to random change. Religious wars demonstrate that extreme military pressure and ruthlessness often fail to change the mentality of the people but instead generate martyrs. Attitudes change only when a new wind and breath, coming from some place, meets a corresponding inner need in man and helps articulate it, just as the early Christians spread the "pneuma" of Jesus. Christianity could grow only because all those different people gathered in Jerusalem for the feast of Pentecost—"Parthians, Medes and Elamites; people from Mesopotamia, Judaea and Cappadocia, Pontus and Asia, Phrygia and Pamphylia, Egypt and the parts of Libya around Cyrene; as well as visitors from Rome, Jews and Proselytes alike, Cretans and Arabs" (Acts 2, 9-11)—could understand all that was articulated by Peter through the force of the breath of Jesus and of the Abba in their own native tongue. In other words, they were able to perceive it as their own innermost yearning which had hitherto remained unrecognized.

"The wind blows wherever it pleases; you hear its sound but you cannot tell where it comes from or where it is going," is the answer Jesus gives the Pharisee Nicodemus, who comes secretly by night, urged by the new wind of Jesus. He cannot understand how he—although he is a "grown man"—could possibly undergo such a radical change of attitude as if he were "born again" from his mother's womb (John 3, 1-13). Humankind was also grown—over one million years old—when it changed to this new way of life. As the numerous and partially contradictory archaeological theories show,[4] it is not possible to identify the cause of this change as a singular empirical phenomenon like population growth, changes of climate, or a heightened imagination due to the growth of the brain.

Jost Herbig, who comes to this conclusion, develops an original explanation of the process that led to an agriculture and settled lifestyle, a theory that, on the whole, seems quite plausible. He talks about plants that "seek out man."[5] That is, he sees the cause of man's transition to agriculture in the existence of certain "colonizing plants" that spread by themselves in those areas in which "at the end of the Ice Age, after the thawing of the glaciers, after avalanches, wild fires, droughts, and river floodings" rich and fertile soil was opened to new vegetation.[6] The camps of hunters and gatherers also "left behind them soils without vegetation that abounded in nutrients: sites of garbage disposal, well-worn pathways, latrines and fire pits"[7] — places where, after the departure of the hunters or gatherers, colonizing plants such as corn, wild beans, and pumpkins found a new habitat. When a group of humans periodically returned to these places, they were surprised to find such plants in great numbers. One day they themselves began small but controlled burnings and cleared the woods to "lure" these nutritional plants.

But even in this theory one wonders why it took a million years before man had been "sought out by the plant" and began changing his way of life. More than all preceding theories, this latest hypothesis makes us ask about the origin of the *inner readiness,* the willingness to react to the colonizing plants. To be sure, it is impossible to determine where this wind comes from (John 3, 8), the "sound" of which becomes audible in this dramatic change of man's way of life. As the question about the motivation of the homo erectus who thrust his spear into the bison's loins and thus became a hunter, cannot be answered by exact science, the question of the origin of this inner readiness, of the wind and breath, of the "pneuma" which allowed such a change of behavior, although it has to be asked by exact science, cannot be answered from within this dimension of science.

We must be aware of this fact: At this point man's exclusively scientific inquiry *cannot* find an answer. For the idea of "God" or of a "transcendent dimension" is not an acceptable answer in empirical science. God cannot be declared the cause of the "Neolithic transformation" within a scientific theory. Such a God would be only a stopgap. But the situation is different if we try to feel our way into that which has moved human beings of all times towards a discourse about God, not as archaeologists, but as theologians, and as persons with religious sensibilities. For exact scientific thought is insufficient to comprehend the processes that generate religious symbols. Such a comprehension requires a religious attitude, an active openness to religious symbols. Within such initially religious and yet also scientific (i. e. theological) thinking, human phenomena — like the specific questions of human prehistory and protohistory — appear in a totally different light than in a science which is based only on facts and conclusions without any religious ties.

Only if we are open from the beginning to a transcendent dimension of reality, thanks to our own religious experiences which cannot be scientifically demonstrated, will we be able to make the wind and breath which shapes human behavior at its very existential (i. e. religious) root the subject of our inquiries. Scientific thought without religious ties can only inquire about the function of religion, not its origin, as is clearly apparent from Jost Herbig's studies. (Because Herbig, Durkheim, and others are not sufficiently explicit on this point, one often gets the impression that some clever people invented religion for their own economic, political and social ambitions, which would be in opposition to Herbig's general anthropology.) From this perspective, prehistoric scholars attempt too much when they try to answer the question of the origin of the Neolithic change in behavior in a radical way, that is, from its roots. They are able to gather the elements that contributed to this change, but they cannot see the "pneuma" which makes the whole change possible and is its ultimate motivation.

Of course, even scientific religious thinking reaches its limits here. It can no longer give phenomenological descriptions and can make no logical deductions. But in contrast to a science without any religious ties, it still can relate to certain experiences which we have as religious persons and which we can communicate to other persons who live and think in a religious way: experiences of the transcedent dimension of reality that go beyond the objective given. In the same way in which we may relive the dimension of the unrestrained power, strength, and vitality in the encounter with the huge and frightening animal, we can also relive the experience of absolute order and transcendent security that emanate from the sun and the stars, from the wide open sea, from the deep roots and the widespread branches of the tree, and from the human mother. From the moment — which no one can define with precision — that human-like beings developed the ability to sense this transcendent dimension, using an ever more highly differentiated nervous system, this dimension was indeed experienced by humans in this form.

Since man has existed, he feels the "solar wind," that calm and steady force which emanates from the sun and other phenomena — like that paranoid patient mentioned in the example from Jung. From that time he lives with the obscure presentiment of an absolute warmth and security, of a steady, universal, and constitutive order and of a never-ending existence and life. In a word, he lives with a longing for a homeland. The earliest signs of this sentiment are burials. They indicate a notion of permanence. Thus it is quite conceivable that man could have moved directly from the biologically determined life style of a gatherer to the life style of a settled farmer. There is no necessity involved, but this move is the result of a free historical decision, namely, the decision to prefer the fascination of large, powerful animals to that of the sun, the stars, and the trees (which the homo erectus had always seen above himself), and above all, to his reaction to the fascination of animals by killing. This deed, central to his adoption of a behavior for which he was not naturally equipped, and which he therefore had to learn anew in each generation, using up all his religious energies, bound him to the animal world and the wilderness and thus to an existence as a hunter for more than one million years.

Only in the later Paleolithic Period, once he was able to purge his soul of the hunter's trauma through paintings on the walls of caves hidden in the depths of the earth, did this fixation slowly begin to loosen its hold. Of course, he remained a hunter—in fact, as shown in the previous chapter, he remains one to this very day. But he also became more open to other experiences and their transcendent dimensions. The solar wind, the longing for lasting order and for a permanent homeland was revived within him. Thus he let himself "be sought out by plants" (Herbig), at first in the plains of the fertile crescent (in the mountain ranges which stretch from Palestine and Syria all the way through Iraq and Iran), and within a few thousand years he learned to domesticate plants and animals.

Sun and Rock: Lost Symbols Regain Speech

As archaeological evidence universally demonstrates, these very symbols which had previously been neglected, were now returning to the foreground. In order to feel our way into these symbols, it is useful to begin, as Sibylle von Reden did in her book on megalithic culture, with a literary example. Although this particular example was composed thousands of years later, it still accurately reflects the structure of feeling and thought, the wind and breath of Neolithic man.[8] The basic motif of the Sumerian myth and its hero Gilgamesh is the search for immortality, for the hidden herb on the bottom of the ocean which grants eternal life. This yearning for eternity is awakened by the experience of the light of the sun which always returns and shines with eternal brilliance. Sibylle von Reden hears the "longing of all mortals" in the cry of Gilgamesh:

> *Let my eyes gaze upon the sun,*
> *that the fullness of light may last forever!*
> *Darkness recedes where light is abundant.*
> *May even the dead see the brilliance of the sun!*

The "solar wind" moves man to look for a permanent, eternal homeland. The most ancient human village with evidence of being occupied the year round was excavated at Ain Mallaha in the upper valley of the river Jordan, and was built about twelve thousand years ago.[9] It is made up of some fifty round houses made with clay bricks that are entrenched in mother earth and arranged around a central plaza: a clearance in the midst of an immense wilderness, imitation of the disc of the sun as a source of light. Sibylle von Reden correctly speaks of a new "spiritual center." "In the midst of the chaos of nature, certain centers emerged in the form of stable communities: in the house, in the enclosure of a sacred space, at the grave of ancestors."[10]

Indeed, this is the spiritual basis for the culture which developed in the following millenia, referred to as the "megalithic culture." The decisive fact is that men no longer needed to leave behind the remains of their deceased ancestors, when, of necessity, they moved to a different camp in search of food. Their dead were no longer dispersed over an immense territory, their graves no longer exposed to vultures and hyenas, but were gathered in cemeteries close to the abodes of the living, at first even under the floors of their houses. These ancestors were equally dreaded and venerated, living on as a presence in the village and forming solid bonds within the community. The ancestral heritage provided the kind of durability which was primarily experienced in the transcendent dimension of towering mountains and rocks. Accordingly, these big stones, these "mega-liths" are the characteristic feature of this culture. Immense blocks of granite, hewn with chisels and weighing up to fifty tons, like some of the blocks at Stonehenge, were dragged great distances (using a technique which still remains a mystery) to the graves of the departed, and erected there as funerary monuments and cultic symbols.

The cult of the stones was always connected to a cult of the sun and of the stars. Especially in Stonehenge (Fig. 32) the astronomical orientation of the whole construction has proven the presence of a sun-cult.[11] In ancient Egypt the combination of the veneration of the sun and of ancestors gave rise to a unique expression. The basic idea of this combination is already explicit in the epic of Gilgamesh which we quoted earlier:

...that the fullness of light may last forever!...
May even the dead see the brilliance of the sun!

Even if the quasi-scientific and astronomical explanation of the stones as a calendar, which some scholars have tried to prove, cannot be accepted, a symbolic, cultic relation between sun, stone and death can be

184

Fig. 32: Stonehenge (England): Stones of up to fifty tons were brought and erected here from distances up to thirty kilometers, using still unknown techniques.

assumed as certain. The stones, as symbols of eternity, also served the purpose of bringing sunlight into the tombs. The clearing that was wrested from the wilderness should not be darkened even by death.

The warm light of the sun which makes plants grow and ripen signifies strength, potency and fertility. The stones upon which the sun shines during the day are charged, as it were, with this force that grants fertility. Long after the sun has disappeared below the horizon, they still radiate that warmth. To this day the freestanding menhirs in Brittany are called the "hot stones." Up to our own time popular belief credited them with fertilizing powers. Girls who wanted to marry or to conceive sat naked on top of this "solar penis." Until the last century the Catholic Church fought vigorously but not always successfully against such customs.[12] This fertilizing solar power, the potent solar wind, is also the bridge towards an understanding of the cult of the great mother and of the bull which arose in the Neolithic Period.

In the oldest wall-paintings of the Ice Age and in the numerous idols found in Paleolithic campsites, the woman and mother appear as an important motif. This will be the theme of the next chapter, when we talk about the symbol of the father and the mother. At present, it is important to note that the representations of animals form the vast majority of motifs in Paleolithic art, and that the figures of women are often associated with those animals, sometimes presented only as the symbol of

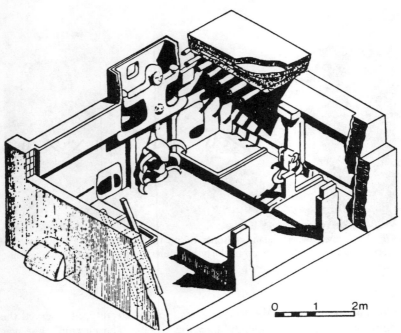

Fig. 33: Relief sculpture of the great goddess (shrine from layer six at Çatal Hüyük).

the vulva, in order to express the erotic aspect of the relation between hunter and animal. Now, in the Neolithic Period, the woman and mother has domination over the animal.

In one of the oldest settlements, in Çatal Hüyük in southern Anatolia, settled from the 8th millenium BC (reaching the peak of its development around the year 6,000 BC), a relief sculpture, standing in a niche above three bull skulls with large horns, shows a goddess enthroned in the so-called Baubo posture with legs and arms spread wide (Fig. 33). Herbig seems to suggest that it is the representation of parturition,[13] a possibility also considered by von Reden.[14] But in certain Sumerian cylinder seals the same position is assumed by a prostitute who is called the "daughter of Inanna," according to an old text (Fig. 34).[15] For Urs Winter, the goddess in this posture embodies the aspect of sexual surrender, which includes an aspect of fertility.[16] In some representations of this kind the goddess holds a plant in her hands as a sign of fertilty and growth, and above it are figures of the sun and of a star. We often see the goddess enthroned in this position in the midst of dangerous and wild

186

Fig. 34: The goddess Innana/Ishtar and her daughter, in the so called "Baubo-posture" with plants in their hands as signs of fertility (central Syrian cylinder seal).

creatures like scorpions, serpents, and ibexes.[17] The woman who is ready for intercourse, thereby granting fertility like the light and the sun, now dominates these wild and dangerous animals.

In Çatal Hüyük, as in later cylinder seals from Syria, Akkadia and Babylonia, she has brought the bull, the ram and the predator "under her control": she stands on top of them. In a little statue her throne is

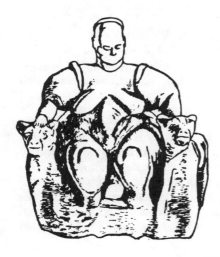

Fig. 35: Ceramic figurine of a goddess in labor, resting on two leopards (discovered in Çatal Hüyük).

Fig. 36: Wild animals tamed by the goddess (ibexes "eat from the hands of the goddess"); cover of an ivory box (Ras Shamra, Syria, Mycenaean culture, 13th century BC).

made of two leopards, on the heads of which she puts her hands while she gives birth to a child (Fig. 35). Her partner is not the bull,[18] but a man, usually a youthful, boyish lover who will later become the light-hero and son/lover of Mediterranean mythologies who, like his mother/mistress, has conquered the wilderness. He rides on a leopard or stands on a bull. The taming of the wilderness, symbolized by the animals, is expressed very nicely when the goddess of Çatal Hüyük holds leopards in her arms or on her lap, a symbolism analogous to later Syrian and Cretan images in which the rampant ibex eats out of the hands of the goddess (Fig. 36). The picture reminds us of Isaiah's eschatological vision of the peace of nature:

> *"The wolf shall live with the lamb,*
> *the leopard lie down with the kid,*
> *calf and young lion shall feed together*
> *and a little child shall lead them..."*

(Isa. 11, 6)

The Old "Hunter's Breath" Fuses with the New "Solar Wind"

Human beings have always longed for a peace within nature, but the reality is different. The wilderness around the small clearings in which man tries to build a permanent home is unconquerable. Man can neither tame it nor pass over it transported by the solar wind, as suggested in those graceful pictures from Çatal Hüyük and Crete of men leaping over wild bulls and goats (Fig. 47). Thus, all these ancient settlements were abandoned at some point. The wilderness re-claimed them. Wherever man confronts the elemental power of the wilderness in the name of the sun, the stone and the stars, of the woman and mother, he is involved in a struggle in which his life is at stake. Sooner or later the breath of the hunter and of the warrior, the breath of the slaying, rises again and, in fusion with the solar wind, it becomes even sharper and more cruel.

Even the goddess of Çatal Hüyük reveals some ambivalent features. She is surrounded by black vultures which eat the flesh of the dead bodies before the skeletons are buried — a practice later adopted by the Persians in their "towers of silence." In one picture the powerful tusks of a boar and the beak of a vulture are protruding from of her breast. Later she is interpreted as Ishtar, in martial attire and holding a sickle-shaped axe in her right hand. Her head is encircled with a wreath of weapons and she puts her foot triumphantly on the back of an open mouthed, crouching lion whom she holds with a leash. The winged sun above her and the wings fixed to her shoulders in this Akkadian cylinder seal show that the solar wind and the breath of the hunter have been fused (Fig. 37). The goddess of love has also become the goddess of warfare. Similarly, even the priestly queen of peaceful Minoan Crete has the features of violence and killing.[19]

This new form of the deadly breath is characterized by the absence of any erotic relation between the "hunter" and his "prey." Indeed, when such a relation occurs, terrible disasters follow, as in the case of Pasiphae,

Fig. 37: Fusion between the solar wind and the hunter's breath: The goddess of love, Ishtar, as goddess of war — winged and heavily armed, she puts her foot on a wild lion, which she holds in check with a leash (Akkadian cylinder seal).

the queen of Knossos, who weds the bull sent by Poseidon instead of killing it: the man-eating Minotaur is born, half man, half bull. There are only two choices. Either submit to the god of the wilderness and cast into his jaws the most beloved possession, one's own children, as a sacrifice,[20] or lead a merciless campaign of subjection and extermination against him. The wilderness-god, against whom the woman or the light-hero, her son/lover, fights, now becomes the dragon of chaos. He is no longer a competitor but merely a monster with no right whatsoever to existence.

In this scheme, man is also seen as a monster of chaos, whether it be as a rebel, as an enemy from within the community, or as an enemy who comes from outside to threaten the bright homeland. There is even an example in the Old Testament. Although the historical settlement of Palestine by the people of Yahweh was relatively peaceful, the book of Joshua recounts it as a ruthless campaign of extermination. The scriptural account reads: "He took Debir and its king and all the cities belonging to it; they put them to the sword, and every living creature there they destroyed utterly. He left none alive" (Josh. 10, 38 f.). Such a narration reveals the breath of a merciless rage of war and battle, a lethal breath against an inhuman enemy, a monster that must be exterminated. For the slain, the God "I-am-here" of the Israelites, who has given them this

190

Fig. 38: Mithras kills the bull and thus brings fertility: The bull's tail ends as ears of grain; the scorpion, dog and serpent lick its blood (cultic image from the second to third century AD; probably from Northern Italy).

land, is a terrible god of horror. The hunter's breath and the solar wind have fused into a deadly power. Similarly, in many representations of Mithras, whose cult was especially popular among Roman soldiers, the sun-god jumps on a fleeing bull, transported by the breath of the hunter and warrior, and thrusts his sword to the hilt into the bull's neck while the dog and the serpent, the powers of chaos, lick the wild animals' blood (Fig. 38). It was with such an attitude that the Roman soldiers went out to conquer the "barbarians."

Jost Herbig's reconstruction, supported by archaeological evidence,[21] of the origin of Monte Albán in Mexico's Oaxaca Valley between 500 and 200 BC shows clearly how this fateful fusion of solar wind and hunter's breath culminates in the foundation of a state. Around 550 BC, the valley of Oaxaca consisted of small hamlets of one or two hectares and fifty or sixty inhabitants, as well as of some larger settlements like those of Ain Mallaha or Çatal Hüyük, with several hundred and sometimes more than one thousand inhabitants. The large settlements were older, the small ones offshoots. In the larger settlements there were public cultic buildings binding the inhabitants of the small hamlets to their mother-villages through their religion. This dependence was also expressed economically in taxes on their production as well as other taxes that had to be paid to the religious leaders of the mother-villages. Despite clear differences in

Fig. 39: The "Danzantes." Tortured village chiefs represented on reliefs found on stone tiles in a temple wall at Monte Albán (ancient Mexico).

rank and wealth, the chiefs and their clans had family ties throughout the entire population and there is no evidence of a class of rulers separated from the people. The settlements were arranged in such a way that they encompassed enough fertile land to feed their inhabitants. The number of inhabitants grew slowly. The population of San José Mogote, the largest and most ancient of these settlements in the Oaxaca valley, did not reach one thousand for nearly one thousand years.

Around 500 BC something strange happened in the valley. Within three centuries the city of Monte Albán emerged in the hills of the valley, centrally located but without fertile land. Monte Albán, whose population had grown to between ten and twenty thousand inhabitants was thereafter the absolute ruler of the entire valley. What had happened? Obviously some chiefs from the larger villages discovered that it was not necessary to grow one's own food in order to feed oneself and one's entourage, but that it was as good or even better to live off the tributes paid by others. The breath of the hunter was aroused in them and turned the possessions of their fellow beings into a potential prey. In a concerted action, they subjugated the older settlements and demanded tribute. Those who rebelled against this new and larger "community" were denounced as a chaotic element threatening the stability of the community and had to be mercilessly destroyed. The so-called "danzantes," relief figures on large stone plates in one of the temples in Monte Albán, show how the leaders of the subjugated villages who had opposed the claims of the new leaders in the city were tortured to death in the most gruesome ways (Fig. 39).[22] Even the Roman Empire and the subsequent Holy Roman Empire of the German Nation practiced this type of execution, particularly for rebels and heretics; and Jesus of Nazareth suffered it as well.

Conquered enemies, whether from outside or inside the community, were considered subhuman. They could be treated in any fashion. Thus the ancient world saw the emergence of huge populations of slaves and pariahs. Whenever larger state structures arose they followed this pattern at least to some extent. For example, the major Sumerian city-states emerged primarily from struggles among traditional, larger settlements for the control of a region. As a result of these wars, the countryside was devastated and the population enslaved. According to some recent though still incomplete archaeological and socio-historical research,[23] during the three centuries from 3100 to 2800 BC there were 124 villages, twenty small cities, two larger cities, and one metropolis, Uruk, in southern Mesopotamia. In the following four centuries, people tried to evade the tributes imposed upon them by Uruk and formed their own urban centers in order to defend themselves. One great city that emerged was Umma. During this period, the number of smaller cities shrank to six and the number of villages to seventeen. Only an estimated seventeen percent of the population still lived in the countryside. The fate which rural people met in the cities is revealed through the cuneiform character of "woman from the foreign mountains" which is synonymous with "slave."[24] Only in certain instances did the establishment of states take place without major violence, as in the huge city-state of Teotihuacán in ancient Mexico, where economic development was the major driving force, and where militaristic tendencies emerged only later, in times of decadence, or in Crete, where the excavated palace-cities show no sign of ramparts, city walls, watch-towers or other fortifications—in this case probably because of its island location.

Eventually, the breath of the preying hunter overcame and usurped the solar wind which emerged during the Neolithic Period and perverted it into a breath of abstract power and destruction. The fruit which Eve, the mother-goddess, hands to her son and lover, her light-hero Adam, as a token of her affection (and which subsequently became the royal orb in the hands of kings and emperors), had within it the poison of this will to usurpation and destruction. It meant that whoever accepted it had to go out as king and war-hero to kill and to be killed without mercy. Therefore the God "I-am-here" from Egypt, the protective god of the enslaved, says of this fruit: "Nevertheless of the tree of knowledge of good and evil you shall not eat; for the moment you eat from it you are doomed to die" (Gen. 2, 17). Thus the author of this story takes the basic pattern of "sin"—the "original sin"—from the power of the state to usurp all authority in the ancient East, according to his own experience. This must have been indeed the origin of his "world." With this material, he accurately describes the basic pattern of that original sin, which for us, in the context of the world as we know it today, lies in the transition from the lifestyle of the gatherer to that of the hunter.[25]

As it is shown in the prophets' criticism of the kings,[26] Israel itself had eaten from the "tree in the middle of the garden" during its founding as a state, as Egypt and Sumer had previously done. This is not only true in respect to Israel's behavior towards the natives of Canaan, but also in respect to the social life within Israel itself. The judge and prophet Samuel's critical prediction in the period before the foundation of the state had come true. A ruling class emerged which appropriated all the power (the "tree in the middle of the garden") and exploited and enslaved the people. "[The king] will take your best fields, your vineyards, and olive groves and give them to his attendants...and you yourselves will be his slaves" (1 Sam. 8, 11-17). The prophet Amos has the exploiters say "We can buy up the poor for silver, and the needy for a pair of sandals" (Amos 8, 4-14).[27] They "deserted" the god who "brought them out of Egypt" and "served other gods" (1 Sam. 8, 8). In their own land they created a new "Egypt." And thus, as shown in earlier chapters, the breath of the hunter, formed over millions of years, blows through many passages of the Bible as well, beginning with Lamech's oath of vengeance, the oath of a descendent of Cain (Gen. 4, 23), through Joshua's narrations, the cursing psalms, the inhumanly abstract black-and-white pictures of universal judgment in the gospel of Matthew (Matt. 25, 31-46), and culminating in the orgy of horror, pain, and destruction in the Book of Revelation.

The Breath of Jesus and the Solar Wind

This is not the breath of Jesus. The original solar breath does have some similarities with the wind and breath of the Abba coming "from the opened sky" (and thus from light and the sun) upon his beloved son and filling him at the baptism in the river Jordan. This breath corresponds as well to man's longing for a permanent homeland and for eternal life. However, as the content of a historical religion, it is of yet a different nature. The light, the sun, flowers and birds, crops growing in the fields, as they are mentioned by Jesus in the Sermon on the Mount and in his parables,[28] are not symbols of the divine as such, as *natural phenomena,* but rather, they exemplify certain *processes* which are metaphors for the "malkût Yahweh," the new power of the God "I-am-here" among men. The analogy is not drawn between something *existing* and a transcendent

194

infinite *essence,* but between a finite *event* and the transcendent *divine operations.*[29] The wind and breath of the comforting, strengthening God "I-am-here," who becomes the Abba, comes forth not in objects and phenomena, not in the large, powerful animal, not in the sun, the sea, or the tree, but in human abandonment and misery. The Egyptians deprived the "wandering Aramaeans" of their rights and forced them into hard labor. "But we called on Yahweh the God of our fathers. Yahweh heard our voice and saw our misery, our toil and our oppression..." (Deut. 26, 6-10). Jesus of Nazareth in Galilee came to the preacher John at the river Jordan, full of the desire for the "malkût Yahweh," and submitted to his baptism of repentance. In answer to this silent crying prayer, the heavens opened and the "ruach Yahweh" descended upon Jesus as the breath of the Abba and of the dove.

It is the condition of finite and limited humanity—the abandoned human, the child—which reveals to Christians the ultimate transcendent dimension from which the "pneuma hagion" emanates, the wind and breath which saves and heals mankind. As witnessed by the criticisms of kingship in the historical writing of the people of Yahweh, and the persistent criticisms by the prophets up to the New Era, this "pneuma" cannot be usurped by the breath of the hunter. It will always find a place in which it can be articulated in a loud and piercing cry, be it in the silent cry of the servant of Yahweh, or in the agony of the Crucified. Wherever this cry is heard, the God "I-am-here" stoops to the crying being and, in the midst of the misery and slavery of Egypt or in the deadly torture of the Crucified, the "malkût Yahweh" establishes—without violence and imperceptible to the empirical experience—a homeland which can never be conquered by the hunter, but grows solely from the experience of a transcendent dimension and thus becomes truly eternal.

2.4. Indian Spirituality: Calming the Breath

Historic Origins: The Civilization of the Indus and the Vedas

Some time after 7000 BC Neolithic settlements sprang up in the valley of the Indus river. They were similar to those which had been formed a little earlier in Anatolia (Çatal Hüyük), Palestine (Ain Mallaha, and Jericho in the Jordan valley) and in other places of the "fertile crescent," as well as to those which would later arise in almost every part of the world, including Sumer, Egypt, and (though much later) Northern China and

Mexico. The forms of spirituality which developed here from about 2500 BC, especially in Harappa and Mohenjo-Daro, were born of the same mentality which we have met earlier in Çatal Hüyük, Sumer, and Crete, and which we described as "solar wind" (the new longing for stability, for warmth and for a homeland). Solid houses were built from mud bricks. Some seals incised in steatite rock depict tree gods; one divinity, sitting in the posture of a Yogi, shows clearly that by then the bodily posture so typical of Indian meditation and spirituality was already in common practice. It is the posture of resting-in-oneself, the posture of one who is in quest of the permanently valid, of one who has achieved at least the first stage, and thereby has become a "sedentary," while continuing to strive for ever greater rest (Fig. 40). Phallic stones were also found, as well as a divine figure surrounded by wild animals obviously obedient to the divinity. Female figurines bear the symbolism of motherhood, and one well-preserved bust shows the partner, the priest-king, who probably also rules over the destinies of a community that wrested its existence from the wilderness. The bull, the wild goat, and the predators symbolize the forces of the wilderness that had to be subjugated.[1]

It is remarkable that there were no actual temple areas. However, in the middle of the city of Mohenjo-Daro a large bathing pool was excavated, flanked by many chambers and side aisles. It reminds one of the baths and ablutions in holy rivers and ponds in temple enclaves that are still a very living part of popular religion in India.[2] Similar cultic bathing pools were discovered in Crete as well (e.g. in Kato Zakros). It is difficult to determine whether these constructions were built with slave labor, as were the temples and cultic buildings in Egypt, Sumer, and Monte Albán. Funeral gifts are evidence of a wealthy upper class which followed quite similar lifestyles in various distant regions. About 2000 BC, only a millenium after the beginnings of these urban centers, the power of the centralized state government disintegrated and was again divided among autonomous villages and communities in which social life was defined by "parental ties." More recent studies have shown that these events were not caused by any major wars — as was previously thought[3] — but were probably the result of natural disasters like droughts or floods. The wind and breath of the central power had proved too weak to hold together a larger community (perhaps because mechanisms of oppression and slavery were not sufficiently developed). At any rate, the comparable states of Egypt and Sumer (where such mechanisms can be shown to have existed) had survived for several thousands of years and they ceased to exist only when they were conquered and subjugated by even larger and more powerful states with better developed mechanisms of power (Egypt by the Romans, Babylon by the Persians).

Before the middle of the 2nd millenium, Indo-germanic tribes, the Aryans, invaded this country in several waves from the West and North-west (over the Punjab), and subjugated the rural village populations. Like the Ionians, Aeolians, Dorians, and the Indo-germanic tribes who had invaded Greece several hundred years earlier and subjugated a peasant population, the Aryan people who came to India were pastoral people with a strong patriarchal and martial structure. They were only slightly influenced by the Neolithic mentality. They domesticated animals but probably learned the values of a settled lifestyle from the subjugated populations. As a result, they eventually settled permanently in the conquered land. Their highest godhead was a stormy god of wind and weather, comparable to the Germanic Wotan who rumbles through the air as a wild hunter in November nights, and to Donar who throws bolts of lightning down to earth. The original features of the Greek god Zeus are quite similar.

Fig. 40: Divinity in the sitting posture of a Yogi (from the culture of the Indus valley).

197

Here, in hot and sunny India, this god of storm and lightning manifested itself as Indra, as a great and radiant conquerer who rips open the belly of the cloud-dragon Vrtra with his sword of lightning and his wedge of thunder freeing the waters of the heavens which were contained in the dragon. He overflows with vitality and the joy of life; he rejoices in combat. The waters run down into the valleys like racing horses or bellowing cows. He is the divine power who, violently drunk with Soma (a sacred, intoxicating beverage which Indra gulps ceaselessly) chases darkness, creates light, gives milk to cows and fertility to all female beings, and conquers all enemies.[4]

According to some texts he drives around the firmament with great skill (like Surya) as a sun-god in a golden chariot drawn by reddish horses, holding a thousand-pointed club in his hand. This image of the sun has many more of the wild and vital aspects of hunting than in the Neolithic perception.[5] In his fight with the dragon, Indra is accompanied by his followers, the Maruts, powerful wind gods, armed with shining spears and dreadful to look at. Like the wild army of Wotan, they roam the skies, mountains and peaks, splitting rocks and producing wind, lightning and rain.

Such is Indra, at the summit of the pantheon as it is described in the Vedas, the most ancient sacred texts of Hinduism. In addition to the brilliant Indra there is Rudra, who retains some aspects of the wilderness-god, and Mithra, the god of contracts who was important in the context of the Aryan-germanic system of allegiance and who later became the light-hero and sun-god of the Mithras-cult which came from Persia to Western Europe. The divinities of the subjugated people have also penetrated the Vedic pantheon, but they are of only minor significance. To this group belongs a mother-goddess, who appears as Sarasvati in the Vedas but is later replaced by the indigenous mother-goddess Tara or Shri Lakshmi, the spouse of Vishnu, symbolized in the lotus blossom, or by her ambivalent apparition as Durga or Kali, the spouse of Shiva.[6] Both Vishnu, who eventually will take on the features of the light-hero, and Shiva, the ambivalent personification of the power of procreation whose wild features are probably pre-Aryan and who is ultimately merged with Rudra, the Aryan god of storm and wilderness, are mentioned in the Vedas, but in a subordinate position. On the other hand, Agni, the god of fire, is of paramount importance in these texts. In him, in the transcendent dimension of the phenomenon of fire, the light of the heavens is joined with earthly human life. Through building and kindling the fire, man can transcend his earthly life. In the Śrauta-ritual, an ancient peasant sacrifice, the master of the ceremony mutters these words when he kindles the fire: "From the human realm I go to the gods; ...kindling the fire I will conquer both realms and overcome death."[7]

198

In the fire, and in the sacrifices linked to it, the new sense of order and permanence manifests itself in the spirituality of the Vedas. The individual ceremonies which assure not only the good luck and well-being of humankind, but also the continuance of the whole universe, are described in minute detail. According to an old saying, the sun would not rise in the morning if the Brahmans did not perform the morning offerings as prescribed before dawn.[8]

The Brahmans are initiated into, and responsible for, the rite of offering. They guarantee the world order and are the highest social class within the society that emerged from the settling conquerers. The second class consists of warriors, among which kings are counted as well, and the third class is comprised of peasants and craftsmen. Far below these three castes are the Sudras, the subjugated indigenous people who are forced into all sorts of menial occupations. This is the origin of the Indian caste system.

The subsequent evolution of these religious traditions will take a peculiar turn which is probably unique to India. The evolution in Greece might serve as a comparison. Here, Indo-germanic tribes also invaded the country and conquered the indigenous population without, however, isolating themselves through any kind of caste system. These tribes also imported their pantheon which was centered around Olympus and was ruled by Zeus. The indigenous divinities were integrated into this pantheon mostly in minor positions, just as Vishnu and Shiva were integrated in the Vedas. But the tensions that appeared in the Greek myth, between Apollo and Dionysus, for example, were always solved to the advantage of the new gods. It is often difficult to see the difference between the divinities imported by the conquerers and the local ones. There are many assimilations. But one thing is clear: The thunder-god Zeus, who is most certainly of Indo-germanic origin (and therefore imported by the conquerers), remains, from the time he overcame the Titans, the unchallenged head of the Pantheon, brilliant and radiant (which is, according to H. J. Rose, the basic meaning of his name).[9] From his eternal throne on top of Mount Olympus, shrouded in clouds, he casts bolts of lightning. In India, however, the evolution is very different. Although the Sudras remain social outcasts and become today's "pariahs," the "untouchables," their gods Vishnu and Shiva, and especially the mother-goddess Sarasvati[10] gain more and more importance in the course of time. Compared to them, the Aryan, Vedic divinities and their highly sophisticated sacrificial cults move to the background.

The Parable of the Ants: the God of the Conquered Teaches the God of the Conquerers

This process is expressed in an unsurpassably poetic way in the Hindu story of the ants's parade as it is told in the Puranas, a collection of stories gathered during the first millenium AD.[11]

During the rule of the dragon Vrtra who withheld the waters and made the countryside dry, the land was deserted and the magnificent "divine cities" with their palaces and temples decayed. After Indra had killed the dragon and the waters were flowing once more, Indra's first act was to reconstruct the cities. Praised by all the gods in the heavens, proud of his triumph and conscious of his power, Indra ordered the god of the arts and crafts to build a residence for him such as no man or god had ever seen. The divine king wished for ever more gardens, towers, lakes and ponds, halls and palaces, until eventually the exhausted architect went to Brahma and Vishnu, moaning and complaining about his burden. They promised to help.

The next morning, a ten-year-old Brahman boy with a shepherd's staff appeared before the palace of Indra and asked to be admitted. The king received the boy with kindness and asked for the purpose of his visit. The child said he would like to see the palace that was larger and more magnificent than any Indra before him had ever built. Somewhat amused, Indra asked whether there had ever been any divine king before him. Thereupon the little guest began a wondrous discourse about old gods — about Kashyapa, the turtle man, the lord and maker of all creatures on earth; about Marishi, the holy son of Brahma; and about Brahma, the creator of the universe who came forth from the calyx of a lotus that grew from Vishnu's navel; and about Vishnu himself, the highest being, who supports Brahma's creative activity. He told of the ages of the universe which comprise millions and millions of years, rising from and sinking back into the infinity of the dark primeval ocean upon which Vishnu rests, dreaming up the new ages. Each age has many gods and god-kings, "Indras," who follow each other on their path, each one rising to kingship and divinity and passing away again.[12] The host of Indras, is as uncountable as the grains of sand on the seashore and the raindrops that fall from heaven.

While the boy was telling his story a large parade of ants crossed the imperial hall. Bewildered, Indra looked at the teeming little creatures on the floor, while the boy laughed quietly. Indra asked him what he had seen in his spirit, and the boy answered hesitantly. "All those many ants that cover the floor in the long parade were once Indras. They rose by good deeds and gained the rank of divine king to become ants again, eventually after many incarnations." An innumerable army of former Indras crossed the floor of the royal hall. The little boy confronted the divine king with the unending wheel of birth and rebirth and the operations of the Karma, which leads all beings either up or down.

In the meantime, a hermit had entered the hall. He looked wild and haggard, wearing a black fur around his loins, with a white mark on his forehead and a wretched grass hat on his head. On his breast grew a circular tuft of hair, which thinned out in the center. Silently, the dark ascetic sat down on the floor between the boy and the king and remained motionless as a rock. Indra, the host and king of the gods, whom the boy's story had caused to "shrink to insignificance in his own sight, despite his celestial brillance,"[13] welcomed the new guest a little hesitantly, but with respect, and asked about his well-being and the purpose of his visit. The hermit presented himself as a Brahman who had realized that this life was too short to own a home, to build a house, to marry and to earn a living in any way that makes sense. He lived from alms and wore a grass hat to protect himself from the sun and rain. The circle of hair on his breast signified the Indras of the present age of the universe. Every time an Indra fell, a hair fell out of the tuft, and that is why the skin at the center of the tuft was already bare.

Anything that lived beneath the sphere of the Brahma was, in the eyes of the hermit, as futile as a layer of fog which is visible for a brief time and then dissolves. The hermit had therefore devoted his whole life only to the contemplation of the incomparable lotus-feet of the highest Vishnu. "This," he said, "is more than all earthly joys and honors, even more than salvation and celestial bliss, all of which are nothing but dreams." Shiva, who was incarnated in him, had told him this.

After this utterance the Brahman boy and the hermit disappeared from Indra's sight. He remained alone, frightened and brooding. He had no desire to continue construction of his palace, but instead wanted to retire into the desert as an ascetic. But with the help of the clever house-priest, his spouse eventually succeeded in dissuading him from this decision and convinced him to play his role as Indra up to the end.

This story expresses some important elements of Indian spirituality in their most authentic form. At a superficial glance one might see here the confirmation of Marx's thesis that religion is the garland of flowers which the people wind around the chains of their oppression at the hands of rulers. Declared "untouchables" by the conquerors and enslaved to do the basest of labors, the people were too weak for an actual insurrection. This story tells of the superiority of the old gods and of the insignificance and futility of the lives of the conquerors and their gods. It is, as it were, a merely verbal protest. But this is only a superficial view. It is significant that both the boy and the hermit in the story are Brahmans, members of the priestly aristocracy, of the highest social class of these Aryan immigrant people. This story, which is such a radical challenge to the religious thought of the immigrants is not told by a dirty Sudra boy or by an untouchable beggar, but by members of that religious authority which was put in place by the immigrants themselves. It is Brahman wisdom. It is true and eternal and teaching, not something prompted by a specific historical event. Ultimately, the issue at hand is not the discrepancy between the natives and the higher castes. Rather, it is the question of and search for the lasting, the valid, the eternal and it is highlighted once more and with particular intensity by this new historical constellation.

The dissolution of the ancient Indus civilization, the inability of the rulers of the time to keep the people permanently in servitude to build their palaces and fortifications, has shown that "divine cities," palaces, residences, gardens and ponds will decay within a short time, and that they are not the expression of the sought-after, lasting, true homeland. It may be that a disastrous drought contributed to the fall of the Indus civilization, as suggested by the mythical motif of the cloud-dragon Vrtra who retains the waters in his belly. At any rate, the formation of states, kingships and cities proved not to have been shaped by the wind and breath of truth and permanence. No, all that we see in those apparently magnificent deeds and works is nothing but "Maya," an illusion without substance; "Samsara," a blind and senseless hunting for prey, an eternal search, a blind cycle.

The Only Permanent Things: Mother (Primeval Ocean), Child (Vishnu), and the Power of Procreation (Shiva)

The Indus people had learned this from their own history, long before the invasion of the Aryans. Every civilization of gigantic size will eventually collapse of its own weight. It is only a question of time — but time is immeasurable. The Indus people were not too weak for revolt, but they would have been disloyal to themselves and to their convictions if they had attempted a violent rebellion to shake off the chains of alien rule. In so doing they would have committed themselves to "Samsara." All the oppression of the caste system notwithstanding, they remained faithful to themselves, to their quest for the lasting, for the "solar wind" which moved them from the beginning. They would not allow it to be mingled with the restless breath of the hunter. They remained loyal to that transcendent dimension which spoke to them in the experience of the mother, the sun, the rock and the endless sea. They opened themselves completely to this yearning for a calm and continuing procreative power and an eternal homeland.

The characteristic symbols of Indian spirituality did not arise from archetypal structures, but from this longing, this solar wind called forth by their experience of the world: Consider the god Vishnu who, like a self-absorbed child, plays on the maternal, primeval ocean, and in his slumber dreams the succession of the worlds.[14] Or the god Shiva, emerging from a phallus which rises from the primeval ocean to the unfathomable heights of the spheres. The god Brahma cannot reach its top when he flies up in the form of a bird. The god Vishnu cannot reach its bottom when, as a wild boar, he dives into the depth of the primeval ocean.[15] There the untamed violence of the wilderness-god has been transformed into an endlessly rising phallus of procreating power whose dance makes and destroys the worlds, continuing the cycle of becoming. Finally there is the goddess, the great mother, unsurpassably symbolized by the primeval ocean, the endless waters upon which Vishnu rests, from which the succession of the world ages arises, and to which they return, as into a mother's womb. Condensed into a "sea of milk,"[16] the primeval ocean makes manifest the superabundance and the richness of the mother who supports and feeds all.

Although this Great Mother does not hold the highest place in the cult, she nevertheless represents even more so than Shiva and Vishnu the all-embracing and protecting foundation of being in the mythical world of Indian spirituality (Fig. 41). This is shown beautifully in the myth of her origin, narrated in the Markendeya-Purana (81-93; also related and interpreted by Zimmer)[17]. She comes into being when all the gods, including Vishnu and Shiva, pour out their dynamic energy (one could say their "pneuma") and make it flow together in one single being, the goddess, just as they themselves had always been embraced and created by the primeval ocean. According to this tale, only this concentration of all divine essence in the mother (not, as one would expect, in Indra) is finally able to slay the terrible bull-demon who appears in ever more frightful figures of warriors and thus peace is brought to the universe. In Indian spirituality this domination of the female and maternal forces is present particularly in the many branches of the tantric tradition.[18] Brahma, the architect of the worlds, who is often named as one of the Indian divine triad, falls short in one dimension compared to this goddess as well as to Vishnu and Shiva: he is mortal. Together with the world cycle which he built, he sinks back into the divine primeval substance.

The concepts of the immensity of time and of the reincarnation of all life so characteristic of Indian thought also fit into this context. The many ages of the world that may last several millions of years—presently we live in the Kali-Yuga, an age (Yuga) of little moral substance—together form one "great Yuga," and one thousand "great Yugas" are one Brahma-day. One world cycle, and thereby one existence of Brahma, comes to an

Fig. 41: The maternal godhead as tree-goddess. She symbolizes fertility and victory over the wilderness-power; just as Baal stands on the bull, so she stands on an elephant (from the Buddhist stupa at Barhut).

204

end after one hundred Brahma-years (that is, 311,040,000,000,000 human years).[19] Any frenzy for world improvement drowns in this infinite space of time. In the unending chain of birth, death and rebirth the suffering and oppressed people find not only the hope that executioners will have no ultimate triumph over their victims — a hope that still belongs to the hunter and warrior — but also the appeasing faith that all, hangman and victim, conqueror and oppressed, hunter and prey, winner and loser, are integrated into the same cycle of becoming and perishing, and that their lives are judged by the same standards in the face of this law. This is not a wishful projection but a set of ideas and images in which man thinks and dreams about the promise of eternity, validity and permanence, that he was given by the transcendent dimension of the world which he encounters, by the mother, the sun, the rocks and the sea. In them the Hindu sees and experiences this lasting quality, the only true reality. Everything else — houses and palaces, plants and animals, men and gods, and the worlds in which they live — is mortal, subjected to the process of becoming and perishing.

The thought that even gods are mortal, which came from Indian spirituality, is alien to us Westerners. But, given the passionate devotion of the Hindu for Vishnu or Lakshmi and his deep veneration for Shiva, this idea must not be misunderstood as an early emergence of nihilistic or atheistic thought. The Great Mother remains, the sea of milk will never dry out, the sleeping child on the primeval ocean will never die, the pro-creating power of Shiva cannot wither. The idea of the mortality of the gods was not born out of sceptical resignation, as was the religious criticism in late Hellenism, but from focussing upon the truly permanent. From this quest for the eternal the Hindu has understood that man can never grasp the transcendent dimension of things which he perceives in animals, people and natural phenomena but he will always perceive it from his own perspective, from within the feeling in which he lives and breathes. Thus the hunter and warrior in the torrid country of India sees the sun-god riding fiery horses across the firmament while the peasant of the Nile delta sees the sun barque gliding peacefully along the belly of the celestial cow. The symbol which signifies the transcendent dimension may change, while that which is expressed in the symbol with differing individual accents — this transcendent dimension of sun and firmament, of mother and sea, of tree and rock, this common entity — remains unchanged. Due to their own special situation, the inhabitants of the Indus valley, subjugated by the Aryans, perceived these changes among the gods especially when they represented power, vitality and strength: Indras die and turn into ants, and ants, the hard working slaves, rise to the divine kingdom.

In a similar situation, the exiled and enslaved people of Israel called the gods of their conquerors "nothing":

They are all vanity;
their works are nothing;
their images are wind and confusion.

(Isa. 41, 29)

But here the tone is more belligerent: Yahweh enters into competition with the foreign gods. They are challenged to prove their divinity by predicting the future or by some miracle:

Tell us the things that are to come,
and so convince us you are gods.
Do something good or evil,
that will fill us with awe and fear.
No, you are nothing and your works are nothing;
to choose you is an abomination.

(Isa. 41, 23-24)

In the face of the foreign gods, the people of Israel, shaped by historical perception and historical experience, do not have the calmness and composure, nor the detachment of the Indian, who is formed more by the observation and experience of nature. This is why they utter terrible threats against the alien divinities and their followers.

But in that genuine "Christian" character which came from the Old Testament, and which the early Christian community related with Jesus was the figure of the suffering servant of Yahweh. Here the particular sensitivity of the Old Testament has created the image of a just man without violence, who, although "despised and rejected by men" (Isa. 53, 3), and "harshly dealt with" (Isa. 53, 7), did not defend himself with violence:

I gave my back to those who struck me...
I did not shield my face
from insult and spittle.

(Isa. 50, 6)

Without violence, he puts his trust in God: "He does not cry out or shout aloud, or make his voice heard in the streets" (Isa. 42, 2) and thus becomes the "light of the people":

to open the blind eyes,
to free the prisoners,
and those who live in darkness from the dungeon.

(Isa. 42, 6 f.)

More than did the people of Israel, the ancient people of the Indus valley lived according to this principle which was personified in our own time in the figure of Mahatma Gandhi. The new gods of the Aryans have raised themselves above the divine symbols of the ancient populations because of their power to kill (or, more accurately, because of that power in their followers), and have tried to subjugate them. But a god whose authority relies on a death-dealing power is perishable by comparison. Although Indra lives for seventy-one eons, it is only after twenty-eight Indras have come and gone that one single Brahma-day is over, and, as the story of the ants' parade makes clear, this is nothing compared to the eternity of Vishnu.[20] The man who approaches the transcendent dimension of reality and is still held in the enchantment of the killing-power will perceive it only in distortion. He can grasp only a relatively insignificant, perishable aspect of it and express it symbolically. If man wants to know and experience the transcendent dimension intensively and in an unobstructed way, he must free himself from the fatal attraction of killing. A man who abandons this attraction steps out of "Samsara," out of the confinement of the blind life, and enters the essential.

Calming the Breath Through Asceticism (Yoga, Jainism, Buddhism)

This is the structure of sensibility and belief which gave birth to the most ancient monastic movement on earth. If we follow recent studies that date the birth of Siddharta Gautama around 450 BC rather than 560 BC,[21] then Mahavira, the founder of Jainism, was active almost a century before Buddha. It is important to note that both Mahavira and Buddha came from the caste of warriors whose trade is killing. Originally Indian monasticism was the radical negation of the wind and breath of the killer, of the hunter and the warrior. "Ahimsa Paramo Dharma" ("Not to kill is the highest religion") is the motto that is inscribed in many Jaina temples and brings into focus the fundamental thought of this monastic religion. "Ahimsa" lies at the very center of Indian monastic spirituality. It marks the way towards salvation, towards the permanent homeland. Even today the Jaina monks express this spirituality symbolically by "breathing through a gauze cloth placed over their mouths, by brushing away insects on the road, and by filtering their drinking water — just to avoid swallowing living beings."[22]

Even today the monks of the Digambara school, the so-called "clothed in air," go naked in order to express their lack of any needs, which makes senseless any rivalry and any killing. Indian monasticism and asceticism is aimed at overcoming "Samsara," the world marked by hunting, preying, and killing. It is the attempt to return to a condition of humanity that predates the fascination with killing, before man's transition from gathering to hunting or, in Christian terms, before original sin. Buddha eventually turned away from the extreme asceticism which he himself practiced for seven years and embarked on the "middle path." He ate food once a day; he dressed, and took care of his body. On this path he achieved illumination after profound meditation and opened the way to Nirvana for his followers.

Buddha realized that the ascetic life which he had previously led was a form of violence against himself — Jainism, for example, accepts suicide by voluntary starvation — and that a fine line divides violence towards others and violence towards oneself. Nevertheless, he adopted the fundamental rules which even today characterize any kind of monasticism including Christian monasticism: celibacy, the renunciation of sexual fulfillment; poverty, the renunciation of the desire to possess; and the renunciation of the imposition on others of one's own will (in Christian terms: obedience). These are supplemented by seven other commandments that also apply to the lay person (e.g. not to lie, not to steal) or are simply elaborations of the basic monastic rules (e.g. not to eat when it is not allowed, not to sleep in a bed that is too large or comfortable, not to take part in feasts, etc.).

But the first and most important commandment, for the lay person as well as for the monk, is the commandment not to kill.[23] It is the foundation and the sum of all other commandments. This is very clear in the three commandments specific to the monks: Whoever renounces the satisfaction of his sexual desires, the greed for possession, and his own will, escapes the danger of having to compete against others, and therefore to be drawn into the malevolent cycle of violence and of killing. In the teachings and commandments of Buddhism this fundamental attitude of "Ahimsa," of not-killing, is much more internalized than in Jainism. Thus, for example, Jainas do not work as peasants because in the course of ploughing and working they would have to kill or damage plants and small animals. Yet, some have become rich industrialists and powerful merchants, even in economic systems that oppress others and in which children die from hunger — as in the Third World today. The Buddhist "Ahimsa," in contrast, internalizes the basic attitude of intending no harm to any creature but meeting them all with kindness. Still they share the idea of rising above a humanity bound by a cycle of violence and killing-power.

It is important to extinguish the breath of the warrior and the preying hunter. The central tenet of Indian ascetic techniques is therefore the so-called "prânâyâma" which is described in one Yoga-Sutra (II, 49) as a "ceasing" or "stopping" of the breath. This exercise consists in a gradual lengthening of inhalation and exhalation, the goal being to interpose an ever longer interval of rest. The religious historian Mircea Eliade, who describes this discipline of the breath in great detail,[24] relates that he himself had observed monks in an ashram who "spent a major part of the day and of the night in profound 'meditation,' during which time their breathing was barely perceptible."[25]

The goal of this calming of the breath is, in the Yoga-tradition of Hinduism, the liberation from the diversions of sensual perception, the overcoming of the multiplicity of activities directed towards individual objects, and the deep, calm concentration on the one act of breathing, in which the essence of life is revealed as something permanent and valid, independent of any action. From eternal becoming and perishing, man thus reaches the permanent and true.

In this form, focused on a definite goal, this breathing discipline still relates to Hinduism. Just as the people of the Megalithic cultures dragged immense rocks weighing over fifty tons for distances of more than thirty kilometers and piled them up with methods still unknown to us, and just as the Egyptians built their gigantic pyramids as funeral monuments in order to create something permanent, something that overcomes death, a lasting homeland, so the Yogi takes spiritual control over his bodily functions through an effort of utmost concentration, freezing into a stonelike trance beyond becoming and perishing. To the degree that the rise and fall, the in and out of breathing is levelled and comes close to stopping, to the degree that he ceases his individual breathing, the individual self, the "Atman" (etymologically related to the German *atmen*, to breathe) dissolves in the unchanging primeval substance of being, in the Brahman. In analogy to the breathing exercises of autogenous training, the "I breathe" becomes "it breathes me,"[26] which frees the individual from the self and produces the effect of levitation.

In the Upanishads, which were added to the Vedas probably after 800 BC, the ultimate goal of the human quest is still described in positive terms: It is "Sat" (essence, reality), "Satyam" (truth), "Jñánam," "Vijñánam" (knowledge), "Ánanda" (bliss, happiness), "Anantam" (eternity).[27] But the seers of the Upanishads were already conscious of the fundamental ineffability of the absolute. When the student comes to his master and tells him about an experience in which he thinks he might have found the Brahman, the Guru's stereotypical answer is: "Néti, Néti," "not this, not this!"[28] Anything that can be expressed (grasped, like the hunter's prey) is still not the ultimate.

On this path of gradual negation and abstraction the absolute becomes Nirvana in Buddhism. Hindu meditation techniques are adopted, of course, but their goal in Buddhism is no longer the active search for a state of being which is described positively, but rather the negative renunciation of all wishing, desiring, aiming. Even the orthodox

Buddhist of the most ancient schools (Hinayana and Teravada), even the ascetic who tries to reach and unite with the absolute through a trance resulting from rigorous control over his bodily functions, is still, as it were, the hunter who goes out for prey, even if that prey be the Brahman and union with it—just as the hunter sought unity with that which fascinated him in the animal by eating it and by wearing its skin.

Western philosophy and theology are also fundamentally skeptical of this arresting and powerful concept and the conscious aiming for a goal (even if it be God). The existential philosophy of Martin Heidegger tries to free thought from grasping and seizing its objects, and to bring it back to *Ver-nunft* (reason), to the *Vernehmen* (perception) of the claim of being which is addressed to man by all that exists. Erich Fromm's apology for *being* instead of *having* also belongs in this category.[29] The New Age movement has found in Fritjof Capra a scientist who sees in this perception of a non-acquisitive way of thinking the salvation of our earth, threatened as it is by scientific-technological *exploitation*.[30] In theology, the "via negationis" of Karl Barth's dialectic theology is in keeping with the way of Buddhism.[31] It understands every religious endeavor of man, including all the manifestations of religious history, as ultimately sinful, as an attempt to usurp God. This includes especially the justification by works which had already been criticized by Luther, and according to which the kingdom of God and eternal bliss can be hunted down by fulfilling the law and by accumulating good works. But it also includes all other forms of pre-Christian and non-Christian spirituality. According to this theology, the tremendous efforts of Megalithic cultures, the construction of the Egyptian pyramids, as well as the trance of the Yogi achieved through the harshest asceticism, are, in the symbolic language which we use here, nothing but gigantic hunting projects, an expression of the breath of the hunter as he goes after his prey. What we had called "solar wind" is interpreted as nothing more than an augmented hunter's breath.

There is, however, a great difference between these two attitudes to life and culture. It is true that even agriculture and animal husbandry can become an exploitation. We certainly experience in our world today a merciless hunt for prey, a squandering of resources, ruthless exploitation of the soil and brutal treatment of animals for the sake of higher "productivity." In such cases, agriculture is practiced in the manner of the game-hunter. But originally the farmer's way of cultivating plants that, as Herbig thinks, sought out man in the first place[32] and the harvesting of the ripened fruits and bulbs was not at all like the hunter's way of going after prey with the intention of killing it. The true farmer adapts to the rhythm of the seasons. He orders his life in accordance with the growing forces of nature. The fear of a weakening of these forces does prompt him to offer sacrifices as well. But this fear of death is an inheritance of the hunter's existence. It is this which eventually changes the "solar wind" into the hunter's breath.

But the very root of the Neolithic effort was a true, fresh beginning. Wherever man looks for a permanent homeland, by opening himself to the transcendent dimension which speaks to him from the woman and mother, from the trees and plants, from the sun and the stars, from the far-reaching ocean and towering cliffs, wherever he tries to establish a close contact with these symbols, and to root his life in them, his endeavor is not a hunt and the result is not a hunted prey. A quest of this kind is not a hunting expedition. Rather, in it man sets out on an extremely difficult but straight path which lies ahead of him. He is not lurking, waiting for the right moment to strike and to kill. It may be true that among these people, who were nomad hunters for hundreds of thousands of years, the passion for the hunt may rise again and again, so that they turn back and hunt their fellow-men as prey. Even so, the effort to keep to the path and resist the fascination of the hunter's life is something new. The aging Hindu, after he has lived in affirmation of the world — sensual pleasure (kama), possessions (artha), civic and ritual obligations (dharma) are also religiously motivated goals for him — and after his children are grown and his duties towards his fellow men are fulfilled, retires into the wilderness or the solitude of an ashram. Under the direction of a master he now strives to achieve this permanence and validity, this homeland from within, which he had honestly tried to achieve through his external activities. This step is neither an escape from the world, nor an attempt to conquer God. It is, rather, the expression of pure loyalty to the "solar-wind" that first animated him.

The monastic movements, however, were more radical. Mahavira, the founder of Jainism, and Buddha, both the sons of warriors, resisted the hunter's and warrior's breath so radically, that they denounced any kind of aiming at a goal. Their followers do not proceed towards a goal, but rather turn away from people who have goals and are trying to achieve them. Buddha does not seek a new breath — a "solar wind" or a "pneuma hagion," for example, instead of the hunting breath — but seeks his "Nibbána," his ultimate extinction. In the most ancient description of Nirvana as the third of the four "Noble Truths," the word Nirvana doesn't even appear, but it is only negatively paraphrased as "the total ending (Niródha), the complete renunciation of desire, liberation (Mutti), the separation from lust."[33] Buddha himself did not speak frequently about the Nirvana. Nobody was to be tempted to desire Nirvana and thus to enter again the cycle of violence and slaying.

Later, however, especially in Mahjájána Buddhism, Nirvana is described positively once again in a way that is similar to the Brahman of the Upanishads. It is peace, comfort, truth, rest, liberation, purity and bliss. But as in the Hindu Bhakti devotion, the speculation over this ultimate goal of human life and the means of attaining it are essentially linked with an attitude of personal love. A person can, and indeed must, help others on his way to the eternal homeland. He can communicate to his fellow men the positive karma that he has accumulated and thereby help them achieve their goal. The ideal figure is the Bodhisattva who has in fact reached his destination, but renounces Nirvana voluntarily and commits himself to entering the cycle of life once again in order to help other men and other beings—until all creatures are rescued and brought to Nirvana. The Bodhisattva is, like the suffering servant of Yahweh of the Old Testament, a sort of antithesis of the hunter. He exposes himself to the cycle of violence and killing without actively involving himself, and thus can break it for himself and for others after a long and difficult journey.

Thus, from its beginnings in the history of the pre-Aryan Indus culture through the various diversified forms of its development and up to the broad, dazzling spectrum of contemporary far-Eastern religions, Indian spirituality is deeply affected by the search for liberation from the chase and the search for rest and peace. Indian spirituality is about calming the breath. It strives to extinguish the breath of the hunter and to keep the solar wind, the quest for permanence, from becoming too violent, from growing into a storm, and thereby changing into a hunting wind. If it seeks motion at all, it is similar to the motion of the "cool of the day" of Paradise in which Yahweh walks, and to the slight breeze in which Yahweh appeared to Elias on sacred Mount Horeb. Heinrich Zimmer, a keen observer of the symbols of Indian spirituality and its iconography, says that Indian representations of super-terrestrial beings are almost never provided with wings, as is customary in the representations of the love-goddess from ancient Sumerian cylinder seals, in the winged sun-disk of ancient Egypt, in the widespread symbolism of birds in the Mediterranean and in American Indian cultures, in the Seraphim of the Old Testament, and in the angels of the New Testament.[34] Only Garuda, the wild duck on which Vishnu rides, soars through the universe in a straight flight and with a rhythmic beating of its wings.

Indian Spirituality and the Breath of Jesus

The "pneuma hagion," the wind and breath of Jesus and of his Abba, is also a soothing breath, in comparison to the "ruach Yahweh." Notwithstanding the gospel story about the expulsion of the merchants from the temple,[35] the breath which moves Jesus is not at all like the breath of Yahweh. The "pneuma hagion" is not a "fuming rage," which drowns

212

the Egyptians in the Red Sea. The wind of war of the Apocalypse, when the horn is blown and the dreadful cups of wrath are poured over the world, is more a recollection of the Old Testament (there are several occurrences in the New Testament) than a manifestation of the breath of Jesus. To be sure, this breath can swell into a "powerful wind" descending from heaven with a great noise and making tongues of fire appear (Acts 2, 2 f.), but its character remains that of the dove's breath which announces, in the sermon given by Peter, salvation to the people and the overcoming of death (Acts 2, 14-36).

The breath of Jesus has much in common with the "solar-wind" and the Indian calming of the breath, yet its origin is entirely different. The experience out of which it comes is not an objective phenomenon, like the sun, the stars, the sea, the mountain, the woman and mother, but a human *event*. Wherever human beings are abandoned—in need, sickness, and distress—and cry for help, it responds. The old, protective God of the nomadic tribes of Israel hears "the groaning of the sons of Israel, enslaved by the Egyptians," and he remembers his covenant and says to them: "I am Yahweh (I am the "I-am-here"). I will free you of the burdens which the Egyptians lay on you...I will adopt you as my people, and I will be your God" (Exod. 6, 5-7). The Old Testament still mentions a salvation "with my arm outstretched and mighty acts of judgment" (Exod. 6, 6), but these features disappear in the figure of the suffering servant of Yahweh. In Jesus' discourse Yahweh becomes the "Father in heaven" who "causes his sun to rise on bad men as well as good, and his rain falls on just and unjust alike" (Matt. 5, 45). When, at the end, despite his defense of his rights, Jesus in his innocence is condemned to die on the cross, he prays for his executioners, filled with this dove's breath (Luke 23, 34).

Both "ruach Yahweh" and "pneuma hagion" are a wind and breath rising from the victim's misery and distress. At the same time, this wind is the force and dynamism that saves the victim from subscribing to the sacrificial ideology and thus consecrating the mechanism of violence and killing. From the victim's cry of distress it produces the force which heals and saves. From the silent cry of the outcast poor of Israel at the time of Jesus, the breath of the Sermon on the Mount ascends and blesses these poor. The cry of distress with which the father of the epileptic boy calls to Jesus: "I do believe. Help the little faith I have" (Mark 9, 24) finds resonance in the breath of Jesus and leads to the healing of the son. The blind beggar at the gate of Jericho, who will not comply with the role forced upon him as someone punished by God and sentenced to silent forbearance, instead shouts out to the Rabbi Jesus for help. Scolded by the by-standers, he is answered: "Your faith has saved you" (Mark 10, 52). At this point Jesus casts off even the symbol of the suffering servant.

Although the earliest sections of the Passion story mention Jesus' silence before the council and before Pilate, it is part of the story's structure that he breaks his silence in the end and cries out his agony on the cross. It was this cry that opened the world to God,[36] and disclosed to all people those heavens that had already opened for Jesus in the baptism at the river Jordan, and had called to him as son in the descending dove-wind.

The "pneuma hagion" articulates the creature's cry of distress that contains the force of salvation. It is an event taking place inside the human person. In his utmost distress the suffering creature is seized by the divine gift of a wind that makes him cry from the depths of his soul, silently or audibly. By the force of this cry he promptly calls forth that presence which grants him salvation. This is the gospel, the good news of the healing wind and breath. None of the innumerable beings who have cried aloud or silently in their agony have cried in vain. Even if it seems as if those cries die away without resonance in the empty and dead spaces of the cosmos — for many this is their understanding of Jesus — Christians have experienced the events surrounding Jesus in a different way. All, good and evil, who have like Jesus cried out in their agony, are confident that "the prayer was heard" (Heb. 5, 7). Thus, despite all its similarities to the Indian calming of the breath (and to "the solar-wind"), the origin of the healing and saving wind of the Abba is different. It is a *new* wind which surges up when the hunter slays his victim and the victim cries out in misery and distress. This wind and breath of the powerless and the persecuted will overcome the hunter's breath, which has been blowing for millions of years, in a historical process that will force it to change direction. When this happens, the seemingly powerless breath of the crying victim is revealed as the wind and breath that liberates the solar-wind usurped by the hunter and thereby fulfills the promise contained in the sun, in the stars, in the woman and mother, and in the lakes and mountains.

3 Father/Mother as Divine Symbol

In a study of religious history or religious psychology it would be well to begin with the divine symbols of the "father" and of the "mother." The great mother and the divine father feature prominently in early religions. In terms of developmental psychology, the mother and the father, on whom the infant and the little child depend totally, appear necessarily as something absolute from the child's perspective, as the basis and shelter of its existence, as an existential point of reference. But Christianity does not begin with such an idea of God. The foundation of Christianity is the crucified Christ who lives beyond death. It is not the merciful, nourishing and sustaining image of the father or mother, leaning down to the small and helpless child, which stands at the origin of this religion. On the contrary, Christianity finds its symbol in God speaking first from within the helpless, abandoned being, from within the child itself. In its cry of distress the divine appears and the breath which carries this cry, the cry for father and mother, is the healing breath of God which changes the world and initiates the history of salvation. Only that which responds to this breath of the child—whoever or whatever comes in response to this childlike cry for nourishment, warmth and security—is "father" and "mother" in the Christian sense, and as such is a divine symbol. Father and mother are the answer to the crying of the child—the holy, helping response to abandonment and need. In their care for the child, the father and mother emanate the same wholesome, healing breath as the child so that they are united by *one* breath.

From a biological point of view, father and mother come before the child. They conceive it. But as procreators they are not yet father and mother. A child who is not personally acknowledged by its procreator or the one who bore it may well have a procreator and a bearer, but no father and mother. The father becomes a father and the mother becomes a mother only in the moment when a helpless child cries, and when they turn to that child to help it. Man and woman conceive the child. But it is only the breath and the cry of the child which conceives the mother in the woman and the father in the man.

Thus, the symbolism of father and mother comes at the end of an examination of the Trinitarian tradition in the light of the "economy of salvation" and of its corresponding symbolism. Only when we are immersed in this breath of childlike existence, when, with the fullest confidence we are borne by the breath of the Abba, do we surrender to the abandonment of the child. (Martin Heidegger speaks of the " 'being-thrown-into' of human existence.") Only when we have been baptized in

215

such a way, can we invoke God as the transcendent dimension of life and of the world, as Abba. Only thus can we be freed from the slavery of finitude and become the sons and daughters of the heavenly father (Rom. 8, 15).

In the next section we will first investigate, as in the preceding chapters, the experience of God corresponding to the experience of father and mother within the Bible. This experience will then be brought into dialogue with corresponding phenomena in religious history in order to reveal its particular character within that context.

3.1 Father/Mother as Divine Symbol in the Bible

God as "Lord and Father"? On the Approach of Dialectical Theology

"Lord" and "Father" are the names for God most frequently used in the Bible. In the Old Testament the word "Lord" is very clearly the predominant one, rather than "Father." In the New Testament the situation is reversed. Here, the name "Father" prevails, especially in Jesus' prayers. Exegetical scholarship unanimously agrees that Jesus never addressed God as "Father" but as "Abba," even if it survives at only one place in the gospel (Mark 14, 36). In all other instances, this Aramaic word has been translated as "Father".[1] The word "Lord" in the New Testament is used above all for the crucified and risen Jesus. The famous hymn to Christ in the epistle to the Philippians says that every tongue should "confess that Jesus Christ is Lord, to the glory of God the Father" (Phil. 2, 11).

How should these names of God be handled? Karl Barth, whose perspective is focused principally on revelation, states: "The fact that God is our Father is not to be measured against our natural human fatherhood (Isa. 63, 16). It is rather from the fatherhood of God that natural human fatherhood derives its significance and dignity."[2] It is not important to Barth that the authors of the biblical texts refer to God as "Father" nor why they do so. These and similar words are only the "instruments" which God uses in order to manifest himself to man despite his total otherness.[3] But when this happens, the traditional content of human words which transmit this event is transcended. The word "father" is used in an "improper" way. "When Scripture calls God the Father, it takes up an analogy and transcends it immediately."[4] God is the father of Jesus Christ. This relation not only defines the fatherhood

216

of God, but should define fatherhood in general. The issue is to go beyond "whatever we know otherwise as relation between father and son" through the word of Christ, the crucified and risen, and to interpret the relation of father and son in his light.

In a certain way this view is correct. The "world" of man, as it is shaped by language, does not emerge from the blind game of evolution, but from the manner in which the transcendent dimension of things is perceived by man and is used as the basis which gives meaning to his existence. When Jesus the Crucified is recognized as the source and meaningful foundation of human existence, rather than all other hierophanies and theophanies; when from this source this ground of existence appears as Abba who hears the cry of agony of the Crucified, and stoops down to save him in his distress — then a man who, for example, would procreate a child by rape, is not yet "father" (as mentioned above) according to the Christian conception (in so far as the word "father" has anything to do with "abba"). But in my opinion Barth's theological insight is erroneous when he says that through the coming of Christ a human word is given a significance "which it cannot have of itself."[5] For human language is in its origin the answer of that living being, who (because of his evolution) was one day able to perceive the transcendent dimension of things and events, and to react to them. Language existed before the Fall. Indeed, the Fall was only possible because of the emerging faculty to perceive the transcendent dimension and to react to it with an answer. To be sure, original sin has shaped our linguistic behavior in a decisive way. In seeking an answer to the transcendent dimension of things, the linguistic behavior of the game-hunter changed from answering as the founder of a community to answering as a predator who captured, analyzed and classified his prey. But this usurpation of words and language is directed precisely against their original meaning and direction. The salvation which occurred in the messiah Jesus does not involve the construction of a new language or new words, but it means that we are freed from our usurping linguistic behavior, and can find our way back to the original use of words which precedes sin. The biblical story of the El-Shaddai, the god of terror who reveals himself first as God "I-am-here," and eventually as Abba in Jesus, can also heal our linguistic behavior and can lead us to the original significance of the word "father" and to the proper way of using it.

If in the course of re-living and re-feeling this history of salvation, we do not remain in our naturally and historically given world and do not bring this story into a healing dialogue with our given universe, but instead interpret the history of salvation as a shattering of the given world which is then to be replaced by a totally new universe sent forth from the God who revealed himself — then, inadvertently, the very same old patterns of behavior and of thought from which we were meant to be saved and freed by the story of Yahweh and Jesus may come creeping in again. This becomes evident in Karl Barth's interpretation of the name of God as "Father." In the following pages we will discuss this, using the example of his interpretation of the parable of the merciful father.

Barth derives the content of the name "Father" for the God of Jesus from the figure of the merciful father and his relation to his son. God as father is "the father of the son, who died and lives again, was lost and is found again (Luke 15, 32)."[6] Indeed, the parable of the merciful father expresses fully what God, Father, and Abba mean for Jesus, and thus for Christians. In this parable Jesus draws the symbol of the father in such a way that it becomes totally transparent, and any man, who enters the world of this symbol, comes face to face with the one and only Abba: before the countenance of the one who has been revealed as God by Jesus.

The association of the prodigal son "who had died and comes to life again" with Jesus and his fate is astounding, especially for Karl Barth. Even most recently, Eugen Biser has drawn this parallel within an existential and biographical interpretation of the parable. And indeed, the point of the parable is not the moral guilt of the son or his liberation from culpability. The father cuts short the confession that the son had prepared for his arrival by embracing him. What is important is not what the son has done but that he was lost and is found again. Now this is precisely the fate of Jesus. Rejected by his people, the chosen people of Israel; sentenced as a blasphemer by its leaders; delivered to the hated, occupying forces, the Romans; cursed and handed over to death on the cross — Jesus suffers the prodigal son's misery and distance from God. But when he turns to his Abba in his cry of agony, he sinks into the arms of the merciful father who has always waited for his son, and in this life beyond death, beyond the reach of any human violence or brutality, proclaims him Son of God (Rom. 1, 4).

In this story the name "father" and its true meaning is saved from the darkness and corruption caused by man's sin, in his transition to unnatural predatory behavior, by his usurpation of the power to kill. The patriarchal features of the father disappear of their own accord, through the dynamics of narrative language. He is infinitely different from the Lord and father, the "pater familias" of the Roman-Hellenistic world, who held the "ius vitae necisque," the authority over the life and death of all the inhabitants of his household, and had the power to dispose of a child, to give it away for marriage or adoption, or to set it free. Parts of the Old Testament also show the signs of such an absolute paternal power, such as the Book of the Covenant, in which we find a discussion of the special status of a female slave who has been sold into slavery by her father (Exod. 21, 7-11). The story of Jesus and the story of the prodigal son make it crystal clear that such an absolute ruling power has nothing at all to do with the reality which is called "Father." Even a sexist separation of the roles of father and mother is overcome. The merciful father is the good mother as well, who sets free her child, the fruit of her womb, by cutting the umbilical cord, and allowing the child to go out into foreign lands. Yet this mother embraces her child even at the greatest distance and in spite of alienation, with that love which in the midst of misery awakens the memory of the father's house and of maternal protection. The arms of the Father, into which the Crucified sinks when he dies, in order to be carried by them into a new life, become one with the arms of the Pietà, which receive the dead body and endow him with new life (Fig. 53).

For Karl Barth, however, the essence of the father revealed by the gospels lies in his patriarchal authority, in total inconsistency with his primary source, the parable of the merciful father. He faces us "...without obligation, but rather with absolute power at his disposal."[7] This is the Roman "pater familias," lord over the life and death of his children. Indeed, this father even *wills* the death of his son and our death: "...his will enters the life of men when he enforces death, when he marks man with the sign of death." Even if he wills our death "in order to lead us beyond death into eternal life,"[8] he nevertheless wills our earthly death. But the merciful father of the parable did not wish for the abandonment and the death of his son, any more than the Abba wished for the rejection and the cruel death of his own beloved son. Both are, rather, the work of sinful humans, who are seaching for prey, trying to usurp a seemingly divine authority by their killing acts. The fact that the Father has let these things happen and did not intervene with twelve legions of angels (Matt. 26, 53 f.) dramatically expresses again the fact that authority and the power to kill are not the attributes of this fatherhood, and that only without violence can love be love. The Father is not the "Lord over life and death" — he is the fount of eternal life.

This and only this is the correct understanding of fatherhood spoiled by sin as it is introduced by the gospels. The patriarchal father is still the hunter, who in the act of procreation uses his phallus as a weapon, like the shaman in the Lascaux cave, in order to appropriate the procreated children as prey. A theology that transfers this understanding of fatherhood to God has not yet abandoned the mentality of the hunter. This mind-set has not yet been abandoned if we imagine God as the "Lord of all being," as the "Lord over life and death," in other words, as the great hunter who, alone among all beings of the universe, has the absolute power to kill, offering the whole world and ourselves as submissive sacrifices, as his prey. But the truth is that Jacob faces the dark godhead at the dangerous ford and wrestles down his dark power in a fierce struggle, until the rising sun drives away all obscurity. Jacob is left with the blessing and only a small scar (Gen. 32, 23-33). This wrestling match is the lasting task of Isra-El, of the fighter with God, until Jesus completes this struggle and sees Satan, the violent-demonic aspect of God, falling down from heaven like lightning (Luke 10, 18).[9]

Even for Paul Tillich, well known as an opponent of Karl Barth in his religious interpretation of culture, lordship and fatherhood belong together. They supplement each other: "A Lord who is not father, is a demon; a father who is not Lord is merely sentimental."[10] This idea is very widespread. In the great dictionary of the New Testament (begun by G. Kittel), H. Kuhn says that "the power of lordship and paternal care" belong together indissolubly and that it is only through this unity that they can answer all petitions "in time and in eternity."[11] For him, 'Father' always and simultaneously signifies 'Lord.'[12] Wherever this equation does not hold, the image of the father is emasculated. The merciful father of the parable would thus be only one aspect of the message of Jesus, the other aspect being that of the universal judge coming on the clouds of heaven to curse the evil and sentence them to eternal torture (Matt. 25, 41).[13]

The Merciful Father is Sufficient

Is this really so? Does the merciful father of the Parable of the Prodigal Son need to be improved upon? Is he "merely sentimental," who is not Lord but pure Abba? This judgment is superficial. Indeed, because the father is and expresses nothing but pure love he is "dangerous" in a certain sense. Because he is only Abba and not the lord over his son's life, the son is free in his decision. The father does not prevent him from making wrong decisions which drag him down into misery. There is no word about any attempts made by the father, either through violence or persuasion, to prevent the son from taking his share of the inheritance and leaving with it for a foreign country. The son wills it and the father complies with his son's will. He does not send any messengers or letters after him to exhort him to lead a good life or to promise help in case he should experience hardship. Love leaves the loved one free. It does not take away his independence by providing a security net, as it were, secretly installed to rescue him from the fall that might follow his free decision. Whatever the son wills happens with all its consequences. Thus the son of the chosen people, the Jew, who becomes unclean by touching animals, especially unclean pigs, ends up as the herdsman of pigs in a pagan household. He craves even the food of the animals entrusted to him. This was really considered death for a Jew in those times. Indeed, the prodigal son might seem even further away from Yahweh than the deceased in the underworld for whom the sun no longer shines and who no longer praise Yahweh.

But one thing accompanies the son on his journey into foreign countries, in his "unbridled lifestyle," and even in the deepest misery of death: the powerless and non-violent love of the father. This love would continue even if the son were to wander to the farthest galaxies and commit the most hateful crimes. The father who has given him absolute freedom is always there for him. In Egypt he has made himself manifest as the God "I-am-here." Never, in all eternity, will he lose this identity. But this means two things. On the one hand, it gives the prodigal son the possibility of remembering his father. He has no reason to erase the memory of his father because he was not insulted or cursed when he left home. In his distress the image of the father rises and invites him back, silently, without violence, and without force. The son is free to accept the invitation or to reject it. In any event, whether explicitly stated or not, the return is a confession of his own failure. There is the obvious danger that the son will harden his heart in obstinacy and prefer to perish in the foreign land with the unclean pigs rather than admit his failure. In a culture of hunters and warriors such obdurate behavior might even seem heroic. But in reality it would be hell.

For hell does not consist in material lack and physical pain. Its essence is rather a sense of absolute deprivation of meaning. It is the unending, desperate clinging to an abysmal "No" towards love. In the meaninglessness of this negation, life simultaneously freezes into an icy desert and melts away into a "lake of burning sulphur" (Rev. 20, 10). The searing emptiness of this negation is the result of its having no enemy to attack. For the father utters no demands against which one might rebel and thus create an existence. Only a free refusal of this invitation is absolutely deprived of meaning and thereby becomes hell.

The son who remained at home is confronted with this decision between heaven and hell even more explicitly than the prodigal son is. When he heard the music and the dancing to celebrate the return of his brother, he became "angry and refused to go in" (Luke 15, 28 f.). But his father comes out to him and turns towards him in his conciliatory love to "plead with him." The son, however, begins to rail against the father as an unjust patriarch: "All these years I have slaved for you and never once did I disobey your orders, yet never did you offer me so much as a kid for me to celebrate with my friends. But, now this son of yours, comes back after gambling away your property — he and his women — and you kill the fatted calf for him." But the negative image of

221

the harsh and all-powerful father, of the patriarchal lord with violence at his command, which the son constructs in order that his rebellion be meaningful, vanishes like a ghost in the embrace of the loving father. "My son, you are with me always and all I have is yours. But it was only right that we should celebrate and rejoice, because your brother was dead and has come to life; he was lost and is found." The story does not go on to tell us whether the older son persisted in his mood of anger and rejection. If he did so, he could articulate it only as a profoundly meaningless "no"; and this would convert his world where he stood outside in his negation, into a hell.

Thus the theological precondition of hell is *not* the commanding overlord, the almighty judge, but, on the contrary, a non-violent, unconditional love. The lord and judge would be an opponent who could give rise to our negation and provide it with meaning. Sisyphus, pushing gigantic rocks to the top of the mountain in his titanic pride, well knowing that they will tumble down again every time, is not a son of hell. For his action, even if it can never achieve its superficial, primary purpose, is nevertheless meaningful, as an expression of promethean and titanic resistance against the arbitrary rule of the gods. Only the existence of a non-violent and absolute love opens the possibility of a hell, because its negation is absolutely without meaning. If that love did not exist, everything—titanic obstinacy, loving surrender, death and life, pain and joy—would sink back into the dark primeval ocean from which the universe arises, as in the story of Vishnu. Everything would dissolve into nothingness. If, on the other hand, this love was also absolute lord, all powerful king, and pitiless judge, life in hell could be understood as a form of heroism and give it a purpose, and thus nullify "hell" in the theological sense.

Thus the symbolic content of the Abba, as it appears in the parable of the merciful father, in no way calls for a complement. On the contrary, any extension of the unconditional love of the father into the form of a lord and judge would reduce the unfathomable and dangerous aspect of this God; it would be truly "sentimental." Only the unconditional love of the Abba holds within it eternal being and life, which takes the form of heaven or of hell, according to man's free decision. The Abba is sufficient: "solo abba basta."[14] He encompasses everything: being and life, heaven and hell.

God as our Mother (Pope John Paul I)

The great theological significance for the Church of the thirty-three day pontificate of the Luciani-Pope John Paul I is that relations of the kind mentioned above were articulated by the highest ecclesiastic authority. In his catechisms and public addresses he interpreted with great insight the father symbols, as expressions of the essence of God, through the mother symbol, because it expresses even more intensely unconditional, non-violent love. In each of his weekly general audiences (he gave only four), he lovingly mentioned his mother and the unconditional love he had experienced from her. He repeatedly mentioned that as a child he was often sick and that his mother had to carry him from one doctor to another, and spent many nights by his bed.[15] His own attitude towards his mother became for him the archetypal image of faith in God. When his mother told him about how she had cared for him and asked him, " 'Do you believe me?', how could I have said: 'No, Mother, I don't believe you! — Of course I believe, I believe what you say, but above all I believe in you.' And so it is with faith. It is not only important to believe what God has revealed, but to believe in him, who merits our faith, who has loved us so much, and who has done so much for us."[16] God's tenderness towards us is so great that "it surpasses even the tenderness of a mother towards her child, as the prophet Isaiah says."[17]

In this attitude of humility the Luciani-Pope knew that he was not facing a "Lord and Father" — whom he had to face like a hunted deer, and to whom he had to surrender — but he felt like a child before his mother. "Before God we have to feel small. When I say: 'Lord, I believe,' I am not ashamed to feel like a child before his mother; one's mother can be trusted."[18] He devoted his last general audience on September 27, 1978, entirely to a "word by word" explanation of a prayer taught to him by his mother. The prayer spoke about our love of God and the love of God for us. "My God, I love you with my whole heart and more than everything else, unending good and eternal blessedness..."[19] And then the Pope (who would die two nights later suddenly and unexpectedly) explained that the love of God means "to begin a journey towards God. This journey is beautiful."[20]

For the Luciani-Pope it is a journey towards his mother. During the few public addresses of the thirty-three days of his pontificate, he repeatedly referred to the passage in Isaiah 49, 15, in which the prophet compares the relation between man and God to the relation between an infant and its mother: "Does a woman forget her baby at the breast, or fail to cherish the son of her womb? Yet even if these forget, I will never forget you." For Pope John Paul I this promise is the biblical answer to the complaint of the Israeli Prime Minister Menachem Begin, when he read this passage in his common prayer with President Carter at Camp David: "You have abandoned us, you have forgotten us." "No," is the answer of the Luciani-Pope: "can a mother forget about her own child? And even if that happened, God would never forget his people...He is our father; even more, he is also our mother."[21]

223

For the Pope, the divinity of God consists in this paternal love which is not lordly, but motherly, in his all-embracing being and life. In his address on the Angelus prayer on September 24, he reminded his listeners of the sixteen Carmelites of Compiègne who were executed during the French Revolution and quoted the words of the prioress when she climbed the scaffold: "Love will always overcome, love can accomplish everything." He added: "That is the right word: Not violence, but love can accomplish everything."[22]

But there is one thing it cannot accomplish. It cannot curse people and send them to eternal torture. One might conceive of a despotic "Lord and Father" who, in the exercise of his sovereign power, rescues the child lying helplessly before him and, because of a perceived worthlessness, abandons it once more in the wilderness. But a paternal symbol interpreted in its motherly quality renders such a possibility inconceivable. Such a maternal father may well punish the child before it comes of age with the intention of correction. "God has to punish—especially if I offer resistance. When he comes running after me, asks me to come back, and I say, 'No!' I literally force him to punish me. That is unpleasant. But it is the truth of the faith."[23] Yet he cannot condemn; as a maternal father he cannot freely and consciously inflict something on his children which, ultimately, is evil. In the same breath with which the pope says of God the Father, "He is also our mother," he adds, "He does not want to do evil to us, he wishes only to do good to all of us. When children are sick, they have an even greater right to be loved by their mother. And we too, when we are sick with evil, or when we stray from the right path, have an even greater right to be loved by the Lord."[24] This is God in the symbol of the Abba, in the symbol of the good shepherd who leaves ninety-nine sheep in the desert, and goes after the lost one until he finds it (Luke 15, 4 f.), and in the symbol of the merciful father who says to the older son who had stayed at home, "My son, you are with me always and all I have is yours. But it was only right we should celebrate and rejoice, because your brother here was dead and has come to life; he was lost and is found" (Luke 15, 31 f.).

From El to Abba: Biblical Truth as History

The present book tries to understand the history of salvation as a history of the revelation of the Abba symbol. At the beginning of this history stands the violent appropriation, the usurpation of that dimension which is perceived by the dawning human conscience as transcending material reality, and therefore as a "divine" dimension in things. Because the primeval gatherer and hunter kills the "great animal" by piercing it with a spear in a perverted, quasi-sexual act, establishing himself as an unnatural predator, the experience of the divine becomes fundamentally linked to death and terror. Through adhering to certain laws and respecting certain taboos, this god of terror, whose reality and presence is made palpable by ever new sacrificial slayings, enters into a contract with mankind, which allows man to live in the face of this divine terror, and to eke out a restricted sort of livelihood. In this relation, shaped by law-abiding behavior and obedience, the god of terror develops paternal and merciful features for those who submit to him, and whom he favors in the writing of the laws. Although he faces the enemies of his chosen people with his original power of terror, he becomes a blessing for his people. He becomes their protector. This situation is set forth very clearly in the often mentioned passage of Exodus (Exod. 6, 3), in which Yahweh says that he had appeared to the forefathers, to Abraham, Isaac and Jacob, not as Yahweh, but as El-Shaddai (god of terror), and had formed a covenant with them. This is also confirmed by the fact that certain texts of the five books of Moses (the Pentateuch) use El or Elohim as the divine name.

In the biblical history of revelation this protective and caring aspect of the original El is intensified in two steps. The first intensification occurs in the liberation of Moses' people from Egypt. Here the experience of God's liberating and protective force was so strong that it was recognized as the true inner essence of El, whose name therefore took on the meaning "I-am-here." In biblical language this means that in the liberation from the slavery of Egypt, El has revealed his name Yahweh, I-am-the-"I-am-here." All the texts of the Old Testament, in which the caring aspect of El is stressed, and his love is expressed in commands and instructions, disclose this Yahweh doctrine as the center and root of the belief of Moses' people. Apart from the psalms, these texts are found for the most part in the books of the prophets, whether they point out the maternal care of Yahweh, or criticize cultic practices and sacrifices by extolling the primacy of ethical actions and of a proper moral attitude, or draw the ideal image of the "son" of Israel in the figure of the suffering servant of Yahweh, who renounces all violence and hands himself over to men in absolute confidence in Yahweh. As is revealed particularly in his parables, Jesus stands precisely in this tradition of thought and feeling, which goes back unquestionably to the revelation of Yahweh. In Jesus, therefore, the self-revelation of El as saving and caring is condensed into maternal, healing love. This is the second step in the intensification of the protective and caring aspect of El. El becomes the maternal, healing Abba of all mankind. As such he becomes alive in a new and powerful way in Jesus and in all men who open themselves to him, thereby ushering in the "malkût Yahweh," the kingdom of God, which for centuries Israel had longed for and which has been realized and perfected in Jesus, a realization and perfection anticipating the ultimate goal of the entire evolution of humankind.

This is, in a nutshell, the history of biblical revelation. It is a history in which the symbolic content of the encounter with the divine is metamorphosed from the terrorizing killing-power into the maternal, loving father. The Bible is a holy, that is, a healing scripture because it tells this story to man in a credible way, and thereby saves him and sets him free from within, from within the realm of his experience of life.

Here, also, is where the *truth* of the Bible lies. This truth does not consist in the correctness of individual sentences, nor in the assumption that each of its parts, from beginning to end, already holds the complete revelation of God (and refers to human actions from within that ethos). It lies instead in the fact that the essence of God as maternal love unfolds in a many-layered process throughout biblical history, beginning with the darkness of the terrorizing power to kill. Because we as human beings, in our earthly life, are only on the way to perfection, we would be ill-served if only the end of the biblical history were revealed to us — God as the love of the Abba. Rather, each of us, like biblical history, must find his own path away from the fascination of the killing-power and towards the veneration of maternal love. Only as a book which also reveals the "dark aspect of Elohim" (Martin Buber) can the Bible be a real help to man, and a protective companion on his life's journey. The triune God, who pours forth his wind and breath from the abandoned being — the child — and whose motherly and healing breath makes visible the loving caring Abba, is not an entity that can be acknowledged in a doctrinal, abstract way; he is rather that which fills man with the hope of being the embraced and perfected child when he dies.

We will now have to bring this biblical revelation of God, as it is articulated in the symbol of father/mother, into a dialogue with religious history.

3.2 Father as Divine Symbol in Religious History

On the Evolution of the Paternal Symbol

A major characteristic of the formation of social hierarchies within higher mammals, "especially among the anthropoid apes, Makaken baboons and humans,"[1] is the fact that not only physical strength and aggressivity but also social skills determine the individual's rank. "The high-ranking individual is selected for, among other things, its ability to settle disputes, to protect the weak, to repel enemies, to take initiative, and to organize activities...Therefore older animals are most often higher in rank."[2] "Lord and Father" symbolizes the transcendent dimension in the perception of the high-ranking fellow beings. The symbol of "lordship" signifies that element of the perception which belongs to the aggressive aspect of the high-ranking individual, arousing fear and terror and commanding humiliating subjection, while the symbol of "paternity" signifies helping and protective aspects. It is also characteristic of groups of primates that the highest ranks may be occupied only by males. This corresponds to the symbol of "Lord and Father" as a correlative of this transcendent dimension.

We do not know how this symbolism evolved in the history of emerging mankind, in the transition from animal to man, and in the early evolution of humanity with the progressive refinement and differentiation of perceptive faculties—especially in view of the transcendent dimension beyond the objective. But it is certain that the quality of "lordship" was significantly enhanced when man (by means of a symbolic and mediated, but nevertheless perverted expansion of his sexuality) turned into a game-hunter (that is, into an unnatural predator), by fatally piercing large animals with his spear. Within a given group, the man who would best master this behavior became the most dangerous to his fellow beings. He had the strongest aggressive aura and was therefore selected as leader of the group.

The ability to kill large animals, and especially fellow beings either within or outside his own group, determined the rank of a man. Greatness within the human community was usually determined by the "vis vitae necisque," the "lordship" over the life and death of other humans. It is exemplified, for example, in the Roman "pater familias," who represented the emperor's divine power within the small circle of his family. The ruler had to affirm his power to kill again and again in order to impose his rank on the other members of the community. This was the purpose of the cultic sacrifices of animals and humans, of wars, and later of public executions, in which the state's power to kill became visible. Even today our military parades serve a similar function. The more forcefully and powerfully the leader asserted his killing-power, the more his activities within the community—his arbitration of its disputes, his attacks on its enemies and his skills in its political organization—were considered as manifestations of divine grace and condescending mercy. Only the superior lord, who nonetheless chooses to act like a kind and merciful father, can arouse that uplifting feeling of being chosen and of having something gracefully and undeservedly bestowed upon oneself.

It is therefore understandable that God, as the transcendent dimension of the high-ranking individual, always has the features of the Lord and Father. This aspect of spirituality—along with the experience of a maternal aspect (see Chap. 3.3)—may be thought of as belonging to the very beginning of humanity, and as constituting, within religious anthropology, the essential mark of the transition from animal to man. Only an anthropology which sees the essence of humanity in economic systems and the working-world, can accept the use and production of tools as the criterion of that transition. From the religious standpoint, however, an animal becomes a man when it perceives the transcendent dimension of the objective world which he encounters with such intensity that the perception generates behavior that can no longer be explained by purely biological necessity.[3]

In this context we must look especially to burials—the burial of an animal or a man, according to a specific symbolism which for the most part cannot be recaptured today. This symbolism is revealed either by the purposeful treatment, disposition and burial of the skulls of bears or humans as is likely in the earliest period or, as in the middle and late Paleolithic Periods, by the covering of the deceased with red ocher, and by ornaments and other burial gifts. Such behavior always indicates that man was able to recognize a dimension beyond the corporeal, biological reality in the buried beast or human with such intensity that this experience lasted even after the body or bodily part was lifeless and subject to organic decay.

As shown by the oldest anthropological excavations (for example in Lantien [China] or in Java, later in the cave of Chou-k'ou-tien, forty-five kilometers south of Beijing, the former approximately 700,000 years old, the latter 300,000 to 400,000 years old),[4] it was above all the human head which received such reverential treatment. It is obviously the part of the human body which emanates a transcendent dimension beyond the corporeal and objective with particular intensity—that which we now call personality. Indeed, in primates we can observe that struggles for social rank are begun by the challengers staring at each other. The one who first turns his face away is defeated. So the head and face emanate that vitality which grants the highest rank even to individuals in animal groups. This emanation exists independently of actual physical strength. An individual can be defeated in such a competition even if it could have easily overcome its adversary through its sheer muscular strength. However, it is defeated because it is unable to withstand the psychic energy emanating from the face of its rival.

Such a behavior becomes religious—and therefore human, from a religious perspective—when this emanation reaches such an intensity that it lasts even beyond the death of the individual, and when man—only at

228

this point is it theologically valid to speak of man — expresses this perception through burial rites of some kind.

From this perspective, the oldest spirituality with social impact was probably some kind of ancestral cult. The high-ranking individual — characterized by the force, vitality, strength, cleverness and kindness emanating from his countenance — continued to exist in the group's experience of his transcendent dimension (and therefore of his rank) even if he died. His head was prepared and carried around by the group (see Fig. 42), and was later set up in the communal hall. Such behavior marked the birth of ancestral cults. The new leader of the group was no longer an autonomous ruler. He had an ancestor above him: the divine lord and father.

No one can give the exact ratio between aggression (that is, a threatening force and strength) and social, protective aspects of the emanation that determined the rank of an individual in the transition from animal to man. According to the observations of Eibl-Eibesfeldt even primates choose their leaders "only secondarily because of their aggressivity."[5] It is therefore likely that the social aspect was predominant during the evolution of man. Thus we see in the evolution of man a possible path which leads directly, according to the degree of the humanization process, to the Abba as the fundamental divine symbol, without any exaltation of the killing-power. This fact is expressed in theological categories in the ancient theological tradition of the first man's primitive, prelapsarian state of grace, (that is, of an original openness to the God who appears in Jesus). It is clear, however, that from the moment man became a game hunter through original sin and developed the faculty to kill great animals (and thus potentially his fellow-being as well), the aggressive element of emanation became the decisive criterion for rank. Therefore, from this original sin onwards, the power to kill more than anything else determined the rank of the individual.

It became the ancestor's characteristic element as well. He was not only venerated, but also dreaded and appeased with gifts.[6] From this point on we find a direct line to the often shocking sacrifices of precious objects, animals and humans that followed the deceased ruler into his grave. Not infrequently the whole court was killed and buried with him.[7] God, as the transcendent dimension of the high-ranking individual, was henceforth and above all the dreadful lord. Only for a few chosen ones or only during a few periods of his life was he the kindly and caring father. This aspect of spirituality is characteristic of societies of peasants as well as societies of hunters. As is strikingly demonstrated by the doubled-headed axes found in Crete in the palace of Knossos, which today can be seen on the back wall of the museum at Herakleion, as well as by the pictures of the sacrificing priestess, this power to kill is used even in those agricultural societies with matriarchal structures, where it identifies the woman and mother as ruling priestess. Moreover, as is shown in the cultures of Mesopotamia and Egypt, a system of social classes often develops among the population of the city and the state cultures. The caste of priests and rulers (and everything belonging to them) enjoys the paternal and caring aspect of the godhead, while the slaves experience it above all as a terrorizing killing-power. Nomadic hunting tribes, on the other hand, do not have such class distinctions. Their divine ancestors act towards the tribe as a whole, without class distinctions. They are kindly and protective at certain times when, for example, they grant abundant prey, and at other times terrifying in their power to kill when earthquakes, storms or sicknesses prompt humans to communicate with them through sacrifices. Corresponding to the sexual element of the hunting process—the great animal is stabbed to death with the phallic spear—it is the male who gains sole possession of the power to kill.

In the tribes of belligerent hunters the male child was often taken away from the care of its mother at an early age and subjected to a harsh discipline of privation, fear and subordination. At his final initiation into the hunting and fighting group of males, cruel pain was often inflicted upon him. He might be flogged, his teeth might be knocked out, or a crocodile-shaped pattern might be carved into his back with stone knives and the wounds sprinkled with ashes and salt to increase the pain and to make permanent scars. His foreskin might be brutally circumcised, and he might be hung for nine nights in the "windy tree," as is said to have been done to Wotan, the Germanic god of male initiation, the so-called "hanging god."[8] Or, as we have described with regard to the pit of the Lascaux cave, he might be lowered by rope into a deep, dark pit with a little oil-lamp. There he might contemplate the gruesome acts of the hunt, pictured in the wall paintings, over the long days and nights in order to fix them in his youthful psyche. All of this had only one purpose: to elevate the killing-power before him as the great *fascinosum et tremendum* (R. Otto), and to move him to an unconditional subjection to this power.

As we have shown in the preceding chapter on the wind and breath as divine symbols, this spirituality of the hunter did not die away with the Neolithic transition to a settled lifestyle and agriculture. On the contrary, it arose with renewed intensity, especially in the context of the foundation of states, with a new dimension of contempt for human life expressed in torture, slavery and bonded labor. As such, it still shapes the lives of many people today. Only a few years ago, in his book on the "poisoning of God,"[9] Tilman Moser described the self-hatred and the deep aggression which the image of a God who threatened eternal dam-

230

nation—that is of a God with an infinite killing-power—had instilled into his soul as a child. The songwriter Konstantin Wecker confessed in an interview at the age of forty-two that in all his texts and songs he fought an "eternal struggle against what I have inherited from my childhood. The fear that was aroused in me is a curse. The threat of hell is one of the most vile threats in world history."[10]

This religious tradition, which extends back over millions of years, is probably the most profound reason why in Judaism, in Islam, and partly still in Christianity, women have played a subordinate role in religion and are not allowed to hold the higher religious offices. For the spirituality which venerates a Lord God is originally the spirituality of the hunter who strikes down and kills large animals or his fellow-being with his phallic weapon. It therefore leaves no room for the activities of women. Very often the boys who are destined to become priests or preachers in these religions are taken away from the home of their caring parents at an early age, as in the old hunting societies, and are trained in special institutions, directed by males, with quasi-military discipline and rigor.

Indeed, Judaism, Islam, and Christianity are characterized among contemporary world religions by a special relation to this spirituality, characterized by the symbolism of "lord and father." However, these religions did not develop the Stone Age spirituality of the hunters in a linear and unbroken way. Rather, they constitute a critical, liberating and humanizing new beginning in contrast to the earlier city and state cultures that were shaped by the transition to a settled life, and by the rise of matriarchal structures.

On the Origin of the Abrahamite Religions

After the original sin, the nomadic game hunter violently and against his nature had appropriated the killing force of nature as he saw it expressed in predators and in such disasters as storms, floods, wildfires, and lightning. He now seemed to be allied with these forces. Nimrod, called the "mighty hunter in the eyes of Yahweh" (Gen. 10, 9) whose name recalls Nimurta, the Babylonian god of war and hunting; Esau, the dark, hairy brother of the biblical light-hero Jacob; or, from another tradition, Wotan, the leader of the wild hunt who roars across the Northern countries during November-nights—these are all incarnations of nature's blind and destructive, yet fascinating power to kill. Just as in nature, the power to kill is closely related to the power of procreation, and just as the hunter activates his sexuality in the act of killing, so do these primeval hunters exhibit some paternal and constructive features. According to the biblical account, Nimrod, Noah's grandchild, was one of the forefathers of mankind and founded the great empires of Babel, Erech, Accad, Kalne, Niniveh, and Calah, "the great city" (Gen. 10, 10 ff.). According to this tradition Esau is the "father of Edom in the mountainous region of Seir" (Gen. 36, 9) and the names of the sons, chiefs and kings who descended from him are numerous (Gen. 36, 10-43). Wotan is the father of the gods in the Germanic pantheon and he explicitly promotes fertility as leader of the Woutis army, the raging army of the dead in the storms at night in winter.

For those groups of men who established during the Neolithic Period, lasting homesteads dependent on sun and fertile soil, the ambivalent power of nature to confer the blessings of sun and rain on crops and to destroy these same crops and their homes as well by drought, flood and raging wind became a force too capricious with which to establish a lasting covenant. As Al, El, or Il, this force demanded cruel sacrifices of adults and children at the beginning of the rainy season, at the mouth of the wadis. Later, as Mot or Moloch, the god of heat and drought, it ordered the burning of the first-born sons — or so it appeared to the sinful man in the Semitic region, fascinated by the killing-power. Thus this gluttonous force of the wilderness becomes the Il-Afrit of the Yemeni fairy tales, the man-eater whose counterpart in our own fairy tales is the devouring force of nature, primarily symbolized by the witch. And yet, as can be observed very clearly in the ancient Yemeni fairy tales collected by Werner Daum,[11] the almighty power still has the features of the father, at least in the beginning. The abandoned maiden cries: "Father, O Father, such a quantity you have to pee! You have filled the wadis and all the flat land!"[12] In one Turkish story the girl, when she suddenly confronts the huge, fat, half-naked ogre, "runs towards him without hesitation, embraces him, kisses his hands and calls him her dear father," whereupon he actually adopts her as his child.[13] The terrible rainbow-serpent of the Pygmies, an incarnation of Mungu, the god of the bush from whom the Pygmies hide in their huts because he kills men, is called by the childlike name of Papa on other occasions. According to Schebesta's extensive reports on the Pygmy people, the Bafwaguda hunter, when hunting, calls into the bush: "Bapae gapae emi nyama!" — "Papa, give me deer!"[14] — in an "utterly unceremonial way," and "without any solemnity," as Schebesta remarks with slight contempt. Yet, it is similar to the manner in which Jesus addresses Abba.

But settlers cannot endure this ambiguity for ever. Eventually, the demonic aspect will predominate in their experiences of having their settlements, wrested from the wilderness at such labor, repeatedly destroyed by the forces of nature. In fairy tales this is expressed in having the adopted child or bride eventually unlock the closed, forbidden chamber of Il-Afrit and make the gruesome discovery of the piled skulls of the "children of Adam," whom the "Garguf" (another name for Il-Afrit) has devoured.[15] This motif also appears frequently in European stories and fairy tales, as in the story of Bluebeard whose wife eventually opens the forbidden door and finds the bodies of Bluebeard's former spouses. Henceforth the girl knows that the occasional kindness of the wild figure is nothing but a veneer and that his inner nature is nothing but evil.[16] Together with her brother or with her bridegroom, who comes as a light-hero from the East to rescue her, the girl lures Garguf into a trap, and the young man, her brother, beheads him with a single stroke of his sword. The wilderness-father has turned into a demon and dragon who must be mercilessly killed by the cooperation of man and woman, in the bond of holy matrimony.

At this point the hunting mentality of the Ice Age catches up with the Neolithic man. The settler — as described in the preceding chapter in the context of the solar wind's change into the hunter's breath — now seizes all power and kills or conquers everyone resisting his construction of a centralized state, in a reenactment of original sin. All that stand against the unlimited growth of the state — primeval forests, neighboring communities, or dissidents within who resist subjection — are mercilessly exterminated, stoned, dismembered, burnt, or, in our century, gassed. This is also the beginning of our lethal exploitation of nature which, we are only beginning to realize, is futile and will not eliminate the destructive force of nature. For in destroying nature we also destroy the foundation of our own lives. The destructive wilderness-force will now face us with a different, perhaps even more terrifying countenance, as acid rain, as poisoned ground water, and as nuclear contamination.

The Religion of Abraham as Father-religion

This situation in human history gives birth to the great historical religions of Judaism, Christianity and Islam. Their common origin, their "ancestor," is the biblical figure of Abraham. The significance of this name is controversial. But the Hebrew word "Ab," father, can be clearly recognized. Greßmann[17] and Noth[18] consider it to be derived from the Hebrew name "Abiram," which means "Father (God) is exalted." This would mean that the symbolism of the name already expresses the insight that the old god of the wilderness, El, Il, or Al, recognized as "Father" by his followers, is still exalted in relation to humans and cannot be pushed aside by any human power, even by the greatest and most powerful state. Biblical narration is quick to point out that Abraham leaves Mesopotamia, the country in which the first great states are founded. (According to Gen. 11, 27 ff. etc. Abraham comes from Southern Ur;

233

see also Neh. 9, 7, Jth. 5, 6; according to a different tradition he comes from the northerly Haran: Gen. 12, 4 and 24, 10, as well as Josh. 24, 2). This motif is especially noteworthy because it is part of a mythical, rather than historical narration. In fact it forms a link between the story of creation, which preceded the account of the patriarchs, and the new mythical cycle. But this is only its external, literary function, which does not explain the motif's central position in the whole of the mythical cycle. This is revealed only when we ask what resonance the name "Ur of the Chaldees" had for the contemporary listener and what religious position he associated with the name of this city which Abraham had left.

As we know today from excavations, Ur was, in its golden age, a powerful city-state and the cultic center of the moon-god Sin with a large temple area and a soaring ziggurat. The story of the sinful construction of the tower in Babel was probably inspired by these impressive towers. "They said 'Come, let us build ourselves a town and a tower with its top reaching heaven'..." (Gen. 11, 4). This is the Neolithic form of man's original sin, raising himself above his position, trying to appropriate and to have at his disposal the divine power of life and death which sends good and bad fortune, rain or burning drought down to man. Violence is no longer aimed at the animal, as it had been with the Stone Age hunters, but against humans in the usurpation of their states. The government of Ur's contempt for human life became manifest in the gruesome discovery of sixteen royal tombs, described by Sir L. Wooley in his book "Excavations at Ur" (London 1954). In many cases, soldiers, servants, and women, along with richly loaded chariots, their animals and drivers, had to follow the king into the pit, in order to be buried alive with the deceased ruler. The value of human life for the rulers of such states is expressed in a subtle observation by N. Davies, who noted that ten women, who were buried with the king, carefully lined up in two rows, had no personal burial gifts "for they themselves were part of the burial furnishings of their king."[19] At the beginning of the first millenium BC, the very time when semi-nomadic tribes migrated from the Syrian-Arabic desert and Mesopotamia into Syria and Canaan, and when the myth of Abraham might have had its historical roots,[20] Ur acquired the political leadership of southern Mesopotamia and, by means of its central administration, strove to establish an immense Sumerian empire, as evidenced in its monumental cultic buildings.[21]

This is the form of human life which Abraham "left behind." He did not seek stately power and grandeur, but was confident that the powerful El — even if at times El appeared as frightening (Gen. 31, 53: the "fear of his father Isaac") — would bless him and his people and give him a new homeland no longer shaped by despotism and a cynical spirituality. Quite apart from the validity of our interpretation of the etymology of his

234

name, Abraham lived according to the principle that "Father (God) is exalted." In other words, it is not possible to declare El a dragon of chaos and to destroy him with the help of the royal light-hero. The transcendent dimension of strength, might, and care (El as lord and Father) "is exalted": It cannot be usurped by men and transferred to the authority of the state. The only choice is to adore him, to humble oneself, and to pray for his blessing. In his semi-nomadic life-style, Abraham adapted to the all-embracing reality in a special way. The nomadic wandering of the gatherers and hunters is motivated by their search for prey, and the transition to a settled life always contains the temptation to erect a "tower of Babel," and usurp the primeval forces of nature and subjugate their fellowmen. On the other hand, the semi-nomad who adopts this life-style in a secondary way, as former peasant and cattle raiser, integrates himself into the fundamental rhythms of the seasons and of the environment with his regular change of grazing-grounds.

Despite the terror and violence which can occasionally plague human existence there are also caring and paternal aspects to the nature of the force man recognizes as embracing and defining his being. To confront this force as a king would, in order to destroy it, is hubris. Whoever attempts to do so, puts himself on the same level as El; he makes himself God. But to want to be like a god is the great temptation that surges from the serpent as the dreadful, destructive aspect of El (see the narration of the Fall: Gen. 3, 1-24 and the temptation by the serpent: Gen. 3, 5). Man can imitate the killing-power of God rather well with sacrificial slayings, war and conquest. Wherever the king gives in to this temptation, his subjects are no longer free human beings with personal dignity. They become the "furniture" of the God-king, be it for his life (to produce food and to build monumental structures), or for his death (to adorn his grave as burial gifts).

Only when the transcendent dimension of the rulers, for example the leader of the tribe, remains truly transcendent and does not descend to a concrete, objective manifestation, is the dignity of the people under the leader's rule preserved. Of course, even in the religion of Abraham, God appears as the God of the leader of the tribe, as the "shield" of Abraham (Gen. 15, 1), as the "fear" of Isaac (Gen. 9, 2), as the "Mighty One" of Jacob (Gen. 49, 24).[22] But this transcendence always remains distinct from its bearer; the leader of the tribe is responsible to him, and he bows before the protector God of his tribe in the same way as the most humble among his people do. Here, all people are in principle equal in dignity before this "exalted" God. Nevertheless, neither the leader nor the members of the tribe are in a relation of despotic dependence on him. It is true that the God-El of Abraham still demands a bloody and painful initiation as symbol of the covenant between him and the people of

Abraham: the circumcision of the foreskin. This is a sort of ritual male fraternity. The men circumcise their phallic weapon and express in this symbolic action that they subject their power to kill and to procreate to El (Gen. 17, 1-27). Accordingly, this El demands that they be *prepared* to sacrifice even their sons, as in the story of Abraham's sacrifice (Gen. 22, 1-19). But this narration already reveals that he does not want the offering itself. In other, probably later, traditions and generations from the time of the patriarchs, the idea arose—incarnated in the figure of the patriarch Jacob—that wherever El did not manifest himself as a protective father, but as terror—Jacob's wrestling with the demon of the river is an example—man was allowed to, and indeed had to fight with him. It was not a fight with the intention of killing and "exterminating" God, but a fight to wrest his blessing from him, that is, to force him to show his caring aspect again (Gen. 32, 23-33).[23]

Judaism: The Religion of the "I-am-here (for you)"

Despite the continuity between the Abrahamite religion of the patriarchs and the religion of Moses which is particularly stressed in the Yahwistic texts (which use the name of Yahweh for the God of the patriarchs),[24] the Mosaic religion constitutes a new beginning. The religion of Judaism is founded in Moses, not in Abraham. To be sure, this beginning is quite analogous to the one characterized by the figure of Abraham. Egypt, from which the people of Moses departed, had a religious and political situation structurally similar to that of ancient Sumer. The ruler was identified with the transcendent dimension. He was the incarnation of the sun-god. Being his son and sharing his nature, he was the absolute ruler over the life and death of men. He demanded human offerings as well, and living people as burial gifts.[25] The inhuman slavery and forced labor are described vividly in the book of Exodus (Exod. 5, 6-19).

In contrast to the story of Abraham, the exodus from Egypt is described as an armed conflict. The Egyptian persecutors drown in the Red Sea. But the decisive new aspect is that God, as the transcendent dimension of the nomadic leader Moses, reveals his new name. He is not only spoken of as "El," as the "Strong," as the "terror" or the "shield" of Moses. This God unveils himself to Moses and his people by his own name, that is, in his real nature: "I am the 'I-am-here' " (Exod. 3, 14).

Thus there are two new elements in contrast to the religion of Abraham. First, the caring aspect of the old ancestral wilderness-god, his paternal/maternal aspect, has been recognized as his *real* aspect, as his *true nature,* in contrast to his terrifying aspect. This and only this introduces the exact opposite of the religious position of the city-cults in the

236

Eastern state religions. There, the demonic, destructive aspect was seen as the true nature of the transcendent dimension (experienced in post-Neolithic times especially in the forces of nature and in enemy attacks). Together, the erotic-maternal woman and the royal light-hero, declared a "total war," of extermination against the dragon of chaos. In the Mosaic religion, on the contrary, paternal care—with a tendency towards maternal love at the core of its symbolism (Isa. 49, 15: "I-am-here" like a mother for her baby, or Isa. 66, 13: "Like a son comforted by his mother will I comfort you")—was recognized as the nature of this transcendent dimension. Its terrifying elements, insofar as they were not directed against the enemies of Israel, as an expression of this same care, were interpreted as a consequence of Yahweh's justice or as a means of correction.

Of course, we have to take into account that the nature of El as "I-am-here" has not yet acquired a universal quality. He is "there" for his own people of Israel, whose distress he has seen in Egypt and whose bitter complaint about the slave-drivers he has heard (Exod. 3, 7). He stoops down to his son to help and to rescue him (Jer. 31, 9; Hos. 11, 1 ff.). For the foreign peoples, on the other hand, he is the terror who goes ahead of Israel and throws everyone into confusion so that they "turn and run" and are filled with "panic" (Exod. 23, 27 f.). However, the nature of El as God "I-am-here" is in much stronger contrast to the cultures of the city-states than was even the religion of Abraham.

The second difference between these cults is that through the revelation of the divine name, this transcendent dimension is even more detached from its bearer than it already was with Abraham, Isaac and Jacob. This divine dimension can now be implored directly by every member of the tribe, independently of the leader's mediation. To enter into its protection, the tribal member need no longer go to the leader and to look up to him—and beyond him. He may himself try to establish contact with this nature which has revealed itself as "I-am-here." He has only to know the commands and the guidelines which express this nature. Then he may, in loyal obedience to these commands, entrust himself to the protection of God, integrating and adapting himself to God's nature, just as the wandering tribes adapted themselves to the rhythms of the seasons when they changed pastures.

This is precisely the function of the "Ten Words" (Exod. 34, 28), the "Ten Commandments" which Moses inscribed on stone tablets following God's command or, according to another tradition, were written by Yahweh himself and handed to the people as a covenant (Deut. 4, 13 and 10, 4). In these commandments, behavioral traditions and customs that were common in other semi-nomadic patriarchal tribes as well, were condensed in a way which makes them appear as an unfolding of the nature of Yahweh, an ethos emanating from the nature of the God "I-am-here." Indeed, both passages which enumerate the Ten Commandments (Exod. 20, 1-17, and Deut. 5, 6-21) begin with the words: "I am Yahweh your God who brought you out of the land of Egypt, out of the house of slavery." The commandments which follow seem to emanate directly from this divine revelation. Whoever experiences and acknowledges the transcendent dimension of existence in such a way will not worship other gods; he will not try to transfer this divinity into a carved image; he will not by magical practices abuse the gift of the divine name; he will observe the day of rest instituted by the caring God "I-am-here" for his people; he will honor his father and mother, in which this God is symbolized; he will kill no one who is, like himself, under the protection of God; he will not break into his marriage, bear false witness against him or steal from him.

For the subsequent religious evolution of Israel this is the starting point for two complementary and yet different spiritual traditions. One of these traditions tries to preserve the origin of the religion founded by Moses by interpreting the current events of history *in light of this original event,* and in this light prescribing the behavior to be adopted by the people. This is the prophetic tradition. It begins during the time of the kings, when the settled life and the founding of state structures threatened to cause Israel to forget its origins and to fall back into the cynical spirituality of the surrounding city-states. And indeed, during that period there was no pure belief in Yahweh. Belief in "Baal and Astarte, wood and stone, rites of fertility and the veneration of a celestial pantheon" was widespread.[26] At this time the word of the prophets escorted the history of Israel and interpreted it in the light of the revelation of Yahweh. Insofar as this history is an apostasy from the faith of Yahweh, this history comes as a punishment. However, as a counterpoint, the maternal-caring countenance of Yahweh is revealed, which preserves his promise of blessing and prophesies a new intervention in the messianic kingdom at the end of time. The purpose of this tradition is to keep alive the countenance of the "Yahweh from Egypt" and to emphasize the nature of this God as protecting love, at least a love for his chosen people.

In the other tradition the purpose is to unfold the *contents* of this nature, the commandments and standards for human life which it contains, and to apply it to the whole scope of life, in order to tell individuals how they should behave in each situation of life to ensure themselves of Yahweh's protection. This tradition is realized within the Old Testament in the Torah. This word means teaching, lesson, instruction. It refers especially to the instructions of Yahweh transmitted by Moses, which are handed down principally in the five books of Moses, the Pentateuch.

238

This is why these books themselves are sometimes called the Torah, and in early Judaism and the New Testament the whole of the Old Testament is sometimes referred to as Torah. The most frequently used translation for Torah is "Law." But it should not be thought of as "law" in the sense of a difficult "burden" (Acts. 15, 10). Originally, the Law (in the sense of the Torah) was a sort of gospel, namely the unfolding of the joyful and liberating message that the nature of the old god of terror is in fact "Yahweh," that is, caring and redeeming love. The Torah unfolds the consequences of this message for the conduct of man's life and is therefore to the devout of the Old Testament a "delight," a "joy for the heart," a "light for the eye" (Ps. 19, 8-11; Ps. 119, 92).

Later, however, a tendency arose within Judaism to see the Law less as the expression of God's nature and a way of entering a blessed relation with this God, than as a series of commands to be taken literally. In this manner, an immense number of specific regulations were formulated which the individual Israelite could obey only with difficulty, especially if he had to work hard for his living. Large segments of the population were consequently considered religiously second-class and excluded from the prophecies and blessings of Yahweh. As the parable of the Pharisee and the publican shows (Luke 18, 10-14), there were Pharisees and scribes who used such a formulistic understanding of the Law to withdraw from their fellow-men and to place themselves, as it were, on the same level with God. Like the royal light-hero in Mesopotamia or in Egypt, the figure in the parable builds, in his fulfillment of the Law, a "tower of Babel," a "tower with its top reaching heaven" (Gen. 11, 4). In other words, he usurps the place of God and revives the original sin of man. Of course, this is only one of many currents within Judaism.

Christianity: The Religion of the Abba

Christianity is not just a further development of Judaism. Jesus was indeed a Jew, and remained so until his death. But the early community recognized that through Jesus' actions "the Law and the prophets" had been suspended in two senses: On the one hand the law is now fulfilled and surpassed; on the other it has thereby come to an end. It is fulfilled insofar as in Jesus and in his actions the "malkût Yahweh," the kingdom of God announced by the prophets, the new liberating and saving activity of the God "I-am-here" among his people (his new being/being present), has already begun. Because of this it has also come to an end, for in this fulfillment of "the Law and the prophets," the religion founded by Moses has a new beginning (Luke 16, 16: "Until John there were the Law and the prophets; since then, the 'malkût Yahweh' has been preached").

239

The transcending of the Mosaic religion means that the dark side of El, his threatening and terrorizing character, disappears through the divine experience and revelation of Jesus. In their escape from enslavement the people of Moses experienced the "Yahweh from Egypt" not so much in his aspect as the frightening and all-powerful El but as one who has chosen Israel from all peoples to be his son and his bride. He has become for them the "I-am-here." He has revealed himself to *Israel* in his paternal-maternal nature. And yet he did not cease to be the wrathful and punishing God of terror to others—and even to Israel itself when it was unfaithful to him. But in Jesus El has disclosed himself as pure love. At the baptism in the river Jordan Jesus saw "the heavens torn apart and the breath of God, like a dove, descending on him," and thus experienced himself as the Son, beloved of an unconditional and absolute love (Mark 1, 9-11). When he began to live in the strength of this experience, to awaken it among his people as well, and to drive out their demons of desperation and depression, Jesus saw Satan, the demonic aspect of El, "fall like lightning from heaven" (Luke 10, 18). Then there was nothing left in the world that could harm the beloved children of Yahweh. His apostles could tread underfoot serpents and scorpions, "nothing shall ever hurt you" (Luke 10, 19).[27]

The terror of El is the projection of the fear and bondage born of original sin. In the parable of the talents (Matt. 25, 14-28), the servant with one talent is scolded because he had projected his own fear and inhibitions onto the master and therefore buried the entrusted sum in the earth, instead of managing it freely and independently. The older son in the parable of the merciful father (Luke 15, 11-32), who served his father for many years without ever acting against his father's will (Luke 15, 29), had lived like a slave in relation to his father. But when his brother, the prodigal son, found his way back to the father and the great feast of the "malkût Yahweh" was begun, the older brother learned that he was his father's child as well, that he was always with him, and that everything that belonged to the father was his.

The experience of Yahweh without terror makes the isolation of Israel from other people spiritually purposeless. Yahweh is no longer the paternal, caring God "I-am-here" to his chosen people and, simultaneously, the dreadful terror against other, hostile peoples or against the renegades within his own people, the terror spreading panic among his enemies and making them flee from him (Exod. 23, 27 f.). No, he is *only* Abba: Mama/Papa, and nothing else. "He causes the sun to rise on bad men as well as good, and his rain to fall on just and unjust men alike' (Matt. 5, 45). Indeed, as is shown by the parable of the prodigal son, and as Pope John Paul I has put it, "when the children are sick—or are plagued by evil or have strayed from the right path—they have an even greater right to be loved by their mother."[28]

Now there is no longer any spiritual justification for isolation from other men. The commandment which emanates from the nature of Yahweh—to love all people for whom El is the "I-am-here" (the Israelites)—is no longer a confining one. Every man, even one who has evil intentions towards me, is my fellow-being, and I am everyone else's fellow-being. The "I-am-here (for you)" has turned into the "I-am-here" for all men. Jesus was a Jew. In his preaching of the coming "malkût Yahweh" he did not transgress the boundaries of Judaism; he did not address the heathens. But when he encountered people in extreme distress, he shared his healing love with pagans as well. When he was sentenced by the Sanhedrin as blasphemous, and handed over to the pagan power of the Romans, he did not defend himself in an agony of spirit. Even on the pagan's gallows he knew that he was in the hands of his heavenly Father (Luke 23, 46). Fifty days after Jesus' death, at the harvest festival and feast of the covenant (Pentecost), the early community recognized this divine experience and revelation of Jesus as unique. Subsequently it began to preach Christianity as a universal religion.

Jesus is therefore not a prophet or religious teacher who continues and broadens the work of Moses, but he is, as Matthew in particular describes him, a second Moses who starts again where Moses began: with the religion of Abraham. The El-Shaddai, the powerful God from whom Jacob wrested the blessing for himself and his people, and who thereby became the protective God and ally of this people, revealed himself a second time, as it were, not only as the caring God "I-am-here" towards his chosen people, but as the Abba of all men. Henceforth, every person is called to relive the experience of Jesus, to unearth the treasure hidden in the field of his life (Matt. 13, 44), to acquire the precious pearl (Matt. 13, 45 f.), to see that the twigs on the tree of his life grow supple and put forth leaves (Mark 13, 28), that is, to hear the voice that says to everyone: You are my beloved son, my beloved daughter, my favor rests on you.

A divine revelation such as this cannot set up another isolated religious group, a new "people" among other people. Rather, the Abba reveals himself to each and every person in such a way that it is ultimately only the person himself who can discover the commandment, the "Torah," which is contained in this newly grasped nature of God, although in communion with others who share this revelation with him. Therefore, wherever Christianity preserves its original impulse, no new conception of "Law" will arise. The way in which the Abba discloses himself to his beloved son or to his beloved daughter is so individual and personal indeed, that the guidelines and commandments—insofar as they really proceed from this new self-disclosure of Yahweh (and not from a repetition of specific divine revelations from the Old Testament)—can no longer petrify into a common Law, into a list of concepts and precepts to

241

be chiselled in stone. The time which the prophet Jeremiah announced has come:

Behold the days are coming, says Yahweh, when I will make a new covenant with the House of Israel and the House of Judah, but not a covenant like the one I made with their fathers on the day I took them by the hand to bring them out of the land of Egypt. They broke that covenant of mine, though I was a husband to them, says Yahweh. No, I will make this covenant with the House of Israel when those days arrive, says Yahweh. I will place my Law deep within them, writing it on their hearts. Then I will be their God and they shall be my people. No longer shall each man teach his neighbor, or say to his brother, "Know Yahweh!" for they will all know me, from the least to the greatest—it is Yahweh who speaks—since I will forgive their iniquity and remember their sin no more. (Jer. 31, 31-34)

As different as human hearts are, and yet of the same structure—so, different and yet of the same structure is the new "Law," written into the living, maturing, and always evolving heart of man. The common structure is the central command of love. It alone is sufficient: "Love—and then do what you please," said Augustine. The concrete manifestation of this love differs according to the period of life and to the maturing process of each person. But at whatever stage one may be, whether young or old, educated or uneducated, rich or poor—every person is always loved by the Abba with endless affection, and can therefore experience him in his own life. Certainly there must always be teachers and educators to watch and guide one's development as a human being. But the potential for that knowledge which is of ultimate importance is written in the human heart. Every human being has the faculty to perceive this transcendent presence and he has it even in his mother's womb. No one need be taught who his or her Abba is. Everyone knows from experience or will never know it.

Only this revelation makes possible a religious community of people who are truly mature, of people who have competence in a spiritual language grounded in personal experience and knowledge, and who are "catholic" in the original sense of the Greek word "kathalon," that is universal. Only such a community allows for a "festive gathering" in the sense of the original meaning of the Greek and Latin word "ekklesia," church, to which *all* are invited, namely all beings who have the faculty to perceive that dimension transcending the objective given in their lives. A festive gathering founded on such a divine experience and revelation can exclude no one. It must be open for as many articulations of experience between the Abba and the son or daughter as there were, are, and will be

242

beloved sons and beloved daughters. Only the exchange and the new and surprising consonance of those very personal experiences that grant new meaning and freedom and are articulated in an authentic way, in a "mother-tongue" — "Each one [heard] these men speaking his own language" (Acts 2,6) — can be the foundation and the contents of that feast at which people gather. This, of course, is the church of the end of time, towards which we are on our way. But we can achieve this goal only when we acknowledge beforehand the religious autonomy of each person and then begin to train ourselves in communication. To do this, we need sensitive directors of such communication. We do not need manipulative rulers acting as God, nor tribal leaders whose experience of the transcendent may represent only that of the members of their clan, nor shepherds who watch over immature sheep (Ezek. 34, 11), but real servants of the unity of all. Sensitive listeners are needed. Listeners who can first sense the consonance of the different words and sounds, and work to interpret them, like sensitive conductors, so that the voices will one day resound in one great concert.

In the divine experience and revelation of Jesus, the spiritual significance of Abraham is supplied as a counterpoint. The name Abraham signifies: the Father (God) is exalted; he is not a dragon of chaos to be conquered by the light-hero, in a heroic struggle. The name Jesus signifies: God is help, the Exalted One is Abba. In our contemporary understanding this means that the terrifying strength and power that attacks man and his human settlements, is only experienced by the sinful man who is confined within the cycle of violence that was initiated by original sin. In reality the "exaltation," the transcendent dimension of our existence as it is expressed in the exalted one (for the child in its father and mother, for the members of a tribe in the emanation of their ancestors, and for the peasants in the overwhelming power of surrounding nature) is nothing other than the selfless, powerless, but almighty love, as it is represented in the parable of the merciful father.

This is, of course, an experience and a revelation difficult to retain and even more difficult to relive for sinful, earthly human beings, even when it shines forth in a sudden brilliant light, as in Jesus' experience at the river Jordan. It shone forth from the son of a people over whom the Roman emperor-god had imposed his rule of terror, at a time and in a country where gallows had been set up at all road-crossings, to affirm and reaffirm the terrifying divine and imperial power to kill and where the Jewish freedom fighters died dreadful, sacrificial deaths. No psychological theory can ever hope to explain adequately that paradox. Soon, the terror of this power to kill turned against Jesus himself, the recipient and bearer of the revelation of love as divine power. Some patriots and collaborators "plotted how to destroy him" (Mark 3, 6), when he healed people on the Sabbath. In the parables we can see how the horizon of Jesus' activity darkens, night threatens to fall, and the sower can no longer work. He must leave his field and sleep, perhaps the sleep of death (Mark 4, 26-28).[29] All four gospels report that the killing-power threatened Jesus more and more, and that he almost broke down the night of his arrest (Mark 14, 32-42). But as the son of Isra-El, of the fighter with God, Jesus wrestled the demonic manifestation of Elohim in a nocturnal struggle of prayer, like his forefather, who had struggled long ago at the ford of the river, and found his way back to the name of the Abba (Mark 14, 36).

Then the killing-power closed in on him — men sent by the "high priests, the scribes and the elders," armed in a terrifying way. They brought Jesus before the "high" council, the "holy" Sanhedrin, the only court authority that remained to the Jews during the time of Roman occupation, and he was sentenced to death. The killing-power raised itself up into a divine terror. But for Jesus and for all who would later tell of him, all of this was ultimately a shallow performance, a ridiculous fuss: "Am I a brigand that you had to set out to capture me with swords and clubs? I was among you daily teaching in the Temple..." (Mark 14, 49). The high-priest had to tear his robes in a theatrical gesture to divert attention from the contradicting witnesses.

Then the profane terror of the Jewish Sanhedrin was united with the divine, imperial power of Rome. The scene was impressive: the fortress Antonia, Roman cohorts with lances and shining swords, the seat of the procurator in the inner court of the fortress. But all this failed to impress Jesus. The reality which he encountered abounded in banality. It lacked any symbolic content, any transcendence. Jesus did not join in the game. He did not answer the grossly exaggerated accusations brought forth by the high priests. By his attitude he threw even the feared procurator Pilate into ridiculous confusion. And indeed, what could Pilate do, in all his display of military might, with a man who said to himself and to his friends: "I say: Fear not those who kill the body and after that can do no more"? (Luke 12, 4).

Thus they did what they could. They mistreated him pitifully and crucified him. Jesus wrestled once again in a struggle of prayer with El — "Eloi, Eloi, lama sabachthani" (Mark 15, 34) — and again he found the Abba. He fell into his hands, free, crying like a child: "Father, into your hands I entrust my life" (Luke 23, 46). In his death Jesus appears again as the beloved, living son of God, who in his fate makes God manifest for *all* — even for the Roman centurion who presided over the execution and who in Mark's gospel speaks for *all*: "In truth this man was the son of God" (Mark 15, 39). Later, the gospel of John quotes Jesus: "To have seen me is to have seen the Father" (John 14, 9), and "the Father and I are one" (John 10, 30). Thus Jesus lived his divine experience and revelation up to the very end and confirmed it in the midst of the imperial terror of the universal Roman rule. God alone is Abba, the terror unsacred and empty.

This is the message of the Christian faith — a message that cannot be pinned down as a doctrine, taught and "accepted as truth." Rather, it has to be discovered anew in each believer's nocturnal struggle of prayer, as it was by our forefather Jacob, and by Jesus. But wherever it discloses itself, it widens and brightens one's life.

Islam: The Religion of the All-Merciful

As Christianity had done earlier, Islam reaches back past the Mosaic religion to the religion of Abraham. Islam defines itself as the "faith of Abraham" (sura 22, 78; 2, 131; 2, 136 etc.).[30] The fourteenth sura of the Koran bears his name, and in many other suras Abraham is called the first Muslim (e.g. 2, 3, 4, 6, and 22). The Koran relates that he founded the Kaaba at Mecca, together with his son Ishmael (sura 2, 125 ff.). Thus Islam sees itself as a reformation of Judaism and Christianity in view of its origin in the religion of Abraham.[31] The Koran eliminates the mistakes and falsifications brought by Jews and Christians to the divine revelation which began with Abraham. These mistakes consist in "worshipping other gods, for which no sanction hath been revealed. Their habitation shall be the Fire, and wretched the abode of the wrong-doer" (sura 3, 152).[32] This holds true especially for Christians who "speak a lie concerning Allah knowingly. It is not possible for any mortal to whom Allah has given the Scripture and endowed with wisdom and the prophethood that he should afterwards have said unto mankind: worship me instead of Allah" (sura 3, 80).[33] But according to the Koran, even the people of Israel fell into idolatry, especially during the time of the kings, and falsified the original revelation to Abraham in many ways. Thus Abraham is the first Muslim, but he was neither Jew nor Christian (sura 3, 67). The sin of both Jews and Christians consists in the fact that they did not remain within Abraham's revelation, but claimed, with Moses and Jesus, a new beginning, a new origin of revelation. "And they say: Be Jews or Christians and you will be rightly guided. Say (to them, O Mohammed): No, we follow the religion of Abraham, and he was not an idolater. Say (O Muslims): We believe in Allah and that which is revealed to us and that which was revealed to Abraham, and Ishmael, and Isaac, and Jacob, and the tribes, and that which Moses and Jesus received, and that which the other prophets received from the Lord. We make no

245

distinction between any of them..." (sura 2, 136 f.).[34] In several places the Koran says: "We believe in Allah and that which is revealed to us; and in what was revealed to Abraham and Ishmael and Isaac and Jacob and the tribes, and that which was vouchsafed to Moses and Jesus and the prophets from their Lord. We make no distinction between any of them, and unto Allah have we surrendered" (sura 3, 85).

Thus Islam has a deeply reformatory character, bringing religion and human life back to their origins in Abraham.[35] This can be understood from the situation in which Islam arose. In Mohammed's time, different religious and political spheres of influence overlapped on the Arabian peninsula. In the north the Byzantine Empire was influential, but was weakened by the christological disputes of Arianism, Nestorianism and Monophysitism, and appeared religiously confused. From the southwest yet a different branch of Christian thought penetrated the Byzantine Empire through the national Christian kingdom of Abyssinia. In the southeast was the Persian Empire, weakened by wars. Its dominant Manichaean religion, which combined Christian, Zoroastrian and Buddhist elements, introduced these various forms of belief into Arabia. Mohammed also encountered Judaism throughout his country and especially in centers of commerce. Thus there was no dominating political and religious orientation. In and around Mecca, different families ruled, whose ethical code and religion followed the primitive ethics of clans, according to which all is good that is useful to one's own clan, and all is evil which goes against its interests. Furthermore, the rising, wealthy class of merchants in the important region around Mecca began to leave their clans and tried to establish their own centers of power.

Mohammed had experienced this lack of religious, moral, and political orientation on the Arabian peninsula over two decades. First as a merchant in his uncle's business, and later in the management of his own business after his marriage to Cadijah, a wealthy merchant's widow. When he was forty years old, the search for the fundamental meaning of life so compelled him that he could no longer live in the surrounding religious and political chaos. He retired from business and lived in meditation for long periods of time in the caves near Mecca. What could be more logical in his quest for meaning than an attempt to return to the roots of the different Jewish and Christian factions that he had encountered and, as scriptural religions, held a better promise of stability than the ancient elements of a spirituality based on stars and fertility that still flourished abundantly in his country but were no longer able to produce a significant accord? He decided to extend the scriptural religion of Judaism and Christianity back to the time of Abraham, to make the scripture-less religion of Abraham a scriptural one. The perspective of an

Abrahamite origin enabled him to discover the points at which the Jews and Christians "took words from their context and forgot much of that whereof they were commanded" (sura 5, 14).

Because of their distinctively different revelations of Allah, Jews and Christians consider themselves to be the "beloved children of Allah." But the God of Abraham has no favorites: "Nay, ye are but mortals of His own creation. He forgives whom He will, and chastises whom He will" (sura 5, 19).[36]

Thus Mohammed writes the "Koran of Abraham" (sura 9, 42): the first and original Torah, "a declaration for mankind, a guidance and an admonition unto the righteous." (sura 3, 139). There is a clear reorientation of the understanding of God, back from the Christian God of love and the Jewish God "I-am-here" to the original Almighty. As is expressed by the name "Allah," it is the old Il, El, Al, the wilderness-god, overwhelming in his power.[37] At the time in which Mohammed lived, he could not relive Neolithic man's original attempt in religions of light and fertility to overcome and to eliminate the wilderness-power. The combative light-heroes and their women are nothing but blind and dull idols for him. Indeed, in their attempts to be like El and to overthrow Allah, they become, like the angel of light from the Old Testament, Lucifer (meaning: "light-bearer"), opponents of Allah. They become Satan. Abraham's exodus from his homeland is a definite refusal of idolatry: "O my father! Why do you worship that which cannot hear or see?...O my father! Do not serve the devil, for the devil has rebelled against the Beneficent.. O my father! I fear lest a punishment from the Beneficent befall you and you become a servant of the devil." Thereupon Abraham was rejected by his father: "Dare you reject my gods, Abraham? If you so reject them, I shall surely stone you. Depart from me immediately!". Then followed the separation on Abraham's side; he responded to his father's rejection: "Peace be with you! I shall ask my Lord to forgive you...I shall depart from you and the idols to which you pray." (sura 19, 43-49).

Thus for the Koran, the origin of the religion of Abraham, which was rediscovered and established as scriptural by Mohammed, began with Abraham's separation from his human father. Abraham can accomplish this separation because he knows that he is protected by a "greater father," the "All-Merciful," who is exalted above all, even above his own father in the flesh. He dreads the punishment of the All-Mighty and trusts in His mercy. This is a clear de-symbolizing of the concept of God. El, Al, Il was originally the transcendent dimension of the ruler, the father, the ancestor, and beyond that the force of the wilderness which surrounds man and shapes his fate. He used to manifest himself in an unpredictable way, caring and kindly at one time, wild and destructive at another. In the conversation between Abraham and his father, this transcendent dimension is, as it were, now detached from its symbol—the father, the ancestor, natural forces—and elevated to a purely spiritual essence.

This is probably the deepest root of the rejection of symbols and images in Islam as well as in Judaism.[38] But man is not capable of thought that is utterly without symbolism. Even Allah continues to bear the prominent features of the "Lord and Father," especially of that father from whom Abraham was separated, and who mercifully lets Abraham go, not without pointing out that he has the power to stone him. Thus the character of the old El, Il, Al clearly survives. His characteristic feature is the abrupt and immediate juxtaposition of mercy and kindness with an arbitrary power to punish, without being accountable to anyone. Even if, on the whole, his mercy is predominant, he is still best described by the name "Lord."[39]

In the figure of Abraham and in his intercession, Allah's merciful nature is particularly evident. The Koran exhorts Muslims: "And when Abraham said: My Lord! Make this land safe and preserve me and my sons from serving idols...But he who follows me, he shall be my brother. But if one should turn against me—Still You art Forgiving, Merciful" (sura 14, 36 f.). Hence, because of Abraham there is also the possibility of Allah's forgiveness and kindness towards non-Muslims. But in Allah the impetuous and unpredictable force of the wilderness is preserved as the free divine power of disposition and almighty despotism. When, at another point, Abraham asks Allah to feed the faithful with the fruit of the land, Allah answers, going even beyond Abraham's request: "As for those who do not believe, I shall leave them in life...," but he adds abruptly: "...I shall leave them in life for a while, then I shall drag them to the doom of fire" (sura 2, 127). In the same breath Allah is called the kindly "Beneficent," and it is said that the criminals and unbelievers will be fed to the fire of hell (sura 3, 9-11). In divine arbitrariness "You bestow sovereignty on whom You will, and You take it away when You will. You exalt whom You will and You humble whom You will. In Your hand is the good" (sura 3, 27). The immediacy of the wild threat and the promise of mercy shocks again and again:[40] "And Allah guides not wrongdoers. As for them, their reward shall be the curse of Allah and of angels and of men. They will abide therein. Their fate will not be lightened, neither will they be reprieved; except those who afterward repent and do right, for Allah is Forgiving and Merciful" (sura 3, 87-90).

This is the feature of Allah in which the old wilderness-god is seen most clearly. But the "Muslim" Abraham and all other Muslims give themselves to Allah in confidence, because they believe in and experience in their own lives the prevalence of his merciful guidance. In sura 93

248

Mohammed mentions Allah's guidance in his own life. He sees in this merciful guidance a symbol of Allah's care beyond death, in a future life: "And truly the life to come will be a richer one for you than this life and truly the Lord will give unto you so that you will know contentment. Did he not find you an orphan and protect you? Did he not find you destitute and enrich you? (sura 93, 5-8).

Of course, grace remains free and arbitrary. Allah remains El, Il, Al, the El-Shaddai, the almighty god of the wilderness, whose mercifulness and caring kindness is a surprise every time, and even a shock. He has not manifested himself in a new nature, as did Yahweh, for example, as the God "I-am-here," or indeed as Abba, as Mama/Papa, so that his love and mercy would flow forth from this newly revealed *nature*. Allah shows his mercy not because he is love, but because he wants to give mercy, and he refuses it because he wants to refuse mercy. The specific forms of religious practice of both religions arise from this peculiarity and from this difference in their spirituality.

Compared to Christianity, the characteristic difference between the two religions is that of a God whose mercy springs from a kind condescension and a God as the Abba, who *is* pure love. To be sure, in contemporary Islam there are certain tendencies to interpret the relation between God and man in a feminine-maternal manner. The reference invoked—analogous to the encyclical of Pope John Paul II, "Dives in misericordia"[41]—is the common stem of the words "mercy" and "womb" in the Semitic language.[42] Just as in the Hebrew "rahamim" (mercy) and "reheb" (maternal womb), the Arabic words "rahma" (mercy) and "rahim" (maternal womb, family relation) have a common stem. The "rahma,"[43] the fundamental property of God, which appears in the Koran more than seven hundred times in different forms of the stem, would therefore contain something feminine and maternal: "The relation between God and man in Islam thus receives maternal, feminine features...His relation to man is not founded in his almightiness, that is, in his strength, but more on the rahma (mercy), which is the highest principle of action, guiding his almightiness in a certain direction."[44]

This spiritual peculiarity is already present in the return to the religion of Abraham. Unlike Moses, Abraham has maternal characteristics, shaped by his experience of God. The Bible repeatedly speaks of "the bosom of Abraham" (Luke 16, 22). In the story of the rich man and the poor Lazarus (Luke 6, 16-31), for example, the bosom of Abraham is Lazarus' resting place after his death. This is perhaps a point at which Islam and Christianity are closer to each other than Judaism and Christianity, although the latter grew from the former.[45] In a certain sense Jesus himself is a religious reformer who wants to renew from its origins the tradition in which he stands, that is, from Abraham's experience.

249

However, the difference remains that *rahma* in Islam "does not contain any notion of compassion *(rigga)*, but is a pure act of kindness *(Ihsàn)*," as Islamic scholar Abdoldjawad Falaturi points out.[46] As such, it is still ultimately founded in sovereignty, that is, in almightiness, even if this almightiness resolves in a sovereign way to be generally kind and merciful.[47] In Christianity, however, mercy is founded in the nature of the Abba. The father "has to" lift up his garment in a most undignified way and run to his boy to clasp him in his arms: "It [is] only right that we should celebrate and rejoice" is the justification the father gives to his older son, "because your brother here was dead and has come to life; he was lost and is found" (Luke 15, 32). God *is* Abba, and therefore every human being is the infinitely beloved son, the immeasurably beloved daughter. This state of being God's child, which is promised to each of us, has no correspondence either in Judaism or in Islam.[48] The maternal womb of Allah is empty. He has no sons and daughters.

3.3 The Mother as Divine Symbol in the History of Religions and in Christianity

On the Evolution of the Maternal Symbol: The Creation of the Woman and Mother (as the First Human) by the Christian God.

According to M. Eliade,[1] everything can reveal a transcendent dimension and thereby transform the being who perceives this transcendent dimension into a human being. In the identification of this dimension, the highest-ranking male of a group of primates became the "father," and those beings who communicated with each other on this level of perception thereby became humans.

The symbol of the mother, however, is perhaps even older and more basic. Here, the following holds true as well: As the sexual procreation of offspring does not make the male, that is the man, a father, so the activities of laying eggs, of breeding, and of parturition do not turn the female, or the woman, into a mother. A female reptile that lays eggs after mating and no longer cares for them is certainly not a mother. But, even in situations in which we see an intensive breeding behavior, as in birds and mammals, our talk of "mothers" or "motherly care" is actually a projection of human concepts onto the animal world. We project our feelings associated with the word "mother" back onto animal behavior.

250

Of course we witness touching behavior of caretaking in the animal world, especially by "mothers," but also by "fathers." The development of perceptive faculties for the transcendent dimension is also an evolutionary process, and thus a flowing process without rigid limits. What is it that turns a being that gives birth to offspring, and feeds and cares for it until it is grown, into a human mother? In general terms, it is the faculty to recognize in the newborn, growing being a transcendent dimension with such intensity that it prompts specific reactions. But how should we identify such reactions? When a cat takes care of her young, licks them tenderly, hides them when she senses dangers, and protects them courageously against attackers, this behavior may be explained in a plausible way by biologists as a behavior which is dictated by what Richard Dawkins calls the "selfish genes" that want to survive and multiply. The situation is different when adult female or male chimpanzees fool around and play with their young. Is this not an extravagant waste of energy and of no use to the preservation of the genes? On the other hand this may be a genetically given training program to envigorate the offspring and make them fit for survival.

But what if one of these young animals dies, through an accident or illness? The female chimp shows signs of great distress, she wails and gently nudges the little body in order to make it respond. Often for a long time the mother cannot believe that her child is dead. In his "Tierleben" (vol. 10, Mammals I, Munich 1979, 536), B. Grzimek recounts the case of a female gorilla who carries her dead baby for four days. There is eventually, however, a sudden realization. It seems as if her perception of the dead being has changed—as if it were a piece of flesh that does not belong to anyone. She drops the body and leaves it there. It makes no difference to her that it will be found and eaten by wild animals or even by her own fellow-beings. The transcendent dimension of the child, which might have dawned on her in her care and play, cannot be perceived independently of its bearer, the living, moving being. The dead body does not have enough symbolic force. The perception of this dimension is not intensive enough to be recalled by the sight of the dead body, by a part of that body, by a "souvenir," or by simple recollection after a length of time following the death—after days, weeks, months later—and to elicit a response.

How different is the picture we get from the earliest human burial sites. As described in the chapter, The Child as a Symbol of God, the most frequently encountered graves and those having the richest burial gifts were the graves of children.[2] The Neanderthal man and woman laid down their child on a bed of flowers and red ocher powder, the color of festive life, and put into its grave necklaces made from sea shells, snail shells and teeth, as well as precious stone tools. They gave special treatment to the head from which the personality, the transcendent dimension, emanated with particular intensity, and may have carried the head with them for some time before burial. They also protected the grave from predators by covering it with heavy stone tiles or the shoulder blades of mammoths.

But these findings from the Mousterian culture (as those from La Ferrassie)[3] are already a late development of burial culture, although they are more than fifty to seventy thousand years old. The human skulls found in Choukoutien near Beijing have also received special treatment.[4] Time has erased such traces in the findings from Southern and Eastern Africa, the cradle of humanity more than one million years ago, but an emotionally motivated treatment of the dead body is in no way excluded. No evidence, even if it did exist, could show us the pain of a female Australopithecus or *Homo habilis* who does not want to be separated from her dead child and carries it around for days, wailing and ignoring the stench of its decay. Finally, when the stench becomes overwhelming, she cuts the head from the body with a sharp instrument, removes the stinking flesh from the bones with a flint scraper and lovingly carries the cleaned skull — as do the Papua women in New Guinea to this day (Fig. 42). This "female" — and only she — has become the human woman and mother. She has experienced the transcendent dimension of her child with such intensity that the "eternal" and "immortal" character of this dimension (the child's personality) lasts beyond death, beyond the body's decay.

Her behavior is the reaction to this perception. Through this perception and this behavior she became a mother and thereby human. The first human was probably the mother. It was not the "selfish gene," nor physical-biological laws that produced her, but God, as the transcendent dimension of the child which she has borne. This God, who created man as mother, does not signify greatness, strength and might. It was not the "divine child" of religious history, not the Pharaoh, who stood upright even as an infant, or the Buddha, who paced through the universe. No, it was God as a child in the sense of the Christian experience of God: the helpless, powerless being, "the child, wrapped in swaddling clothes and lying in a manger" (this is the sign of the messianic child in the Christmas story, Luke 2, 12). *This* child-God has created man and his world, according to Christian belief — until the power of his symbolism was obscured by the god of terror who rose through killing, and thereby turned the child into the victim par excellence, the scapegoat, the crucified. But in Jesus, the beloved son of the heavenly father, in whom the dynamic of terror found its climax, the original symbolic power of the child shone forth again, and in its light the god of terror reveals himself as Abba. Thus the crucified son has become the Messiah, the bearer of the

Fig. 42: A Papuan woman with the skull of her deceased husband.

hope that, thanks to the strength of this symbolism, man may be freed from the paralyzing fascination of the killing-power, a power that distorts all perception, and man and the world can therefore be created anew.

In the preceding description of the process of becoming human — the awakening of the woman and mother — we must take into account the fact that our imagination and our power of empathy has been shaped over millions of years by the god of terror who was conceived by original sin. From the moment he stabbed the mighty bull mired in a bog with a sharpened stick of wood, man knew death only as something frightful. He saw every kind of death only in the dreadful image of the strong and vital animal fighting for its life until the very end but eventually slain by repeated thrusts. Since then man has understood death as the result of being fatally stabbed. As through a thick, impenetrable mist, we can hardly sense the way in which the first human being who had not yet grasped at the killing-power (the "tree in the middle of the garden") experienced death. Perhaps it was for him something very natural, self-evident, as it is for the old, sick and dying animal, that retires into the bush and returns its body to the cycle of birth and death.

But in that case the picture we drew of the behavior of the distressed *Homo habilis* women would be false. Not desperation but simple, pure love for her child, the simple perception of an angel who continued to talk to her, even after the child's body had died and begun to decay, may have motivated her behavior. The cruelty and brutality which we might see in this behavior appears unnatural to man perhaps only when seen through the tainted vision of violent killing. It may be inconceivable for us, but for this woman, the cutting and preparation of the head may have been only the natural continuation of the care that she had given to the child's body when it was alive — or more precisely, given to the angel of the child. She simply tried to save as much as possible of the symbol through which the angel had spoken to her (the symbolic message of the child, the hierophany).

Of course, from a Christian point of view and hierophantic order, the child-angel who turned the female Australopithecus or *Homo habilis* into a human woman was not an angel, but God himself. It is God as child, as son and daughter, who integrated the living being leaning towards him into his own, inner divine dynamic, into the breath of life pouring forth from the child, from the caring mother, and from the protective father, and which, when blown into a being shaped by this love, makes this being into a living and feeling man: "Yahweh fashioned man...breathing into his nostrils a breath of life, and thus man became a living being" (Gen 2, 7).

When the caring and protective being opens itself to the divine, transcendent dimension of the being entrusted to it, to the strength and

254

dynamic of its symbolism, to the wind and breath of the child, and reacts to it—even if only subconsciously—it begins to emanate divinity itself. The mother and, analogously, the father, are born as symbols of the divine—as Abba. The mother's actions have a dimension that transcends death. This dimension is transmitted in all aspects of maternal, caring behavior, once the female has become a woman and mother. For in every act of nursing, rocking, fondling, carrying, feeding and caressing, that dimension of the child which transcends death and motivates the behavior of burial, is also met.

In his popular book "Rumor of Angels"[5] the religious sociologist P. L. Berger has given a simple and convincing example of this specifically human behavior of the mother that contains a religious dimension, transcending death—whether it be conscious and accepted, or unconscious, or even denied. It is a world-wide phenomenon, independent of culture. A small child cries in the night. It has had a bad dream, or it suffers pain. The mother takes the child in her arms, nurses it, rocks it and says—even non-verbally in the international language of gesture: "Be quiet, go to sleep. *All is well.*" The mother says this even in a world menaced by ecological and nuclear destruction. Indeed, she has said it in times of war, during bombing raids, knowing that in the next moment a shell could kill them both. She also says it when the child in her arms is handicapped or is close to death. Berger asks the question: "Does the mother *lie* to the child?" The answer has to be: The mother cannot lie to the child, because, whether she wants it or not, in her specifically human maternal behavior she expresses a dimension which transcends death and the objective given. As a mother she is always a divine symbol, the bearer of the hope for eternal life.

To be a mother means to feed, to take care of, and thereby to comfort beyond death. This behavior, and nothing else, makes a human being into a mother. A surrogate "mother," who may have given birth to five children and given them away right after their birth, is not a mother. On the other hand a Mother Teresa of Calcutta is a mother in the true sense of the word, although she has never given birth and does not work only with children, but mainly takes care of older, dying people. All human care is directed not only to the suffering body and perhaps the ailing soul, but also to the transcendent, immortal dimension of one's fellow-being. Its inner essence is care beyond death—and in this sense it is maternal.

The evolutionary origin of this symbolism is the feeding behavior of mammals. In his ethology I. Eibl-Eibesfeldt explains that the rich repertory of social behavior in animals—gestures of friendship, feeding and greeting ceremonies—derives mostly from the primal experience of

255

feeding the young and from the repertory of childlike behavior.[6] Apart from some species of coral reef fish only those animals that care for their offspring form exclusive groups, mostly structured by parental ties.[7] Much of the sexual behavior in mammals comes from the feeding of the young—and all the more so the closer they are related to man: fondling, kissing, caressing and mouth-to-mouth feeding. Through this behavior the distance between each being is lessened and mating is thus facilitated. However, in certain groups of apes one can observe that the eventual copulation is not the ultimate goal of the friendly behavior, but, on the contrary, copulation is used to strengthen social ties. An obviously sexual gesture, like the presentation of the sexual organs, is used as greeting ritual, and certain baboons engage in binding, or social copulation without ejaculation.[8] Here the symbolism of this behavior is not aimed beyond death, but nevertheless reaches beyond the biological function in order to stabilize the group.

This combination of feeding and mating behavior in primates helps us understand that in humans, too, maternal and sexual attractions often overlap. Eibl-Eibesfeldt agrees with the philosopher Schopenhauer who pointed out in his study of the metaphysics of sexuality that "a full bust exerts such a strong attraction on males because it is in direct relation to the female's ability to propagate and promises rich food for the newborn."[9] Of course, the signals of attraction in humans are subject to cultural influences. But the prehistoric wall paintings and figures of female idols show very clearly that in those times the fascination of women was determined by physical characterstics that imply motherhood, such as large hips and broad buttocks. But this fascination, as it emanates from the woman and mother, becomes human—and thereby religious—only when the force of a love beyond death is also perceived and experienced in this emanation with one's heart, even if it remains unspoken or unidentified.

The Maternal Symbol in Prehistoric Times

An art which touches us existentially always contains man's reflection upon his own finitude and his death. The cave paintings of the Ice Age are such works of art. These representations of animals are manifestations of the breath of the hunter that seizes the young man of the hunting society at the beginning of adulthood, shapes his behavior and motivates him beyond individual death. In the same caves in which the young man is thus initiated into the society of hunters and into the struggle with death, there are also numerous representations of the woman and mother

(Fig. 3, the "Venus of Lausalle"; similar representations in the Trois Frères cave picture a woman in several overlapping scenes, immediately before parturition, Fig. 43).[10]

A. Leroi-Gourhan found that in many caves the feminine element is present in geometric figures: the triangle, the curve and the cleft (representing female genitalia). These and similar symbols add a female and maternal presence in the cave.[11] Men and male symbols are much less frequent. When they do appear, they are hunters (mostly with erect penises expressing aggression) and are usually pictured with animals. On the other hand, the woman appears most often independently of both. In the representations of woman the predominant aspects are fullness, maternity and parturition. In this symbolism she represents the all-embracing being who always brings forth new life from her womb and feeds it from her breasts. Research in prehistory often points to a possible analogy between the female figures of the later Paleolithic period and the notion of the "mistress of the animals" that appears in many hunting cultures.[12] It is said that she gives life to men and beasts. The skulls and skeletons of hunted animals are often given back to her for regeneration in cultic rituals, placing them on stakes or in trees, or submerging them in water.[13] The mother is meant to tend them and, as it were, restore them to life. Thus the woman and mother is the symbol of returning and regenerated life. Her image helps man overcome his fear of death and of transience.

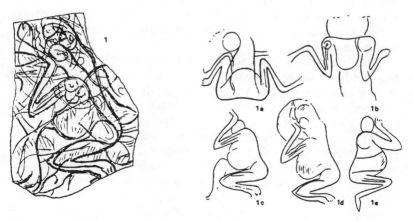

Fig. 43: A woman in labor; different phases of parturition are drawn, superimposed; see the individual figures on the right (rock-drawing from the early Paleolithic period; cave of Trois-Frères, France).

Many small, modelled female figures similar to the wall paintings have been found, especially at the fireplaces of campsites. Here, in the center and sanctuary of the gathering and hunting community, was obviously the place and seat of the woman and mother. After the hunt one returned to this "place." The food was prepared and handed out here. One found the warmth and light of the fire and experienced a regeneration of vital forces. The symbol of the woman and mother stood for this "place."

This transcendent dimension of the woman and mother appears only relatively late in Ice Age art. While animal representations extend in part back as far as the Mousterian culture (75,000 to 47,000 BC), female figurations are not found before the Aurignacian period (32,000 to 23,000 BC), but are very numerous in the Gravettian (23,000 to 18,000 BC) and in the Magdalenian periods (18,000 to 11,000 BC). Of course, this evidence could be interpreted differently. A. Leroi-Gourhan gives a plausible explanation. In his book "Hand und Wort," he has proved the close connection between manual and linguistic activities in man, particularly with his medical examination of the different regions and functions of the brain. Throughout his evolution, man's way of making tools corresponds to the nature of his language. The cause of the change in both is seen by Leroi-Gourhan as changes in the brain.

The author takes this "development" of the brain as a final, given fact that no longer needs to be explained. He does not examine the many circumstances to which the human being adapted in this change through mutation just as the giraffe, with its oversized neck, adapted to the lofty food supply on the solitary trees in the prairie. From the perspective of religious history and cultural anthropology, man's growing and increasingly differentiated brain serves his growing sensitivity to the transcendent dimension of reality.[14]

This is especially applicable to the brain's evolutionary step from Neanderthal man to modern man or Neanthropus. In this step the volume of the brain remained constant, or, indeed, decreased slightly. However, we may suppose that a transformation of different parts of the brain occurred, a higher density of cells and connections between cells and thereby a higher efficiency in the given space. In the course of these transformations the "unbolting of the forehead" (Leroi-Gourhan) took place, that is, the expansion of the brain's frontal lobes.[15] These parts of the brain serve as a "regulating mechanism" between the part that controls motor coordination and the part that creates emotions.[16] This allows for a better control of the emotions on the one hand and, on the other hand, for a greater detachment from the emotions in the mastery of technical movements.[17] Together, these elements create a greater distance from the experience of reality, a greater variety and differentiation in the reality which touches man emotionally, and more scope for reacting to it. The one-sided fixation of emotional perception on the great and the strong, on the power to kill, had perhaps been somewhat eased, and man became more and more able to perceive the transcendent dimension of the woman and mother as well, and to represent her image within the "mythographical art" which already existed in a rough form.[18] About 40,000 years ago this transformation began to take place gradually, and we find, in Ice Age art of approximately 32,000 years ago, female idols — an essential step in mankind's withdrawal from the dark fascination of the killing-power, to which he had succumbed, and his move towards (and back to) the Abba, the mother.[19]

The symbolism of fire may have been a bridge to the discovery of the transcendent dimension of the woman and mother. Joseph Campbell, the American scholar, claims to have discovered that for a very long time, that is, from the first appropriation of fire (as we know today, more than a million years ago[20]) up to the time of the cave paintings and female figurations (30,000 to 20,000 years ago) man used fire not for mundane uses such as heating, cooking or grilling, but exclusively for cultic veneration. The first fireplaces were sacred places (shrines), where fire was venerated and guarded as a sort of "fetish," while man ate his food raw.[21] This would mean that he was extremely sensitive to the transcendent dimension of fire — the later Vedic god Agni — the sacredness of the phenomenon preventing him from using it for the purpose of grilling and cooking. However, Campbell does not produce any proof for his thesis. He contends that Peking man and even Neanderthal man ate their meals "absolutely raw,"[22] but he does not specify how he comes to this conclusion (one could think of a proof based on the shape of the teeth and jaw bones).

All this evidence makes sense only when we see in man's transition towards game hunting an original act (original sin) that is contrary to his physical and psychic evolution. Through this act man came under the spell of the (male) killing-power in such a way that all transcendence which had previously been perceived by him, as the child, the fellow-being and the fire, was caught in this circle and could not escape into autonomous activity. Only when the "unbolting of the forehead" enabled him to paint this conflict of animal and killing on the walls of caves, and thus to gain a certain distance from it, did the spell loosen somewhat. Man then became able to perceive the realities of the world — the child, the woman and mother, the fire, the animals and plants — as independent entities, and became aware of their individual transcendent dimensions.

If Campbell's thesis is correct, then man would have been free to put fire to practical use. But a close relation between the symbolism of fire and the symbolism of woman exists even independently of Campbell's thesis. Of course, fire was probably first perceived as killing-power — created by a bolt of lightning, and experienced in the disastrous wildfires which consumed men and animals alike. Thus fire fell under the overwhelming spell of the power to kill that blocked the perception of other symbols and hierophanies. The symbol of this relation between fire and the sacred killing-power is the burnt offering, which exists in all ancient religions, and in which the victim is first killed and then burnt. The burning of heretics and witches during the Middle Ages was also a manifestation of the frightful killing-power of fire.

But the guarding of this fascinating phenomenon was probably a female task from early on. Even in ancient Rome the highly respected vestal virgins, the priestesses of Vesta, goddess of the hearth, had the task of guarding and caring for the sacred flame. The precious fire was too easily snuffed out to be taken on the hunt by the males. It had to be preserved and guarded at that place where the women took care of the children and were not allowed to take part in larger expeditions. Thus the camp with its holy flame soon became the domain of the mother. And indeed, almost all female idols were found at fireplaces, and it is always a goddess — Hera for the Greeks, Vesta for the Romans, Freya for the Germans — who incarnates the transcendent dimension of fire. With the discovery of the woman and mother (and perhaps simultaneously the usefulness of fire) as a transcendent dimension independent of the complex of killing and killing-power, the possibility is opened up for the investment with symbolic meanings of other objects and situations. Characteristically, however, these symbols remain more or less related to the symbol of the woman and mother in early civilizations: campfire, hut, home, sun, moon, stars, immobile rock, mountains, hills, refreshing and revitalizing water, the tree with deep roots and great height, fertility and growth, sexual experience — all this was now being gradually discovered in a symbolic meaning, transcendent to the objective reality, but remained linked to the symbol of the woman and mother. The transcendent dimension of these phenomena is almost always expressed by female divinities or by their heroes.

Along with this liberating and broadening religious-symbolic experience arose the psychological readiness to quit following the herds, to abandon the divine power to kill during the hunt, to "be found out by the plants" (Herbig),[23] and to establish a permanent homestead. It is striking that all the evidence from the early settled cultures — Çatal Hüyük, Sumer, ancient Egypt, Crete, the Indus culture — points clearly towards the symbol of the woman as the focal point of religious symbolism. And in their relation with this maternal symbol, in their different graduations and accentuations, all those things and situations of life which we have mentioned take on a religious, symbolic meaning. In Çatal

Hüyük, in Jericho, in early Mesopotamia, in the Indus culture and in the Minoan culture of Crete, we find sacred trees, sanctuaries in rocks and caves, the veneration of the sun and the moon, religious ablutions, and the cult of holy matrimony. These elements of a culture shaped by the maternal symbol were developed particularly in the insular situation of Crete over a longer period of time, and thus more clearly than in other locations. We will therefore devote closer attention to Crete as an example of a culture shaped by the maternal symbol.

A Culture Shaped by the Maternal Symbol: Crete

Such cultures as we have just mentioned are often referred to as "matriarchal cultures." However, the term "matriarchy" is contradictory insofar as it joins the word "mother" to the Greek word "arché," which means "beginning," "origin," as well as "power," "domination." But the archaeological evidence does not allow us to determine the precise division of roles and of power between the genders in these cultures, and even less of their history. In the context of religious history, it is therefore preferable to speak about a religion and culture shaped by the maternal symbol instead of a "matriarchy." Such a highly developed culture existed in Crete from the earliest traces of settlement until the conquest by the Mycenaeans. A Cretan did not talk about his fatherland, but about his motherland. In the following section we will highlight some of the characteristic aspects of this culture.

— An Architecture Shaped by the Maternal Symbol

In contrast to the cultures of Sumer and Egypt and to corresponding cultures in Mexico, that of Crete is characterized by the absence of large temples and cultic buildings. A similar situation is encountered in the Indus culture, as long as one does not interpret the bathing facility excavated at Mohenjo-Daro as a cultic building or temple.[24] In Crete the cult was practiced mainly in caves. The caves remained the cultic places during all periods of development and survived even beyond the Minoan culture, until late in the Hellenistic period. The cave of Eileithyia, the goddess of birth, near Amnissos served as a cultic place until the fifth and sixth centuries AD.[25] Other cultic places were situated on mountain tops or in the courts of Minoan palaces. The rites of the cult were practiced outdoors, as is evidenced by excavated altars and sacrificial stones. The symbols of trees, the sun, the moon, and double-headed axes were integrated into their rituals. Processional trails are found all around the palace courts. In Animospilia a temple-like building was excavated, but it

261

is so small that it cannot be compared to the well-known Sumerian, Egyptian and Mexican structures.

The monuments we know from other highly developed cultures are absent not only from the religious world in Crete. Monumental and tall buildings tend to be associated more with the symbolism of the killing-power than with the woman and mother. This can be seen characteristically in the urban and palace architecture of ancient Crete. Palaces from both the early and the later periods are built from the inside out, differing in this respect from any other known palace construction. The architect did not start with a given ground plan, a given outer limit, in order to divide it according to need. Rather, the first consideration was obviously the inner court, around which all the different buildings were grouped. The principle of construction is not consistent planning. Rather, the rooms surrounded the court according to a principle of growth. Growing from the inside outward, we find first the living, sleeping, and eating rooms, as well as stairs to the lower rooms for cultic ablutions, and then, spreading to the outskirts, rooms for the servants, storage space and corridors. Outer courts with large open stairs and processional trails to the inner court were added to the outside, without really separating the palace from its environment.

A good example of this architecture of palaces and cities is Kato Zágros on a small bay on the east coast of Crete. At the bottom of a rounded slope, the inner court is built in a sort of depression. The rooms of the palace are built adjacent to it, and these seem to flow seamlessly into the city houses on the slope, connected through rising stairs. Thus, while in our medieval towns, the palace or the fortress is usually located on a mountain, towering majestically over the town, the royal palace and its court are here at the lowest point and the center of the urban structure. One goes up to the lord and father, but the mother is found below, in the center, in the midst of her children. It is also surprising that the whole city has no outer limit, but seems to fade into the landscape. There are no city walls, no gates, no fortifications. Very few weapons have been found. And yet there were approximately sixty towns and at least four major city-states which excavations have revealed—Knossos, Festos, Zágros and Malia—which obviously did not fear invasion and conquest by their neighbors. The insular location of Crete and its naval force protected the whole of Crete against enemies from outside. From this example we might catch a glimpse of what a culture and civilization could look like in which the maternal symbol shapes belief and practice.

262

The people who first arrived on this island some six thousand years ago brought with them the female and maternal idols known from the Later Palaeolithic period, as is confirmed by the oldest excavated evidence. They probably came from Anatolia. Many symbols and scenes resembling those from Crete were found in Çatal Hüyük. But in Crete this culture, with its maternal symbolism, was further developed and more highly refined. From the full features of the Venus of Lausalle (Fig. 3), or of the "toad-goddess" from Hakilar in Anatolia (Fig. 44) figures arise which still have maternal features with large hips, but whose upper bodies are slender, their heads raised with an ecstatic expression, and their hands lifted in a gesture of blessing (see the "poppy-goddess" with poppy-capsules on her head, Fig. 45).

Fig. 44: The "toad-goddess" of Hakilar.

Different symbols define the character of the goddess. She is frequently pictured with a bird. It sits on her head like a dove, as in the figure from Gazi or as in the serpent-goddess (Fig. 46), or it sits on the double-headed axe, the symbol of the priestess' rule. It also appears hovering freely. In general, the bird expresses man's yearning for lightness, flight and ecstasy. We have already seen this symbol in the pit of the Lascaux cave, as an expression of the hunter's wind and breath, which still holds and embraces the hunter thrown down by the wounded buffalo, even if he suffers death as an individual. In the intoxication of the hunt, his death was nullified. But the bird of the Cretan goddess is not a predator—an eagle or a falcon, as suggested by the shape of the hunter's head at Lascaux—but is a dove. Even at the time of Jesus, when the narrator saw the divine breath descending upon Jesus in the form of a dove, this creature was the symbol of the goddess of love and fertility throughout the Near East (Ishtar, Anat, Astarte, Aphrodite). Accordingly, it is not the intoxication of the prey and the hunt, the ecstasy of hunting down and of killing, which emanates from the goddess, but erotic and sexual ecstasy. This element, overtly expressed in the female figures from the Stone Age by the exaggerated representations of sexual attributes, has been refined into the image of the dove. Some impressions from seal-stones show dancing women in ecstasy or the figure of the poppy-goddess and seem to suggest that during the celebration of the cult, the element of ecstasy was not only achieved by the sexual act of the holy wedding, but also by drugs (poppy?), and undoubtedly also by music. The fact that the bird and its wings do indeed symbolize sexual ecstasy is proved by the motif of the "Phallus-bird," the winged phallus known throughout the Greek world. Other symbols surrounding the Cretan goddess are the trees, flowers, and bees. Sacred trees seem to have had a prominent place in the inner courts of the palaces, for example at Zágros. Along with flowers and bees, trees represent life, fertility, and growth, and also beauty and sweetness. The goddess personifies and bestows these gifts.

— *The Bull of the Sea and of the Underworld as Opponent of the Goddess*

The goddess grants and symbolizes fertility, growth, beauty and the sweetness of life. But oppressive, primeval forces of nature threaten this divinely protected life. Floods and earthquakes plague the island repeatedly and totally destroy the old palaces. On the fresco at the north entrance of the palace at Knossos (Fig. 10), a raging bull charges with lowered horns towards a tree. The bull is therefore the power opposing

Fig. 45: The "poppy-goddess" from Crete.

Fig. 46: The "serpent-goddess" from Crete.

the goddess. He is present everywhere, on wall paintings and seals, in ivory carvings and soapstone jars. His horns are lined up like trophies on the frieze of the palace.

However, the religion of Crete, with its maternal symbolism, is not a dualistic one. One of the most respected scholars of Cretan culture, Klaus Gallas, writes: "In the Minoan religion the bull never appears as an attribute of the godhead. Its special status is due to the fact that its primeval power has to be overcome by man..."[26] In contrast to Israel, which had experienced the wilderness-god as the caring God "I-am-here," and for whom the maternal divinities and their heroes were no longer true godheads, but only blind powers that tempted man to fall away from Yahweh, the wilderness-force symbolized by the bull was no longer itself of a divine nature, but was the element that had to be overcome by the maternal divine power.

This conquest of the bull was performed in a twofold manner, according to Klaus Gallas: by ritual killing, and by games involving bulls.[27] In the west court of the Knossos palace archaeologists found three huge pits, paved with stones, that were filled exclusively with the bones of bulls and held two sacrificial altars. Pictorial representations (like the sacrificial scene on the sarcophagus of Hagia Triada) suggest that the bulls were butchered here, the blood gushing into a cultic vessel, the drinking horn, called a rhyton, which was often adorned with emblems of bulls. Then this rhyton, brimming with the blood of the bulls, was probably carried south along the excavated processional trails, around the palace and into the inner court, where the blood was poured out on a stone altar in the northwest corner of the court. The force of the wilderness was thus spilled in the inner court of the maternal palace.

The "bull-jumping" fresco was also found in the palace of Knossos (Fig. 47): A man, marked by his darker skin, performs a back flip or handspring over the back of the galloping bull. Two large female figures seem to illustrate the starting and ending points of this acrobatic performance. What is the meaning of this mysterious picture? On the one hand, the best Spanish bullfighters of our day, to whom this picture was shown, thought that such a jump would be impossible to perform. On the other hand, it is represented so frequently in other pictures, on seals, vessels and sculptures, that it could not have been the product of a single artist's imagination. It is striking that in other cultures in which the maternal symbol is most prominent, namely the culture of the Indus valley and possibly Çatal Hüyük, similar representations appear as well. The realism of the representation is especially conspicuous in the rhyton at the museum of Herakleion. It is called the "boxer's rhyton" as it has

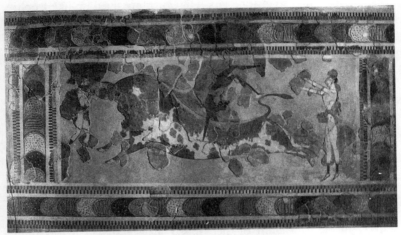

Fig. 47: The "fresco of the bull-jumper" in Knossos, Crete.

some representations of fist-fights. In one scene a bull jumper is gored to death by a bull (Fig. 48). H. G. Wunderlich interpreted the bull-jumping as a human sacrifice, obviously without knowing of this picture.[28] In fact, human sacrifices did indeed exist in ancient Crete, a fact that Wunderlich could not have known. But this discovery, which we will discuss soon, differs in one crucial respect from the "bull-games": Human sacrifices were conducted more or less in secret, in a small, secluded temple at the north slope of the Iuktas mountain. The bull-games, on the other hand, were performed for a large public, probably in the inner courts of the palaces, as can be seen from the representations.

Perhaps the solution to the mystery of the bull games lies in a motif that is present in many fairy tales. The young hero, who wants to marry the princess and become a king, has to fulfill difficult, almost superhuman tasks. The public and festive character of the bull-jumping seems indeed more appropriate to a wedding than to a human sacrifice. The "lily-prince" in one of the frescoes at Knossos embodies the force of the fertility that he gains from his encounter with the woman and mother, just as does the priest-king whose bust was excavated in the Indus valley. Such a king, who symbolized and granted fertility to the land in his function as the husband of the priestess, the representative of the goddess, had to be very strong and athletic. Even today the solo dances of men express virility and the power of procreation by high and powerful jumps,

Fig. 48: The "boxer-rhyton" from Hagia Triada, Crete. The middle section shows a raging bull who has apparently gored a jumper.

whether in classical ballet or in the dances of the Cossacks. It would be in perfect keeping with the refined culture of Crete if the pretender to or the holder of the royal throne, who wished to become the husband of the priestess queen, had to demonstrate time and again his superior strength and virility by jumping over a bull. In so doing he showed that he knew how to subjugate the primeval forces of nature not with armed threats of death, but in a playful way.[29] As we can see in paintings and sculptures,[30] the jump could be made most easily by holding down the head of the bull by the horns; or by standing on an altar approximately as high as the bull in order to jump more easily over the bull's back. Nevertheless, the jump in all likelihood often ended in the way depicted on the "boxer rhyton" from Hagia Triada.

From the point of view of religious history, it is of course not correct to speak of human sacrifice in this context.[31] For the purpose of the cultic game was not to exalt the dreadful power to kill and thereby to deify the bearer of this power (as in the Roman gladiator games in which the emperor decided the life or death of the loser with a thumb signal). Rather, the jumper died in the attempt to overcome the dark, primeval power of nature, the bull of the underworld, who makes the earth tremble and palaces collapse, much like the light-hero and the dragon-slayer—although without weapons and in a more playful fashion, confident of his athletic skill. He danced on the back of the bull, as it were. If one were still to consider this scene to be one of sacrifice, then this is precisely the point at which the mortal sacrifice and the offering of the first-fruit are fused. On the one hand at the fertility feasts and sacred weddings human life is strewn before the goddess, who grants light and a permanent homeland to man. On the other it is a living human being who bleeds to death under the horns of the bull. Intentionally or not, the killing-power comes to the forefront in these events and is associated with the woman and mother who presides over the game.

— *The Weakness of the Maternal Symbol in the Face of Individual Death: The Sarcophagus of Hagia Triada*

This aspect is conspicuously evident in a sarcophagus that was discovered almost intact in a chamber tomb close by the little palace of Hagia Triada. The four sides are painted with frescoes that probably express the general attitude of Minoan man towards death—since it is the decoration of a sarcophagus. On one side we find, inside an ornamental frame, the image of a two-wheeled chariot, drawn by winged lions, in which two women stand as rulers, holding the reins. On the back of the winged lions stands a small bird facing the women. The lions' heads are also turned towards the women (Fig. 49). The picture expresses the ecstasy and energy of life—even in its colors: reddish-brown and blue are predominant—as it is manifested in the features of the goddesses: The powerful but tractable lions, expressive of the virile, vital force of nature, are held in check by the goddesses. This force thus loses its threat. It even develops long wings and turns back towards the women in the form of a bird. Thus the women do not lose their ruling power even in the face of death. The death of the individual is encompassed by the vital force of the woman and mother, who has the power to kill the bull of the underworld and to grant life and fertility.

This power of the woman is represented on the fresco on a second side of the sarcophagus (Fig. 50). A bull lies on the sacrificial altar, tied up and bleeding to death. Its blood flows into a rhyton standing underneath the altar. A woman stands before the altar and puts her hands on the bull in an upright and lordly gesture. She seems to be in charge of the events. Two goats under the altar are probably the next offerings. A man plays an accompaniment to the ceremony on a wind instrument. Another priestess makes an offering of gifts at a smaller altar next to the sacrificial altar, in the same posture, offering fruits, bread, and wine. A small tree rises from a larger altar, covered with bulls' horns. Between these two altars is a double-headed axe, the Minoan symbol of power, rising to the top of the picture. A bird perches on the axe. This part of the picture expresses the life, the order, and the fertility which the killing of the bull makes possible. The bird on the double-headed axe is a motif that is found in many representations in this area. The axe is at the woman's disposal. It is a symbol of power similar to the sword in the

Fig. 49: A chariot drawn by winged lions. Narrow side of the sarcophagus of Hagia Triada, Crete.

Fig. 50: Sacrifical scene on the long side of the sarcophagus of Hagia Triada, Crete; to the left the sacrifice of a bull, to the right an offering of food. Note the bird (dove) on top of the two-headed axe.

hands of medieval kings—and yet the weapon which symbolizes the killing-power is the resting place for the dove: the sacred symbol of the goddess of love. (This motif reminds one of contemporary photographs of a child in invaded Prague putting flowers in the muzzle of a Soviet gun.) The power is there, but it is integrated into the ecstasy of life emanating from the woman and mother.

The third side again shows a two-wheeled chariot and two women, the one on the right with a whip in her hand, and with her companion controlling with strong reins huge, dark-colored horses with powerful chests and necks. Here, the subjected power of nature is symbolized by the horses.

The fourth side of the sarcophagus is especially instructive (Fig. 51). This picture is obviously divided in two. On the left side we see two women pouring some sacrificial liquid, probably the blood of a slain bull, from the rhyton into a larger container placed between two double-headed axes. Birds once again perch on the axes. A man accompanies the ritual by playing a cithara. The women have the blood of the bull, the life-force of wild nature, in their hands. It is integrated into the power of the bird-bearing double-headed axes.

While this half of the picture has a bright background and its motion is directed towards the left side, the right half has a dark background and is directed towards the right edge of the sarcophagus. In this right half, only men are depicted. In the far right corner there is a rigid, almost wooden, bust-like figure without arms, standing in front of a ledge the height of a man and next to a cactus-like tree without leaves. Three men approach this figure. The first bears a model of a ship and the others have

272

Fig. 51: Left side: the pouring of sacrificial blood; right side: gifts for the deceased. Second long side of the sarcophagus of Hagia Triada, Crete.

two differently colored, probably live, calves in their arms. The motif of the sides of the sarcophagus decorated with twisted meandering lines, is repeated on the wall of the building in front of which the stiff, armless figure stands. This figure represents the dead man who came out of his sarcophagus, as it were, and now stands rigidly in front of it with the stiffness of a dead body. His posture seems a threatening and awesome one. His dark skin identifies him as a male. This figure has the features of an ancestor in whom the terror of death is reflected. Obviously, this terrifying figure is to be appeased by the gifts brought by the men. The picture is in peculiar contrast to the other images on the sarcophagus. While the other pictures are characterized by a predominance of the maternal symbol, this symbol is altogether absent here. Men bring offerings to appease their male ancestor. In the artistic style of the frescoes the graceful and delicate lines which characterize the woman, despite all her power, give way to the threatening "wooden" stiffness of the ancestral figure.

This picture highlights the existential weakness of a culture under the influence of the maternal symbol. One's individual death and the terror of its prospect cannot be explained and appeased by the maternal symbol. Man's personal emanation, the transcendent dimension which was perceived in his personality even in prehistoric times, can not be reassuringly fitted into the feminine and maternal cycle of death and becoming. The new "lily-prince," who takes the place of the former one, who was perhaps killed during a bull-game, *is* not the same. And when he himself is one day gored by the bull's horns, an unbridgeable gulf will open before him too, a gap, a bottomless abyss from which rises the horror of death. The maternal life force and love cannot assuage his distress. In the individual human being who is deeply influenced by the original sinful perversion of the power of life and love into the power to kill, death and destruction provoke a shudder of terror more powerful than the fiercest bull, and therefore cannot be expressed in the symbol of the bull, as the Israelites correctly recognized. No hierophany and no symbol, not the

273

stone, not the tree, not the revitalizing power of water or the sexual experience — not even the image of the woman and mother, insofar as it is itself linked with power — can overcome such terror.

The immediate proximity of these two images on the long side of the sarcophagus illustrates how, in the midst of a culture dominated by the maternal symbol, the very ancient cult of the ancestor, of the lord and father whose rule is absolute and who must be appeased by offerings, resurfaces in the face of individual death, even though it had been thought to have been long since overcome. In the midst of a world of imagery dominated by the figure of the woman and her attributes, a cultic rite evolves which is performed exclusively by men and which is marked by gestures of subjection.

— The Secret Capitulation to the Bull of the Underworld: The Human Sacrifice of Anemospilia

Equally remarkable is the gruesome discovery made at Anemospilia some ten years ago, on the northern slope of the Iuktas mountain, where the grave of the Cretan Zeus is located, according to an old legend. A small temple of three chambers and a transversal corridor was excavated there (see the reconstruction according to K. Gallas, Fig. 52). The building had

Fig. 52: Reconstruction of the temple of Anemospilia with the scene of human sacrifice, as it was occurring at the moment of the temple's collapse.

274

collapsed, probably because of an earthquake, at the very moment a human sacrifice was being performed. Apart from the victim there were only three people involved in the act. It seems almost as if it had been performed quietly and in secret at this remote location. In the western chamber three skeletons were discovered. On a small, narrow altar lay the skeleton of a man perhaps eighteen years old and 1.65 m. in height, as determined by a careful medical examination. He was lying sideways on his right shoulder, his legs folded and bound to his lower body. Under the bones there was a bronze dagger more than 40 cm. long with which the young man had been killed. The color of the bones revealed that he had been killed, as was the bull of the Hagia Triada sarcophagus, by a cut throat (the upper bones were white, because the blood flowed down from there into the lower right side of the body, where it caused the bones to turn black when the dead body was cremated).[32] Behind the victim lay the skeleton of a man approximately thirty years old and 1.80 m. in height, who apparently had performed the sacrifice. In the far corner of the room lay the remains of a young woman. The fourth skeleton lay in the corridor in front of the door of the central chamber. In front of its hands, pieces of a rhyton were found which, when reassembled, showed the figure of a bull on the rhyton's front side.

It is assumed that this young man was carrying the blood of the victim into the central chamber, in order to pour it out at the feet of the idol over a rock that was protruding from the ground. From two earthen feet and some charred pieces of wood it was possible to reconstruct a monumental wooden statue which is strikingly similar in posture and expression to the ancestral figure on the sarcophagus of Hagia Triada. It also has no arms and is stiff and "wooden," the image of a terrifying killing-power.

This discovery is unique, because the sudden collapse and burning of the building has fixed the sacrificial scene as if in a snapshot. In its type, it does not fit into the seemingly peaceful, paradisal world of the other excavations, where scenes of cruelty and war are altogether absent. Accordingly, the evidence is generally interpreted as a singular event. The earthenware dates it to 1,700 BC. This is the time in which the "old palaces" were destroyed by earthquakes (and were completely rebuilt 150 years later in the same location). It is thought that at the peak of their distress, when several heavy shocks had begun to destroy the palaces and the city, people as a last resort turned to human sacrifice in the hope of appeasing the powers of the underworld. As in the experience of individual death, the old symbols of the ancestor as the lord and father resurfaced. The bull of the sea and the underworld appeared once again as a raging god of death and caused a secret capitulation, performed in the remoteness of the Iuktas mountain. Instead of killing the bull symbolically and jumping over its back in a playful way, man subjected himself to this force. In the "bull-rhyton" in which the blood of the sacrificial animals had been collected to be poured out before the altar and the insignia of the goddess and queen, the blood of a sacrificed human was now collected in order to be spilled at the earthen feet of the all-powerful godhead of death. But the god did not accept this offering. At the very moment when the servant stood with the human blood in his hands in front of the central door of the idol's chamber, the beams and stones collapsed, burying the victim and the priests.

This scene demonstrates the vulnerability of a culture under the domination of the maternal symbol. This symbolism is no match for the terrifying power of death and destruction, as it is experienced by sinful humans and their heritage of the primeval deed of murder. Sooner or later this symbolism will collapse in the face of death. Of course, the palaces were rebuilt, even bigger than the earlier ones. Art and the style of life became ever more refined and there was no sign of war or strife on this celestial Mediterranean island. But again, this second blossoming of Minoan culture, the time of the "new palaces," lasted only 250 years, no longer than the period of the old palaces. Around 1450 BC the new palaces and the surrounding cities collapsed again — it is believed because of a volcanic eruption on the nearby island of Santorin.

At this point the fascination exerted by the maternal symbol was broken for good. Just as the immigrating Aryans found in the Indus culture[33] the deteriorating phase of a culture grounded in maternal symbols and met little or no resistance to their immigration, the martial Mycenaeans, "filled with the pride of their forefathers,"[34] came to Crete from Greece and took over the island. The maternal symbol was still woven into the legends, myths, dramas and epics of Greek culture in manifold ways. Everyday and political life, however, was now influenced by the instincts of the hunter. In the tragedies of Sophocles, Orestes could kill his mother without being condemned by the court of male judges. Although it was a strong divine symbol, the symbol of the woman and mother was still too weak to overcome the fascination of the power to kill that dominated the human world.

Christians believe that in the Judeo-Christian tradition the cycle of violence and killing was successfully broken when the god of terror *himself* changed in a credible way. He altered his appearance and let his true maternal countenance shine forth, thus becoming the Abba, the Mama/Papa. Such a transformation follows a long and difficult course. Only at the end of Jesus' life does this process reach its climax and its fulfillment. As the ancient Minoans turned back to the primeval cult of the divine ancestor in their utmost distress, so Jesus turned in his moment

276

of real agony back to El, the God of the forefathers: "Eloi, Eloi, lama sabachthani?" (Mark 15, 34). But with Jesus the story continues. There would be no salvation from the breath of the hunter if Mark had not told us that Jesus cried out once more before his death "with a loud voice," and if Luke had not found a tradition that interprets Jesus' cry of agony in a credible and convincing way as the beloved son's ultimate and irrevocable acceptance by the Abba: "Abba, into your hands I commend my spirit" (Luke 23, 46). In the life of Jesus, and in the way it is narrated, the maternal and caring Abba is manifested as the last embrace of human life *and* death, and not, as in the story of ancient Crete, as El, the bull-like god of terror.

Maternal Religion in Fairy Tales

All tribes and peoples of this earth have gone through a phase of maternal spirituality to some extent, or have at least been exposed to it. This must be assumed to be the case in view of the fact that there is no group of humans that has not "let itself be found by the plants" (Herbig) and thereby developed elements of a settled life style. Populations like the nomadic Eskimos or the Indians of Tierra del Fuego have not lived in these inhospitable regions since the Early Paleolithic period. Instead they were pushed there at a secondary stage and were forced once again to adopt a nomadic life style, but this time in a confined region. They longed for a homeland, too. Wherever man became so sensitive to the emanations of the hearth, its fire and the mystery of the newly discovered plants that he yearned for something lasting and permanent, for a homeland, he was possessed by such a desire that he actually changed his pattern of life and tried to organize his activities in such a way as to assure himself of this settled existence. It is no wonder that symbols of the mother became for him the images of this new way of life and overcame — at least for a time — the fascination with hunting and killing.

Indeed, in the course of history the sinful fascination of the power of terror and killing has proved stronger. In Crete and probably in the Indus culture as well it became clear that in the human experience under the influence of original sin the maternal symbol is too weak to support and motivate a human community permanently in the face of individual deaths and natural disasters. In Sumer and Monte Albán in the Oaxaca valley of ancient Mexico the breath of the hunter and the fascination of the killing-power have prevailed not from conquest but from within, as we have explained previously,[35] because the mother village or a new central authority took the filial communities as their "prey," cruelly and mercilessly subjugating great numbers of the population and exploiting them through demands of tribute and forced labor. In other tribes, like those of the Celtic, the German and the Slavic people, a balanced co-existence between the maternal symbolism and the fascination of the male power to kill emerged from the very beginning, in a way characteristic of each people, and shaped their religions and life styles. At the period of the great migrations those peoples in whom the martial and hunting element was stronger usually conquered those cultures in which the maternal symbolism predominated. But sometimes, as in the case of India, the conquerors were influenced from below, as it were, by the conquered and their ways of thinking and living in maternal images and symbols.

It is true that the maternal symbol could not sustain its dominance any place in this world marked by original sin. In all peoples and cultures the final victory belonged to the patriarchy. But the possibility of living within the maternal symbol is engrained in human memory. This memory has been recorded in our fairy tales.

— Historical Roots of the Magical Fairy Tales (V. Propp)

Fairy tales are stories with a symbolic content. If, as we have contended in the introduction, the origin of symbols is not in some "archetype of the soul," in the sense of a structure of ideas and feelings that is innate in man, but rather in a "perceived reality"[36] (namely, in a transcendent dimension to be perceived in phenomena), then it is possible to explore the social and historical reality which underlies the fairy tales. This approach to the interpretation of fairy tales is most prominently represented by Vladimir Propp.[37] He sees the fundamental problem of research in fairy tales to be the "worldwide similarity" of their motifs.[38] According to this scholar the solution to this problem may be found in the fact that "almost all"[39] the principal elements of fairy tales are grounded in and derived from prehistoric rites of initiation, and in the accompanying ideas about death, that were spread throughout the whole world. A particular difficulty for him arises in the obvious significance of the women and young girls, especially in the genre which he studies most, the magical fairy tale. His main source for the motifs in fairy tales is the rite of initiation which is primarily the introduction of young men into a male society. The rites of initiation for girls are less prominent.

Propp leaves one part of the question open,[40] and the other part he explains as a "reflection of matriarchal structures" in the fairy tale.[41] He seems to accept the Bachofen thesis, according to which the matriarchy is the most ancient form of human society and the formation of

278

male fraternities and rites of initiation are a secondary development. Thus for him the origin of fairy tales lies in the post-matriarchal, male-fraternal society, the significant role of the woman in fairy tales being explained as a relic of former matriarchal structures. However, this explanation is not conclusive. For if male fraternities and rites of initiation were formed as a reaction to female dominance, then one would expect that in these rites, and in the stories related to them, all elements which point to the dominance and the greater importance of the woman would be avoided. The substantial significance of the woman and of the young girl in fairy tales cannot be explained in that manner.[42]

On the whole, the historical space in which magical fairy tales have their historical roots remains quite unspecific in Propp's work.[43] He speaks in general terms of a "pre-class society,"[44] but does not specify where and when it was realized historically. He uses ethnological material without discrimination, without asking what prehistoric or protohistoric conditions were present in a given ethnic people, and to what later influences they might have been exposed. (Such undifferentiated ethnological comparisons used to explain archaeological evidence are viewed very critically today.)[45] But in fairy tales we do often find class differences (e.g. king-servant) that are essential to the plot and cannot be explained as secondary transformations. The king is originally the light-hero, who defends the settlement against the powers of the wilderness and assures the fertility of the land.

Werner Daum's view of the "thousands of years during the transition to settled life" as the time of the birth of fairy tales has therefore some justification. The sacrificing of children and young girls (abandoned in a dark forest) and the conquest of this darkness and death by the light-hero, who thereby becomes a king, and the sacred wedding giving liberation and fertility, is indeed a fundamental structure of many fairy tales.[46] However, Propp has traced so many motifs back to elements of initiation rites that he demonstrates convincingly these rites certainly are part of the historical roots of fairy tales as well. But the origins of these rites do not lie in a post-matriarchal society. Instead they come from a pre-matriarchal and pre-Neolithic hunting society, as evidenced in the pit of the Lascaux cave. The worldwide similarity of fairy tale motifs can be explained only by a similar unity in that early form of society. Later, in the Neolithic transition to a settled life style, the transcendent dimension of the woman and mother appeared as a shaping force for human life and culture in a similar, worldwide and unified way.

These difficulties are best resolved when we place the origin of fairy tales at a time in which all ethnic groups on earth were under the in-

279

fluence of the maternal symbol, some more strongly than others, but all only temporarily. They were all in search of a permanent homeland, but eventually failed—in one way or another—and were overtaken again by the hunter's breath. Only then does it become clear why fairy tales preserve the gruesome initiation rites in such a detailed way, although presenting them strongly devalued or revalued. They are expressed in the motifs of devouring, dismembering and torturing, so that the hero comes forth—the light-hero and king—and puts an end to the power that demands such behavior.

On the other hand, the circumstances of this culture's failure explains the existential impulse for the birth and tradition of fairy tales throughout the centuries. For it sounds logical, as Propp suggests, that a fairy tale cannot come into being while the fairy tale motifs are still part of a functioning complex of rites and myths that have a social significance. In this phase they are sacred and protected by taboo and secrecy. But Propp's explanation fails when he suggests that after the decline of these rites and myths, the motifs that they contained were taken freely as material for man's creative imagination, and further elaborated. For, as can be seen in the most ancient artistic monuments—Ice Age cave paintings—art always elaborates on that which concerns man existentially. It does not serve as curator and preserver of elements of rites and myths that have become meaningless.

Like any artistic or intellectual creation, narrative imagination handles issues that "are of fundamental concern" to man (Paul Tillich), issues that touch upon his existence. If, in the time of the decaying matriarchal cultures, elements of religious ideas that had lost their ritual and mythological context would have seemed "profane" to the people of that time, as they are today for Propp, who declares them from a Leninistic perspective to be "primitive nonsense,"[47] then one would perhaps have witnessed the emergence of scholarly collections of this "nonsense," but certainly not collections of fairy tales. Only because the people of that time had the dim impression, or indeed knew in their innermost heart, that this culture shaped by the maternal symbol, and the life dominated by its symbols, contained an unfulfilled promise, and because they sensed that it was not the weakness of the symbol as such, but rather the blindness and lacking sensitivity of man, which had caused the decline of this life and these cultures (a decline caused by their fascination with the newly established killing-power)—only then did they settle into their houses after the labor of the day to share among themselves and their children the fantastically elaborated accounts of mysterious matters which had formerly been enshrouded by rites and cults.

For this is the basic premise of the fairy tales, comforting and yet provocative—offering the hope for an alternative to people's ordinary lives. They all begin, either explicitly or implicitly with "Once upon a time...," that is, with a nostalgic look back into the past. They end, after the sacred wedding in which all darkness and evil is dissipated and life and joy are victorious, with the formula "...and they lived happily ever after." The narrator and the listener know of course that in reality the people in the tale died and that their life was as ordinary and burdensome as are the lives of people today. But the narrator and listener also know and express in the telling of the fairy tale, that death is not a necessity and that life holds infinite promise.[48]

This is not the place to reinstate Propp's detailed analysis of individual motifs in fairy tales by placing the mythological elements of the maternal symbolism after the hunter's initiation rites and examining these rites from the perspective of such a culture instead of suggesting 'rudiments' of a maternal culture in later rites of initiation. Everything Propp named and that which he finds significant in fairy tales—the hut in the woods serving for the ceremony of initiation, the great house for initiated males separated from other dwellings, the abandonment of children in the forest and their return to the village—is based on a sedentary or settled life-style. It is thus also profoundly influenced by the maternal symbol which is, in turn, recalled and made present nostalgically in a world which has again been blown down by the breath of the hunter and warrior.

— *Stages in Religious History as Elements of the Religion of the Fairy Tale*

In a nutshell, we may describe the following elements of the religion of the fairy tale as a way of thinking that is symbolized by the mother symbol. In the first phase of settled life, the wilderness—the forest, the wild animals, rain and thunderstorms—from which the community tries to distance itself by making a clearing and by protecting itself with a wall, is still an object of great fascination. It is that all-embracing and almighty wilderness-power, which man can survive only by approaching it and trying to establish a dialogue with it through the cruel sacrificial slaying of his most beloved possession, his children. In the Yemeni fairy tale, "The Fourteen Princesses" it is said: "There is the Afrit...he chooses the daughters of the king. And he withholds the waters from us. He has come today and he will wait until tomorrow. When the sun rises, a maiden is pushed out to him. The Afrit will seize her and release enough water for one year into the wadi."[49] Thus, in the most ancient

281

settled culture, the children, especially young girls who had just reached the age of fertility, are not led into the wilderness to be initiated, but they are buried alive in the wadi, or offered to the wilderness-god through abandonment. He usually demands the sacrifice of young girls because, as the transcendent dimension of the powerful, as the personification of the killing-power, he is at least initially perceived as male. This explains the motif of the "sleeping beauty" in the wilderness, which was a stumbling-block to Propp's theory. "Sleeping Beauty" sleeps for a hundred years, surrounded by wild thornbushes; Snow-White lies in a glass coffin in the deep forest "behind the seven mountains, with the seven dwarfs"; and Little Red Riding Hood is devoured by the evil wolf in the deep forest.

But the god of woods and the wilderness is not only a devouring monster. People try to communicate with him because they know that he also gives them the essentials of life. Indeed the violent rainstorm fills the wadis whose roaring floods later turn into "quiet water after the rainy season,"[50] pouring into the irrigation systems and making the earth fertile. This god grants success in the hunt because, in the beginning, hunting was still necessary for survival. The plants and animals that man raises and domesticates come from him as well. Therefore Il Afrit, the old man of the woods, can also be thought of as a kindly father who marries the abandoned maiden and brings her to his beautiful castle in the middle of the wilderness, where he lives beyond the reach of any human. Even in his later form, shrunk to a dwarf in the woods, he may appear in a kindly and caring way, like the seven dwarfs in "Snow-White." And even if he asks for the daughter of the queen, as in the case of "Rumpelstiltskin," it is still he himself who does what the young woman will do as the future queen, as the center of community life: spinning the dark straw into gold at night, so that the golden sun will rise again, flooding the land with its bright and warm radiance and granting life.

In the second phase of settled life man can no longer stand the ambiguity of the wilderness-god. The maiden opens the hidden and forbidden chamber in the castle and discovers human bones, dismembered bodies that disclose the ultimately gruesome nature of this god and turn him into the evil ogre, the wolf, dragon or sorcerer, and his castle into a lair of bandits. Later, when, as we have shown,[51] the mother-village ruthlessly conquers its filial settlements and subjects them to tribute, when the image of the mother has been fused with the killingpower, this god, ogre, wolf, dragon and sorcerer also becomes the evil witch. He is now a power against which a desperate struggle, a "total war" must be fought. The woman now needs a hero who defends the clearing. She gives him the sword, the charm, the strengthening fruit, the apple that later becomes the imperial orb. With this strength granted by the woman, the light-hero sets out and conquers the power of the wilderness, having himself become a bearer of the power to kill (in the Yemeni fairy tales he has seized the sword of the man-eater). Now the time has come when the evil spell of the witch is broken and the wild thornbushes wither, allowing the light-hero access to the "sleeping beauty," whom he saves from her death-like sleep through a sacred marriage. Now the light-hero is victorious over the dragon and the wild lion and opens the belly of the man-eating wolf. Given bird's claws, he climbs the mountain of glass at the end of the universe and frees the beautiful maiden who had been handed over to the wilderness. As Gilgamesh, he builds the unconquerable walls of Uruk, whose friezes are as brilliant bronze and eternally protect the city against the powers of chaos.[52] Dams are built — for example the rudimentary structure from Ma'rib in the old land of Sheba, dating from the first millenium, one of the "wonders of antiquity,"[53] which was intended to collect ever after the water that came streaming down the mountain during the rainy season, and with it the humus that it carried, in order to irrigate and to make fertile the dry and barren desert. Now huge ziggurats were built, to root the community in a central place and guarantee its survival forever. With these constructions bonded labor and slavery also began.[54] All of these were signs of a resurgence of the hunter's breath and of his fascination with the killing-power that gradually obscured the original brilliance of the maternal symbol and established the despotic rule of man over man, and of man over nature, from which Abraham moved away. Abraham put his trust in the kindly aspects of the god of the wilderness, aspects that are disclosed to whoever places his wandering life into this god's hands and recognizes him humbly and devoutly as his lord and father.

Thus, from a wider perspective of religious history, the origin of despotic oppression and of the exploitation of nature that has led to the threat of an ecological crisis as we know it today, is not rooted in the Judeo-Christian tradition as an Abrahamite religion, but in the perversion of the maternal religion by the hunter's breath, that caused Abraham's exodus. The "order to subdue the earth" from Genesis (Gen. 1, 26-28: "...let them be masters of the fish of the sea, the birds of the air...fill the earth and conquer it...") could prove of such disastrous historical consequence only because it was understood and applied literally, taken out of its historical context.[55] From an historical perspective, the older Yahwistic account of creation, of the "garden of Eden" and its "enticing" trees and four streams, still reflects the unspoiled culture and its maternal symbol. But man is not placed in this universe to rule and to conquer it. He is ordered instead to "cultivate and take care of it" (Gen. 2, 15). The grasping for the tree in the middle of the garden, which is recounted as the original sin of man, is the perversion of this culture—an attempt to subdue and rule the force belonging to that central power (the tree in the middle of the garden)—and is thereby a regression into the fascination with the killing-power.

What is known in scripture as the priestly account, however, was written down in the time of the exile. The author of this text is himself a victim of the perversion of the maternal culture by the killing-power. For him, the symbols of this culture, which were still spiritually alive—the dove as the sacred bird of the goddess of love Ishtar (who was also the goddess of war), the sacred hills and trees, sun and stars, streams and rivers—became the symbols of oppression and exploitation. At a time and in a world in which fathers and mothers burned their children in sacrifice ("caused them to pass through the fire," 2 Kings 21, 6; Jer. 7, 31 etc.), emulating the searing and burning sun, the followers of Yahweh had a vital interest in desacralizing the transcendent dimension of phenomena, and in interpreting these symbols simply as creations that Yahweh had given to man for man's benefit (for example, sun and moon as "lights in the vault of heaven," Gen. 1, 14-19). In this historical context, these elements lost their transcendence and became profane and trivial objects—as the Roman procurator Pilate, the representative of Roman imperial power, had become a profane figure for Jesus and the early Christians. The "instruction" to consider these elements in a secular way, to "put one's foot on their necks" (the basic meaning of the Hebrew "kabasch," "to rule"), calls for liberation from a humiliating oppression and an enslaving spirituality.

But in only a few peoples did the perversion of the culture shaped by the maternal symbol happen in such a way that large empires emerged and left archaeological traces. In other, smaller tribes, the transformation resulted in the formation of male fraternities. These fraternities wielded the killing-power and, as holders of that power, identified themselves to some extent with the wilderness-god from whom, as heroes of light, they had stolen this power. They built huts outside their settlements in which they performed initiation rites and constructed large fenced houses—off limits for women and non-initiated males—in which these fraternities met and received the newly initiated into the community.

The initiation did not turn the young man into a hunter, for the culture was now a settled one, but rather into a light-hero. The painful process which often ended with the symbolic death of the initiate, represents a struggle with the wilderness-god, from which the young man emerges (insofar as he survives physically) as a victorious light-hero. Circumcision, probably the most widespread rite of initiation, expresses in particular the fact that the young man who has reached sexual maturity fights with the wilderness-god for his fertility in this bloody struggle. He loses his foreskin in the process, but prevails in the end as the winner[56] who is now ready to enter marriage and to procreate children. (This is expressed in fairy tales by the sacred wedding.) During the preparation for this rite and in its performance all of the young man's social bonds are suspended. He lives secluded in the wilderness, apart from the community, and after the initiation returns to the village from faraway as the victorious light-hero. In the village he finds the bride who had been assigned to him and weds her. This is the primary motif of the hero in the fairy tale who, coming from afar, or struggling in the wild forest, liberates the bride assigned to him and celebrates a sacred wedding. Thus it is clear from the beginning—and not from a later re-evaluation and critique of the rite, as suggested by Propp[57]—that the hero of the fairy tale confronts the evil witch, the sorcerer, the robbers' den, the ogre, the poisonous dwarf or the dragon in the forest or wilderness. He kills or eliminates his opponent with his wits or with force, and thus gains the happiness of the sacred wedding, the full life in the clearing wrested from the wilderness. The woman and the matrimonial union with her is, from the beginning, the goal and often the power instrumental in the struggle against the forces of evil and darkness.

— *Specifically Christian Elements in the Religion of the Fairy Tale*

In this sense the religion of the fairy tale is a religion centered on the symbol of the woman and mother. The core of this religion is the belief that it is possible, with the help of this symbol, to overcome the wilderness and chaos and to gain a life of potentially eternal happiness and fertility: "...and they lived happily ever after." Therefore, the creation and narration of fairy tales is the enactment of a critical, liberating spirituality. For it keeps alive the memory that the conditions of man's life (all but the permanent "magical" happiness of sacred marriage, which is considered to be the ideal relationship) are not necessary evils but are the expression of the evil force conquered in the fairy tale. Fairy tales bear witness to the power and the promise of the maternal symbol in a world in which the light-hero himself has appropriated in a sudden raid, as it were, the same killing-power that he had originally set out to fight, and by which he himself now rules like a despotic wilderness-god, like a perverted and unloving lord and father.

In a few fairy tales the images also reflect the central reason for the failure of this maternal culture. Indeed, in the Yemeni story "The

285

Leopards Kolbi and Fuadi and the Horse Buzzard-snapper"[58] the son of the sultan as a light-hero prevents his sister from being buried alive as a sacrifice, and frees another maiden from the hand of the evil Il Afrit by killing him with his own sword. But then he takes possession of the two leopards and the powerful horse of the dead wilderness-god and identifies with them to such an extent that he himself becomes a sort of Il Afrit. First he locks up his sister and prevents her marriage of love, and then, when she tricks him, he kills her. Eventually he destroys the whole army of the king. He is the sole survivor of the encounter, a dreadful god of terror flying along on his giant horse, the two leopards at his side. In this story's images we can see how the light-hero himself becomes the holder of the killing-power in his struggle against the wilderness force — which can only be destroyed with its own weapons — and how he falls prey to the fascination of violence: *La révolution dévore ses enfants!*

At this point the religion of the fairy tale reveals features of the religion of Jesus, who prefers to hand over his life to a bloody execution rather than seize the sword and fight as a light-hero against the sinister pagan force of the evil Romans and their collaborators among his own people. He knows that whoever lives by the sword will die by the sword (Matt. 26, 52), falling prey to the fascination of the sword (the killing-power). The god of terror cannot be overcome by violence. But a non-violent human existence, founded in fundamental trust and lived with constancy even through a bloody death can overcome the apprehension and anxiety rooted in original sin. This is true to such an extent that the countenance of this God becomes manifest in its maternal emanation as the countenance of the Abba, the Mama/Papa, at least in principle and at moments of crisis. That which frightens — in Jesus' life it was the ruthless exercise of the killing-power by the Roman state — is then perceived as merely a military power, trivial, temporal, vain, lacking any transcendent dimension. The Abba, on the other hand, to whom Jesus has committed his fate, appears as the very ground of existence, protective in a motherly way, granting a new life transcending death — a life both tangible and real.

Indeed, this theme is expressed in quite a few fairy tales. In the story "The Singing Soaring Lark" the maiden first goes full of courage to the wild lion in the woods. "I will go in and appease the lion, so that I may come back to you unharmed," she says to her father.[59] And indeed she finds that, in reality, the lion is an enchanted prince, who regains his human features during the night. But he loses them when, at her sister's wedding, light from a candle falls on him. She wanders through the forest for seven years, asking the sun and the moon for his whereabouts. She is deterred from her purpose neither by set-backs nor by humiliations, and thus her loyalty wins back the prince in his human form. Similarly, Cinderella finds the redeeming sacred wedding by waiting patiently in her abandonment — she must sleep next to the stove in the ashes. She is taken care of by kindly doves and supported by her loyal love for her mother whose grave she maintains. Eventually the little tree which she planted on her mother's grave provides her with the pretty clothes, which help her to gain the love of the prince. The beautiful princess in "Allerleirauh" also goes voluntarily into the deep forest and becomes one with the wilderness, as it were, by blackening her face and hands with soot and clothing herself with a coat of patched fur. When she is discovered by royal hunters, she is taken to live in a closet under the stairs, doing the basest of labors, until she dances with the king at a great feast, wearing her golden dress, and celebrates the sacred wedding with him. In the fairy tale "The Brother and Sister" the little sister lovingly takes care of her brother who has been turned into a deer in the deep forest, and brings him with her when the king finds her in the woods and takes her to his castle to celebrate the sacred wedding. Even after she has been killed in childbirth by the evil witch, she comes back in the night as a ghost to take care of and caress her child and the little deer. Thanks to this unabating motherly care she eventually comes back to life and frees her brother from his animal form. In the fairy tale "The Hut in the Forest" the oldest, the middle and the youngest daughters are sent out one after the other into the wild forest and come to the cabin where a white-haired old man lives among animals. While the older girls fall through a trap-door into the cellar, the youngest one, through her loving care of the animals and of the old man, frees all the persons who had been imprisoned in animal forms. The old cabin is transformed into a royal palace, the white-haired old man into a handsome young prince, and the animals into his servants. Similarly, the maiden in the fairy tale "The Old Woman in the Wood" who is abandoned in the wilderness, frees the enchanted prince from the witch's spell by faithfully performing the tasks she is given, and she too has the sacred wedding. In the well-known story of "Mother Holle" the "Golden maiden" achieves happiness and fulfillment through the loyal and careful accomplishment of her nursing tasks. In the fairy tales "Faithful John," "The Six Swans," "The Seven Ravens" and "The Iron Stove" it is always loyalty and constancy, love and sympathy, faithful persistence on the path of love, that break the spell of evil and make salvation possible.

These and other fairy tales reveal a core of authentic Christian sensibility and thought, if one understands their symbolism. The liberating figure in these stories is an "alter Christus," another Christ, who, through his dedication to love and his unlimited maternal mercy, his death and resurrection, unmasks the god of terror and reveals him as the Abba. Thus in these fairy tales a truth is revealed that goes back to Tertullian, who spoke of the "anima naturaliter christiana." Certainly this does not mean the "archetype of Christ," to use Jung's phrase, is innate to the human soul, but it is present rather in a storied way. Fairy tales of this type demonstrate that original sin and the fascination with the killing-power did not totally smother man's original openness to the transcendent dimension of the realities which he encounters, but that the fundamental ability to experience and to think of God as love remains, an ability that has become a redemptive reality in Jesus. In the motifs we have mentioned and in the basic point of view of the fairy tale, maternal-erotic care and love are able to conquer the power of terror and the wilderness in a non-violent way. A "paradisal," pre-sinful feeling of life penetrates the human world, dominated as it is by the fascination of the power to kill. It is a feeling of life that, especially in light of evolution and of those species that are closely related to us, might well have filled the living beings of the genus *Homo* before it was perverted into predatory behavior. At any rate, the fairy tales recall the promise symbolized by the woman and mother that has not been fulfilled historically and they make people receptive to that promise. In this way they contribute to a receptiveness to the "Good News" of Jesus, the gospel of God as the loving Abba, the caring mother, who loves each of her children with eternal love, even and especially those who "are ill with evil."[60]

On the History of the Maternal Symbol in Christianity (the Veneration of Mary)

— On the Integration of the Maternal Symbol into the Christian Faith through the Veneration of Mary

Jesus reveals God as Abba. This word—as a babbling word: Mama, Papa—contains the element of care and loving concern that a father and mother have towards the baby and towards the little child, and that turns them into what we call "father" and "mother" in a Christian sense. This, of course, is a significant change in the history of the meaning of the words "father" and "mother." In a universal human history dominated by the fascination of the (male) killing-power, the word "father" has primarily the connotation of lordship and authority. In matriarchal cultures these aspects have also adhered to the symbol of the woman and mother. The goddess of love also becomes the goddess of war; the mother becomes a witch. Only the reevaluation of the name of "father" in the life and death of Jesus releases it from this frightful aspect and brings it close to a pre-matriarchal, maternal symbolism, free of the insignia of power. Thus the name of Abba signifies that which hitherto has been expressed by the everyday, childlike use of the word "mother" (mama), although without the devaluation which the mother as a woman had to suffer in the patriarchy.

As I have pointed out in the introduction, the revelation of God as Abba is not realized in a pure way in the texts of the New Testament. It can probably not be expected to be purely realized as long as it is mortal and sinful human beings, fearful of death, who try to understand and take to heart Jesus and his revelation. In some texts the *tremendum et fascinosum* (R. Otto) of the god of terror can be sensed, and in connection with it, the idea of the sacrificial killing. The most obvious indication that the first Christian community was not yet able to accept emotionally the full meaning of Jesus, is the fact that they hesitated to adopt the Abba name in spite of the consistent use Jesus is historically reported to have made of it in his prayerful address. Except for the passage on Gethsemane, where Jesus fled to his "Abba" in anguished distress, this word was replaced in all instances by "father."

But those who appreciate the circumstances of the time and take into account how deeply conditioned people were by the patterns of thought and feeling in their society, can understand this phenomenon. Indeed, it could not be otherwise from a human point of view. Only at certain moments, when man was seized and penetrated in a special way by the childlike breath of Jesus, did he dare to repeat Jesus' use of the name Abba (Rom. 8, 15 and Gal. 4, 6). As has been shown in the chapter on the significance of the paternal/maternal symbol in the Bible (chap. 3.1), almost 2,000 years had to pass before one successor to the office of Peter (whose duty it is to preserve, protect and interpret the revelation of God through Jesus), Pope John Paul I, recognized the maternal symbolism in Jesus' form of addressing God, and used it in his own discourse.

If this had happened in early Christian times the cult of Mary would almost certainly not have emerged, at least not in the form in which it comes down to us today. It was the veneration of Mary that introduced the symbol of woman and mother into the Christian cult and religious practice. This symbol could then be experienced in a new way and more intensively through the divine experience of Jesus. It is an attempt to introduce, peripherally, as it were, the riches of the maternal symbol of God as Abba which had been revealed in Jesus.

In principle Jesus had opened the way to an integration of the maternal symbol. However, the dogmatic conflicts that accompanied the veneration of the Virgin Mary in the course of history are a clear reflection of the resistance against integrating the maternal symbol into religious experience that arose from circumstances of time and tradition. Nestor, the patriarch of Constantinople, who came from the Judeo-Christian school of Antioch and was deeply influenced by the Old Testament and Judaism, resisted the suggestion that Mary be given the title "Theotókos," bearer of God, and be thereby acknowledged as the "mother of God" in the proper sense.[61] At the Council of Ephesus in 431 AD he confronted the Alexandrian Cyril and his Egyptian bishops, who, influenced by Hellenism, were less dominated by an exclusively male perception of monotheism—in Greece as well as in Egypt maternal divinities played an important role—and thus perceived this maternal element even in the new Christian religion. Although Cyril's Christology, which in the early dogmatic conflicts was closely connected to Mariology, was condemned, the formula of the "mother of God" was legitimized in the faith of the early church. Even though the Church stressed with great doctrinal consistency that Mary was in no way elevated to the rank of a divine being, thoughts and feelings within popular devotion throughout the centuries were shaped more by the symbolism of the words and images than by dogmatic pronouncements. In popular experience the mother is always of the same nature as the being to whom she has given birth. Indeed, she even antecedes him and is thus "greater." She embraces and holds her child. With the title "Mother of God" the maternal symbol has been recognized and venerated in popular devotion as a divine symbol.

How very true that influence still is today in popular devotion was made evident to me in one incident on a visit to Crete. We drove in a taxi at breakneck speed through the narrow mountain passes from Matala across the island to the airport at Herakleion. Before each dangerous turn the driver made the sign of the cross. The young woman sitting next to him, and probably even more aware of the danger of his maneuvers than we in the back of the car were, became quite nervous and eventually asked him why he kept crossing himself. In lieu of an answer he pointed to the little replicas of orthodox churches that stood by the roadside at particularly dangerous spots, and that usually contained a statue of Mary and the Child on her arm. He then pointed to a large bronze medal of the Virgin and Child dangling from his rear-view mirror and explained in broken German, "I am Greek Orthodox. We have Mary." Whereupon the woman somewhat resignedly replied, "Ah, so. I am Protestant. We have Christ." The cab driver contented himself with that remark. The many women and mothers, and the men and fathers as well, who prayed to the Mother of God for her intercession with her Son in their existential distress have always turned, like the cab driver, to the last and absolutely secure foundation of being.

— *On Marian Doctrine: Immaculate Conception, Perpetual Virginity, Assumption of her Body and Soul into Heaven*

The doctrines on Mary are designed to integrate the symbol of the woman and mother of popular devotion without conflict with either the monotheism of the Old Testament or the doctrine of the Trinity which has come down to us in patriarchal discourse. These doctrines often prevailed against the magisterial teaching of high theological authorities. In fact, Bernard of Clairvaux, and later Bonaventure, Albert the Great, and even Thomas Aquinas opposed the prevalent theory that Mary was without original sin from the first moment of her existence, that is from her conception (the doctrine of "Mary's immaculate conception").[62] In popular spirituality this doctrine has always been fused with Mary's "perpetual virginity," relating the "immaculate conception" to the way in which Jesus was "conceived" by Mary. Intensive catechetical instruction and innumerable sermons could not prevent this completely erroneous doctrinal combination from penetrating popular faith and it remains there even today. Symbols have their own logic. And in people who have a rich emotional life the logic of symbols is usually stronger than the logic of definition.

In symbolic experience the "immaculate conception" and "perpetual virginity" have become associated. This association has often been criticized as hostile to the body, as a devaluation of human sexuality—and with good reason. Indeed, it often served in that sense. The exaltation of an "immaculate" and "virginal" conception easily made normal sexual procreation and conception seem impure and defiling. But this is a tendency that is irreconcilable with a culture shaped by the maternal symbol, as we have seen in Crete and in the fairy tales. This culture is characterized by a resolutely erotic view of life. But perhaps the tendency of Marian devotion that is hostile to the body and to sexuality was more widespread in clerical circles, where celibacy was predominant. Among the people the feeling was rather the opposite. The courtly love poetry of the Middle Ages was not at all hostile to sexuality but deeply influenced by Marian devotion, and Marian pilgrimages were a thorn in the clerics' sides even as late as the 19th century. Time and again these pilgrimages were suppressed because of the excesses of behavior that occurred when the pilgrims lodged in barns overnight.[63]

291

Against the background of the understanding of original sin as it is developed in the present book, the question arises whether the symbolism of the immaculate conception and perpetual virginity, related to the mother of God, does not have a deeper meaning which is the unconscious root of popular devotion. Original sin as a violent act, as the ruthless and brutal stabbing to death of the big animal occurred, as I have explained,[64] by a change in sexual behavior originally aimed at social communication and procreation. The erect penis was lengthened and hardened into a lance, the killing tool of the primeval hunter. The woman was integrated into this process from the very beginning. For it is she who causes the male's sexual excitement and turns his penis into the erect phallus, and symbolically into a thrusting lance. As is clear from the Stone Age wall painting in Algeria (Fig. 19), woman grants luck in the hunt through her sexuality—depicted as a line between the woman's vagina and the man's penis. By the same means she also grants luck in war and royal power insofar as the excited killing-power is also aimed at fellow beings.

This primordial sense of a connection between sexuality and the act of killing is still present in popular understanding. When woman surrenders to man she creates his thrusting lance, as it were, and at the same time is integrated into the cycle of killing. H. P. Duerr offers many examples of this connection. For example, when in the African Luo Tribe the young married couple walk out of their hut after the wedding ceremony and the first wedding night, the virgin maidens of the village run to the husband, beating him and crying, "You have killed our sister!".[65] He has dragged her into the cycle of violence and killing which is felt to be related to sexuality. Being struck by an arrow is the worldwide symbol for the beginning of a romantic relationship. And it has to be realized that at the time of this symbol's origin, the shot of an arrow was equivalent to today's gun shot. It was an act of killing. The deep roots of these ideas in popular imagery are evident in the little stanza by Germany's popular poet Wilhelm Busch, in which he says to the young people who have resolved to marry but who, in his opinion, are too young:

>»Kinder seid ihr denn bei Sinnen,
>überlegt euch das Kapitel!
>Ohne die gehörigen Mittel
>soll man keinen Krieg beginnen.«[66]

"Children, are you out of your minds,
Think it over carefully!

292

> Without the appropriate means
> One should not begin a war!"[66]

Could it be possible that in a deep layer of consciousness, the notions of the immaculate conception and of perpetual virginity as aspects of the primeval symbol of the woman and mother—which must always contain love and eroticism—form a single association that spells out the vision of a sexuality, a relationship between man and woman extending beyond original sin—that is, beyond the connection between sexuality and the power to kill? The immaculate and virginal conception would then be a conception that was not overshadowed by the fascination of the killing-power, symbolized in male potency—a conception and a relationship that are "radically" free, in the deepest layers and roots of life and experience, from any physical or psychological violence, even the most subtle and disguised. It would be a relationship that is never a "war."

From a theological point of view the "immaculate conception" and "perpetual virginity" are closely related to the redemptive action of the Messiah Jesus. But if salvation means the liberation from the cycle of violence and its enthrallment with the killing-power; if Jesus brings man this liberation through his life, death and resurrection in a radical way; if he is the first human being to enact the redemption from his conception to his death as model and guide for all men before and after him—then we are justified in assuming that he comes forth from a relationship in which the sinful perversion of male potency into the power to kill does not exist (a sort of "niche" in human evolution). As the medieval Franciscan philosopher Duns Scotus expresses it theologically, the savior has already cast his shadow in view of his origin by means of a pre-redemption ("praeredemptio").[67]

In any case, the motif of Mary's virginity has a meaning which is clearly distinct from similar motifs in religious history. As we have explained in the chapter on the child as a divine symbol,[68] the motif of the unnatural conception, not from a man but from God, is essential to the symbolism of the child. But this motif expresses only the uniqueness, the force and the divinity of the child, which—in direct contrast to the helplessness of Christ at birth—is demonstrated by the fact that these other newborns can immediately stand upright (Pharaoh), grab a bow and arrow (Apollo), strangle a poisonous snake in its cradle (Hercules), or pace through the universe with giant steps (Buddha). And the woman who becomes the divine child's mother for the god who impregnates her is "virgin," "tabula rasa," only at the moment of this divine conception. Drewermann, who sees a very close connection between the myth of the virginal conception and birth of the Egyptian Pharaoh, and the childhood narrative in Luke, stresses that the Pharaoh may have older siblings, sisters or brothers who died prematurely "without jeopardizing the idea of the divine bride's virginity."[69] The difference between this motif and the Christian idea of the "perpetual virginity" of Mary is then blurred by Drewermann when he holds "moral or some kind of ethical motivations, as they were construed in Hellenistic thought with exaggerated imagination" responsible for the development of the Christian motif.[70]

The symbol of the perpetual virgin who, as such, is nevertheless a woman and mother, the mother of God in her whole body and soul, and in whom the transcendent dimension of this reality becomes visible in a special way, also contains that dream which is so deeply rooted in fairy tales. It is the dream of the woman who is not forced by loving surrender into the cycle of violence and killing in which humanity has been chained since original sin, but who, on the contrary, brings liberation from that cycle to both the man and to herself as woman.

This image of Mary, then, corresponds to the idea that Mary has been "assumed into heaven with her body and soul," that is, that she has received perfection in eternity—an idea that has been proclaimed dogma only in our century. In the insoluble relation between the virgin on the one hand, and the woman and mother on the other, she is the feminine image of redeemed humanity, freed from the cycle of violence and killing. The most ancient primeval images of the transcendent dimension of woman are realized in her. "Assumed into heaven" and exalted above all the choirs of angels and saints, more radiant in her symbolic strength than the transcendent dimension of sun, moon and stars, of seas and mountains, and of powerful or fascinating human beings, Mary rules together with Christ, her divine son. This radiant image of maternal humanity is absent when mother and child are seated upright in a stiff posture, identified as rulers by a crown and scepter (Fig. 22a). One encounters it rather in the image of the sorrowful mother of God, the Pietà (Fig. 53), who holds her son, killed by the Roman god-emperor, in her lap. Like the first human mother, the Australopithecus-woman, who would not leave her dead child—she is absorbed by the transcendent dimension of her child, which appears before her eyes, beyond the dead body, as a living reality.

With this maternal quality she is in a new, original way the "great mother" and even the "mistress of the animals." She is celebrated by the church fathers as the heavenly mother, the patron of all women and men, the "mistress of all creatures" (John of Damascus).[71] She is the Queen of Heaven of whom the prophet Jeremiah speaks, for whom the

Fig. 53: Pietà by Michelangelo (St. Peter's, Rome): The Christian mother of God holds her son, who was killed by the Roman god-emperor, in her lap.

children light the fire and the women knead the dough to make sacrificial cakes for her (Jer. 7, 18). But in contrast to the situation in Jeremiah's time she has been freed from her ambivalence. From the very beginning she is removed from the cycle of violence. Although she lives fully as woman and mother, she does not enter into any relation with the male killing-power. No one will build sanctuaries for her or for her son (at least not without a renewed perversion) in which they "burn their sons and daughters" as sacrifice, the practice Jeremiah denounced in his time (Jer. 7, 31).

— On a Possible Integration of the Maternal Symbol into the Symbolism of the Trinity

Of course, this tradition of the maternal symbol is, from the perspective of the entire history of the Christian faith, a somewhat esoteric diversion. This became obvious during the time of the Reformation. As in Islam, the Reformation signifies the return of the Christian faith to the religion of Abraham, but now in a personal way, focused on the individual. All that counts is the individual's faithful devotion and submission ("Islam"), his confidence in the grace of God, and his loyalty to the Scripture in which this grace has been made manifest. These three elements — *sola fides, sola gratia, sola scriptura* (faith alone, grace alone, Scripture alone) — are at the heart of Luther's experience of conversion which opened the way for the Reformation. This re-orientation to the God of the ancestors, in the face of whom all men become free and mature Christian people in the same way, left little room for the perception and religious integration of any symbolism beyond that of the Lord and Father. As we have indicated[72] this is evidenced not only in the dialectical theology of Karl Barth, but even in the quite different theology of Paul Tillich.

This urge for reform is a parallel to prophetic criticism in the Old Testament and remains justified, as Paul Tillich stresses, insofar as the distinction between the symbol and that which is symbolized is obscured in the veneration of the transcendent dimension of created realities. When that happens creatures, human beings, even animals, are selected as "holy" and elevated into the realm of the divine. Thus a religiously motivated hierarchy of men and animals emerges that tends to legitimize the division of men into classes and castes. It thereby also legitimizes the physical and psychological enslavement of large groups of the population, as in the early establishment of states that grew from matriarchal cultures. This is also the root of the violent and exploitative oppression of so-called "sub-human" creatures. At the time of the

296

Reformation, after the Renaissance, people became aware that during the Middle Ages freedom and maturity in matters of faith were the privilege of a very small, almost exclusively clerical population who had mastered Latin as a theological and cultic language and were therefore entitled to participate in discussions of religious matters. Princes and noblemen formed an alliance with this class, and consequently held the people in their power, physically and spiritually.

Thus, wherever the transcendent dimension of reality is not perceived and venerated in one symbol alone—after original sin, in the Abrahamite context, it was the symbol of the Lord and Father—the danger of oppressing men (and creatures) arises together with the danger of idolatry (that is, the identification of the symbol with the symbolized). In the history of religions the symbol of the woman and mother, together with the symbolic power of fire, has opened man's eyes to the fact that in all things—in mountains and lakes, in trees and fountains, in children and in cooing turtle doves—a transcendent dimension can be encountered. Or, as Eliade puts it, a hierophany can be experienced. In religious history polytheism appears only in connection with the maternal symbol. However, such a highly differentiated universe and such a variety in manifestations of the transcendent creates the danger that the hunter's instinct may reawaken in sinful man who would then seek to construct a hierarchy of higher and lower ranks in order to capture the universe and his fellowmen as prey.

But as the history of Islam and of medieval Christianity demonstrates (and as Metz and Moltmann show in their political theology),[73] even strict monotheism can provide religious legitimation to despotic and imperialistic rule—as with the motto: "One God, one ruler, one empire." A truly free society, a true communication between human beings relating to one another in fundamental equality of importance and dignity, arises only when the transcendent dimension of reality is thought of and experienced as a true unity—without subordination but yet with inner differentiation, as in the case of the Christian symbolism of the Trinity. The Trinity can reveal this political implication, of course, only when it is not presented as an abstract doctrine, but as a symbolic complex that can be internalized and associated with human life and action.

Seen in relation to the maternal symbol this consideration implies that it would be necessary to free the maternal symbol from its more or less esoteric and marginal tradition, as it is manifested in the veneration of Mary, and to integrate it into the symbolism of the Trinity. But it is not necessary to expand the Trinity into a Quaternity, as C. G. Jung suggested.[74] Rather, the maternal symbol could and should be thought of and experienced within the symbol of the Abba, as the present discourse has tried to show, and as Pope John Paul I had begun to explain. This does not mean that the first person of the Trinity should be thought of as androgynous, in the manner of Melanesian or other ancestral figures. Rather, religious thought and feeling, in both the concrete life of prayer and in liturgy and spirituality, should proclaim what has always been clear from a doctrinal point of view, namely that God is neither man nor woman, but a dimension which transcends both. However, when man thinks of God's reality as a person and prays to this divine being, he can only feel and think of God as a man or woman, because of his creaturely limitation.[75] Therefore the manner in which God is to be addressed, as male or female, as "Father" or "Mother," as "Papa" or "Mama," should be freely determined in each specific situation by the individual or the celebrating and praying community.

Conclusion:

Open, childlike receiving and selfless motherly giving as the "inner court" of a Christ-centered way of life

Anything can become a hierophany. God or his angel can appear in anything. If a true dialogue is to be established, nothing in the history of religion that claims divinity should be labeled as an "-ism" ("polytheism," "pantheism," "dualism," "monism," etc.) and thereby (pierced by a lance, as it were) be dismissed from living dialogue. Everything must be seen and understood in the way it understands and manifests itself: Lakshmi, Kali, Demeter as the great mothers who grant eternal life through the force of their love; Cora, Hainuwele, Artemis-Britomartis, and Athena as the divine daughters, the divine maidens, who make grains and vegetables grow and grant wisdom and luck in the hunt; Baal, Ishtar, Vishnu-Krishna, Apollo, and the Bodhisattva as divine sons, who fight to provide man with the sun, life, fertility, light and knowledge; and El, Allah and Yahweh (and similarly Shiva) as the unique, great God in relation to whom the other godheads are nothing but angels, created spiritual beings, good and evil; and he alone, freely and without obligation, disposes man to salvation or damnation. Every one must be allowed to raise his voice in the dialogue, just as he understands himself and wants to be understood.

The same applies to Jesus and his Abba. He must appear and enter the dialogue in just the way in which he is seen and understood by the gospels: as "beloved son" (Mark 1, 11) of the Heavenly Father; more precisely, of the Abba, of the Mama/Papa, who reveals himself in and through Jesus as pure love and who, in the abandoned child, in the crucified son, releases his divine breath, as a dove-like wind, a wind and breath that turns all those who are enveloped in it into his beloved sons and daughters.

Some of the characteristics of this understanding of Jesus himself and of his God unfold only through dialogue with other hierophanies from religious history as, for example, when the miraculous light-hero and the raging and punishing El-Il-Al, who still appear in the gospels, reveal their true origins to be from a different tradition. Indeed every true dialogue increases the self-understanding of both the speaker and the listener.

In this dialogue we also increase our understanding of others. For ours would not be a dialogue if we were to leave the statement by which the other introduced himself hanging in the air and did not try to integrate what the other says into our own horizon of understanding, thus accepting it in a genuine way. The sign of such a true dialogue is the ever present tension between the way one introduces himself into a dialogue and the way this introduction is received and integrated into the other's horizon of understanding. The conversation is born of this tension.

"Understanding" in this context does not simply refer to an intellectual conception, but to a holistic perception. Intellectually a Muslim can understand quite well the meaning of the statement that God is pure love. But his existential perception understands this to be mere "feeling," which remains far beneath the powerful meaning of "Allah-Il-Allah-Il-Allah," the most-most-most high, who stands above feelings and gives or refuses out of free grace. Conversely, a Christian may grasp this most high and most exalted God intellectually. He may even have met him in his childhood as the god of terror. But he has learned through Jesus' parables and through the passion that such an absolute authority is ultimately unholy and enslaving.

Similar things hold true for the relation with other religious and cultural phenomena. In the present book, written by a Christian, it was and is only possible to articulate one Christian's understanding of a different religion—in a critical way, of course, and refined through dialogue. I have tried to free myself as best I could from the current prejudices of the speculative worldview. I attempted to listen to, understand and accept the different hierophanies from religious history in an experiential way. But precisely because of this I perceive, as a Christian, that the intimidating and commanding postures that bring about subjection and fear often are blended with the unholy killing-power which, through usurpation, man has appropriated in original sin. I also see that in reality the vital, sympathetic light-hero and god of fertility is mostly the blood-smeared warrior who himself eventually takes on the features of that demon from whom he wanted to free his people. The German fairy tales and legends tell us that the "green one," the god of vegetation disguised as a hunter, is usually hooved or has horns under his hunter's hat. His green cloak hides the fuming, destructive horses of Poseidon, and the raging, deadly bull of the underworld, both of which are powers that fell from the heavens (in the light of Jesus' experience of the Abba) and no longer hold any divine power, for they may "kill the body and after that can do no more" (Luke 12, 4).

To us, whose sensitivity has been shaped by the parable of the wicked servant which prefigures the passion of Christ, the beautiful maturing girl, at whose sight "you will grow radiant, your heart throbbing and full" (Isa. 60, 5) seems predestined, by the way she is depicted, to become a sacrificial victim. Like the "beloved son" she will be seized and killed (Mark 12, 6 ff.) because in the slaying of such a victim the slayer can set himself up with authority over the sacred. And to us who have meditated upon the life and death of Jesus, the great mother, with her promise of eternal life, surrounded by the radiance of the sun, the moon and the stars, by doves, fountains and trees, seems ultimately unable to conquer the fear of death or to provide a transcendent home to man in this world, structured as it is by original sin. Furthermore, wherever man faces the tasks he has been given, inspired with high-minded zeal, heroically and unselfishly ignoring his own life and health, perhaps even joyously offering his life, this image dissolves into the scene in the pit of the Lascaux cave, in which the wind and breath of the hunter, the fascination of the killing-power, are painted on walls, dark and deluding. And behind man's amazing cultural achievements—the great walls around Jericho and Uruk, the towering ziggurats and pyramids, and the mighty dam of M'arib, these wonders of antiquity, as also behind the castles, palaces, and cathedrals of the Middle Ages—masses of people appear to us, people who carry stones all their lives, enslaved, chained, guarded and mistreated, and who may eventually follow their king as decorative burial gifts into his grave.

...and Developing One's Understanding of One's Self

Christianity is still too young and its history too laced with failures for the growth of a culture rising from an Abba-related attitude to life which would replace those profanations of the sacred resulting from a religious and cultural history inspired by a flawed Christianity. It is equally impossible to draw up a specific master plan, for such a culture and to look for strategies to engineer it. Such an attempt would ultimately be only another regression into the wind and breath of the hunter who spots his prey and pursues it. A genuine Christ-centered culture and way of life which reveals the Abba would have to grow from below and from within, like the palace cities of Crete. The "interior court" of this new city and way of life from which everything evolves would be symbolized in countless ways by the figure of the helpless child, handed over to the powerful elders.[1]

In our world, shaped by the sinful preoccupation with violence and the power to kill, the child represents the victim. Wherever someone suffers; wherever he is handed over as prey to some greater power—be it as a starving child in the Third World, an adolescent suffocating in the plenty of Western consumer society, a working-ant in a centralized state-system, a jobless person no longer needed in a free, competitive society, a newborn entering a threatening world, or an old, helpless man seeking to leave this world in a dignified way, or any lonely, sick, or persecuted human being—we always meet the child who cries for help, aloud or in silence, for the Abba, the Mama and the Papa who stoop down to help and comfort. This event should be the "interior court" of a Christian culture. There we would meet the triune God, the child, the breath of life that emanates from it, and the Abba, who then is called forth, animated by the same breath. Everything would have to be grounded in this sacred event: the social structure, the rules of the working world and of the economy, the relations between the generations, the relations between man and woman, the life within groups of all sizes, the cooperation of all the people, in science and art, rite and religion.

It would be a culture of an open, reciprocal, giving and receiving nature. This strikes a controversial note in our own culture, dominated by the hunting mentality. The oldest document of German poetry, a fragment of the *Hildebrandlied* (The Song of Hildebrand) is centered around this conflict as it poisoned the common life of man in a way typical of a hunter's society. Hildebrand and Hadubrand face each other at the head of their two armies. A duel between the two leaders will decide the victory. Hildebrand recognizes his adversary as being his son. He takes from his own arms "wuntane bauga, cheisuringu gitan, so imo der chuning gap" (that is, the brilliant ornament which the king had given to him), in order, to give it to his son "bi huldi" (out of free, spontaneous grace and love). But giving and receiving are extremely sensitive acts in the hunting society. In answer, Hadubrand expresses the same attitude in which the solution of such a crisis is looked for even today, in however refined a form: "Mit geru scal man geba infahan, ort widar orte..." (With the lance one should give and receive gifts, point against point). Here the epic rises to its peculiar tragic dimension: "Welaga nu, waltant got, wewurt skihit" (Woe now, ruling god, woeful fate happens) — these are the words with which the father sets about killing his son ("suasat chind" — the sweet child) as atonement for the offence to his honor.[2]

Everywhere in the world, in all cultures, giving and receiving is a problem. To accept a present signifies either subjection, or it obligates us to give a present in return (preferably an even larger one), in order to express our superiority. Giving and receiving the things necessary for human existence have become a strategy of battle in which rank and power are at stake. Hadubrand is not the only one to see the gift offered to him as a trap, which the "Old Hun" sets for him, "ummet spaher" (lurking about): "Wili mih dinu speru werpan" (You intend to throw your spear at me). Therefore it is dangerous to reveal one's wishes and to express one's needs. Such behavior makes man vulnerable, and the hunter, who takes advantage of this weakness and strikes like lightning, is in all of us.

The only place in which giving and receiving still happens in an unspoiled way, as primeval human communication that causes joy to both the giver and the receiver, is in the relation between the little child and his parents. The infant and the toddler are so abandoned and vulnerable in their whole being that they can afford the luxury of expressing their needs and desires without restraint. The parents' happiness consists in the fact that they may respond to this need without any afterthought, in an equally free and unconditional way: in nurturing the child by surrounding it with affection and love.

For the Christian, this is not only the experience of an angel, as P. L. Berger says in his book "Rumor of Angels" (see 3.3, note 5), but an immediate experience of the triune divine life. In it the "malkût Yahweh," the kingdom of God, as Jesus manifests it, becomes reality—as a communication between the prodigal son and the merciful father (Luke 15, 11-32), between the Jew who was attacked by robbers and the helpful Samaritan (Luke 10, 30-35), the sower and the fertile soil which receives the seed and brings forth fruit (Mark 4, 3-8). One need only remove the violent and threatening framework of the parable of universal judgment in Matthew (Matt. 25, 31-46), in order to see what goes on in the "inner court" of a Christ-centered way of life. "I was hungry." One might add: "and I expressed this openly,"—"and you gave me food." "I was thirsty"—and I said so—"and you gave me drink." "I was a stranger"—and dared to knock at your door—"and you made me welcome." "I was naked"—and I dared to show myself—"and you clothed me." "I was sick"—and I showed my weakness—"and you visited me." "I was in prison"—and I accepted my confinement—"and you came to see me." Of such divine simplicity is the fulfilled human life.

Religion and life form a unity in such a genuinely Christian culture. In the New Jerusalem (Rev. 21, 9-22), there is no temple. The experience of God is everywhere. There is no longer need to classify the manifold variety in which humans perceive the transcendent dimension of physical dimension of physical reality or to organize the myriads of angels (Heb. 12, 22) into a hierarchy of ascending choirs at the top of which the triune God is enthroned. The Pseudo-Dionysius did so in a way that became authoritative for the church and for its theologians. (Again an image of the hunter-hierarchy: the great hunter and the hierarchy of his retinue). But equally, there is no need for a reformation-style iconoclasm, no need to renounce these rich experiences and symbols and to flee back to the Lord and Father of the Abrahamite religion, in order to find a clear orientation in life. The order will now be within us. The force of the crying child, calling forth the Abba in its need will always be renewed, in our thoughts, speech, feelings and acts, many times each day and even at night in our dreams. We will also recognize whether or not, and to what extent, we have moved and still move within or outside this redemptive cycle.

The perception of the transcendent dimension of a multifaceted reality, and man's reaction to it, will be integrated into this impelling experience. Man will be liberated from the dilemma of either becoming lost in the multiplicity of his world and of his history (including his personal history), or of betraying his own self by seeking the transcendent dimension in only *one* symbol, thus denying the possible plurality of religious experience. If one day all were integrated into the dynamism of desiring, giving, and receiving, that proceeds from the child, then the prophecy made in the first letter to the Corinthians about the end of time would be fulfilled. God will then rule as child, as the breath of life emanating from the child, and as the Abba who turns to the child in the same breath — "all in all" (1 Cor. 15, 28).

Ideas of this kind can be expressed only in images and symbols. "It is in images, nothing but images that the whole treasure of human knowledge and bliss consists" (J. G. Hamann). Truth that liberates and delights can not be expressed in conceptual, lifeless language. For if truth, as a conceptual utterance, were the possession of a specific group — which does not mean that truth does not exist — a dialogue of religions would be meaningless. For the purpose of the dialogue is to reveal the truth more and more — as living and beyond manipulation. It is not to be usurped by the killing-power, not to be pierced through by the thrusting lance of concepts. Therefore a book with a similar aim would be equally desirable from the pen of a Muslim, a follower of Vishnu, or a Buddhist.[3] The goal would be neither to "convert" the other, nor to found yet another religion, as a mediation containing the essence of all the others. Rather, the goal would be to increase each person's understanding of his own confession, to help him become more a part of it. In the process, he would learn to understand the other better and to accept the other and his intentions. The goal would be a harmonious symphony of these different voices. This would be the deepest experience of the divine: "God is sound; his essence is chant."[4]

The ultimate truth which cannot be manipulated, and which man must try to discover in this dialogue of religions (even on another level in conceptual language) can probably not be expressed, once and for all and in a way valid for everyone, through only *one* of the historical religious traditions and its symbols. Instead, we need the free and harmonious symphony of as many central symbols as possible, from as many traditions as possible. Music is the primeval and universal language of mankind. As a Christian I believe that those who were present at the first feast of Pentecost in Jerusalem heard its first sounds (Acts 2, 4-11). The goal of the dialogue would be the composition and the orchestration of this music in which the many symbols from myths, fairy tales and religions merge harmoniously in the excitement of one single concert.

Footnotes

Introduction

[1] "Erklärung über das Verhältnis der Kirche zu den nichtchristlichen Religionen 2", in: *K. Rahner, H. Vorgrimler,* Konzilskompendium, 19th ed. (Freiburg, 1986): 356.

[2] See ibid. 1, 355. See also the document of the Roman secretariat for non-Christians (Pentecost 1984): "Die Haltung der Katholischen Kirche gegenüber den Anhängern anderer Religionen. Gedanken und Weisungen über Dialog und Mission", in: Una Sancta 43 (1988), 201-209.

[3] This was also the main issue of the International Congress "Geist und Natur" in Hannover, May 21 to 27, 1988.

[4] See *M.-L.v.Franz,* "Der Individuationsprozeß", in: *C. G. Jung* etc., Der Mensch und seine Symbole, (Olten-Freiburg, 1979): 160-229, especially 177-188. The same holds true for the Animus, the inner representation of man within women. See ibid. 189-195.

[5] Besides some later studies of C. G. Jung, the theory of archetypes has entered the intepretation of myths and the history of religions especially through the important systematic works of *E. Neumann* (especially Ursprungsgeschichte des Bewußtseins, (Frankfurt, 1984) 4th ed. and *K. Kerényis* (see especially Einführung in das Wesen Der Mythologie, 4th ed. (Zürich, 1951), and Die Mythologie der Griechen vol. 1: Die Götter und Menschheitsgeschichten, (Munich, 8th ed. 1985).

[6] See for example *H. Gottschalk,* Lexikon der Mythologie der europäischen Völker. Götter, Mysterien, Kulte, Symbole-Heroen und Sagengestalten der Mythen, (Berlin, 1973): 22; *R. Cavendish, T. O. Ling,* Mythologie. Eine illustrierte Weltgeschichte des mythisch-religiösen Denkens, (Munich, 1981): e.g. 11; *K. Hübner,* Die Wahrheit des Mythos, Munich, 1985 is probably right in assuming that the "mythical" man did not experience himself "psychologically", that for him there was no difference between "inside" and "outside". For Hübner, therefore, the psychological interpretation of myths is "only one possibility of interpretation that has to be understood historically" and cannot be transposed "ahistorically upon a totally different past" (see 86 and 60)

[7] C. G. Jung sometimes characterizes his psychology as "empirical science" and sees himself as physician and natural scientist. See e.g. *C. G. Jung,* Collected Works vol. 9, 1: Die Archetypen und das kollektive Unbewußte, 2nd ed. (Olten-Freiburg, 1976): 17, 61 etc. But other remarks seem to contradict that position, see ibid. 40. *W. Schmidbauer,* Mythos und Psychologie. Methodische Probleme, aufgezeigt an der Ödipus-Sage, (Munich-Basel, 1970): 73, points out that C. G. Jung fails to provide a "unified hypothesis about the genesis of myths", that he assumed at one time that the archetypes were given, never "developed", at another that they were the "reflexion of

the powerful affective and experience of all ancestors in father, mother, child, man and woman," and then again that they were "demonstrably inherited instincts and preformations". See also *G. Baudler,* Zum Ursprung der religiösen Symbolik: "Archetypen der Seele (C. G. Jung) oder erfahrbare Wirklichkeit", in : *W. Bies, H. Jung* (ed.), Mnemosyne. Festschrift für Manfred Lurker zum 60. Geburtstag (Bibliographie zur Symbolik, Ikonographie und Mythologie, Suppl. 2), (Baden-Baden, 1989):71-91.

8   *C. G. Jung,* Collected Works, vol. 10: Zivilisation im Übergang, Olten, 1974): 190.

9   See for example *C. Schneider,* Ursprung und Ursachen der christlichen Intoleranz, in: Zeitschrift für Religion und Geistesgeschichte 30 (1978): 193-218.

10   See for this whole question issue 22, 1 (1986) of Concilium; therein especially the article of *P. Knitter,* Die Religionstheologie am Scheideweg, 63-68, and *L. Rouner,* Die Religionstheologie in der jüngeren protestantischen Theologie, ibid., 69-75; *H. Küng,* Zu einer ökumenischen Theologie der Religionen", ibid. 76-80, clarifies the view that one prerequisite for religious dialogue is that each partner holds on to his own faith; important also: *L. Swidler,* Interreligiöser und interideologischer Dialog. Die Matrix aller systematischer Reflexion heute, in Pastoraltheologie 75 (1986/87): 305-327, as well as *W. Kern,* Disput um Jesus und um Kirche, Innsbruck-Vienna-Munich, 1980: 88-112; a careful assessment of different positions in the history of doctrines is found in *H. Sonnemans,* "Außerhalb der Kirche kein Heil"? Ein theologischer Grundsatz uns seine Auslegung im geschichtlichen Wandel." Gastvortrag an der Philosophischen Fakultät der RWTH Aachen am 19.4.1988; recently, see also *P. Kniter,* Ein Gott, viele Religionen. Gegen den Absolutheitsanspruch des Christentums, (Munich, 1988).

11   See for example *F. Wilfred,* "Der Dialog ringt nach Luft. Auf dem Weg zu neuen Ufern des religiösen Dialogs", in: Zeitschrift für Missionswissenschaft und Religionswissenschaft, 1988, 2: 97-117.

12   See for example *C. Schütz,* Art. Gott im Christentum, in: *F. König, H. Waldenfels,* Lexikon der Religionen, Phänomene-Geschichte-Ideen, (Freiburg-Basel—Vienna, 1987): 225. The author summarizes his article as follows: "Jesus Christ therefore is part of a Trinitarian groundplan, he contains and unfolds the mystery of God. The christological Kerygma brings us close to the mystery of the Trinity. What Jesus Christ is, lives, causes, prophesies and does, stands in a Trinitarian context". During my work with the existential interpretation of Jesus' parables I, myself, realized that even the poet of these stories, the prepaschal Jesus, is already inwardly moved by the experience that the lonesome and helpless being—the child, the son, as he experiences himself and whom he depicts in the parables of the murder at the vineyard (Mk 12, 1b-8), of the sower (Mk 4, 3-8), of the praying son (Mt 7, 9-10), the persistent widow (Lk 18, 2-5), as well as the parable of the Samaritan (Lk 10, 30-35), of the merciful father (Lk 15, 11-32), and the dishonest steward—in the open expression of its distress, in the realization of its childlike breath, finds the loving Abba. The promised kingdom of God begins in this experience for which Jesus eventually dies on the cross. See *G.*

Baudler, Jesus im Spiegel seiner Gleichnisse. Das erzählerische Werk Jesu-ein Zugang zum Glauben, 2nd ed. (Stuttgart-Munich, 1988): esp. 261-286. When this same experience is revealed to the apostles in their recollection of the life of Jesus, God is disclosed to them as Son, Spirit, and Father. See also *B. Forte,* Jesus von Nazaret. Geschichte Gottes-Gott der Geschichte, (Mainz, 1984): 177.

[13] See *Wilfred,* Der Dialog ringt nach Luft, op. cit. 111-114.

[14] This is pointed out in several papers read during the conference referred to in note 3 (e.g. by *C. F. v. Weizsäcker* and *Hans Peter Duerr).* Some of these papers were accessible to me in manuscript only.

[15] The text is edited with a commentary in *C. G. Jung,* Symbolik des Geistes, (Olten-Freiburg 1972): 453 f.

[16] *I. Eibl-Eibesfeldt,* Grundriß der vergleichenden Verhaltensforschung. Ethologie, 7th ed. (München-Zürich 1987): 235.

[17] On the biological concept of rituals see *K. Lorenz,* Das sogenannte Böse, 25th ed. (Vienna 1970): 89-127.

[18] See for this question *W. Burkert,* Homo necans. Interpretationen altgriechischer Opferriten und Mythen, (Berlin-New York 1972): 39-45.

[19] *A. Hardy,* Der Mensch-das betende Tier. Religiosität als Faktor der Evolution, (Stuttgart 1979). In this book biology and theology are too confused (see the original title: "The biology of God"). Hardy tries to solve theological problems with biological methods.

[20] See *K. Rahner,* Hörer des Wortes. Zur Grundlegung einer Religionsphilosophie (Munich 1969).

[21] See *P. Ricoeur's* well-known statement about the function of symbols: "The symbols make you think" (Id., Symbolik des Bösen (Freiburg-Munich 1971): 395 ff.)

[22] See on this topic *G. Bateson,* Geist und Natur. Eine notwendige Einheit (Frankfurt 1982): 189 f.

[23] The term of "Horizontverschmelzung" (amalgamation of horizons) in human perception and understanding was coined by *H. Gadamer,* Wahrheit und Methode. Grundzüge einer philosophischen Hermeneutik 2nd ed. (Tübingen 1985).

[24] According to I. Kant the unknowable "Ding an sich" affects the process of knowing. The necessary relation between subject and object in the process of knowing is stressed by scientists like *H. R. Maturana/F. J. Varela,* Der Baum der Erkenntnis. Die biologischen Wurzeln des menschlichen Erkennens (Bern-Munich-Vienna 1987).

[25] On this particular concept of symbol see *M. Lurker,* Zur sym-bolwissenschaftlichen Terminologie in den anthropologischen Disziplinen, in: Id. (ed.), Bibliographie zur Symbolik, Ikonographie und Mythologie, Ergänzungsband 1 (Beiträge zu Symbol, Symbolbegriff und Sym-bolforschung) Baden-Baden, 1983: 95-108; Lurker's concept of symbol is very close to that used by Paul Tillich, following therein the contemporary science of religious education. See e.g. *G. Baudler,* Korrelationsdidaktik: Leben durch Glauben erschließen (Paderborn, 1984): 32-67. Important ad-

ditions to the understanding of symbols by Paul Ricoeur in: *P. Biehl* etc: Symbole geben zu lernen. Einführung in die Symboldidaktik anhand der Symbole Hand, Haus und Weg (Neukirchen-Vluyn, 1989): 51-58.

[26] See *M. Eliade,* Die Religionen und das Heilige (Salzburg 1954): 33 in which he speaks of "hierophanies" in this context.

[27] Idolatry occurs only when the symbol and that which is symbolised are identified as one. See *P. Tillich,* Geo. Werke, vol. VIII (Stuttgart 1970): 147.

[28] See *J. Kreiner,* Art. Shinto/Shintoismus, in: *König/Waldenfels,* Lexikon der Religionen, op. cit. 607-610, esp. 610.

[29] See *H. Halbfas,* Das dritte Auge. Religionsdidaktische Anstöße, (Düsseldorf 1982).

[30] See *M. Kassel,* Das Auge im Bauch. Erfahrungen mit tiefenpsychischer Spiritualität 2nd ed. (Olten-Freiburg 1986).

[31] See *I. T. Ramsey,* Religious Language. An Empirical Placing of Theological Phrases, 4th ed. (London 1974), his most important work.

[32] In the exegetical literature, for example, *R. Schnackenburg,* Maßstab des Glaubens. Fragen heutiger Christen im Licht des Neuen Testaments (Freiburg-Basel-Vienna, 1978): by *F. Mußner,* "Ursprünge und Entfaltung der neutestamentlichen Sohneschristologie. Versuch einer Rekonstruktion" in: *L. Scheffczyk* (ed.), Grundfragen der Christologie heute (Freiburg-Basel-Vienna, 1975); and *P.-G. Müller,* Der Traditionsprozeß im Neuen Testament. Kommunikationsanalytische Studien zur Versprachlichung des Jesusphänomens (Freiburg-Basel-Vienna, 1982): in dogmatics, especially: *E. Schillebeeckx,* in: Id., Jesus. Die Geschichte von einem Lebenden (Freiburg-Basel-Vienna, 1980), and in: Id. Jesus und die Christen. Die Geschichte einer neuen Lebenspraxis, 2nd ed. (Freiburg-Basel-Vienna, 1980): *W. Kasper,* Der Gott Jesu Christi (Mainz, 1982): in fundamental theology and philosophy of religions: *M. Seckler, "Dei Verbum Religiose Audiens: Wandlungen im christlichen Offenbarungsverständnis"; J. J. Petuchowski/W. Strolz* (eds.), Offenbarung im jüdischen und christlichen Offenbarungsverständnis (Freiburg-Basel-Vienna, 1981); *K.-H. Weger,* Gott hat sich offenbart (Freiburg-Basel-Vienna, 1982); as well as *P. Ricoeur,* "The Language of Faith" in: *Union Seminary Quarterly Review 28* (1973); *B. Casper,* Sprache und Theologie. Eine philosophische Hinführung (Freiburg-Basel-Vienna, 1975); *B. Welte,* Religionsphilosophie 3rd ed. (Freiburg-Basel-Vienna, 1980): see ibid. note 1; *E. Biser,* Religiöse Sprachbarrieren. Aufbau einer Logaporetik (Munich, 1980): 54; in moral theology and pedagogy of religion *R. Zerfaß,* Grundkurs Predigt 1: Spruchpredigt, (Düsseldorf, 1987); R. Sauer, Religiöse Erziehung auf dem Weg zum Glauben (Düsseldorf, 1976); *J. Wohlmuth,* Religiöse Erfahrung und christliche Sprache. Bemerkungen zur Theologie I.T. Ramseys und zu deren religionspädagogischer Auswertbarkeit, in: Katechetische Blätter 100 (1975); and *G. Baudler,* esp. id. Der Religionsunterricht als curricular strukturierter, offener Sprach- und Denkprozeß, in: id. (ed.), Religionsunterricht im Primarbereich (Zürich-Einsiedeln-Köln, 1973); id. Religiöse Erziehung heute, Paderborn, 1979; see the recent monograph by *C.*

Schwark, "Die Sprachtheologie I.T. Ramseys und ihre Bedeutung für die Religionspädagogik-"Disclosure-Erfahrungen" im religiösen Lernprozeß," unpublished diss. at the Pädagogische Fakultät of the RWTH Aachen, 1988.

[33] See for this term *Schwark,* "Die Sprachtheologie I. T. Ramseys, op. cit. 37-43. A less thorough portrayal of Ramsey's theology of language is found in *W. A. Pater,* Theologische Sprachlogik, (Munich, 1971).

[34] See above, note 26.

[35] See *L. Ott,* Grundriß der Katholischen Dogmatik, 8th ed. (Freiburg-Basel-Vienna, 1970), 140.

[36] See *J. B. Metz,* "Theologie gegen Mythologie. Kleine Apologie des biblischen Monotheismus," in: Herder-Korrespondenz 42 (1988): 187-193. A detailed discussion of biblical monotheism is found in the special issue "Der Monotheismus" of the periodical Concilium, 21st issue.

[37] See *Metz,* "Theologie gegen Mythologie," op. cit., 192.

[38] See *Wilfred,* "Der Dialog ringt nach Luft," op. cit., 112.

[39] See together with the articles by Halbfas and Drewermann especially *G. Bekker,* Die Ursymbole in den Religionen, (Graz-Vienna-Cologne, 1987).

[40] See *Wilfred,* "Der Dialog ringt nach Luft," op. cit., 112.

[41] Ibid. 113.

[42] See *H. J. Rose,* Griechische Mythologie. Ein Handbuch, 6th ed. (Munich, 1982): 49 f.

[43] Schütz, Art. Gott im Christentum, op. cit., 224.

[44] See *M. v. Brück,* Art. Buddhismus, in: *König/Waldenfels,* Lexikon der Religionen, op., cit., 76-94.

[45] Even in Mohenjo-Daro, a city from the oldest civilization of the Indus valley, a vast bathing complex has been excavated in the city-center (see *M. Jansen,* Die Indus-Zivilisation. Wiederentdeckung einer frühen Hochkultur, Cologne 1986, 62-66).

[46] See *C. Dohmen,* Das Bilderverbot. Seine Entstehung und seine Entwicklung im Alten Testament, Königstein-Bonn 1985.

[47] See *E. Spiegel,* Pferd oder Gott, in: Bruder Franz 36 (1983), 70 sq.; *id.,* Einer Theologie des Gewaltverzichts auf den Spuren, in: ru. Zeitschrift für die Praxis des Religionsunterrichts 17 (1987), 142-145.

[48] When in 734/733 Judah was forced into an anti-Assyrian alliance and king Ahaz began to build a defense wall around Jerusalem, Isaiah confronted the king and the people with a clear choice: "If you do not stand by me, you will not stand at all." (Is 7, 9). See on this: *E. Spiegel,* Gewaltverzicht. Grundlagen einer biblischen Friedenstheologie, Kassel 1987, 178-188.

[49] See *K. Jaspers,* Die maßgebenden Menschen (Special edition from: Die großen Philosophen, vol. 1), München 1967, 186 sq.

[50] See note 27.

[51] *D. Zilleßen,* Symboldidaktik. Herausforderung und Gefährdung gegenwärtiger Religionspädagogik, in: Der evangelische Erzieher 36 (1984) 626-642, esp. 632 sq. and 635 sq. (part 5: "Christologische Begrenzung und Zerbrechen des Symbols"); Zilleßens' critique is aimed especially at *H. Halbfas'* didactics of symbols; see *id.,* Das dritte Auge, op. cit.

Exposition 1

1   *A. Falaturia* et al (ed.), Universale Vaterschaft Gottes. Begegnung der Religionen, Freiburg 1987, 173-199; here, see 183.

2   For the question of whether one can meaningfully speak of "major" and "minor" religions, see *J. F. Thiel,* Religionsethnologie. Grundbegriffe der Religionen schriftloser Völker, Berlin 1984, 16-18. Both terms imply an a priori evaluation that is questionable to the degree that every religion, even that of Australian aborigines, for example, has its own system of values, and a major or minor distinction would thus be imposed from outside.

3   See *W. Sparn,* Leiden-Erfahrung and Denken. Materialien zum Theodizeeproblem, Munich 1980; *H. Wiersinga,* Leid: Herausforderung des Lebens. Auseinandersetzung mit einer Grundfrage, Munich 1982; *H. Sonnemans,* Zum Verhältnis von Gott und Mensch angesichts des Leidens, in: Theologie und Glaube 75 (1985), 286-297; *H.-M. Barth,* Angesichts des Leidens von Gott reden, in: Pastoraltheologie 75 (1986), 116-131; *R. Sauer,* Die Rede von Gott angesichts des Leids in der Welt, in: Universitas 41 (1986), 361-370.

4   See *C. F. Keyes/E. V. Daniel,* Karma. An Anthropological Inquiry, Berkeley-Los Angeles-London 1983, and the fundamental work by *M. Vereno,* Karma. Betrachtungen zu einem Schlüsselbegriff des indischen Denkens, in: Kairos 23 (1981), 189-205, in which Karma is presented as a fundamental unifying doctrine in Hindu writings, from the most ancient of the Upanishads, the Brihad-âranyaka-Upanishad, to the Bhagavadgita. Parallels and differences with the "synthetical conception of life" of the biblical and extra-biblical worlds cannot be discussed here. See on this topic *K. Koch* (ed.), Um das Prinzip der Vergeltung in Religion und Recht des Alten Testaments, Darmstadt 1971.

5   See *I. Yamaguchi,* Die Lehre vom Leiden im Buddhismus, in: Neue Zeitschrift für systematische Theologie und Religionsphilosophie 24 (1982), 216-232; *H. Waldenfels,* Sprechsituationen: Leid-Vernichtung-Geheimnis. Zum buddhistischen und christlichen Sprechverhalten, in: id., *T. Immoos* (ed.), Fernöstliche Weisheit und christlicher Glaube, Mainz 1985, 289-312, esp. 291-297; see also, id., Religionen als Antworten auf die menschliche Sinnfrage, Munich 1980, 23-33.

6   Attempts to explain illness, birth defects and natural disasters as necessary consequences, as by-products of the trial and error of evolution, as found in *G. Greshake,* Der Preis der Liebe. Besinnung über das Leid, Freiburg-Basel-Vienna 1978, 44, cannot remain unchallenged. See e.g. *I. Mieth,* Katechese in der Küche. Kinderfragen verlangen Antwort, Mainz 1979, 74: "...speaking of the physically handicapped as by-products of evolution is an atrocity."

7   See his principal book, *R. Girard,* Violence and the Sacred, Johns Hopkins 1977. See also Girard's, Das Ende der Gewalt. Analyse des Menschheitsverhängnisses, Freiburg-Basel-Vienna 1983. Unfortunately *R.*

8   *Girard's* The Scapegoat, Johns Hopkins 1986, could not be dealt with in this book because it was released only after my manuscript was finished. But the book does not add essentially new aspects to the previous works. See in chapter 2 of Exposition the section *Excursus: The Path of Christian Salvation and Theology*, esp. note 50, 51, and 52.

9   This type of religious education was adopted by the synod of German bishoprics ("Würzburg synod"). See the section "Religious education in the schools," in: Gemeinsame Synode. Offizielle Gesamtausgabe I, Freiburg-Basel-Vienna 1977, 123-152.

10 See *Halbfas*, Das dritte Auge, op. cit.; *P. Biehl/G. Baudler*, Erfahrung-Symbol-Glaube. Grundfragen des Religionsunterrichtes, Frankfurt 1980; *Baudler*, Korrelationsdidaktik, op. cit.; *A. Bucher*, Symboldidaktik, in: Katechetische Blätter 113 (1988) 23-27.

11 *H. Müller-Karpe*, Handbuch der Vorgeschichte, Vol. I (Paleolithic time), Munich 1966, 228.

12 Ibid.

13 Ibid.

14 See for example "Symbole" in Herder-Lexikon, Freiburg-Basel-Vienna 1978, 162.

15 See *W. Daum*, Ursemitische Religion, Stuttgart-Berlin-Cologne-Mainz 1985, 182-188.

16 See *H. Bächthold-Stäubli* (ed.), Handwörterbuch des deutschen Aberglaubens, vol. VIII, Berlin-Leipzig 1936/37, 482.

17 On the interpretation of this picture see chap. 2.2 of the section: *The Baptism of the Hunter: The Lascaux Cave Pictures* and notes 2-10.

18 *Daum*, Ursemitische Religion, op. cit., see esp. 22-47 and 78-81.

19 Ibid. 31.

20 Ibid. 80.

21 Description of *W. Daum*, ibid. 46.

22 See ibid. 188.

23 See the thorough study by *J. Hahn*, Das "goldene Kalb". Die Jahwe-Verehrung bei Stierbildern in der Geschichte Israels, Frankfurt 1981, for example, the summaries pp. 194 and 364.

24 According to *Dohmen*, Das Bilderverbot, op. cit., it is especially the danger of a confusion with Baal, of an idiosyncratic mix of the half-nomadic religion of Yahweh and elements of the religion of Canaan that prompted Hosea's criticisms and the subsequent interdiction of images. See also the review by *E. Zenger*, Der Gott JHWH im Spannungsfeld von Politik und Kult, in: Theologische Revue 82 (1986), 441-450 who agrees with Dohmen.

25 *G. Weiler*, Ich verwerfe im Lande die Kriege. Das verborgene Matriarchat im Alten Testament, Munich 1984. This study develops the bull characteristics of Yahweh from a feminist perspective. But the author takes the bull primarily as a symbol of fertility and procreation, as a symbol of Baal, so that Yahweh, like Athtar and Baal, would be brought into a "holy wedding" with the female mother goddess. Yet, the bull as symbol of El is an opponent of Baal, and therefore also of his female ally. It is true that

Yahweh takes on certain features of Baal once the people of Israel become settled. He becomes, for example, a dragon fighter—but his Baal-aspects are not expressed through the symbolism of the bull.

26 In this sense we agree with the article Kanaanäische Religion, in *G. Cornfeld/G. J. Botterweck,* Die Bibel und ihre Welt. Eine Enzyklopädie zur Heiligen Schrift. Bilder-Daten-Fakten, vol. 2, Bergisch-Gladbach 1969, 885, that points out the differences in character between the Israelite and the Canaanite Els. However, both are related: see Exod. 6, 3 where Yahweh identifies himself as the former "El-Shaddai"—who is similar to the Canaanite El in his might.

27 *A. Falaturi,* Der Islam-Religion der Rahma, der Barmherzigkeit, in: id. etc. (ed.), Universale Vaterschaft Gottes, op. cit., 67-87.

28 Ibid. 84.

29 *M. Lurker,* Adler und Schlange. Tiersymbolik im Glauben und im Weltbild der Völker, Tübingen 1983, 51 f.

30 Compare the horned dragon in the Apocalypse 12, 1-6.

31 See *M. Burkolter-Trachsel,* Der Drache. Das Symbol und der Mensch, Bern 1981, 103.

32 *Bächthold-Stäubli,* Handwörterbuch des deutschen Aberglaubens, op. cit., 483 and 482.

33 See *U. Steffen,* Drachenkampf. Der Mythos vom Bösen, Stuttgart 1984, 51 f.

34 See *Burkholter-Trachsel,* Der Drache, op. cit., 92 f.; *Lurker,* Adler und Schlange, op. cit., 219 ff.

35 *Burkholter-Trachsel,* Der Drache, op. cit., 6.

36 Ibid.

37 See also chapter 3.3 in Development, the section on *"Maternal Religion in Fairy Tales."*

38 See *Daum* on this interpretation of the "Hänsel and Gretel" story, Ursemitische Religion, op. cit., 218 f.

39 See *M. Lurker,* Adler und Schlange, op. cit., 185.

40 Ibid. 136. Elsewhere (ibid. 19 f.) Lurker refers to the creation myth of the North American Tlinkit, in which the raven, Yehl, hovers over the primeval mist which he beats down with his wings until dry land appears.

41 See *M. Landmann,* Das Tier in der jüdischen Weisung, Heidelberg 1959, 31.

42 *Lurker,* Adler und Schlange, op. cit., 40 sq.

43 *F. Heiler,* Die Religionen der Menschheit in Vergangenheit und Gegenwart, Stuttgart 1962, 429.

44 See *V. E. Frankl,* Logotherapie und Existenzanalyse. Texte aus fünf Jahrzehnten, Munich 1987; id., Der Wille zum Sinn. Ausgewählte Vorträge über Logotherapie, Bern 1982; *R. Zimmermann,* Logotherapie und Existenzanalyse bei Viktor E. Frankl, in: Stimmen der Zeit 109 (1984), 111-123; *B. Grom,* Sinnzentrierte Lebens- und Heilkunst. Die Logotherapie Viktor E. Frankls, in: Stimmen der Zeit 110 (1985), 181-192.

45 See the distinction made in logotherapy between "intrinsic and extrinsic religion," that is of a "religion that focuses on genuine religious thoughts and values, and a religion that stresses its institutional aspects;" *H. Faber,* Das Problem der Projektion in der Religion, in: Pastoraltheologie 75 (1986/87), 327-337; 335. See also *E. Biser,* Die glaubensgeschichtliche

Wende. Eine theologische Positionsbestimmung, Graz-Vienna-Cologne 1986, 171-208.

[46] According to the guidelines, "Das katechetische Wirken in der Kirche," of the synod of German bishoprics ("Würzburg synod") "the main goal of teaching catechism is to help man lead a successful life by responding to God's call and his comforting" (Gemeinsame Synode. Offizielle Gesamtausgabe II, Freiburg-Basel-Vienna 1977, 41). Only through traditional religious symbols, and not through religious authority and theological phrases, does the "call and comfort" of God appear in a way that leaves man free and autonomous.

[47] See in Introduction chap. 2 the Section *"Perception of Symbols and Empirical Reality"* and notes 31 and 32.

[48] This is especially true for the image of Satan. See the well-known work by the Old Testament scholar *H. Haag,* Abschied vom Teufel, Einsiedeln 1984; see also his more recent publication: Der Teufel, Mythos und Geschichte, in: Katechetische Blätter 111 (1986), 778-781.

[49] See above in chap. 2 of Introduction the section *Perception of Symbols and Empirical Reality.*

[50] For this "oral" aspect of original sin see especially the psychological hermeneutics of *E. Drewermann,* Strukturen des Bösen, vol. II (Die jahwistische Urgeschichte in psychoanalytischer Sicht), Munich-Paderborn-Vienna 1983, 185-202. In this interpretation "sin" is the "devouring" of that which man encounters in his own life as divine fascination—in nature or in his fellow men. In developmental psychology this happens first in the "oral conflict" of the infant who tries to suck in not only the needed food, but also the divinely fascinating aspect of the mother, and who consequently experiences the weaning as a rejection by God, as an expulsion from paradise.

[51] The French literary critic and cultural anthropologist René Girard, to whom we have repeatedly referred, defines this imitating (mimetic) desire as the origin of human violence. According to Girard, the human community is founded on the lynching of a fellow member of the tribe, a scapegoat who takes all violence upon himself, and thus unites men by liberating them from their self-destructive rivalry—at least for a certain time, before the "sacrifice" has to be renewed. This is where Girard sees the violent origin of all human culture and religion. See also the whole of chap. 2 of the Exposition, esp. note 2.

[52] See in Development chap. 2.3, the section: *The Old "Hunter's Breath" Fuses with the "New Solar Wind."*

[53] R. Pesch sees the behavior of the tenants as usurpation, and therefore as related to original sin, as well. See *R. Pesch,* Neues Testament-Die Überwindung der Gewalt, in: *N. Lohfink/R. Pesch,* Weltgestaltung und Gewaltlosigkeit. Ethische Aspekte des Alten und Neuen Testamentes in ihrer Einheit und ihrem Gegensatz, Düsseldorf 1978, 62-80, esp. 68 f.

[54] On the interpretation of this passage, see *R. Schwager,* Brauchen wir einen Sündenbock? Gewalt und Erlösung in den biblischen Schriften, Munich 1986, 165. On pp. 152-172 Schwager elaborates on how lying and the "subliminal will to kill"—that is, human violence—cause the death of Jesus.

315

55   On Peter's denial see the subtle psychological study by *Girard,* The Scapegoat.

56   *Girard,* Ende der Gewalt, op. cit., 187 ff.

57   See in addition to Raymond Schwager, whom we have mentioned several times, *B. Häring,* Die Heilkraft der Gewaltfreiheit, Düsseldorf 1986, 121 ff., who points to the results of a speculative, nonhistorical theology of "theories about sacrificial death," that "misinterpret the death of Jesus on the cross according to the model of earthly 'justice of revenge' "; according to this interpretation "God himself, in order to satisfy his honor, and in view of a complete payment of the guilt, could not have asked for less than the death of his Son who became man," a view that "not only dangerously obscures the image of God, but also minimizes the healing power of Jesus' agony for the subsequent evolution of history."

58   See also *F. Varone,* Ce Dieu censé aimer la souffrance, Paris 1984; *E. Staimer,* Wollte Gott, daß Jesus starb? Jesu erlösender Weg zum Tod, Munich 1983; also *J. Moltmann,* Der gekreuzigte Gott. Das Kreuz Christi als Grund und Kritik christlicher Theologie, Munich 1972, and the response of *H. Sonnemans,* Hoffnung durch Gott? In Konfrontation mit Ernst Bloch, Freiburg-Basel-Vienna 1973, esp. 71-81, to Bloch's contention that in this perspective, the Christian God reveals himself as a "cannibal in heaven."

59   See the assessment of Girard's theses by the conference of the "Arbeitsgemeinschaft deutschsprachiger katholischer Alttestamentler," August 24 to 28, 1981, in Neustift bei Brixen. Papers and texts in: N. Lohfink (ed.), Gewalt und Gewaltlosigkeit im Alten Testament, Freiburg-Basel-Vienna 1983, with contributions by *Ernst Haag, Norbert Lohfink, Lothar Ruppert* and *Raymund Schwager.*

60   See the section *The Offering of the First-Fruits and the Sacrificial Killing* in chap. 2 of the Exposition.

61   See *Schwager,* Der wunderbare Tausch. Zur Geschichte und Deutung der Erlösungslehre, Munich 1986, 306 f.

62   The use of a flint for circumcision originates from ancient customs that go back to the Stone Age. See article "Beschneidung" in Lexikon für Theologie und Kirche, vol. II, Freiburg i. Br. 1958, 290.

63   See the bibliography for the Hebrew word "dam" — blood, given by *N. Lohfink* (ed.), Gewalt, op. cit., 225.

64   *W. Beltz,* Gott und die Götter. Biblische Mythologie, Düsseldorf 1977, 127.

65   In the most ancient parts of the Old Testament "Israel" is the name of a sacred bond between several tribes (e.g. in the song of Deborah, Judg. 5, 2). Later it is extended in a political sense to the kingdom, and in a religious sense to the entire people of Yahweh. See also *G. W. Ahlström,* Who were the Israelites?, Winona Lake, Indiana 1986, 39 f. in which the author speculates whether the "people of Jacob" had not already brought this name to central Palestine.

66   See *Daum,* Ursemitische Religion, op. cit., 188, in which the author shows that the bull is not the symbol of Baal, but of El. In all Ugaritic myths, El has the name 'thr il', 'bull El' "; for a similar view see *W. H. Schmidt,*

Königtum Gottes in Ugarit and Israel, Berlin 1966, 6.

[67] One cannot say that Jacob fought as "representative of Yahweh" against El or Elohim (*Beltz,* Gott und die Götter, op. cit., 128). In the oldest parts of the Bible, Yahweh and El do not appear as opponents. Rather, the "powerful El" (El Shaddai) later reveals himself to Moses as Yahweh (see Gen. 6, 3).

[68] See *Haag,* Abschied, op. cit., 34. In the context of ancient Hindu religion a similar phenomenon can perhaps be observed for the gods Indra, Vishnu, and Shiva; see on this topic *J. Gonda,* Die Religionen Indiens, vol. 1 (Stuttgart 1960) and II (Stuttgart 1963).

[69] In the Christian teaching on Satan, even according to the early Church Fathers (like Irenaeus, Origen, Augustine, Gregory the Great), this is explained in the following way: The devil (like the other demons) was "created by God with a good nature," but turned evil of his own choice (see the council of Braga). See *J. Michl,* Art. Satan (history of theology), in: Handbuch theologischer Grundbegriffe, ed. *H. Fries,* vol. 4, Munich 1970, 26-35. Thus the devil was not initially created as an evil being. He is not an eternal evil principle as in Parsee dualism.

[70] See *K. Galling,* Die Bücher der Chronik, Esra, Nehemia (Das Alte Testament Deutsch, Teilband 12) Göttingen 1954, 61, who sees the "transformation of the earlier view" as a result of the intention to "keep pure the belief in God's untainted justice;" *F. J. Schierse,* the article Satan (biblical), in: *H. Fries* (ed.), Handbuch theologischer Grundbegriffe, vol. IV, op. cit., 22-26; *A. B. Ehrlich,* Randglossen zur hebräischen Bibel. Textkritisches, Sprachliches und Sachliches, vol. III, Hildesheim 1968, 343 (what was first "ascribed to the wrath of Yahweh" in 1 Sam. 24 "was interpreted differently later"); *F. Stolz,* Das erste und zweite Buch Samuel (Zürcher Bibelkommentare: Altes Testament, vol. 9), Zürich 1981, 301 explains the variant in the Chronicles by contending that in later times "one could no longer stand this rash and unpredictable feature of Yahweh."

[71] See *K. L. Schmidt,* Lucifer als gefallene Engelmacht, in: Theologische Zeitschrift 7 (1951), 161-179, who sees a parallel between rebellious angels and kings, between demonic and earthly powers, and interprets the myth of Lucifer from this perspective. See also *A. Rosenberg,* Engel und Dämonen. Gestaltwandel eines Urbildes, Munich 1986, esp. 147-151.

[72] See *Daum,* Ursemitische Religion, op. cit., 25-31.

[73] Ibid. 124-128.

[74] *W. Daum* (ed.), Märchen aus dem Jemen. Mythen und Märchen aus dem Reich von Saba, Cologne 1983, 84-96.

[75] On this interpretation of the tale of "Donkey skin", see *Daum,* Ursemitische Religion, op. cit., 112, f.

[76] See *Baudler,* Jesus im Spiegel seiner Gleichnisse, op. cit.

[77] For example Origen, Gregory Nazianzen, Gregory of Nyssa, John Scotus Erigena etc.

[78] See *K. Rahner, H. Vorgrimler,* Kleines theologisches Wörterbuch, Freiburg. 1981, 31: "The positive affirmation of a universal reconciliation was rejected by the magisterium as heretical."

79 See for example *John Paul II,* encyclical "Dives in misericordia", in: Verlautbarungen des Apostolischen Stuhls, no. 26, ed. by the secretariat of the German conference of bishops, Bonn, 1980; see also *K. Heinen,* Der barmherzige Gott. Zum biblischen Hintergrund der Enzyklika "Dives in misericordia," in: Lebendiges Zeugnis 37 (1982), 5-11.

80 Yet another particularly fond name for Israel.

81 On the symbolism of the dragon see *Steffen,* Drachenkampf, op. cit., and *Burkolter-Trachsel,* Der Drache, op. cit.

82 The fish is one of the oldest symbols for Christ. During the times of persecution it was used as a secret symbol. In many cultures it signifies both fertility and death. A frequently suggested relation of this symbol with baptism in water is not really convincing, because Jesus baptizes *not* with water, but with the "Holy spirit," as opposed to John the Baptist (Acts 1, 5 and John 1, 31-33); In fact, Jesus himself never baptized with water. The derivation from the acrostic for the Greek word for "fish" is certainly secondary (Ichthys = Iesous Christos Theou Yios Soter); see Herder-Lexikon "Symbole", op. cit., 52. On the other hand, Matt. 12, 38-41 and Luke 11, 29-32 specifically mention the "sign of Jonah" that is given to Christians as the "only sign."

Exposition 2

1 See *Girard,* Violence and the Sacred, op.cit., in the preceding chapter of this section, note 7.

2 *Girard,* Das Ende der Gewalt, op.cit., 36. In our present context we would have to specify the following: The murder of the scapegoat does not really *found* human community in the original sense (as before sin). It merely enables people to live together after original sin (after the unnatural usurpation of divine power), albeit only under "law and order".

3 Ibid. 105.

4 See *N. Davies,* Opfertod und Menschenopfer. Glaube, Liebe und Verzweiflung in der Geschichte der Menschheit, Düsseldorf-Vienna 1981, as well as *G. Widengren,* Religionsphänomenologie, Berlin 1969, esp. 308 ff., and the fundamental work by *Burkert,* Homo necans, op. cit., esp. 8-96. *Gottschalk,* Lexikon der Mythologie der europäischen Völker, op.cit., 249 f., 275 and 356 describe how human sacrifice occurs among the Celtic as well as the Baltic peoples—thus in very different cultural realms. See also *H. Döbler,* Kultur-und Sittengeschichte der Welt. Magie, Mythos, Religion, Munich-Gütersloh-Vienna 1971, 72-79.

5 *Müller-Karpe,* Handbuch der Vorgeschichte, op.cit., 234.

6 According to *Becker,* Die Ursymbole in den Religionen, op.cit., 122.

7 See *Burkert,* Homo necans, op.cit., 29; also ibid., note 34. Burkert sees man and animal as interchangeable in ritual sacrifice from the very beginning. Even in the story of the order to sacrifice Isaac, the original victim is replaced by an animal.

318

8   On this point see *Girard,* Das Ende der Gewalt, op.cit., 236 ff. On the theological possibility of a non-sacrificial interpretation see *R. Schwager,* Brauchen wir einen Sündenbock?, op.cit., as well as ibid., Der wunderbare Tausch, op.cit., and ibid., Für Gerechtigkeit und Frieden. Der Glaube als Antwort auf die Anliegen der Gegenwart, Innsbruck-Vienna 1986.

9   *Girard,* Das Ende der Gewalt, op.cit., 18 ff.

10 *Burkert,* Homo necans, op.cit., esp. 8-96.

11 *Burkert,* Anthropologie des religiösen Opfers: Die Sakralisierung der Gewalt. Veröffentlichung der Carl-Friedrich-von-Siemens-Stiftung, Munich 1984.

12 *Burkert,* Homo necans., op.cit., 25.

13 See *E. Fromm,* Anatomie der menschlichen Destruktivität, Stuttgart 1974, 112-114. Fromm demonstrates that even the Australopithecus as "ancestor" of man did not possess the instincts of a predator.

14 See for example the description of an elephant hunt by the Pygmies in *P. Schebesta,* Die Bambuti-Pygmäen von Ituri, vol. II, pt. 1, Brussels 1941, 114 ff.

15 *M. Stanek,* Geschichte der Kopfjäger. Mythos und Kultur der Iatmul auf Papua-Neuguinea, Cologne 1982, 198 f.

16 Paradoxically, ethological research has shown that wild wolves do not actually consider each other as prey. Man is definitely an unnatural or supernatural predator.

17 *Müller-Karpe,* Handbuch der Vorgeschichte, op.cit., 228.

18 *W. Köhler,* Intelligenzprüfungen an Menschenaffen, Berlin 1921, 76 f.

19 According to *J. M. Cordwell,* The Very Human Arts of the Transformation, in: *J. M. C. Schwarz, R. A. Schwarz* (ed.), The Fabric of Culture, The Hague 1979, 49.

20 See *S. K. Langer,* Philosophie auf neuem Wege. Das Symbol im Denken, im Ritus und in der Kunst, Berlin 1965, esp. 109-146.

21 See also below in chap. 3.3 of the *Development* section "On the Evolution of the Maternal Symbol: The Creation of the Woman and Mother (as the First Human) by the Christian God."

22 For a convincing description of the peacefulness of the ancient people's lives see *J. Herbig,* Am Anfang war das Wort. Die Evolution des Menschlichen, Munich-Vienna 1984 (see esp. 37 ff.: "Das Lager"). This author does not describe the decisive changes in living habits that were brought about by the transition to game-hunting (Burkert). Nor does he take into account Girard's sacrificial theories.

23 On the topic of female figures in the Stone Age, compare the stone engravings in the cave of Laussel, among which is the well known "Venus of Laussel" (Fig. 3). See also *H. P. Duerr,* Sedna oder die Liebe zum Leben, Frankfurt 1985, 94 f. who interprets the figure as the "Mistress of the Beasts." In this cave there is also a small female figure holding her crooked legs with her hands, and below, as a mirror, a human head and shoulders. This figuration is usually interpreted as a scene of birth *(Müller-Karpe,* Handbuch der Vorgeschichte, op.cit., plate 93, fig. 13; description on p. 271). On the so-called female idols see *W. G. Haensch,* Die menschlichen Statuetten des mittleren Jungpaläolithikums aus der Sicht der somatischen Anthropologie, Bonn 1982.

24 See *Burkert,* Homo necans, op.cit., 70-85 "Sexualisierung der Tötungsriten".

25 Apostolic Letter no. 86, sct. 9. The emphasis is from the pope.

26 See *I. Eibl-Eibesfeldt,* Liebe und Haß. Zur Naturgeschichte elementarer Verhaltensweisen, Munich 1976, 40-44.

27 *Müller-Karpe,* Handbuch der Vorgeschichte, op.cit., 169.

28 See below in chap. 3.3 the section "On the Evolution of the Maternal Symbol: The Creation of the Woman and Mother (as the First Human) by the Christian God."

29 *Müller-Karpe,* Handbuch der Vorgeschichte, op.cit., 228.

30 *J. Blank,* Weißt du, was Versöhnung heißt? Der Kreuzestod Jesu als Sühne und Versöhnung, in: *J. Blank, J. Werbick,* Sühne und Versöhnung, Düsseldorf 1986, 21-91; see 28.

31 *Widengren,* Religionsphänomenologie, op.cit., 280 f. distinguishes gift offerings, atonement offerings and communion offerings. With reference to our present terminology a gift offering corresponds to a first-fruits offering and an atonement offering to an offering of sacrificial slaying. Although these two forms of offering differ fundamentally they have in common the purpose of establishing a certain community between the celebrants and the divinty. In this sense they are both communion offerings.

32 *Blank,* Versöhnung, op.cit., see. esp. 28.

33 This remains true even if we assume, following recent historical research, that Israel originated basically from an insurgence of marginal groups within Canaan; see the contributions of *H. Engel, N. Lohfink, H.-W. Jüngling,* and *P. J. King* in the special issue "Bibel und Kirche" 38 (2/1983). It is again a situation of an oppressed people that tries to free itself from enslavement by the central power, and finds a religious legitimation.

34 *K. Jaspers,* Einführung in die Philosophie, Munich 1972, esp. 77 f.f. The "axis," in the sense of a common framework of "historic self-interpretation," is fixed by Jaspers around 800 to 200 BC. It is a time when man strove for a liberation from the abysses of this world, in China, India, Persia, Palestine and Greece, and when the "struggle of rationality and real experience against the myth, the struggle for the transcendence of the one god against the demons..." (78) began.

35 See *Blank,* Versöhnung, op. cit., 43 f.f.

36 See *O. Loretz,* Leberschau, Sündenbock, Asasel in Ugarit und Israel, Altenberge 1985, esp. 50-57.

37 *Blank,* Versöhnung, op.cit., 54.

38 On the criticism of cults by the prophets see ibid. 32-40.

39 See for example *Schwager,* Für Gerechtigkeit und Frieden, op. cit., esp. 33-38 and 42.

40 *Blank,* Versöhnung, op.cit., 69 (note 97); for the following see ibid. 68 f.f.-In the apocalyptic vision of John there is no longer any temple in the new Jerusalem: "I saw that there was no temple in the city since the Lord God Almighty and the Lamb were themselves the temple" (Rev 21, 22).

41 For the classification and interpretation of Jesus' parables of conflict see *Baudler,* Jesus im Spiegel seiner Gleichnisses, op.cit., 169-199.

[42] Translation according to *Blank,* Versöhnung, op.cit., 73.
[43] *Schillebeeckx,* Jesus, op.cit., 283.
[44] *Blank,* Versöhnung, op. cit., 75, note 111.
[45] Ibid.
[46] See in chapter 1 of Exposition the section *"The Profanation of Evil in the History of Biblical Thought: the Fall of Satan"; Girard,* Das Ende der Gewalt, op.cit., 192, sees a "decisive argument" in the fact that the gospels do not link God to the apocalyptic violence, which they announce, but see violence always in relation to man, not to God. But this argument does not hold: especially the image of the lake of sulphur (Rev. 20, 7 f.f.) into which the beast, the false prophet, death and the underworld and everyone who was not marked in the book of life, are cast, and in which they are tortured "day and night, for ever and ever" (Rev. 20, 10). This obviously depicts a violence that comes from God.
[47] This is what I tried to show in Jesus im Spiegel seiner Gleichnisse, op.cit.
[48] On the details of this interpretation see ibid. 204-206 and 277; bibliography on the evaluation of the authentic texts ibid. 205 (note 143) and 206 (note 145).
[49] G. *Greshake,* Der Wandel der Erlösungsvorstellungen in der Theologiegeschichte, in: *L. Scheffczyk* (ed.), Erlösung und Emanzipation, Freiburg i.Br. 1973, 69-101.
[50] *Schwager,* Brauchen wir einen Sündenbock?, op.cit.
[51] *Schwager,* Der wunderbare Tausch, op.cit., Munich 1986, id., Der Richter wird gerichtet. Zur Versöhnungslehre von Karl Barth, in Zeitschrift für katholische Theologie 107 (1985), 101-141.
[52] See above in Chap. 1 of Exposition, note 59.
[53] Blank, for example, voices this reproach in Versöhnung, op.cit., note 64.
[54] This concept is often used and misused in the theological discussions about Eugen Drewermann's essays.
[55] *Blank,* Versöhnung, op.cit., 51.
[56] Ibid.
[57] After a physical breakdown during mass on December 6, 1273 he said, at the age of 49, that all he had systematically assembled in his "summae" was like "straw" compared to the mystical revelations that had been granted him. Henceforth, he no longer worked at his scientific studies. See *J. A. Weisheipl,* Friar Thomas Aquinas. Doubleday, N.Y. 1974.

Development: Preliminary

[1] See below, the chapter 2.1 "Spirit" as Wind and Breath — a Mistranslation by Irish-Scottish Monks.
[2] *Ott,* Grundriß der katholischen Dogmatik, op. cit., 91; see also *M. Schmaus,* Art. Trinität, in: *H. Fries* (ed.), Handbuch theologischer Grundbegriffe vol. 4, Munich 1970, 264-282, esp. 264 f.

3   *J. Neuner, H. Roos* (ed.), Der Glaube der Kirche in den Urkunden der Lehrverkündigung, Regensburg 1958, no. 43 (p. 47).

4   *E. Drewermann,* Religionsgeschichtliche und tiefenpsychologische Bemerkungen zur Trinitätslehre, in: *W. Breuning* (ed.), Trinität. Aktuelle Perspektiven der Theologie, Freiburg-Basel-Vienna 1984, 115-142; here 125.

5   See *K. Rahner,* Theological Investigations, Crossroad/Seabury. "The 'economic' Trinity is the 'immanent' Trinity and vice versa."

6   *J. Wohlmuth,* Zum Verständnis von ökonomischer und immanenter Trinität-eine These, in: Zeitschrift für Katholische Theologie 110 (1988) 139-162, here 140-143.

7   Ibid. 144 f.

8   See ibid. 141 and 144.

9   See also *W. Breuning,* Art. Gott/Trinität (theologisch), in: *P. Eicher* (ed.), Neues Handbuch theologischer Grundbegriffe, vol. 2, Munich 1984, 133-149, 144: "Our access" is granted by "the totally congruent nature of the divine message from God's side, by the economic Trinity".

10 See above, Introduction, chap. 3, esp. the section *On the Distinctiveness of Jesus as Divine Symbol in the Context of Other Divine Symbols.*

11 In our opinion, the dialogue between religions is not helped by discarding Christology and Trinity as "intellectual constructions", locking it up in the history of theology, and beginning the dialogue only with a most general concept of "God" (see *J. Hick,* Gott und seine vielen Namen, Altenberg 1985). That might prove helpful for the dialogue between Christians, Jews, and Muslims (which is Hick's main concern), but it further deepens the gulf between the Abrahamite religions and the other religions of the world. It also means paying for dialogue by giving up one's own identity.

12 This formulation corresponds to the definition of religion by *H. Müller-Karpe* in the Handbuch der Vorgeschichte, op. cit., 228, which we have often quoted.

13 *Drewermann,* Religionsgeschichtliche und tiefenpsychologische Bemerkungen zur Trinitätslehre, op. cit.

14 See ibid. 121 and 128 ff.

Development 1.1

1   *Eliade,* Die Religionen und das Heilige, op. cit., 33.

2   See *W. Schmithals,* Das Evangelium nach Markus, Kap. 1-9, 1 (Ökumenischer Taschenbuchkommentar zum Neuen Testament 2/1), Gütersloh-Würzburg 1979, 46 f. See also *J. Schmid,* Das Evangelium nach Markus (Regensburger Neues Testament vol. 2), Regensburg 1954 , 159.

3   See *Drewermann,* Religionsgeschichtliche und tiefenpsychologische Bemerkungen zur Trinitätslehre, op. cit., as well as *C. G. Jung,* Versuch einer psychologischen Deutung des Trinitätsdogmas, in: id., Symbolik des

Geistes, Olten 1972, 323-446, esp. 379 ff. ("Christ as archetype").

[4] *Jung,* Versuch einer psychologischen Deutung des Trinitätsdogmas, op. cit.

[5] Ibid. 382.

[6] See *Drewermann,* Religionsgeschichtliche und tiefenpsychologische Bemerkungen, op. cit., 118 f.

[7] More specific questions—such as W. Schmithals' well-taken point, that the current form of the gospel according to Mark is the re-elaboration of an "original" by Mark, the structure of which is retraced by Schmithals, (see *Schmithals, Das Evangelium nach Markus,* Kap. 1-9, 1, op. cit., 50-51), can be neglected here. Our concern is the basic form of the Christian creed, which, as Schmithals says, comes before the narrative gospels—even before what he considers the oldest gospel, that according to Mark, and the later writings of Luke, Matthew, and John.

[8] See ibid. 51-52.

[9] See the survey of the history of interpretations of this myth in *Hübner,* Wahrheit des Mythos, op. cit., 48-92; also: *H. H. Schmid* (ed.), Mythos und Rationalität, Gütersloh 1988; *W. J. Hollenweger,* Umgang mit Mythen, Munich 1982; *A. Halder/W. Keinzler* (ed.), Mythos und religiöser Glaube heute, Donauwörth 1985. The difference in linguistic character remains despite the same grammar: see above.

[10] See *M. Eliade,* Myth and Reality, New York 1968, 168 f.

[11] According to *Schmithals,* Das Evangelium nach Markus, Kap. 9, 1-16, op. cit. 681 f., the motif of the witness is already present in the "original": Simon of Cyrene, who helps Jesus to bear the cross, testifies to the crucifixion; Mary Magdalene, Mary, and Salome are witnesses of Jesus' death and burial; Simon and others are witnesses of his life after death. Schmithals suggests that the author of the "original" of the gospel according to Mark intended thus to distance the events around Jesus from the myths of dying and rising Gods as they were known to the ancients. The purpose is not to give historical credibility to the event—"none of the readers doubted the reality of the 'crucified', 'died', and 'buried' "—but rather to characterize it as a single, unique event in the course of history.

[12] Of course, it took centuries of disputes among the early Christians before the Council of Nicaea (787 AD) finally decreed the possibility of making images of the Son of God. See *Freih. v. Campenhausen,* Die Bilderfrage als theologisches Problem der alten Kirche, in: *W. Schöne/J. Kollwitz/Freih. v. Campenhausen,* Das Gottesbild im Abendland, Witten 1957.

[13] See *Rose,* Griechische Mythologie, op. cit., 75.

[14] See *Drewermann,* Religionsgeschichtliche und tiefenpsychologische Bemerkungen, op. cit., 131-133; further developed in id., Dein Name ist wie der Geschmack des Lebens. Tiefenpsychologische Deutung der Kindheitsgeschichte nach dem Lukasevangelium, Freiburg-Basel-Vienna 1986, 32-66.

[15] *Drewermann,* Dein Name ist wie der Geschmack des Lebens, op. cit., 52 f.

[16] See ibid., 167 (description of the figure); also ibid., Religionsgeschichtliche und tiefenpsychologische Bemerkungen, op. cit., 132.

[17] *Neuner/Roos,* Der Glaube der Kirche in den Urkunden der Lehrverkündigung, op. cit., no. 829 and 831.

[18]   *A. Franzen,* Kleine Kirchengeschichte, Freiburg-Basel-Vienna 1965. 79; For the influence of Constantine's political conscience and experience on Christology see: *H. J. Vogt,* Politische Erfahrung als Quelle des Gottesbildes bei Kaiser Konstantin dem Großen, in: *H. Feld* etc., Dogma und Politik. Zur politischen Hermeneutik theologischer Aussagen, Mainz 1973, 35-61.

[19]   See for example *Schwager,* Für Gerechtigkeit und Frieden, op. cit., 26-38 and 41 f; *Häring,* Die Heilkraft der Gewaltfreiheit, op. cit., 25 and 37; *N. Füglister.* Deuterojesaja als Evangelium, in: Bibel und Liturgie 60 (1987), 145-154.

[20]   *Schmithals,* Das Evangelium nach Markus, Kap. 9, 2-16, op. cit., 599.; see also *R. Medisch,* Der historische Judas — und was aus ihm gemacht wurde, in: Theologie der Gegenwart 31 (1988), 50-54, esp. 51; as well as *G. Schwarz, Jesus und Judas.* Aramäistische Untersuchungen zur Jesus-Judas-Überlieferung der Evangelien und der Apostelgeschichte, Stuttgart-Berlin-Cologne-Mainz 1988, e.g. 24-26, who propose to have the word "to betray" and its synonyms "banished from modern vernacular translations of the New Testament."

[21]   According to *G. Lohfink,* Erzählen als Theologie. Zur sprachlichen Grundstruktur der Evangelien, in: Stimmen der Zeit 192 (1974), 521-532, here 527, the earliest gospel has the structure of a Passion with an extended beginning.

[22]   The "third day" is a symbolic expression in the Bible for the peak of a crisis. See Hos. 6, 2: "...on the third day he will raise us" (see the commentaries by *A. Deissler,* Zwölf Propheten. Hosea-Joel-Amos (Die Neue Echter Bibel), Würzburg 1981; *H. W. Wolff,* Dodekapropheton 1. Hosea Neukirchen-Vluyn 1976, 149 f.). Jonas was in the belly of the sea monster for three days; Mary and Joseph found Jesus after three days in the temple; Paul remained blind for three days after his experience at Damascus; etc. See on this symbolism *K. Lehmann,* Aufgeweckt am dritten Tag nach der Schrift, Freiburg 1968; *Schillebeeckx,* Jesus, op. cit., 466-471.

[23]   *W. Kern,* Der Gekreuzigte als der Erhöhte, in: Geist und Leben 49 (1976), 87-91; here 91.

[24]   See *G. Schneider,* Das Evangelium nach Lukas. Kap. 1-10 (Ökumenischer Taschenbuchkommentar zum Neuen Testament 3/1), Gütersloh-Würzburg 1977, 63-68, here esp. 65.

[25]   Ibid.

[26]   In his commentary on the Christmas story, *G. Schneider* (ibid., 67) substitutes the phrase "feeding trough" for "crib." This phrase seems more fitting to the smallness, the insignificance, and the abandonment of the child — important motifs of the story, since they were named as "signs" of the Messiah by the angels (Luke 2, 12) — than the word "crib" which has taken on the somewhat pastoral and idyllic connotation because of our Christmas traditions.

[27]   This important distinction is neglected by *Drewermann,* Dein Name ist wie der Geschmack des Lebens, op. cit.; see my recension in Theologische Literaturzeitung 113 (1988), 226-228.

[28]   *Schneider,* Das Evangelium nach Lukas, op. cit., 57.

29 This interpretation seems more plausible than the one offered by *Schwarzenau*, Das göttliche Kind, op. cit., 77, as another instance of the Jung-Neumann thesis of the ambivalence of the Great Mother who emasculates her son.

30 See *Schwarzenau*, Das göttliche Kind, op. cit., 60.

31 Because, as shown above (see chap. 1 of the Exposition, the section *The Profanation of Evil in the History of Biblical Thought: the "Fall" of Satan*, in the oldest layer of the religion of Yahweh, God still has demonic features, and is the creator of both good and evil, fortune and misfortune. The idea that God stands behind all is still present, in spite of the insight that "our crimes" make the servant of Yahweh suffer: "Yahweh burdened him with the sins of all of us" (Isa. 53, 6). But this verse is not elaborated in any way. It also seems to contradict the statement that we wrongly thought of him as "struck by God" (Isa. 53, 4). The decisive statement is that not God, but the criminal acts of men are responsible for the misery and abandonment of the servent of Yahweh.

Development 1.2

1 See the section "Menschenbilder" in: *Müller-Karpe*, Handbuch der Vorgeschichte, op. cit., 249-256.

2 Ibid. 253; see fig. 43.

3 Ibid. 230; see also below the section *The Creation of the Woman and Mother (as the First Human) by the Christian God in chap. 3.3 of Development*.

4 Ibid. 169.

5 Ibid. 235.

6 Ibid. 169.

7 As with the two skulls discovered in the Vogelherd cave near Stätten in the Lohne valley, in a layer dating from about 30,000 years ago.

8 Ibid. 340. The fact that not all skulls have such injuries does not prove that the persons died a natural death. The slaying could have been caused by other means than a blow to the skull. Different procedures would have been used for particularly precious heads that were to be treated in a special way.

9 According to *Müller-Karpe*, ibid., note 2. The alternative suggested by Obermaier (who considers the findings analogous to the customs of head-hunters e.g. of New Guinea) is not a real alternative to the sacrificial interpretation because recent ethnological studies have shown that the head-hunting of these tribes also has a ritual character, and thus has to be viewed as "religious human sacrifice" which secures the tribe's prosperity.

10 See above, note 4 in chap. 2 of Exposition.

11 From a psychoanalytic perspective, E. Drewermann convincingly shows that fear is the root of all evil. See "Exegetische, tiefenpsychologische und philosophische Analyse der jahwistischen Urgeschichte," in: ibid., Strukturen des Bösen II, op. cit., 559-571.

12 *Becker,* Die Ursymbole in den Religionen, op. cit., 120.

13 *Burkert,* Homo necans, op. cit., 25.

14 *H. Ringgren,* Israelitische Religion, Stuttgart 1965, 160; on the sacrificing of children in the Old Testament, see *Schwager,* Sündenbock, op. cit., 98, who says that such sacrifices were not uncommon in Israel. A thorough study of sacrifice to Molech can be found in *R. de Vaux,* Das Alte Testament und seine Lebensordnungen, vol. 2, Freiburg-Basel-Vienna, 1966, 294-296. See also *R. Golling,* Zeugnisse von Menschenopfern im alten Testament, Berlin 1975.

15 See *C. Westermann/G. Gloege,* Tausend Jahre und ein Tag. Einführung in die Bibel, Stuttgart-Berlin 1977, 3-270, 30: "Behind this story there is a historic process of great significance, not only for the people of Israel, but for many peoples: the replacement of human sacrifice with animal sacrifice." In the same sense *G. von Rad,* Das Opfer des Abraham, Munich 1971, 26, sees in the early form of the story "the reflection of a divinely ordered replacement of the sacrifice of a child by an animal offering". Of course, this is not the only issue of the story; see *v. Rad,* Opfer, op. cit., 26, or *W. Zimmerli,* 1 Mose 12-15: Abraham, Zürich 1976, 110.

16 See *Dohmen,* Das Bilderverbot, op. cit.; according to the review by *E. Haag* in Trierer Theologische Zeitschrift 97 (1988) 159 f., the author could have put more emphasis on the background of the prohibition of images, namely the idea of God's unmanipulability.

17 *Daum,* Ursemitische Religion, op. cit., esp. chap. 3 (32-41). See also *J. Henninger,* Neuere Untersuchungen über Menschenopfer bei semitischen Völkern, in: Al-Hudud, Festschrift für Maria Höfer, Graz 1981, 67-78.

18 For criticism of W. Daum see the (too polemical) review by *U. Marzolphus,* in: Fabula, vol. 3-4/86, 336 f.

19 See *Daum,* Ursemitische Religion, op. cit., 101, the summary of the primeval Semitic myth.

20 Nonnos dionysika, 6th chant, German translation by *T. von Scheffer,* Breman s.d., verse 174 f.

21 Rig-Veda X, 90; from the German translation in: *F. König,* Der Glaube der Menschen. Christus und die Religionen der Erde, Vienna-Freiburg-Basel 1985, 188 f.

22 *F.X.D. 'Sa,* Gott der Dreieine und der All-Ganze. Vorwort zur Begegnung zwischen Christentum und Hinduismus (Theologie interkulturell, vol. 2), Düsseldorf 1988, 29 ff.

23 The enormous popularity of the feast of Corpus Christi, introduced in the 13th and 14th centuries, may be due to the old primeval pattern of feeling and thought, in which the salvation of mankind grows from the body of the sacrifice (as in the myths of Purusha and of Dionysos-Zagreus).

24 On the dating of the idea of redeeming sacrifices see *Widengren,* Religionsphänomenologie, op. cit., 289 ff.

Development 1.3

1   See *Girard*, The Scapegoat, op. cit., 30 ff.
2   See above in chap. 2 of the Exposition, the section *Violence and Terror (Lynching) the Foundation of Human Community (R. Girard)*.
3   See *C. G. Jung/K. Kerényi*, Das göttliche Mädchen (1941), in: *C. G. Jung*, Gesammelte Werke, vol. 9, pt. 1, Olten-Freiburg 1976, 197-220 ("Die Archentypen und das kollektive Unbewußte"); *Drewermann*, Strukturen des Bösen II, op. cit., 603-614.
4   See *Rose*, Griechische Mythologie, op. cit., 107 ff.
5   Ibid. 112 f.
6   Ibid. 115.
7   Ibid. 103.
8   Ibid. 47 f.
9   See *A. E. Jensen*, Die getötete Gottheit. Weltbild einer frühen Kultur, Stuttgart-Berlin-Köln-Mainz 1966, 115 ff.
10 *Drewermann*, Strukturen des Bösen II, op. cit., 609.
11 Ibid. 610.
12 It is truly regrettable that Drewermann—with all his admirable scholarship—does not discuss the fundamental anthropological theses of R. Girard. Nor does he discuss W. Burkert's "Homo necans" (op. cit.). On the character of original sin as violent act refer to our Exposition, esp. chap. 1, section *Evil as Sin (and Satan) in the Bible*, and chap. 2 of the section *The Origins of Violence in Man's Transition to Game Hunter*.
13 This is the basic insight of Anselm of Canterbury's teaching on redemption, developed in his "Cur deus homo" ("Why God had to become man"); see also in chap. 2 of our Exposition the section *Deterioration in the Historical Reception of Jesus' Divine Revelation* esp. note 49.

Development 1.4

1   *König*, Der Glaube der Menschen, op. cit., 81 f.
2   *Schwarzenau*, Das göttliche Kind, op. cit., 61.
3   For example in the Yemeni story of "The Fourteen Princesses," in: *Daum* (ed.), Märchen aus dem Jemen, op. cit., 134: "For Afrit can only be killed by his own sword, and with one stroke;" see also the story "The two leopards Kolbi and Fuadi and the horse Buzzard-snapper," ibid. 76.
4   See *Schwarzenau*, Das göttliche Kind, op. cit., 61.
5   See the psychoanalytical interpretation of the story of Esau and Jacob in Genesis by *M. Kassel*, Biblische Urbilder, Munich 1980, 258-279; the story is used here as an illustration of C. G. Jung's archetype of the "shadow" (see the heading "Jacob's fight with the shadow," ibid. 258): Jacob fights with himself, integrates the "shadow" and thus gains the fundamental experience of God.

6   See *König,* Der Glaube der Menschen, op. cit., 97.

7   See *Schwarzenau,* Das göttliche Kind, op. cit., 32 ff.; *H. Zimmer,* Indische Mythen und Symbole, Cologne 1986, 94 ff.

8   See *Zimmer,* Indische Mythen und Symbole, op. cit., 51.

9   See *Schwarzenau,* Das göttliche Kind, op. cit., 19 ff.

10   *H. R. Niederhäuser,* Von griechischen Göttern und Helden, Stuttgart 1967, 35 f.

11   See *Drewermann,* Dein Name ist wie der Geschmack des Lebens, op. cit., 85-98.

12   This motif of the myth of Aesculapius which marks the difference between Jesus and Aesculapius, is underrated by Drewermann when he interpets its "message" in analogy to the fairy tale "Brother Death" in the sense that the divine healer does not have power over death, but is only "a power within the limits of death" (ibid. 94 f.). For the story from Grimm expresses precisely the same experience over which Christians have triumphed in Jesus, for the terrifying power of death no longer has the last word.

13   *Girard,* Violence and the Sacred, op. cit. (see also above Exposition chap. 2, section *"Violence and Terror (Lynching) as the Foundation of Human Community (R. Girard)*

14   In India, the elephant is often the "big animal" expressing the violent and powerful aspect of the divine, as the bull, the dragon, or the horse does elsewhere. The white elephant is then the manifestation of the bright and good side of the wilderness god, similar to Zeus' apparition as a white bull when he abducts Europa to Crete.

15   Following *Schwarzenau,* Das göttliche Kind, op. cit., 40 ff.

16   See *A. Waiblinger,* Große Mutter und göttliches Kind, Zürich 1986, 26-29.

17   See *M. M. J. Marasinghe,* Der Theravada-Buddhismus, in: *R. Cavendish/P. O. Ling* (ed.), Mythologie der Weltreligionen, Munich 1985, 34-39.

18   In Matt. 21, 32 the standard expression "tax collectors and sinners" is more exactly translated "tax collectors and harlots."

19   See above chap. 1 of Exposition (section *The Profanation of Evil in the History of Biblical Thought).*

20   On the interpretation of these parables see *Baudler,* Jesus im Spiegel seiner Gleichnisse, op. cit., 209 ff. (parable of the importunate friend, Luke 11, 5-8), and 210-213 parable of the unscrupulous judge and the insistent widow, Luke 18, 2-5).

21   See my interpretation ibid. 217-230.

22   See *Spiegel,* Gewaltverzicht, op. cit., 59-62.

Development 2.1

1   See also *G. Baudler,* Geist als Wind, Atem, Luft und Vogel. Ein Übersetzungfehler als Ursache für die Schwierigkeiten bei der Wiedergabe des

Glaubens an den Heiligen Geist, in: Schule und Mission, vol. 2 1987/88, 86-89.

2   *R. Albertz/C. Westermann,* Art. ruach, Geist, in: *E. Jenni, C. Westermann,* Theologisches Handwörterbuch zum Alten Testament, vol. II, Munich-Zurich 1976, 726-753.

3   Ibid. 736.

4   Ibid. 752.

5   Ibid.

6   See *H. Kleinknecht,* Art. pneuma, in: *G. Kittel/G. Friedrich,* Theologisches Wörterbuch zum Neuen Testament, vol. 6, Stuttgart 1959, 333.

7   Ibid. 334.

8   Kleinknecht in particular insists on that fact, ibid. 336 f., 355, 357, 365, 398 etc.

9   After *M. Lurker,* Wörterbuch biblischer Bilder und Symbole, München 1987, 371.

10   See *Kleinknecht,* in: *Kittel/Friedrich,* Theologisches Wörterbuch zum NT, op. cit., 356.

11   Ibid. 355.

12   Ibid.

13   Ibid.

14   Ibid. 356.

15   Ibid. 357, following Büchsel (in *Kittel/Friedrich,* Theologisches Wörterbuch zum NT vol. 6, op. cit., 497).

16   *L. Wittgenstein,* Tractatus logico-philosophicus. Logisch-philosophische Abhandlung, Frankfurt 1971, 7 (preface).

17   See Introduction, chap. 2, section *The Perception of Symbols and Empirical Reality,* as well as notes 31, 32, and 33 of the same chapter.

18   *Kleinknecht,* in: *Kittel/Friedrich,* Theologisches Wörterbuch zum NT, op. cit., 335.

19   Ibid. 357.

20   Ibid. 432.

21   Compare, for example, the stiff "Glory be to the Father..." with the following proposal of re-translation (a translation which makes the Trinitarian symbols eloquent as symbols in a theologically sound way): "Glory be to the child and to the mother and to the breath, which unites them, as it was in the beginning, is now, and ever shall be. Amen" (see chap. 3.3, the section *On the Evolution of the Maternal Symbol: The Creation of the Woman and Mother (as the First Human) by the Christian God).* The words "father" and "mother" are interchangeable in the prayer (in accordance with the children's babbling words Abba/Mama/Papa).

22   *Kleinknecht,* in: *Kittel/Friedrich,* Theologisches Wörterbuch zum NT, op. cit., 355 f.

Development 2.2

1   Lob der Musik. Gedanken und Aussprüche, collected by *A. Klose,* Kassel-Basel, 57.

2   See *M. Raffael,* Wiedergeburtsmagie in der Altsteinzeit, Berlin 1979, 55 f. Like Duerr (see below, note 7), Raffael overlooks the big spear that slashed the lower body. He interprets the hanging bowel as oversized testicles.

3   See *F. Schmeidler,* Malereien in der Höhle von Lascaux. Beweis astronomischer Kenntnisse der Steinzeitmenschen, in: Naturwissenschaftliche Rundschau 37 (1984), 218-222. As a possible *addition* to the interpretation of this picture as an image of religious initiation (see below), Schmeidler's views are valuable. Perhaps initiation into the skill of orientation by using the stars was part of the "hunting-baptism," of the immersion into the breath of the hunter (see in the same issue of "Naturwissenschaftliche Rundschau" the article by *A. Weiss,* Orientierung der Wanderjäger im Paläolithikum, ibid. 312-319).

4   This was the view of the discoverer of the cave, Abbé Breuil. See *M. Ruspoli.* Lascaux. Heiligtum der Eiszeit, Freiburg-Basel-Wien 1986 (original edition: Lascaux—un nouveau regard, Paris 1986).

5   See for example *A. Leroi-Gourhan,* Prähistorische Kunst, Freiburg 1971, 156.

6   *Müller-Karpe,* Handbuch der Vorgeschichte, op. cit., 271.

7   See *Burkert,* Homo necans, op. cit., 70-78 ("Sexualisierung der Tötungsriten"). A great wealth of materials on the sexual/erotic relation between the primeval hunter and the animal is provided by *Duerr,* Sedna, op. cit., esp. 83-94, 290, notes 25, 26 and 27; 300 f., notes 35 and 37. However, this material is often over-interpreted by the author, e.g. when he rejects as "speculation" the quite obvious interpretation of the scene in the Lascaux pit as a fight between the hunter and the bison (given for example by Leroi-Gourhan; see *Duerr,* Sedna, op. cit., 322 f., note 38). Duerr himself sees the hanging bowels of the bison as a figuration of a vulva, making the animal a "bison-woman" whom the shaman approaches with sexual intentions (ibid. 92). In doing so Duerr completely overlooks the barbed spear that sticks out of the bison's body. Quasi-erotic relations between hunters and prey are described even today by *Karin Hutter* in her "Anti-hunting book:" Ein Reh hat Augen wie ein sechzehnjähriges Mädchen, Freiburg 1988. On the significance of sexuality in the (sinful) transition from gatherer and scavenger to game-hunter, see above in chap. 2 of the Exposition, section *God as the Killing Power and the Other "Gods,"* esp. Fig. 19 and its commentary; also Fig. 20 and 21.

8   See ibid. 89; J. Ozolts, Zur Frage des paläolithischen Lochstäbe, in: Kölner Jahrbuch für Vor- und Frühgeschichte, vol. 14, Berlin 1974, 9-16.

9   Staves or stakes of this kind can be found in many shamanistic cultures; see e.g. *M. Eliade,* Shamanism: Archaic Techniques of Ecstasy, Princeton Univ. Press 1964. For the Dolgan people the world is signified by stakes with wooden birds fixed to the tops, the birds signifying the shaman's abili-

ty to fly. The same occurs with some variation among the Buryat. Here the shaman's staff is shown with a horse head and serves as a riding horse for his travels in heaven and the underworld. Staves adorned with feathers or with a bird are also used in burial rites. My own subsequent interpretation of the bird staff is confirmed by Eliade's observation that the Maori put them on their graves to serve as vehicles and as guides for the souls of the dead. Detailed descriptions of this kind are found also in *U. Harva,* Die religiösen Vorstellungen der altarischen Völker, FF Communications No. 125, Porvoo-Helsinki 1938; here especially 43 ff, 459, 547 ff.

[10] According to Eliade the Maori people sing and raise the bird-staff higher and higher in the air when a chief dies; see also the well-known representations of Egyptian scenes of death, where the "soul-bird" rises from the body of the deceased; in a similar way Luke 23, 46 relates how Jesus gives his "pneuma" into the hands of his Abba when he dies (this "pneuma," however, is *not* the breath of the hunter).

[11] See *Eliade,* op. cit.

[12] For example, "le sanctuaire" is the name of a deep chamber in the caverns of Pech-Merle, the ceiling of which is covered with red-brownish dots of ocher; see *J. Herbig,* Die Magie der Bilder und Zeichen. Wie Kunst zum evolutiven Erfolg des Menschen beitrung; in: Bild der Wissenschaft 22 (1985) 108-120.

[13] See ibid., as well as *Herbig's* Nahrung für die Götter. Die kulturelle Neuerschaffung der Welt durch den Menschen, Munich-Vienna 1988, 55-93.

[14] See *Herbig,* op. cit., 60 f.

[15] See *A. Leroi-Gourhan,* Höhlenkunst in Frankreich, Munich 1981; this conclusion of Leroi-Gourhan's research is generally accepted today, while his reconstruction of the world view of Ice Age man, which for him is based upon the duality of the sexes — and this is the perspective from which he interprets the abstract signs and lines on the cave walls — remains controversial.

[16] See *E. Durkheim,* Die elementaren Formen des religiösen Lebens, Frankfurt 1981.

[17] See *Herbig,* Nahrung für die Götter, op. cit., 60 f.

[18] See *Eliade,* op. cit., chap. XIII; here, especially the description of the "magical flight," on ecstatic techniques in ancient India. The Vedas also describe shamanistic trance: "In the drunkenness of ecstasy we have mounted the chariots of the winds. You mortals can only see our bodies..." The ecstatic person is the horse of the wind, the friend of the storm-god, spurred by the gods.

[19] *R. B. Lee/R. Devore* (eds.), Man the Hunter, Chicago 1968, enjoyed particular popularity; also see *L. Tiger/R. Fox,* The Imperial Animal. Preface by *K. Lorenz,* Dell, New York 1972.

[20] See note 19.

[21] See, for example, the report of the Hessischen Rundfunks of September 22, 1988: "Sport als Opium für das Volk oder Religionsersatz?." In the Aztec and Toltec cultures of Central America the ball game was a rite in which the ball symbolized the sun. The losing team was sacrificed by the priests who

acted as referees during the game. On violence in the world of sports see also *G. Gebauer,* Gewalt und Ordnung. Bemerkungen über die Feste des Sports, in: *D. Kamper/C. Wulf* (eds.), Das Heilige. Seine Spur in der Moderne, Frankfurt 1987, 275-291.

[22] See above, esp. in chap. 2 of Exposition, the sections *Reversion to the Fascination of the Killing Power in the Old Testament,* and especially *Deterioration in the Historical Reception of Jesus' Divine Revelation.*

[23] See *G. Baudler,* Gott im Gekreuzigten sehen. Eine christliche Sehschule für die Passions- und Osterzeit, mit Bildern von R. P. Litzenburger (slide-show with commentary), Stuttgart 1988.

Development 2.3

[1] Lecture given on October 10, 1936 in London; German translation published in *C. G. Jung,* Gesammelte Werke, vol. 9, 1, op. cit., 63 ff.

[2] *I. Kant,* Gesammelte Werke, ed. by the Königlich Peußischen Akademie der Wissenschaften, vol. V: Kritik der Praktischen Vernunft/Kritik der Urteilskraft, Berlin 1908, 161.

[3] See *Herbig,* Nahrung für die Götter, op. cit., esp. 65-145.

[4] The most important theories are summarized in ibid., 106-113. See also *L. R. Binford,* Die Vorzeit war ganz anders. Methoden und Ergebnisse der Neuen Archäologie, Munich 1984, 208-228.

[5] *Herbig,* Nahrung für die Götter, op. cit., 120-125.

[6] Ibid. 123.

[7] Ibid. 145.

[8] *S. von Reden,* Die Megalith-Kulturen. Zeugnisse einer verschollenen Urreligion, Köln 1984, 25.

[9] See *Herbig,* Nahrung für die Götter, op. cit., 167, as well as *von Reden,* Megalith-Kulturen, op. cit., 29-31.

[10] *Von Reden,* Megalith-Kulturen, op. cit., 28.

[11] See ibid. 130 and 311 f.

[12] See ibid. 235 and 241.

[13] *Herbig,* Nahrung für die Götter, op. cit., 228.

[14] *Von Reden,* Megalith-Kulturen, op. cit., 63.

[15] See *U. Winter,* Frau und Göttin. Exegetische und ikonographische Studien zum weiblichen Gottesbild im alten Israel und in dessen Umwelt, Freiburg (Switzerland) and Göttingen 1983, 342-346, esp. 344.

[16] Ibid. 343.

[17] There is a bull's head on the lower left corner of Fig. 34. See similar images in *U. Winter,* Frau und Göttin, op. cit., nos. 332, 333, 336 and 337.

[18] Even *von Reden (ibid.)* speaks of the "bull-god as partner of the Magna Mater," in accordance with the widespread idea of the bull as symbol of fertility, without backing up this identification with any archeological

evidence. We have tried above to show that the bull originally did not symbolize fertility but the *force of the wilderness* based on the wall-painting of the north entrance of the Knossos palace, in which the bull charges aggressively at a tree, a symbol of fertility (see chap. 1 in the Exposition, the section *God and Evil as Bull-Power in Archaic Religions.* The *white* bull appears relatively late, when the wilderness-power has apparently fused with light and has begun to function as a blessing, a fertilizing force, as in the myth of Zeus abducting the princess Europa to Crete and mating with her, by assuming the form of a white bull; or in the story of Pasiphae, the queen of Knossos, who falls in love with the sea-bull sent by Poseidon and conceives with him the man-eating Minotaur (here, the dangerous wildness of the bull is immediately evident as the message of the myth); or in the Egyptian bull Apis who is created "by the touch and breath of Zeus" according to Aeschylus, and "by the brilliance of the heavens," in other words: the "solar wind," according to the older account of Herodotus. An analogy to the fusion of light and wilderness-power in the white bull is found in the white elephant of India who mated with the queen on the roof of her palace in order to procreate the Buddha, the forceful conquerer of the darkness of human feelings and thought.

[19]   See also the section *A Culture Shaped by the Maternal Symbol: Crete* in the following chap. 3.3; also *J. Makkay,* Über neolithische Opferformen, in: Actes du Valcamonica Symposium 1972: Les Religions de la Préhistoire, Brescia 1975, 161-172.

[20]   See in Exposition, chap. 1.2, on the sacrificing of children.

[21]   *Herbig,* Nahrung für die Götter, op. cit., 324-359.

[22]   See ibid. 324. These figures are called "danzantes," dancers, because they were first believed to be dancing priests who, in their ecstasy, went into strange convulsions and maimed themselves in the process.

[23]   See *R. M. M. Adamas/H. J. Nissen,* The Uruk Countryside, Chicago 1972.

[24]   See *Herbig,* Nahrung für die Götter, op. cit., 398-405, as well as 393.

[25]   See above in Exposition, chap. 1, the section *Evil as Sin (and Satan) in the Bible* and in chap. 2, the section *The Origins of Violence in Man's Transition to Game Hunter.*

[26]   See *W. Lienemann,* Gewalt und Gewaltverzicht. Studien zur abendländischen Vorgeschichte der gegenwärtigen Wahrnehmung von Gewalt, Munich 1982, 36-41; *Spiegel,* Gewaltverzicht, op. cit., esp. 192-199.

[27]   *Herbig,* in Nahrung für die Götter, op. cit., 416-421 makes well-founded comparisons between the situation in Israel and in the early Sumerian city-states.

[28]   See for example the parable of the mustard seed (Mark 4, 30-32), of the seed that sprouts by itself (Mark 4, 26-28), of the fig tree (Mark 13, 28) and others.

[29]   See *C. Westermann,* Vergleiche und Gleichnisse im Alten und Neuen Testament, Stuttgart 1984, esp. 105-135; as well as *Baudler,* Jesus im Spiegel seiner Gleichnisse, op. cit., esp. 35-79.

1   On the Indus civilization see *Jansen,* Die Indus-Zivilisation, op. cit., as well as *H. Mode,* Das frühe Indien, Stuttgart 1959. An excellent survey was provided by the exhibit "Vergessene Städte am Indus. Frühe Kulturen in Pakistan vom. 8.-2. Jahrtausend v.Chr." in Aachen in 1987 (and subsequently in Munich, Arnhem, Münster, Paris, Brussels and Frankfurt). The catalogue of this exhibition (same title), Mainz 1987, contains many important articles (in the following, quoted as "Vergessene Städte").

2   See *Zimmer,* Indische Mythen und Symbole, op. cit., 107.

3   See *Jansen,* Die Indus-Zivilisation, op. cit., 10; *J. -F. Jarrige,* Der Kulturkomplex von Mehrgarh (Periode VIII) und Sibri. Der "Schatz von Quetta"; in "Vergessene Städte," op. cit., 102-111; here 111. *Mode,* in Das frühe Indien, op. cit., has already suggested alternatives to the traditional view that the end of the Indus civilization was brought about by Aryan invasions (an opinion popularized by the English archaeologist *Sir N. Wheeler,* The Indus Civilization, Cambridge 1968.) According to Mode it has not been proven that "the Aryan invasion occurred immediately after the Harappa-culture; in other words: that the Aryans were indeed responsible for the destruction of that civilization."

4   On Indra and the Vedic pantheon see *Gonda,* Die Religionen Indiens I, op. cit., here esp. 53, 57, 61.

5   This holds true for the sun-god Surya as well. He is also represented on reliefs in which he races through the firmament on a one-wheeled chariot, drawn by four or seven horses. Besides these divinities, there is also Savitar, the "driver who forces the sun on its course with raised arms" (*Gonda,* Die Religionen Indiens I, op. cit., 230, 94); see as a contrast the Egyptian idea that during the course of the day the barque of the sun sails alongside the belly of the nourishing celestial cow Hathor. The steady, calm character of the light is also the transcendent dimension expressed in the Greek sun-god Apollo.

6   See *Zimmer,* Indische Mythen, op. cit., 102-114.

7   From *Gonda,* Die Religionen Indiens I, op. cit., 139; more thoroughly: *H. Krick,* Das Ritual der Feuergründung (Agnyadheya), Vienna 1982.

8   See *Gonda,* Die Religionen Indiens I, op. cit., 139.

9   *Rose,* Griechische Mythologie, op. cit., 43.

10   According to *Zimmer,* Indische Mythen, op. cit., 108 f., the mother-godhead has always retained the highest place in the religious consciousness of the indigenous population—despite her absence in the Vedas: "...with the gradual fusion, over hundreds of years, between the Vedic and the pre-Vedic traditions, she slowly regained her place of honor. She is ubiquitous in early Buddhist sanctuaries and in the works of the classical period she stands triumphantly at every sacred place. Nowadays she is one of the greatest powers in the East." According to popular belief, the Hindu kings are married to her and receive from her the "raja-lakshmi," the regal power (see ibid. 103, note 22).

[11] Brahmavairta Purana, Krishna-Jamna, Kahnda, 47.50-161; narrated by *Zimmer,* Indische Mythen und Symbole, op. cit., 7-15.

[12] Ibid. 10.

[13] Ibid. 11.

[14] Ibid. 44 ff.

[15] On the myth of the "Origin of the Lingam" (Phallus) from which Shiva proceeds, see ibid. 143 f.

[16] On the motif of the sea of milk see ibid., 23, 119.

[17] Ibid., 210-219.

[18] The word "Tantra" (Sanskrit; meaning "texture," "text," a very polyvalent word) designates a large group of heterogeneous writings, dating mainly from the 7th to the 9th centuries AD (including some later texts). Tantra probably originated in Kashmir and Assam, but it is based upon very ancient maternal cults. The goal of all tantric dialogues is "salvation." The most noteworthy detail of the way of salvation is the "sacred libido," sexuality as a sacrament, celebrated after the transubstantiation of man and woman into god and goddess. See on the Hindu Tantra: *A. Bharati,* The Tantric Tradition, London (Methuen) 1965, and on the Buddhist Tantra: *M. Eliade,* Yoga: Immortality and Freedom, Princeton Univ. Press; *C. S. George,* The Candamaharosana Tantra, New Haven (American Oriental Society) 1974.

[19] *Zimmer,* Indische Mythen, op. cit., 21-24.

[20] See ibid., 10.

[21] See *U. Tworuschka,* Die vielen Namen Gottes. Weltreligionen heute, Gütersloh 1985, 127.

[22] Ibid. 168.

[23] See ibid. 136.

[24] *Eliade,* Yoga, op. cit.

[25] Ibid.

[26] See *I. H. Schultz,* Das autogene Training. Konzentrative Selbstentspannung. Versuch einer klinisch-praktischen Darstellung, Stuttgart 1986; see also *E. Müller,* Bewußter leben durch Autogenes Training und richtiges Atmen. Übungsanleitungen zu Autogenem Training, Atemtraining und meditative Übungen durch gelenkte Phantasien, Reinbek bei Hamburg 1983; *E. Postmeyer,* Autogenes Training für Christen, Düsseldorf 1985.

[27] See *A. Thannippara,* Art. Brahman, in: *König/Waldenfels,* Lexikon der Religionen, op. cit., 74.

[28] See ibid.

[29] See *E. Fromm,* To Have or to Be. Harper and Row, New York; 1976; but see also *B. Staehelin,* Haben und Sein. Vom Wesen der zweiten Wirklichkeit der Natur jedes Menschen, Hamburg 1972.

[30] See *F. Capra,* Wendezeit. Bausteine für ein neues Weltbild, Bern-Munich, Vienna 1984. See also the extensive discussion of New Age literature in *J. Sudbrack,* Neue Religiosität — eine Herausforderung für die Christen, Mainz 1987.

[31] See *K. Barth,* Epistle to the Romans, Oxford University Press; *I. Spieckermann,* Gotteserkenntnis. Ein Beitrag zur Grundfrage der neuen Theologie

K. Barths, Munich 1985, as well as *C. Frey,* Die Theologie Karl Barths. Eine Einführung, Frankfurt 1988. See also in the following chap. 3.1 the section *God as 'Lord and Father'? On the Approach of Dialectical Theology.*

32 See above, in chap. 2.3 the section *Where Does the New Behavioral Pattern (the Transformation within the Soul) Come From?*

33 See *A. Thannippara,* Art. Nirwana, in: König, Waldenfels, Lexikon der Religionen, op. cit., 461.

34 See *Zimmer,* Indische Mythen und Symbole, op. cit., 105.

35 See *E. Spiegel,* War Jesus gewalttätig? Bemerkungen zur Tempelreinigung, in: Theologie und Glaube 75 (1985), 239-247.

36 See *Kern,* Der Gekreuzigte als der Erhöhte, op. cit., 91.

Development 3.1

1 See *G. Kittel,* Art. Abba, in: *F. Gerhard* (ed.), Theologisches Wörterbuch zum Neuen Testament, vol. I, Stuttgart 1957, 4-6, here 5.

2 *K. Barth,* Kirchliche Dogmatik vol. I/1, Zollikon-Zürich 1952, 410.

3 *K. Barth,* Kirchliche Dogmatik vol. I/2, Zollikon-Zürich 1948, 589.

4 *K. Barth,* Kirchliche Dogmatik vol. I/1, op. cit., 410.

5 Ibid.

6 Ibid. 408.

7 Ibid. 408 f.

8 Ibid.

9 See also above chap. 1 of Exposition, esp. the section *The Profanation of Evil in the History of Biblical Thought: The "Fall" of Satan.*

10 *P. Tillich,* Systematische Theologie, vol. I, Stuttgart 1977, 329.

11 *K. G. Kuhn,* Art. Pater, in: *G. Kittel* et al. (eds.), Theologisches Wörterbuch zum Neuen Testament, vol. 5, Stuttgart 1954, 946-1016, here 992.

12 Ibid. 991.

13 The Greek word "kolasis," translated in the standard German edition by "Feuer" (fire), has the basic meaning of "torture".

14 See the well-known prayer of St. Teresa of Avila: "Solo dio basta," in: *E. Lorenz,* Theresa von Avila, "Ich bin ein Weib und obendrein kein gutes." Ein Portrait der Heiligen in ihren Texten, Freiburg i.Br. 1987, 130.

15 *Paul VI, John Paul I, John Paul II,* Wort und Weisung im Jahre 1978, Kevelaer 1979; here from the section: John Paul I, 16 (General audience, September 13), see also 11 and 12 (General audience, September 6).

16 Ibid. 16.

17 Ibid.

18 Ibid. 11.

19 Ibid. 25.

20 Ibid. For an analysis of the circumstances surrounding the sudden death of John Paul I see *D. Yallop,* In God's Name: The Mysterious Death of Pope

John Paul I. Bantam Books. New York 1984. For a counter-presentation see *John Cornwell,* A Thief in the Night. Simon and Shuster, New York 1989.

21 Ibid. 69 Address on the Angelus, September 10.

22 Ibid. 85.

23 Ibid. 17 General audience, September 13.

24 Ibid. 69 f.

Development 3.2

1 *Eibl-Eibesfeldt,* Grundriß der vergleichenden Verhaltensforschung, op. cit., 595.

2 Ibid.

3 Wherever biology attempts to extend its intellectual approach in such a way that *all* behaviors, including religious behaviors, seem to be explainable through mathematics and natural sciences, it turns itself into ideology—as can be witnessed in modern socio-biology—into a pseudo-religion, postulating certain behaviors as absolute (e.g. competitive behavior). Biology thus loses its sensitivity to the multiplicity and differentiation of human and natural life. See for example *R. Dawkins,* The Selfish Gene, Oxford Univ. Press 1976; *E. O. Wilson,* Biologie als Schicksal, Berlin 1980. This kind of socio-biological reductionism is convincingly criticized by *H. Hemminger,* Der Mensch—eine Marionette der Evolution? Eine Kritik an der Soziobiologie, Frankfurt 1983; as well as by *A. Knapp,* Soziobiologie und christliche Moral, in: Internationale Katholische Zeitschrift 17 (1988), 227-241.

4 The dating of this evidence is still quite uncertain.

5 Eibl-Eibesfeldt, Grundriß der vergleichenden Verhaltensforschung, op. cit., 595.

6 Whenever the wilderness-god appears as an ancestral godhead, the victims increasingly show gestures of subjection and surrender. The difference between the killing sacrifice where the executioner originally deploys and activates his own killing-power (and thereby ascends to the same level as the godhead, entering into a dialogue with it), and the offering of the first fruits, or offering of gifts, in which man expresses his vital joy and gratefulness by the laying out of gifts, becomes very indistinct (see above chap. 2 of Exposition, esp. the section *The Offering of the First-Fruits and the Sacrificial Killing.* This can be observed, for example, in Shintoism which, in its most ancient form, is an ancestral cult ("Clan-Shintoism").

7 *Davies,* Opfertod und Menschenopfer, op. cit., 28-41, describes evidence of that nature from Mesopotamia, Egypt, and Kenya in a vivid way.

8 See *H.-P. Hasenfratz,* Art. Germanische Religion, in: *König/Waldenfels* (ed.), Lexikon der Religionen, op. cit., 194.

337

9   *T. Moser,* Gottesvergiftung, Ulm 1980. See *G. Baudler,* Geglückte Kindheit-geglücktes Leben. Zur Bedeutung des christlichen Gottesglaubens für die frühkindlichen Entwicklungs- und Lernprozesse, in: Theologisch-Praktische Quartalschrift 127 (1979), 239-247; *J. Richter,* Himmel, Hölle, Fegefeuer. Versuch einer Befreiung, Reinbek bei Hamburg 1985.

10   Interview with *K. Wecker,* in: Publik-Forum 17 (1988), 29-30, under the title "Kampf gegen den kleinlichen Gott," ibid. 29.

11   *Daum* (ed.), Märchen aus dem Jemen, op. cit.

12   Ibid. 8, 9, 10.

13   "The Old Ogre," Turkish fairy tale, in: *S. v. Massenbach* (ed.), Es war ein-mal...Märchen der Völker, Baden-Baden 1958, 328-338; here 330.

14   *P. Schebesta,* Die Pygmäen-Völker, vol. I, Bambuti, 2nd book, Brussels 1948, 67; as well as ibid., Religiöse Ideen und Kulte der Ituri-Pygmäen, in: Archiv für Religionswissenschaften 30 (1933), 110-140, here: 114.

15   *Daum* (ed.), Märchen aus dem Jemen, op. cit., 55-69, here 61 ff.

16   After the girl has opened the forbidden door and seen the "skulls and bones of the children of Adam" before her, the narrator says, "Now she knew that he ate people, that he was evil and dangerous, dangerous for her as well" (ibid. 61).

17   See *H. Greßmann,* Sage und Geschichte in den Patriarchenerzählungen, in: Zeitschrift für Alttestamentliche Wissenschaft 30 (1910), 1-34, here 1 f. See also *J. V. Seters,* Abraham in History and Tradition, New Haven-London 1975, 41.

18   *M. Noth,* Die israelitischen Personennamen im Rahmen der ge-meinsemitischen Namengebung, Stuttgart 1928, reprint Hildesheim 1966, 145.

19   *Davies,* Opfertod und Menschenopfer, op. cit., 27.

20   See *A. v. d. Born,* Art. Abraham, in: *H. Haag* (ed.), Bibellexikon, Einsiedeln-Zürich-Cologne 1968, col. 13. Even if the legendary figure had to be attributed historically to the so-called "Apiru-people," i.e. to that group of people which had fallen socially and emigrated from the cities in order to avoid slavery, taking up a nomadic life-style, the motif of the exodus from "Ur of the Chaldees" fits them very well: it is the exodus from an inhuman oriental city-culture. See also *H. Donner,* Geschichte des Volkes Israel und seiner Nachbarn in Grundzügen. Part I: Von den Anfängen bis zur Staaten-bildungszeit, Göttingen 1984, 49. Donner counts the so-called Apiru among the socially fallen "outlaws," pushed out of the cities and villages, "who were forced to take up a nomadic life-style in a secondary way as it were." See also ibid. 71 and 125. In the same sense also *J. A. Soggin,* A History of Ancient Israel, Philadelphia 1985, 102 ff., and *J. M. Miller/J. H. Hayes,* A History of Ancient Israel and Judah, London 1986, 64 ff.

21   *W. Rölling,* Art. Ur, in: *Haag* (ed.), Bibellexikon, op. cit., col. 1802.

22   On the so-called "God of the fathers," who is characterized in the Bible by the fact that he has no name but is called the "God of XY," see: *A. Alt,* Der Gott der Väter, in: id., Kleine Schriften zur Geschichte Israels. Vol. I, Munich 1953, 1-78. The validity of these conclusions about religion in the

time of the patriarchs even today is shown by *E. S. Gerstenberger*, Yahweh—ein patriarchaler Gott? Traditionelles Gottesbild und feministische Theologie, Stuttgart-Berlin-Cologne-Mainz 1988, 78-81.

[23] On this passage, see chap. 1 of Exposition, the section *The Profanation of Evil in the History of Biblical Thought: The "Fall" of Satan.*

[24] Today the continuity between the religion of the patriarchs and Judaism is stressed especially by orthodox Jewish theologians and by American scholars of religious history: see *F. M. Cross*, Yahweh and the God of the Patriarchs, in: Harvard Theological Review 55 (1962), 225-259.

[25] See *Davies*, Opfertod und Menschenopfer, op. cit., 32-37.

[26] *Gerstenberger*, Yahweh, op. cit., 48.

[27] See Exposition chap. I, section: *The Profanation of Evil in the History of Biblical Thought: The "Fall" of Satan.*

[28] *John Paul I*, in: *Paul VI/John Paul I/John Paul II*, Wort und Weisung im Jahre 1978, op. cit., 17.

[29] This biographical interpretation of the parable is further developed in *Baudler*, Jesus im Spiegel seiner Gleichnisse, op. cit., 131-243, here: 231 ff.

[30] English language readers are referred to N. J. Dawood's lucid translation of "The Koran" (Viking-Penguin Books, New York). On the significance of Abraham for Islam, see also *R. Paret*, Der Koran. Kommentar und Konkordanz, Stuttgart-Berlin-Cologne-Mainz 1971, 28 (but Paret does not number the verses according to what he calls "standard numbering," see ibid. 33).

[31] See *K. W. Tröger*, Mohammed und Abraham, in: Kairos 22 (1980), 188-200, esp. 193, where Abraham is pointed out by Mohammed, already in Mecca, as "defender of the pure faith in God"; see also sura 53, 38; 37, 81 ff.; 51, 24 ff., etc. See *Paret*, Der Koran, op. cit., 28 (on sura 2, 124-141): "Mohammed himself believed he was able to identify his own religion with the faith of the forefather Abraham and thus claimed for himself and for his community priority over Judaism (and Christianity)." See the biography of Mohammed: *E. Dinet/El Hadj Sliman Ben Ibrahim*, La vie de Mohammed. Prophète d'Allah, Paris 1975.

[32] Nevertheless, Jews and Christians enjoy as "holders of scripture" a special status in conquered regions. They were treated as "dhimmis" (entrusted ones) who were allowed to practice their religion and manage their own affairs on the condition of the payment of a certain tax. See *T. Mooren*, "Kein Zwang in der Religion." Zum Verständnis von Sure 2, 256 mit einem Beispiel aus einem indonesischen Korankommentar, in: Zeitschrift für Missions- und Religionswissenschaft 72 (1988), 118-136; here esp. 118 f; also *K. W. Tröger*, Kein Zwang in der Religion? Zur Frage der Toleranz im Islam gegenüber Nichtgläubigen, Andersgläubigen und den eigenen Glaubensgenossen, in: Kairos, NF 26 (1984) 89-101; here esp. 94-98.

[33] However, it is said in sura 5, 83 that they are closest to the faithful "in love," whereas "Jews and idolators are the worst enemies" (see *Tröger*, Kein Zwang in der Religion?, op. cit., 95).

[34] See *J. Horovitz*, quoted from *Paret*, Der Koran, op. cit., 33 (on sura 2, 136): "When it is said in verse 130 (standard counting 136) of the prophets that

"we make no difference between them," what is meant is that all their revelations have the same content of truth, but not that there are no differences in rank, for such differences are recognized expressively in sura 2, 254 (253)...."

35 This reforming zeal is expressed in the well-known term of "jihad" (most frequently translated as "holy war"). But originally the term meant "to be eager," "to toil," "to commit oneself with one's life and possessions" (including armed struggle). See *M. Tworuschka,* Gihad im Islam-Bedeutung und Wandel eines Phänomens, in: Symbolon, vol. 8 NF, Cologne 1986, 60-74; here esp. 61 ff.; as well as: *H. Zirker,* Allah—ein kriegerischer Gott?, in: Katechetische Blätter 113 (1988), 171-179.

36 For more details, see the section "Islam and the Holders of Scripture—The Relation between Muslims, Jews, and Christians" in the article by *Trüger* mentioned in note 32, ibid. 94-98.

37 According to Islamic commentaries on the Koran, the genuine Islamic understanding of God is expressed particularly in sura 2, 256, called "On the Throne": "Allah! There is no God save Him, the Living, the Eternal. He neither slumbers nor sleeps. To Him belongs everything in the heavens and in the earth. Who can intercede with him except by his leave? He knows what is in front of men and what is behind them, but they grasp nothing of his knowledge save what he wills. His throne includes the heavens and the earth, and he never wearies of preserving them. He is the Sublime, the Immense." According to the commentary of the well-known Indonesian scholar *Hamka,* Tafsir al-Azhar, vol. III, Jakarta 1968, the Islamic idea of God, and therefore the very core of Islam is expressed in this verse "in its entirety" (according to *Mooren,* "Kein Zwang in der Religion," op. cit., 122).

38 See note 16 in chap. 1.2 (Development).

39 See *H. Zirker,* Die Rede zu Gott im Koran, in: Zeitschrift für Missionswissenschaft und Religionswissenschaft 72 (1988), 14-32: "The only way in which God is addressed in the prayers of the Koran is 'lord' (rabb); the believers therefore see themselves in the role of 'servants' or 'slaves' ('abd')."

40 *H. Küng* sees in the promise of grace the crucial point, both in the Bible and in the Koran, but he admits that "God can appear in certain sentences of the Bible and of the Koran as an arbitrary God"; see *H. Küng,* in: ibid., *J. v. Ess/H. v. Stietencron/H. Bechel,* Christentum und Weltreligionen. Hinführung zum Dialog mit Islam, Hinduismus und Buddhismus, Munich-Zürich 1984, 142.

41 *John Paul II,* encyclical "Dives in misericordia," op. cit. See also *Spiegel,* Gewaltverzicht, op. cit., 103-107.

42 See *Falaturi,* Der Islam-Religion der Rahma, op. cit., esp. 77 ff.

43 Ibid. 69.

44 Ibid. 78.—However, according to the comprehensive monograph by *J. Bouman,* Gott und Mensch im Koran. Eine Strukturform religiöser Anthropologie anhand des Beispiels Allah und Mohammed, Darmstadt 1977, 178, the "principal dogma (remains) the strict dichotomy of justice, which

sets a limit to God's mercifulness, forgiveness and love."

45   When *Falaturi,* Der Islam-Religion der Rahma, op. cit., 78, remarks that in this point there is a difference between Islam and Christianity—according to him the relation between God and man in Christianity has "paternal, therefore male features"—he did not grasp the nature of the relation of Jesus to his Abba-God in its fundamental significance (and did not take into account the more recent literature on the maternal qualities of the Christian God, e.g. the encyclical "Dives in misericordia," see above note 41).

46   *Falaturi,* Der Islam-Religion der Rahma, op. cit., 78—Besides the "religion of Law" represented by the theologians and students of law, Islamic mysticism knows a God of love, as is expounded by *J. v. Ess* in *Küng* etc., Christentum und Weltreligion, op. cit., 122. Thus we read the text of a woman who lived in the 8th century AD, in the Iraqi city of Basra: "I served God not because I feared hell, for I would be nothing but a miserable hireling, if I did it out of fear. Neither did I serve him because I loved paradise, for I would be a bad servant if I served for the sake of what is given to me. But I served him eternally out of love for him and out of desire for him" (quoted from ibid. 123).

47   See *G. C. Anawati,* Die Botschaft des Korans und die biblische Offenbarung, in: *A. Paus* (ed.), Jesus Christus und die Religionen, Graz-Vienna-Cologne 1980, 136: "The relations between God and believers are the relations between the Lord and his creatures, not between the father and his sons." See also above, note 39.

48   This is also confirmed by *Falaturi,* Der Islam-Religion der Rahma, op. cit., 78 f.

Development 3.3

1   *Eliade,* Die Religionen und das Heilige, op. cit., 33.

2   See above chap. 1.2, section *Traces From the Paleolithic Period.*

3   See *Müller-Karpe,* Handbuch der Vorgeschichte, op. cit., 264. This find is described in the context of the social situation on 168 f.

4   See ibid. 230: "The suggestion that man took part in their selection and preservation is compelling."

5   *P. L. Berger,* Rumor of Angels. Doubleday, New York.

6   *Eibl-Eibesfeldt,* Grundriß der vergleichenden Verhaltensforschung, op. cit., 598 ff.

7   Ibid. 590.

8   Ibid. 588.

9   Ibid. 737.

10   According to *Müller-Karpe,* Handbuch der Vorgeschichte, op. cit., 253, fig. 1 on plate 135.

11   See *A. Leroi-Gourhan,* Hand und Wort. Die Evolution von Technik,

Sprache und Kunst, Frankfurt 1980, 470, fig. 143, and the explanation 514.

12 See especially *Duerr, Sedna,* op. cit., 71-82, as well as 39 ff., 73 ff., 83 ff., 146 ff. etc. *Müller-Karpe,* Handbuch der Vorgeschichte, op. cit., 167 and 251, note 3; *E. Neumann,* Die Große Mutter. Eine Phänomenologie der weiblichen Gestaltungen des Unbewußten, Olten 1974. 255-266; *J. Haekel,* Art. Herr der Tiere, in: RGG III, Tübingen 1959, 270 f.

13 The findings in Stellmoor from the Magdalenian period (ca, 18,000 to 11,000 BC) are characteristic of this: a reindeer skull was found at the top of a cultic stake and the hunters had dumped thirty reindeer-cows in a lake. This and similar evidence is described in *Müller-Karpe,* Handbuch der Vorgeschichte, op. cit., 225 f.; on the interpretation see ibid. 227 f. Many parallels to this custom in modern hunting societies are found in *Duerr,* Sedna, op. cit., 81 f. etc.

14 See chap. 2 of Introduction, section *The Perception of Symbols.*

15 *Leroi-Gourhan,* Hand und Wort, op. cit., 169.

16 Ibid.

17 See on this whole question ibid., 168-171.

18 See ibid. 249; Leroi-Gourhan compares Ice Age art with the spiral-shaped figures that the Australian Aborigines draw in the sand to illustrate symbolically the myth of the lizard or of the honey ant (ibid. 247). Thus, the pictures in the caves are neither hieroglyphs of hunted animals, nor paintings in the modern sense, but rather a particular way of reacting to the transcendent dimension of reality, in accordance with the rite and in the myth that accompanies the rite.

19 *L. Mumford,* Myth of the Machine, Harcourt Brace Jovanovich, New York. Mumford sees an inner connection between game hunting and the "increase of aesthetic sensitivity and emotional richness," as he finds them expressed in Ice Age art and in the feminine idols that stress sexuality. But the connection he sees is too immediate, as proven by the temporal dimensions: When Ice Age art and, tens of thousands of years later, the representations of women began, man had already been game hunting for over a million years. If the relation had been that close, art and the representation of women would have had to appear much earlier. It is therefore more plausible that man blocked his aesthetic and emotional faculties in a radical way with the fascination of the killing-power, and that only a new organization of his brain could remove the obstacle in such a way that he discovered art and the transcendent dimension of the woman and mother.

20 This vast period of the continuous use of fire is made clear by the most recent excavations in Swartkrans (South Africa). See *C. K. Brain/A. Sillen,* Evidence from the Swartkrans Cave for the Earliest Use of Fire; in: Nature. International Weekly of Science 336 (1988), 464-466. However, conditions at the site do not allow us to determine whether the Australopithecus, the homo habilis, or both, used fire, nor can the specific purpose of the fire be determined (see ibid. 466).

21 *J. Campbell,* The Masks of God. Primitive Mythology, Viking, New York 1976.

22 Ibid.

[23] See chap. 2.3 *A Failed Neolithic Experiment: The "Solar Wind," or the Search for a Permanent Homeland,* especially the section *Where Does the New Behavioral Pattern (the Transformation within the Soul) Come From?*

[24] See the beginning of chap. 2.4 *Indian Spirituality: Calming the Breath* on the historical origin of the Indus culture and the Vedas (with bibliography). On the bathing complex see *Jansen,* Die Indus-Zivilisation, op. cit., 63-66.

[25] According to *S. P. Marinatos/N. Hirmer,* Kreta, Thera und das mykenische Hellas, Munich 1986, 24.

[26] *K. Gallas,* Kreta. Ursprung Europas, Munich 1984, 127.

[27] Ibid.

[28] *H. G. Wunderlich,* Wohin der Stier Europa trug, Reinbek 1972, 261.

[29] According to *Eibl-Eibesfeldt,* Grundriß der vergleichenden Verhaltensforschung, op. cit., 600, the behavior of climbing or jumping over the lower-ranking individual (the so-called "bluff over") is a sign of extreme "arrogance" and manifestation of power in the conflicts of hierarchy among herds of chimpanzees.

[30] E.g. on an earthenware rhyton from Kumasa. See also *Duerr,* Sedna, op. cit., 179 and 180.

[31] *Wunderlich's* somewhat somber interpretation of Crete in Wohin der Stier Europa trug, op. cit., according to which the Minoan palaces are nothing but huge cemeteries ("Burial palaces," see ibid. 155 ff.), has not been adopted by the community of scholars.

[32] See the detailed description of the discovery in *Gallas,* Kreta. Ursprung Europas, op. cit., 148-150.

[33] On the decline of this culture see chap. 2.4 the section *Historic Origins: The Civilization of the Indus and the Vedas.*

[34] *Gallas,* Kreta. Ursprung Europas, op. cit., 30.

[35] See chap. 2.3 the section *The Old "Hunter's Breath" Fuses with the New "Solar Wind."*

[36] See *Baudler,* Zum Ursprung der religiösen Symbolik: "Archetypen der Seele" (C. G. Jung) oder wahrgenommene Wirklichkeit, op. cit.

[37] *V. Propp,* Die historischen Wurzeln des Zaubermärchens. Translated from Russian by M. Pfeiffer, Munich-Vienna 1987. The earlier work of *V. Propp,* Morphologie des Märchens, Vienna-Munich 1972, which has gained international attention, views fairy tales from the same historical perspective. Recently this perspective has also been taken by *W. Daum,* Ursemitische Religion, op. cit.; in a similar way: *A. Nitschke,* Soziale Ordnungen im Spiegel der Märchen, vol. I: Das frühe Europa, Stuttgart-Bad Cannstatt 1976, and vol. 2: Stabile Verhaltensweisen der Völker in unserer Zeit, Stuttgart-Bad Cannstatt 1977; *H. Gehrts/G. Lademann-Priemer* (ed.), Schamanentum und Zaubermärchen, Kassel 1986; see also *F. von der Leyen/K. Schier,* Das Märchen. Heidelberg 1959; as well as *W. E. Peuckert,* Deutsches Volkstum in Märchen und Sage. Schwank und Rätsel, Berlin 1938.

[38] *Propp,* Historische Wurzeln des Zaubermärchens, op. cit., 462.

[39] Ibid. 452.

40 Ibid. 158, here in relation to the motif of the "sleeping beauty" (as in the fairy tales of Snow-White and Sleeping Beauty).

41 Ibid. 132.

42 The inappropriate treatment of the thematic fusion of the woman and maiden in fairy tales is also criticized by *W. Scherf* in his review in Bayerischen Jahrbuch für Volkskunde, Volkach am Main 1988, 225-226.

43 This is also criticized by *G. Ueding* in his discussion of Propp's work in the series "Das wissenschaftliche Buch" of the Hessischer Rundfunk radio station, in a broadcast of June 25, 1987.

44 *Propp,* Historische Wurzeln des Zaubermärchens, op. cit., 454.

45 See *Müller-Karpe,* Handbuch der Vorgeschichte, op. cit., 170, concerning the hypothesis of "priests," "sorcerers," "shamans" etc. for the later Palaeolithic period: "It should be clear that we cannot get any specific idea about these persons of exceptional spiritual awareness by referring to cultic persons from contemporary ethnic groups." A similar argument might also apply to the question of the origins of the motifs from the magical fairy tale. See also *Thiel,* Religionsethnologie, op. cit., 10: "...we know that we cannot reach primeval people with the help of ethnology" (Despite such reservations *Duerr,* Sedna, op. cit., uses ethnological comparisons in a sometimes immoderate way).

46 See *Daum,* Ursemitische Religion, op. cit., 216 ff.

47 *Propp,* Die historischen Wurzeln des Zaubermärchens, op. cit., 24.

48 See *M. Lüthi,* Es war einmal..., Göttingen 1977, as well as: Ibid., ...so leben sie noch heute, Göttingen 1976.

49 *Daum* (ed.), Märchen aus dem Jemen, op. cit., 130-145.

50 *Daum,* Ursemitischer Mythos, op. cit., 26 f., 50 f.

51 See chap. 2.3 the section *The Old "Hunter's Breath" Fuses with the New "Solar Wind."*

52 Eventually it is this wall that grants Gilgamesh the immortality he had been longing for. The epic begins and ends with a hymn of praise for this wall. See *H. Schmökel* (ed. and transl.), Das Gilgamesch-Epos, Stuttgart etc. 1966, 23 and 112.

53 See *Daum,* Ursemitischer Mythos, op. cit., 15 ff.

54 See the complaint of the citizens of Uruk about the bonded labor during the building of the wall in the Gilgamesh epic: "...Gilgamesh does not let the son go to his father, nor the girl to her lover...toil without end by day and by night." In another story, the drum with which Gilgamesh urges the citizens of Uruk "by day and by night" to build the wall becomes a sort of mythical object, falling into the underworld and being rescued by Gilgamesh's friend Enkidu (see *Schmökel,* Das Gilgamesch-Epos, op. cit., 27 and 113 f.).

55 On the history of the reception of Genesis 1, 28 see — besides the bitter complaints in *C. Amery,* Das Ende der Vorsehung, Reinbek 1972, and *E. Drewermann,* Der tödliche Fortschritt, Von der Zerstörung der Erde und des Menschen im Erbe des Christentums, Regensburg 1981 — *U. Krolzik,* Umweltkrise-Folge des Christentums, Stuttgart-Berlin 1979, as well as *K. Koch,* Gestaltet die Erde, doch heget das Leben! Einige Klarstellungen zum

dominium terrae in Genesis 1, in: *H. -G. Geyer* (ed.), Wenn nicht jetzt, wann dann?, Neukirchen 1983, 23-26, and especially *E. Zenger,* Gottes Bogen in den Wolken. Untersuchungen zu Komposition und Theologie der priesterschriftlichen Urgeschichte, Stuttgart 1987 (here especially the postscript to the 2d edition, ibid. 213-220, with an up-to-date and expanded bibliography).

[56] See *Daum,* Ursemitische Religion, op. cit., 166 f., who reports specifically on rites of circumcision in Southern Arabia and describes them as a struggle against the "powers of evil." Even in Israel the element of struggle against El is not altogether overcome. The patriarchs tell stories about the fight of the light-hero Jacob with El at the ford of the river (Gen. 32, 23-33), in which Jacob prevails although injured, and thus becomes the "Isra-el," the fighter with God. From this perspective it is understandable that circumcision becomes the sign of the covenant between Yahweh and his people, as expounded in Gen. 17, 1-27.

[57] See *Propp,* Die historischen Wurzeln des Zaubermärchens, op. cit., 23 f.

[58] See *Daum* (ed.), Märchen aus dem Jemen, op. cit., 73-83.

[59] See the *Brothers Grimm,* The Complete Grimm's Fairy Tales, Pantheon Books, New York 1944. 399

[60] *Paul VI/John Paul I/John Paul II,* Wort und Weisung im Jahr 1978, op. cit. (69) (John Paul I).

[61] See on this issue the recently published encyclical "Mulieris dignitatem" by *John Paul II,* op. cit. 11.

[62] See *L. Ott,* Grundriß der katholischen Dogmatik, Freiburg-Basel-Vienna 1970, 243.

[63] See *D. P. J. Wynands,* Rhein-maasländische Wallfahrten des 19. Jahrhunderts im Spannungsfeld von Politik und Frömmigkeit, in: Annalen des Historischen Vereins für den Niederrhein, vol. 191, Pulheim 1988, 115-131; the Archbishop of Cologne, Ferdinand August Graf Spiegel, complained, for example, in his pastoral letter of May 12, 1826 that on longer pilgrimages the "most crude excesses" had occurred (ibid. 123), and a mayor from the region of Trier complained to the bishop and county council as late as the end of the 19th century about the "public exchanges of signs of affection" (ibid. 130).

[64] See in chap. 2 of Exposition the section *God as Killing Power and the Other "Gods"* (especially on the "division of roles" and of "culpability" between man and woman).

[65] See *Duerr,* Sedna, op. cit., 69 f.

[66] Quoted after glauben-leben-handeln. Arbeitsbuch zur Glaubensunterweisung, ed. by the German bishops, Freiburg i.Br. 1969, 262.

[67] See *Ott,* Grundriß der Dogmatik, op. cit., 243.

[68] See chap. 1.4, especially the section *The Divine Son as Light-Hero (Independent of Women).*

[69] *Drewermann,* Dein Name ist wie der Geschmack des Lebens, op. cit., 49.

[70] Ibid.

[71] *Ott,* Grundriß der Dogmatik, op. cit., 254.

[72] See chap. 3.1 the section *God as "Lord and Father"? On the Approach of Dialectical Theology.*

[73] See esp. *J. B. Metz/J. Moltmann/W. Oelmüller,* Kirche im Prozeß der Aufklärung, Mainz 1970; also, *Moltmann,* Der gekreuzigte Gott, op. cit., 293-315.

[74] See *C. G. Jung,* Symbolik des Geistes, op. cit., 395-435; see also *H. Unterste,* Quaternität. Theologische Aspekte der Tiefenpsychologie von C. G. Jung, Düsseldorf 1977.

[75] I have tried to spell out the significance of these considerations for sexual partnership in *G. Baudler,* Einführung in symbolisch-erzählende Theologie. Der Messias Jesus als Zentrum der christlichen Glaubenssymbole, Paderborn-Munich-Vienna-Zürich 1982, 146-177 ("Sexuality, Love, God. Sexual Partnership and the Christian Trinitarian Understanding of God"). See also *H. Mühlen,* Der Heilige Geist als Person in der Trinität, bei der Inkarnation und im Gnadenbund: Ich-Du-Wir, Münster 1968.

Conclusion

[1] For an attempt to build a religious socializing process for children within a religiously indifferent society following this principle see *G. Baudler,* Kindern heute GOTT erschließen. Theorie und Praxis einer Evangelisation durch Erzählen, Paderbron 1986.

[2] See *W. Braune/K. Holm,* Althochdeutsches Lesebuch, Tübingen 1985, 81-82; the alliterations characteristic of old High German poetry express the warrior's thrust ("Weh nun, Waltender Gott, Weh-Geschick geschieht").

[3] Of course, insights for a dialogue between religions and cultures could and should be gained from other Christian perspectives as well, although no Christian will deny that he experiences the God revealed by Jesus in the harmony between child, father-mother, and healing breath of life, so that he might (and must nowadays) enter into the dialogue from the perspective of this experience of the divine.

[4] *Schwark,* Die Sprachtheologie I. T. Ramsey und ihre Bedeutung für die Religionspädagogik — "Disclosure-Erfahrungen" im religiösen Lernprozeß, op. cit., 503.

Bibliography

1. Theology

Ahlström, G. W.: Who Were the Israelites? Winona Lake/Indiana 1986

Albertz, R./Westermann, C.: Art. ruach, Geist, in: *E. Jenni/C. Westermann,* Theologisches Handwörterbuch zum Alten Testament, vol. II, Munich 1976, 726-753

Alt, A.: Der Gott der Väter, in: *id.,* Kleine Schriften zur Geschichte Israels, vol. I, Munich 1953

Amery, C.: Das Ende der Vorsehung, Reinbek 1972

Anawati, G. C.: Die Botschaft des Korans und die biblische Offenbarung, in: *A. Paus* (ed.), Jesus Christus und die Religionen, Graz-Vienna-Cologne 1980

Barth, H.-M.: Angesichts des Leidens von Gott reden, in: Pastoraltheologie 75 (1986) 116-131

Barth, K.: Church Dogmatics. Allenson, Naperville, Illinois

Barth, K.: Epistle to the Romans. Oxford University Press

Baudler, G: Zum Urpsrung der religiösen Symbolik: »Archetypen der Seele« (C. G. Jung) oder erfahrbare Wirklichkeit, in: *W. Bies/H. Jung* (ed.), Mnemosyne. Festschrift für Manfred Lurker zum 60. Geburtstag (Bibliography on symbolism, iconography, and mythology, suppl. 2), Baden-Baden 1989, 71-91

Baudler, G.: Einführung in symbolisch-erzählende Theologie. Der Messias Jesus als Zentrum der christlichen Glaubenssymbole, Paderborn-Munich-Vienna-Zürich 1982

Baudler, G: Religiöse Erziehung heute, Paderborn 1979

Baudler, G.: »Geist« als Wind, Atem, Luft, Vogel. Ein Übersetzungsfehler als Ursache für die Schwierigkeiten bei der Wiedergabe des Glaubens an den Heiligen Geist, in: Schule und Mission, vol. 2, 1987/88, 86-89

Baudler, G.: Gott im Gekreuzigten sehen. Eine christliche Sehschule für die Passions- und Osterzeit, mit Bildern von R. P. Litzenburger (slide-show with commentary), Stuttgart (Calwer) 1988

Baudler, G.: Jesus erzählt von sich. Die Gleichnisse als Ausdruck seiner Lebenserfahrung, Freiburg-Basel-Vienna 1989

Baudler, G.: Jesus im Spiegel seiner Gleichnisse. Das erzählerische Lebenswerk Jesu — ein Zugang zum Glauben, Stuttgart-Munich 1986

Baudler, G.: Geglückte Kindheit — geglücktes Leben. Zur Bedeutung des

christlichen Gottesglaubens für die frühkindlichen Entwicklungs- und Lernprozesse, in: Theologisch-Praktische Quartalschrift 127 (1979) 239-247

Baudler, G.: Korrelationsdidaktik: Leben durch Glauben erschließen,
Paderborn 1984

Baudler, G.: Der Religionsunterricht als curricular strukturierter, offener
Sprach- und Denkprozeß, in: *id.* (ed.), Religionsunterricht im
Primarbereich, Zürich-Einsiedeln-Cologne 1973, 13-33

Baudler, G.: Rez. E. Drewermann, Dein Name ist wie der Geschmack des
Lebens in: Theologische Literaturzeitung 113 (1988) 226-228

Becker, G.: Ursymbole in den Religionen, Graz-Vienna-Cologne 1987

Beltz, W.: Gott und die Götter. Biblische Mythologie, Düsseldorf 1977

Berger, P. L.: Rumor of Angels. Doubleday, N.Y.

Biehl, P.: Symbole geben zu lernen. Einführung in die Symboldidaktik
anhand der Symbole Hand, Haus und Weg, Neukirchen-Vluyn 1989

Biehl, P./Baudler, G.: Erfahrung-Symbol-Glaube. Grundfragen des
Religionsunterrichts, Frankfurt 1980

Biser, E.: Religiöse Sprachbarrieren. Aufbau einer Logaporetik, Munich
1980

Biser, E.: Die glaubensgeschichtliche Wende. Eine theologische Positionsbestimmung, Graz-Vienna-Cologne 1986

Blank, J: Weißt du, was Versöhnung heißt? Der Kreuzestod Jesu als Sühne
und Versöhnung, in: *J. Blank/J. Werbick,* Sühne und Versöhnung,
Düsseldorf 1986, 21-91

Born, A. v.d.: Art. Abraham, in: *H. Haag* (ed.), Bibellexikon, Einsiedeln-
Zürich-Cologne 1968, col. 13

Breuning, W.: Art. Gott/Trinität (theologisch), in: *P. Eicher* (ed.), Neues
Handbuch theologischer Grundbegriffe, vol. 2, Munich 1984 113-149

Bucher, A.: Symboldidaktik, in: Katechetische Blätter 113 (1988) 23-27

Campenhausen, H. Freih. v.: Die Bilderfrage als theologisches Problem der
alten Kirche, in: *W. Schöne/J. Kollwitz/H. Freih. v. Campenhausen,* Das
Gottesbild im Abendland, Witten 1957

Casper, B.: Sprache und Theologie. Eine philosophische Hinführung,
Freiburg-Basel-Vienna 1975

Cross, F.M.: Yahweh and the God of the Patriarchs, in: Harvard
Theological Review 55 (1962) 225-259

Deissler, A.: Zwölf Propheten. Hosea—Joël—Amos (Die Neue Echter
Bibel), Würzburg 1981

Dohmen, C.: Das Bilderverbot. Seine Entstehung und seine Entwicklung im
Alten Testament, Königstein-Bonn 1985

Dokument des Römischen Sekretariats für die Nichtchristen (Pfingsten 1984): Die Haltung der Katholischen Kirche gegenüber den Anhängern anderer Religionen. Gedanken und Weisungen über Dialog und Mission, in: Una Sancta 43 (1988) 201-209

Donner, H.: Geschichte des Volkes Israel und seiner Nachbarn in Grundzügen. Part 1: Von den Anfängen bis zur Staatenbildungszeit, Göttingen 1984

Drewermann, E.: Religionsgeschichtliche und tiefenpsychologische Bemerkungen zur Trinitätslehre, in: *W. Breuning* (ed.), Trinität. Aktuelle Perspektiven der Theologie, Freiburg-Basel-Vienna 1984, 115-142

Drewermann, E.: Der tödliche Fortschritt. Von der Zerstörung der Erde und des Menschen im Erbe des Christentums, Regensburg 1981

Drewermann, E.: Dein Name ist wie der Geschmack des Lebens. Tiefenpsychologische Deutung der Kindheitsgeschichte nach dem Lukasevangelium, Freiburg-Basel-Vienna 1986

Drewermann, E.: Strukturen des Bösen, vol. II (Die jahwistische Urgeschichte in psychoanalytischer Sicht), Munich-Paderborn-Vienna 1983

D'Sa, F.X.: Gott der Dreieine und der All-Ganze. Vorwort zur Begegnung zwischen Christentum und Hinduismus, Düsseldorf 1988

Ehrlich, A.B.: Randglossen zur hebräischen Bibel. Textkritisches, Sprachliches und Sachliches, vol. 3, Hildesheim 1968

Engel, H: Grundlinien neuerer Hypothesen über die Entstehung und Gestalt der frühisraelitischen Stämmegesellschaft, in: Bibel und Kirche 38 (1983) 50-53

Faber, H.: Das Problem der Projektion in der Religion, in: Pastoraltheologie 75 (1986/87) 327-337

Forte, B.: Jesus von Nazaret. Geschichte Gottes—Gott der Geschichte, Mainz 1984

Franzen, A.: Kleine Kirchengeschichte, Freiburg-Basel-Vienna 1965

Frey, C.: Die Theologie Karl Barths. Eine Einführung, Frankfurt 1985

Fries, H. (ed.): Handbuch theologischer Grundbegriffe vol. 4 (of the paperback-edition), Munich 1970

Galling, K.: Die Bücher der Chronik, Esra, Nehemia (Das Alte Testament Deutsch, part 12), Göttingen 1954

Gemeinsame Synode. Offizielle Gesamtausgabe I and II, Freiburg-Basel-Vienna 1977

Gerstenberger, E.S.: Jahwe—ein patriarchaler Gott? Traditionelles Gottesbild und feministische Theologie, Stuttgart-Berlin-Cologne-Mainz 1988 glauben—leben—handeln. Arbeitsbuch zur Glaubensunterweisung, edited by the German bishops, Freiburg i. Br. 1969

Greshake, G.: Der Preis der Liebe. Besinnung über das Leid, Freiburg-Basel-Vienna 1978

Greshake, G.: Der Wandel der Erlösungsvorstellungen in der Theologiegeschichte, in: *L. Scheffczyk* (ed.), Erlösung und Emanzipation, Freiburg i. Br. 1973, 69-101

Greßmann, H.: Sage und Geschichte zu den Patriarchenerzählungen, in: Zeitschrift für Alttestamentliche Wissenschaft 30 (1910) 1-34

Haag, E.: Book review of C. Dohmen, Das Bilderverbot, in: Trierer Theologische Zeitschrift 97 (1988) 159f.

Haag, H: Abschied vom Teufel, Einsiedeln 1984

Haag, H. (ed.): Bibellexikon, Einsiedeln-Zürich-Cologne 1968

Haag, H.: Der Teufel. Mythos und Geschichte, in: Katechetische Blätter 111 (1986) 778-781

Häring, B.: Die Heilkraft der Gewaltfreiheit, Düsseldorf 1986

Hahn, J.: Das »goldene Kalb«. Die Jahwe-Verehrung bei Stierbildern in der Geschichte Israels, Frankfurt 1981

Halbfas, H.: Das dritte Auge. Religionsdidaktische Anstöße, Düsseldorf 1982

Halder, A./Kienzler, K. (ed.): Mythos und religiöser Glaube heute, Donauwörth 1985

Heinen, K.: Der barmherzige Gott. Zum biblischen Hintergrund der Enzyklika »Dives in misericordia«, in: Lebendiges Zeugnis 37 (1982) 5-11

Hick, J.: God Has Many Names. Westminster, John Knox

John Paul II.: Apostolic Letter "Mulieris Dignitatem", National Council of Catholic Bishops, Washington, D.C. 1988

John Paul II.: Encyclical "Dives in misericordia", National Council of Catholic Bishops, Washington, D.C. 1980

Jüngling, H.-W.: Die egalitäre Gesellschaft der Stämme Jahwes, in: Bibel und Kirche 38 (1983) 59-64

Kasper, W.: Jesus the Christ. Paulist Press

Kassel, M.: Das Auge im Bauch. Erfahrungen mit tiefenpsychischer Spiritualität, Olten-Freiburg 1986

Kassel, M.: Biblische Urbilder, Munich 1980

Kern, W.: Disput um Jesus und um Kirche, Innsbruck-Vienna-Munich 1980

Kern, W.: Der Gekreuzigte als der Erhöhte, in: Geist und Leben 49 (1976) 87-91

King, Ph.J.: Die Archäologische Forschung zur Ansiedlung der Israeliten in Palästina, in: Bibel und Kirche 38 (1983) 72-76

Kittel, G.: Art. abba, in: *id./G. Friedrich* (ed.), Theologisches Wörterbuch zum Neuen Testament, vol. 1, Stuttgart 1957, 4-6

Kleinknecht, H.: Art. pneuma, in: *G. Kittel/G. Friedrich,* (ed), Theologisches Wörterbuch zum Neuen Testament, vol. 6, Stuttgart 1959, 333ff.

Knapp, A.: Soziobiologie und christliche Moral, in: Internationale Katholische Zeitschrift 17 (1988) 227-241

Knitter, P.: Ein Gott—viele Religionen. Gegen den Absolutheitsanspruch des Christentums, Munich 1988

Knitter, P.: Katholische Religionstheologie am Scheideweg, in: Concilium 22 (1986) 63-68

Koch, K.: Gestaltet die Erde, doch heget das Leben! Einige Klarstellungen zum dominium terrae in Genesis 1, in: *H.-G. Geyer* (ed.). Wenn nicht jetzt, wann dann?, Neukirchen 1983, 23-36

Koch, K. (ed.): Um das Prinzip der Vergeltung in Religion und Recht des Alten Testaments, Darmstadt 1972

König, F.: Der Glaube der Menschen. Christus und die Religionen der Erde, Vienna-Freiburg-Basel 1985

König, F./Waldenfels, H. (ed.): Lexikon der Religionen. Phänomene—Geschichte—Ideen, Freiburg-Basel-Vienna 1987

Krolzik, U.: Umweltkrise—Folge des Christentums, Stuttgart-Berlin 1979

Küng, H.: Zu einer ökumenischen Theologie der Religionen, in: Concilium 22 (1986) 76-80

Küng, H. et al.: Christianity and the World Religions: Path to Dialogue with Islam, Hinduism & Buddhism. Doubleday, N.Y.

Kuhn, K. G.: Art. pater, in: *G. Kittel/G. Friedrich* (ed.), Theologisches Wörterbuch zum Neuen Testament, vol. 5, Stuttgart 1957, 946-1016

Lehmann, K.: Auferweckt am dritten Tag nach der Schrift, Freiburg 1968

Lienemann, W.: Gewalt und Gewaltverzicht. Studien zur abendländischen Vorgeschichte der gegenwärtigen Wahrnehmung von Gewalt, Munich 1982

Lohfink, G.: Erzählen als Theologie. Zur sprachlichen Grundstruktur der Evangelien, in: Stimmen der Zeit 192 (1974) 521-532

Lohfink, N.: Die segmentären Gesellschaften Afrikas als neue Analogie für das vorstaatliche Israel, in: Bibel und Kirche 38 (1983) 55-58

Lohfink, N. (ed.): Gewalt und Gewaltlosigkeit im Alten Testament, Freiburg-Basel-Vienna 1983

Lorenz, E.: Theresa von Avila, »Ich bin ein Weib und obendrein kein gutes«. Ein Portrait der Heiligen in ihren Texten, Freiburg i. Br. 1987

Loretz, O.: Leberschau, Sündenbock, Asasel in Ugarit und Israel, Altenberg 1985

Medisch, R.: Der historische Judas—und was aus ihm gemacht wurde, in: Theologie der Gegenwart 31 (1988) 50-54

Metz, J. B.: Theologie gegen Mythologie. Kleine Apologie des biblischen Monotheismus, in: Herder-Korrespondenz 42 (1988) 187-193

Metz, J. B./Moltmann, J./Oelmüller, W.: Kirche im Prozeß der Aufklärung, Mainz 1970

Michl, J.: Art. Satan (theologiegeschichtlich), in: Handbuch theologischer Grundbegriffe, edited by *H. Fries,* vol. 4 (of the paperback edition), Munich 1970, 26-35

Mieth, J.: Katechese in der Küche. Kinderfragen verlangen Antwort, Mainz 1979

Moltmann, J.: The Crucified God. Harper & Row

Mühlen, H.: Der Heilige Geist als Person in der Trinität, bei der Inkarnation und im Gnadenbund: Ich-Du-Wir, Münster 1968

Müller, J. M./Hayes, J. H.: A history of Ancient Israel and Judah, London 1986

Müller, P.-G.: Der Traditionsprozeß im Neuen Testament. Kommunikationsanalytische Studien zur Versprachlichung des Jesusphänomens, Freiburg-Basel-Vienna 1982

Mußner, F.: Ursprünge und Entfaltung der neutestamentlichen Sohneschristologie. Versuch einer Rekonstruktion, in: *L. Scheffczyk* (ed.), Grundfragen der Christologie heute, Freiburg-Basel-Vienna 1975, 77-113

Neuner, J./Roos, H. (ed.): Der Glaube der Kirche in den Urkunden der Lehrverkündigung, Regensburg 1958

Noth, M.: Die israelitischen Personennamen im Rahmen der gemeinsemitischen Namensgebung, Stuttgart 1928, reprint Hildesheim 1966

Ohlig, K.-H.: Fundamental-Christologie. Im Spannungsfeld von Christologie und Kultur, Munich 1986

Ott, L.: Fundamentals of Catholic Dogma. Tan Books

Pater, W. A.: Theologische Sprachlogik, Munich 1971

Paul VI./Johannes Paul I./Johannes Paul II.: Wort und Weisung im Jahre 1978, Kevelaer 1979

Pesch, R.: Neues Testament—Die Überwindung der Gewalt, in: *N. Lohfink/R. Pesch,* Weltgestaltung und Gewaltlosigkeit. Ethische Aspekte des Alten und Neuen Testamentes in ihrer Einheit und ihrem Gegensatz, Düsseldorf 1978, 62-80

Rad, G. v.: Das Opfer des Abraham, Munich 1971

Rahner, K.: Der dreifaltige Gott als transzendenter Urgrund der Heilsgeschichte, in: Mysterium Salutis, vol. 2, Einsiedeln-Zürich-Cologne 1967, 317-401

Rahner, K.: Hörer des Wortes. Zur Grundlegung einer Religionsphilosophie, Munich 1969

Rahner, K.: Theological Investigations, vol. 4, Crossroad/Seabury

Rahner, K./Vorgrimler, H.: Konzilskompendium, Freiburg 1986

Rahner, K./Vorgrimler, H.: Kleines theologisches Wörterbuch, Freiburg i. Br. 1981 [13]

Ramsey, I. T.: Religious Language. An Empirical Placing of Theological Phrases, London 1974

Ringgren, H.: Israelitische Religion, Stuttgart 1965

Rouner, L.: Die Religionstheologie in der jüngeren protestantischen Theologie, in: Concilium 22 (1986) 69-75

Sauer, R.: Religiöse Erziehung auf dem Weg zum Glauben, Düsseldorf 1976

Sauer, R.: Die Rede von Gott angesichts des Leids in der Welt, in: Universitas 41 (1986) 361-370

Schierse, F. J.: Art. Satan (biblisch), in: Handbuch theologischer Grundbegriffe, (ed.) *H. Fries,* vol. 4 (of the paperback edition), Munich 1970, 22-26

Schillebeeckx, E.: Jesus. Die Geschichte von einem Lebenden, Freiburg-Basel-Vienna 1980

Schillebeeckx, E.: Jesus und die Christen. Die Geschichte einer neuen Lebenspraxis, Freiburg-Basel-Vienna 1980

Schmid, J.: Das Evangelium nach Markus (Regensburger Neues Testament, vol. 2) Regensburg 1954

Schmidt, K. L.: Lucifer als gefallene Engelsmacht, in: Theologische Zeitschrift 7 (1951) 161-179

Schmidt, W. H.: Königtum Gottes in Ugarit und Israel, Berlin 1966

Schmithals, W.: Das Evangelium nach Markus (Ökumenischer Taschenbuchkommentar zum Neuen Testament 2/1), Gütersloh-Würzburg 1979

Schmithals, W.: Das Evangelium nach Markus (Ökumenischer Taschenbuchkommentar zum Neuen Testament 2/2), Gütersloh-Würzburg 1979

Schnackenburg, R.: Maßstab des Glaubens. Fragen heutiger Christen im Licht des Neuen Testaments, Freiburg-Basel-Vienna 1978

Schneider, C.: Ursprung und Ursachen der christlichen Intoleranz, in: Zeitschrift für Religion und Geistesgeschichte 30 (1978) 193-218

Schneider, G.: Das Evangelium nach Lukas, Kap. 1-10 (Ökumenischer Taschenbuchkommentar zum Neuen Testament 3/1), Gütersloh-Würzburg 1977

Schütz, C.: Art. Gott im Christentum, in: *F. König/H. Waldenfels,* Lexikon der Religionen. Phänomene-Geschichte-Ideen, Freiburg-Basel-Vienna 1987, 223 sqq.

Schwager, R.: Für Gerechtigkeit und Frieden. Der Glaube als Antwort auf die Anliegen der Gegenwart, Innsbruck-Vienna 1986

Schwager, R.: Der Richter wird gerichtet. Zur Versöhnungslehre von Karl Barth, in: Zeitschrift für Katholische Theologie 107 (1985) 101-141

Schwager, R.: Brauchen wir einen Sündenbock? Gewalt und Erlösung in den biblischen Schriften, Munich 1986

Schwager, R.: Der wunderbare Tausch. Zur Geschichte und Deutung der Erlösungslehre, Munich 1986

Schwark, C.: Die Sprachtheologie I. T. Ramseys und ihre Bedeutung für die Religionspädagogik—»Disclosure-Erfahrungen« im religiösen Lernprozeß, unpublished dissertation at the Pedagogical Faculty of the RWTH Aachen 1988

Schwarz, G.: Jesus und Judas. Aramäistische Untersuchungen zur Jesus-Judas-Überlieferung der Evangelien und Apostelgeschichte, Stuttgart-Berlin-Cologne-Mainz 1988

Seckler, M.: Dei Verbum Religiose Audiens: Wandlungen im christlichen Offenbarungsverständnis, in: *J. J. Petuchowski/W. Strolz* (ed.), Offenbarung im jüdischen und christlichen Offenbarungsverständnis, Freiburg-Basel-Vienna 1981, 214-236

Seters, J. V.: Abraham in History and Tradition, New Haven-London 1975

Soggin, J. A.: A history of ancient Israel, Philadelphia 1985

Sonnemans, H.: Hoffnung ohne Gott? In Konfrontation mit Ernst Bloch, Freiburg-Basel-Vienna 1975

Sonnemans, H.: Zum Verhältnis von Gott und Mensch angesichts des Leidens, in: Theologie und Glaube 75 (1985) 286-297

Sparn, W.: Leiden—Erfahrung und Denken. Materialien zum Theodizeeproblem, Munich 1980

Spieckermann, J.: Gotteserkenntnis. Ein Beitrag zur Grundfrage der neuen Theologie K. Barths, Munich 1985

Spiegel, E.: Gewaltverzicht. Grundlagen einer biblischen Friedenstheologie, Kassel 1987

Spiegel, E.: War Jesus gewalttätig? Bemerkungen zur Tempelreinigung, in: Theologie und Glaube 75 (1985) 239-247

Spiegel, E.: Pferd oder Gott, in: Bruder Franz 36 (1983) 70-71

Spiegel, E.: Einer Theologie des Gewaltverzichts auf den Spuren, in: ru. Zeitschrift für die Praxis des Religionsunterrichts 17 (1987) 142-145

Staimer, E.: Wollte Gott, daß Jesus starb? Jesu erlösender Weg zum Tod, Munich 1983

Stolz, F.: Das erste und zweite Buch Samuel (Züricher Bibelkommentare: Altes Testament, vol. 9), Zürich 1981

Sudbrack, J.: Neue Religiosität — eine Herausforderung für die Christen, Mainz 1987

Swidler, L.: Interreligiöser und interideologischer Dialog. Die Matrix aller systematischen Reflexion heute, in: Pastoraltheologie 75 (1986/87) 305-327

Tillich, P.: Systematic Theology. Univ. of Chicago Press

Tillich, P.: Gesammelte Werke, vol. VIII, Stuttgart 1970

Unterste, H.: Quaternität. Theologische Aspekte der Tiefenpsychologie von C. G. Jung, Düsseldorf 1977

Varone, F.: Ce Dieu censé aimer la souffrance, Paris (Du Cerf) 1984

Vogt, H.-J.: Politische Erfahrung als Quelle des Gottesbildes bei Kaiser Konstantin dem Großen, in: *H. Feld* etc., Dogma und Politik. Zur politischen Hermeneutik theologischer Aussagen, Mainz 1973, 35-61

Waldenfels, H.: Religionen als Antworten auf die menschliche Sinnfrage, Munich 1980

Waldenfels, H.: Sprechsituationen: Leid-Vernichtung-Geheimnis. Zum buddhistischen und christlichen Sprechverhalten, in: *id./T. Immoos* (ed.), Fernöstliche Weisheit und christlicher Glaube, Mainz 1985, 289-312

Wecker, K.: Kampf gegen den kleinlichen Gott, in: Publik-Forum 17 (1988) 29-30

Weger, K.-H.: Gott hat sich offenbart, Freiburg-Basel-Vienna 1982

Weiler, G.: Ich verwerfe im Lande die Kriege. Das verborgene Matriarchat im Alten Testament, Munich 1984

Weisheipl, J. A.: Friar Thomas Aquinas. Doubleday, N.Y. 1974

Welte, B.: Religionsphilosophie, Freiburg-Basel-Vienna 1980

Westermann, C.: Vergleiche und Gleichnisse im Alten und Neuen Testament, Stuttgart 1984

Westermann, C./Gloege, G.: Tausend Jahre und ein Tag. Einführung in die Bibel, Stuttgart-Berlin 1977

Wiersinga, H.: Leid: Herausforderung des Lebens. Auseinandersetzung mit einer Grundfrage, Munich 1982

Wilfred, F.: Der Dialog ringt nach Luft. Auf dem Weg zu neuen Ufern des interreligiösen Dialogs, in: Zeitschrift für Missionswissenschaft und Religionswissenschaft 72 (1988) 97-117

Wohlmuth, J.: Religiöse Erfahrung und christliche Sprache. Bemerkungen zur Theologie I. T. Ramseys und zu deren religionspädagogischer Auswertbarkeit, in: Katechetische Blätter 100 (1975) 37-45

Wohlmuth, J.: Zum Vernhältnis von ökonomischer und immanenter Trinität—eine These, in: Zeitschrift für Katholische Theologie 110 (1988) 139-162

Wolff, H. W.: Hermeneia: A Critical & Historical Commentary on the Bible. Augsburg Fortress 1973 (original title: Dodekapropheton)

Yallop, D.: In God's Name: The Mysterious Death of Pope John Paul I. Bantam Books. New York

Zenger, E.: Gottes Bogen in den Wolken. Untersuchungen zur Komposition und Theologie der priesterschriftlichen Urgeschichte, Stuttgart 1987

Zenger, E.: Der Gott JHWH im Spannungsfeld von Politik und Kult, in: Theologische Revue 82 (1986) 441-450

Zerfaß, R.: Grundkurs Predigt. 1: Spruchpredigt, Düsseldorf 1987

Zilleßen, D.: Symboldidaktik. Herausforderung und Gefährdung gegenwärtiger Religionspädagogik, in: Der evangelische Erzieher 36 (1984) 626-642

Zimmerli, W.: 1 Mose 12-15: Abraham, Zürich 1976

Zirker, H.: Allah—ein kriegerischer Gott?, in: Katechetische Blätter 113 (1988) 171-179

Zirker, H.: Die Rede zu Gott im Koran, in: Zeitschrift für Missionswissenschaft und Religionswissenschaft 72 (1988) 14-32

2. Cultural and Religious History, Philosophy and Psychology

Adams R. M. M./Nissen H. J.: The Uruk Countryside, Chicago 1972

Bächthold-Stäubli, H. (Ed.): Handwörterbuch des deutschen Aberglaubens, vol. VIII, Berlin-Leipzig 1936/37

Bharati, A.: The Tantric Tradition, London (Methuen) 1965

Binford, L. R.: Die Vorzeit war ganz anders. Methoden und Ergebnisse der neuen Archäologie, Munich 1984

Boumann, J.: Gott und Mensch im Koran. Eine Strukturform religiöser Anthropologie anhand des Beispiels Allah und Muhammad, Darmstadt 1977

Brain, C. K./Sillen, A.: Evidence from the Swartkrans Cave for the Earliest Use of Fire, in: Nature. International Weekly of Science 336 (1988) 464-466

Braune, W./Holm, K.: Althochdeutsches Lesebuch, Tübingen 1985

Brothers Grimm.: The Complete Grimm's Fairy Tales. Pantheon Books 1944

Burkert, W.: Anthropologie des religiösen Opfers: die Sakralisierung der Gewalt. Published by the Carl-Friedrich-von-Siemens-Stiftung, Munich, 1984

Burkert, W.: Homo Necans: The Anthropology of Ancient Greek Sacrificial Ritual and Myth. Univ. of California Press

Burkolter-Trachsel, M.: Der Drache: Das Symbol und der Mensch, Bern 1981

Campbell, J.: The Masks of God. Penguin Books

Capra, F.: The Turning Point. Bantam Books 1987

Cavendish, R.: Man, Myth and Magic: The Illustrated Encyclopedia of Mythology, Religion and the Unknown. Marshall Cavendish

Cordwell, J. M.: The Very Human Arts of Transformation, in: *J. M. C. Schwarz/R. A. Schwarz* (ed.), The Fabrics of Culture, The Hague 1979

Daum, W. (ed.): Märchen aus dem Jemen. Mythen und Märchen aus dem Reich Saba, Cologne 1983

Daum, W.: Ursemitische Religion, Stuttgart-Berlin-Cologne-Mainz 1985

Davies, N.: Human Sacrifice in History and Today. (Dorset Press Reprints Series) Hippocrene Books 1988

Dawkins, R.: The Selfish Gene. Oxford Univ. Press 1978

Dinet, E./El Hadj Sliman Ben Ibrahim: La vie de Mohammed. Prophète d'Allah, Paris 1975

Döbler, H.: Kultur- und Sittengeschichte der Welt. Magie, Mythos, Religion, München-Gütersloh-Vienna 1971

Duerr, H. P.: Sedna oder Die Liebe zum Leben, Frankfurt 1985

Durkheim, E.: The Elementary Forms of the Religious Life. Free Press 1965

Eibl-Eibesfeldt, J.: Grundriß der vergleichenden Verhaltensforschung. Ethologie, Munich-Zürich 1987

Eibl-Eibesfeldt, J.: Love and Hate: The Natural History of Behavior Patterns. Schocken Books 1987

Eliade, M.: Myth and Reality, Harper-Row, New York 1968

Eliade, M.: Die Religionen und das Heilige, Salzburg 1954

Eliade, M.: Shamanism: Archaic Techniques of Ecstasy. Penguin Books 1989

Eliade, M.: Yoga: Immortality and Freedom. Princeton Univ. Press 1970

Falaturi, A.: Der Islam — Religion der Rahma, der Barmherzigkeit, in: *id.* et al. (ed.), Universale Vaterschaft Gottes. Begegnung der Religionen, Freiburg 1987, 67-87

Falaturi, A. et al. (ed.). Universale Vaterschaft Gottes. Begegnung der Religionen, Freiburg 1987

Frankl, V. E.: Psychotherapy and Existentialism. Pocket Books 1985

Frankl, V. E.: Der Wille zum Sinn. Ausgewählte Vorträge über Logotherapie, Bern 1982

Franz, M.-L. v.: Der Individuationsprozeß, in: *C. G. Jung* et al., Der Mensch und seine Symbole, Olten-Freiburg 1979, 160-229

Fromm, E.: Anatomie der menschlichen Destruktivität, Stuttgart 1974

Fromm, E.: Haben oder Sein. Die seelischen Grundlagen einer neuen Gesellschaft, Stuttgart 1976

Gadamer, H.: Truth and Method. Continuum 1988

Gallas, K.: Kreta. Ursprung Europas, Munich 1984

Gallas, K.: Kreta. Von den Anfängen Europas bis zur kreto-venezianischen Kunst, Cologne 1986

Gebauer, G.: Gewalt und Ordnung. Bemerkungen über die Feste des Sports, in: *D. Kamper/C. Wulf* (ed.), Das Heilige. Seine Spur in der Moderne, Frankfurt 1987, 275-291

Gehrts, H./Lademan-Priemer, G. (ed.): Schamanentum und Zaubermärchen, Kassel 1986

Girard, R.: Das Ende der Gewalt. Analyse des Menschheitsverhängnisses, Freiburg-Basel-Vienna 1983

Girard, R.: Violence and the Sacred. Johns Hopkins 1979

Girard, R.: The Scapegoat. Johns Hopkins 1989

Gonda, J.: Die Religionen Indiens, vol. I (Stuttgart 1960) and II (Stuttgart 1963)

Gottschalk, H.: Lexikon der Mythologie der europäischen Völker. Götter, Mysterien, Kulte und Symbole—Heroen und Sagengestalten der Mythen, Berlin 1973

Grom, B.: Sinnzentrierte Lebens- und Heilkunst. Die Logotherapie Viktor E. Frankls, in: Stimmen der Zeit 110 (1985) 181-192

Haekel, J: Art. Herr der Tiere, in: RGG III, Tübingen 1959, 270 sq.

Haensch, W. G.: Die menschlichen Statuetten des mittleren Jungpaläolithikums aus der Sicht der somatischen Anthropologie, Bonn 1982

Hardy, A.: Der Mensch—das betende Tier. Religiosität als Faktor der Evolution, Stuttgart 1979

Harva, U.: Die religiösen Vorstellungen der altarischen Völker, FF Communications No 125, Porroo-Helsinki 1938

Hasenfratz, H.-P.: Art. Germanische Religion, in: *F. König/H. Waldenfels* (ed.), Lexikon der Religionen. Phänomene-Geschichte-Ideen, Freiburg-Basel-Vienna 1987, 194

Heiler, F.: Religionen der Menschheit in Vergangenheit und Gegenwart, Stuttgart 1962

Hemminger, H.: Der Mensch—eine Marionette der Evolution? Eine Kritik an der Soziobiologie, Frankfurt 1983

Henninger, J.: Neuere Untersuchungen über Menschenopfer bei semitischen Völkern, in: Al-Hudhud, Festschrift für Maria Höfer, Graz 1981, 67-78

Herbig, J.: Am Anfang war das Wort. Die Evolution des Menschlichen, Munich-Vienna 1984

Herbig, J.: Die Magie der Bilder und Zeichen. Wie Kunst zum evolutionären Erfolg des Menschen beitrug, in: Bild der Wissenschaft 22 (1985) 108-120

Herbig, J.: Nahrung für die Götter. Die kulturelle Neuerschaffung der Welt durch den Menschen, Munich-Vienna 1988

Herder-Lexikon Symbole, Freiburg-Basel-Vienna 1978

Hollenweger, W. J.: Umgang mit Mythen, Munich 1982

Hübner, W.: Die Wahrheit des Mythos, Munich 1985

Hutter, K.: Ein Reh hat Augen wie ein sechzehnjähriges Mädchen, Freiburg 1988

Jansen, M.: Die Indus-Zivilisation. Wiederentdeckung einer frühen Hochkultur, Cologne 1986

Jarrige, J.-F.: Der Kulturkomplex von Mehrgarh (Periode VIII) und Sibri. Der »Schatz von Quetta«, in: Vergessene Städte am Indus. Frühe Kulturen in Palästina vom 8.-2. Jahrtausend v. Chr. (exhibition catalogue), Mainz 1987, 102-111

Jaspers, K.: Einführung in die Philosophie, Munich 1972

Jaspers, K.: Die maßgebenden Menschen (special edition from: Die großen Philosophen, vol. I), Munich 1967

Jensen, A. E.: Die getötete Gottheit. Weltbild einer frühen Kultur, Stuttgart-Berlin-Cologne-Mainz 1966

Jung, C. G.: Symbolik des Geistes, Olten-Freiburg 1972

Jung, C. G.: Versuch einer psychologischen Deutung des Trinitätsdogmas, in: *id.,* Symbolik des Geistes, Olten 1972, 232-446

Jung, C. G.: Gesammelte Werke, vol. 9, 1. Halbband: Die Archetypen und das kollektive Unbewußte, Olten-Freiburg 1976

Jung, C. G.: Gesammelte Werke, vol. 10: Zivilisation im Übergang, Olten-Freiburg 1974

Jung, C. G./Kerényi, K.: Das göttliche Mädchen (1941), in: C. G. Jung, Gesammelte Werke, vol. 9, 1. Teil, Olten-Freiburg 1976, 197-220

Kant, I.: Gesammelte Werke, edited by the Königl. Preuß. Akademie der Wissenschaften, vol. V: Kritik der Praktischen Vernunft/Kritik der Urteilskraft, Berlin 1908

Kerényi, K.: Einführung in das Wesen der Mythologie, Zürich 1951

Kerényi, K.: Die Mythologie der Griechen, vol. 1: Die Götter und Menschheitsgeschichten, Munich 1985

Keyes, C. F./Daniel, E. V.: Karma. An Anthropological Inquiry, Berkeley-Los Angeles-London 1983

Kohler, W.: The Mentality of Apes. Liveright 1976

Der Koran. Das heilige Buch des Islam. Revised edition ofLudwig Ullmann's translation with commentary, by Leo Winter, Munich 1954

Kreiner, J.: Art. Shinto/Shintoismus, in: *F. König/H. Waldenfels,* Lexikon der Religionen. Phänomene-Geschichte-Ideen, Freiburg-Basel-Vienna 1987, 607-610

Krick, H.: Das Ritual der Feuergründung (Agnyadheya), Vienna 1982

Landmann, M.: Das Tier in der jüdischen Weisung, Heidelberg 1959

Langer, S. K.: Philosophy in a New Key: A Study in the Symbolism of Reason, Rite and Art. Harvard Univ. Press 1957

Lee, R. B./Devore, R. (ed.), Man the Hunter, Chicago 1968

Leroi-Gourhan, A.: Hand und Wort. Die Evolution von Technik, Sprache und Kunst, Frankfurt 1980

Leroi-Gourhan, A.: Höhlenkunst in Frankreich, Munich 1981

Leroi-Gourhan, A.: Prähistorische Kunst, Freiburg 1971

Leyen, F. v. d./Schier, K.: Das Märchen, Heidelberg 1958

Lob der Musik. Gedanken und Aussprüche, gesammelt von *A. Klose,* Kassel-Basel

Lorenz, K.: Das sogenannte Böse, Vienna 1970

Lüthi, M.: Once Upon a Time: On the Nature of Fairy Tales. Indiana Univ. Press

Lüthi, M.: ...so leben sie noch heute, Göttingen 1976

Lurker, M.: Adler und Schlange. Tiersymbolik im Glauben und Weltbild der Völker, Tübingen 1983

Lurker, M.: Zur symbolwissenschaftlichen Terminologie in den anthropologischen Disziplinen, in: *id.* (ed.), Bibliographie zur Symbolik, Ikonographie und Mythologie, suppl. 1 (Beiträge zu Symbol, Symbolbegriff und Symbolforschung), Baden-Baden 1983, 95-108

Makkay, J.: Über neolithische Opferformen, in: Valcamonica Symposium '72 »Les Religions de la Préhistoire«, Capo di Ponte (Brescia), Italy 1975

Marasinghe, M. M. J.: Der Theravada-Buddhismus, in: *R. Cavendish/P. Ling* (ed.), Mythologie der Weltreligionen, Munich 1985

Marinatos, S. P./Hirmer, N.: Kreta, Thera und das mykenische Hellas, Munich 1986

Marzolph, U.: Rez. W. Daum, Ursemitische Religion, in: Fabula, vol. 3-4/1986, 336 sq.

Massen, S. V. (ed.): Es war einmal ... Märchen der Völker, Baden-Baden 1958

Maturana, H. R./Varela, F. J.: Der Baum der Erkenntnis. Die biologischen Wurzeln des menschlichen Erkennens, Bern-Munich-Vienna 1987

Mode, H.: Das frühe Indien, Stuttgart 1959

Mooren, T.: Kein Zwang in der Religion. Zum Verständnis von Sure 2,256 mit einem Beispiel aus einem indonesischen Korankommentar, in: Zeitschrift für Missions- und Religionswissenschaft 72 (1988) 118-136

Moser, T.: Gottesvergiftung, Frankfurt 1980

Müller, E.: Bewußter leben durch Autogenes Training und richtiges Atmen. Übungsanleitungen zu Autogenem Training, Atemtraining und meditative Übungen durch gelenkte Phantasien, Reinbek bei Hamburg 1983

Müller-Karpe, H.: Handbuch der Vorgeschichte, vol. I (Alsteinzeit), Munich 1966

Mumford, L: The Myth of the Machine. Harcourt, Brace Jovanovich 1967

Neumann, E.: The Great Mother: An Analysis of the Archetype. Princeton Univ. Press 1964

Neumann, E.: Ursprungsgeschichte des Bewußtseins, Frankfurt 1984

Niederhäuser, H. R.: Von griechischen Göttern und Helden, Stuttgart 1967

Nitschke, A.: Soziale Ordnungen im Spiegel der Märchen, vol. 1: Das frühe Europa, Stuttgart-Bad Cannstatt 1976

Nitschke, A.: Soziale Ordnungen im Spiegel der Märchen, vol. 2: Stabile Verhaltensweisen der Völker in unserer Zeit, Stuttgart-Bad Cannstatt 1977

Ozolts, J.: Zur Frage der paläolithischen Lochstäbe, in: Kölner Jahrbuch für Vor- und Frühgeschichte, vol. 14, Berlin 1974, 9-16

Paret, R.: Der Koran. Kommentar und Konkordanz, Stuttgart-Berlin-Cologne-Mainz 1971

Perrar, H.-J.: Mit Märchen dem Leben zuhören, Düsseldorf 1979

Peuckert, W.-E.: Deutsches Volkstum in Märchen und Sage, Schwank und Rätsel, Berlin 1938

Postmeyer, E.: Autogenes Training für Christen, Düsseldorf 1985

Propp, V.: Morphology of the Folktale. Univ. of Texas Press 1968

Propp, V.: Die historischen Wurzeln des Zaubermärchens. Aus dem Russischen übersetzt von *M. Pfeiffer,* Munich-Vienna 1987 (Russian original ed. Leningrad 1946)

Raffael, M.: Wiedergeburtsmagie in der Altsteinzeit, Berlin 1979

Reden, S. v.: Die Megalith-Kulturen. Zeugnisse einer verschollenen Ur-religion, Cologne 1984 [3, revised]

Richter, J.: Himmel, Hölle, Fegefeuer. Versuch einer Befreiung, Reinbek bei Hamburg 1985

Ricoeur, P.: The Language of Faith, in: Union Seminary Quarterly Review 28 (1973) 213-224

Ricoeur, P.: Symbolism of Evil. Beacon Press 1969

Rölling, W.: Art. Ur, in: *H. Haag* (ed.), Bibellexikon, Einsiedeln-Zürich-Cologne 1968, 1801 sq.

Rose, H. J.: A Handbook of Greek Mythology. Dutton 1959

Rosenberg, A.: Engel und Dämonen. Gestaltwandel eines Urbildes, Munich 1986

Ruspoli, M: The Cave of Lascaux: The Final Photographs. Abrams 1987

Schebesta, P.: Die Bambuti-Pygmäen von Ituri, vol. II, pt. 1, Brussels 1941

Schebesta, P.: Religiöse Ideen und Kulte der Ituri-Pygmäen, in: Archiv für Religionswissenschaften 30 (1933) 110-140

Schebesta, P.: Die Pygmäen-Völker, vol. I, Bambuti, pt. 2, Brussels 1948

Scherf, W.: Rez. V. Propp, Historische Wurzeln des Zaubermärchens, in: Bayerisches Jahrbuch für Volkskunde, Volkach am Main 1988, 225-226

Schmeidler, F.: Malereien in der Höhle von Lascaux. Beweis astronomischer Kenntnisse der Steinzeitmenschen, in: Naturwissenschaftliche Rundschau 37 (1984) 218-222

Schmid, H. H. (ed.): Mythos und Rationalität, Gütersloh 1988

Schmidbauer, W.: Mythos und Psychologie. Methodische Probleme, aufgezeigt an der Ödipus-Sage, Munich-Basel 1970

Schmökel, H. (ed. and transl.): Das Gilgamesch-Epos, Stuttgart 1966

Schultz, J. H.: Das autogene Training. Konzentrative Selbstentspannung, Stuttgart 1986

Schwarzenau, P.: Das göttliche Kind. Der Mythos vom Neubeginn, Zürich-Stuttgart 1984

Sport als Opium für das Volk oder Religionsersatz? Broadcast of the Hessischer Rundfunk Radio Station on Sept. 22nd, 1988

Staehelin, B.: Haben und Sein. Vom Wesen der zweiten Wirklichkeit der Natur jedes Menschen, Hamburg 1972

Stanek, M.: Geschichten der Kopfjäger. Mythos und Kultur der Iatmul auf Papua-Neuguinea, Cologne 1982

Steffen, U.: Drachenkampf. Der Mythos vom Bösen, Stuttgart 1984

Thannippara, A.: Art. Brahman, in: *F. König/H. Waldenfels,* Lexikon der Religionen. Phänomene-Geschichte-Ideen, Freiburg-Basel-Vienna 1987, 74

Thiel, J. F.: Religionsethnologie. Grundbegriffe der Religionen schriftloser Völker, Berlin 1984

Tiger, L./Fox, R.: The Imperial Animal. Henry Holt 1989

Tröger, K. W.: Mohammed und Abraham, in: Kairos 22 (1980) 188-200

Tröger, K. W.: Kein Zwang in der Religion? Zur Frage der Toleranz im Islam gegenüber Nichgläubigen, Andersgläubigen und den eigenen Glaubensgenossen, in: Kairos NF 26 (1984) 89-101

Tworuschka, M.: Gihad im Islam — Bedeutung und Wandel eines Phänomens, in: Symbolon vol. 8 (NF, Cologne 1986) 60-74

Tworuschka, U.: Die vielen Namen Gottes. Weltreligionen heute, Gütersloh 1985

Ueding, G.: Book Review of V. Propp, Historische Wurzeln des Zaubermärchens, in: »Das wissenschaftliche Buch« broadcast of the Hessischer Rundfunk Radio Station on June 6th, 1987

Vereno, M.: Karma. Betrachtungen zu einem Schlüsselbegriff des indischen Denkens, in: Kairos 23 (1981) 189-205

Vergessene Städte am Indus. Frühe Kulturen in Pakistan vom 8.-2. Jahrtausend, v. Chr. (exhibition catalog), Mainz 1987

Waiblinger, A.: Große Mutter und göttliches Kind, Zürich 1986

Weiss, A.: Orientierung der Wanderjäger im Paläolithikum, in: Naturwissenschaftliche Rundschau 37 (1984) 312-319

Wheeler, N.: The Indus Civilization, Cambridge 1968

Windengren, G.: Religionsphänomenologie, Berlin 1969

Winter, U.: Frau und Göttin. Exegetische und ikonographische Studien zum weiblichen Gottesbild im alten Israel und in dessen Umwelt, Freiburg (Schweiz) und Göttingen 1983

Wittgenstein, L.: Tractatus Logico-Philosophicus. Routledge Chapman & Hall 1981

Wunderlich, H. G.: Wohin der Stier Europa trug, Reinbek 1972

Wynands, D. P. J.: Rhein-maasländische Wallfahrten des 19. Jahrhunderts im Spannungsfeld von Politik und Frömmigkeit, in: Annalen des Historischen Vereins für den Niederrhein, vol. 191, Pulheim 1988, 115-131

Yamaguchi, I.: Die Lehre vom Leiden im Buddhismus, in: Neue Zeitschrift für Systematische Theologie und Religionsphilosophie 24 (1982) 216-232

Zimmer, H.: Myths and Symbols in Indian Art and Civilization. Princeton Univ. Press 1971

Zimmermann, R.: Logotherapie und Existenzanalyse bei Viktor E. Frankl, in: Stimmen der Zeit 109 (1984) 111-123

Picture Credits

1   From: H. Müller-Karpe, Handbuch der Vorgeschichte, vol. I, Munich: C. H. Beck'sche Verlagsbuchhandlung 1966, plate 44, fig. 39.

2   Photo: G. Baudler, Aachen.

3   From: G. Baudler, Gott im Gekreuzigten sehen. Slide show, Stuttgart: Calwer Verlag 1988. Photo: G. Baudler, Aachen.

4   From: G. Baudler, Gott im Gekreuzigten sehen, op. cit.

5   Photo: Photographic archives Kösel-Verlag.

6   © Estate R. P. Litzenburger (pen and ink 1955).

7   © Estate R. P. Litzenburger (drawing 1967).

8   © Estate R. P. Litzenburger (ink and watercolor 1971).

9   From: H. Müller-Karpe, Handbuch der Vorgeschichte, op. cit., plate 44, fig. 38.

10 Private photograph.

11 Paris, Louvre.

12 From: M. Lurker, Adler und Schlange. Tiersymbolik im Glauben und Weltbild der Völker. Tübingen: Ranier Wunderlich Verlag Hermann Leins 1983, p. 53, fig. 107.

13 From: H. Müller-Karpe, Handbuch der Vorgeschichte, op. cit., plate 235, fig. 44.

14 From: J. Campbell, The Mythic Image, Bollingen Series C, Princeton, New Jersey: Princeton University Press 1974, V. 422, fig. 371.

15 Photo: G. Baudler, Aachen.

16 From: H. Müller-Karpe, Handbuch der Vorgeschichte, op. cit., plate 137, fig. 1.

17 From: H. Müller-Karpe, Handbuch der Vorgeschichte, op. cit., plate 237, fig. 2.

18 Photo: C. Hansmann, Stockdorf (Germany)

19 From: Frobenius/Obermaier, Hádschra Máktuba, vol. II, fig. 78.

20 Drawing: Photographic archives Kösel-Verlag.

21 From: P. Lüth, Der Mensch ist kein Zufall. Umrisse einer modernen Anthropologie. Stuttgart: Deutsche Verlags-Anstalt 1980, p. 175.

22 Graphics: Abdel Gaffar Shedid.

22a Paris, Louvre.

23 From: H. Müller-Karpe, Handbuch der Vorgeschichte, op. cit., plate 191, fig. 1.

24 From: J. Campbell, The Mythic Image, op. cit., V. 424, fig. 378.

25 From: J. Campbell, The Mythic Image, op. cit., V. 424, fig. 377.

26 From: J. Campbell, The Mythic Image, op. cit., V. 423, fig. 374.

27 From: Bild der Wissenschaft 22 (1985), p. 112.
28 From: M. Ruspoli, Lascaux. Heiligtum der Eiszeit. Freiburg-Basel-Vienna: Verlag Herder 1986, p. 100; © Bordas éditeur s.a., Paris.
29 From: M. Ruspoli, Lascaux, op. cit., p. 143. © Bordas éditeur s.a., Paris.
30 From: H. Müller-Karpe, Handbuch der Vorgeschichte, op. cit., plate 75, fig. 52.
31 Photo: Photographic archives of the Preußischer Kulturbesitz, Berlin.
32 Photo: Ministry of Works, London.
33 From: S. von Reden, Megalith-Kulturen. Zeugnisse einer verschollenen Urreligion. Cologne: DuMont Buchverlag 1978, p. 62.
34 Drawing of a middle Syrian cylinder seal. Baltimore, Walters Art Gallery.
35 From: S. von Reden, Megalith-Kulturen, op. cit., p. 63.
36 Paris, Louvre. Photo: Archives photographiques.
37 Drawing of an Akkadian cylinder seal. Chicago, Oriental Institute Museum.
38 Photo: C. Hansmann, Stockdorf (Germany).
39 From: K. Flannery/J. Marcus (eds.), The Cloud People. New York 1983, p. 90.
40 Photo: G. Helmes, Aachen.
41 Calcutta, Indian Museum. Photo: India Office.
42 Photo: Museum für Völkerkunde, Vienna.
43 From: H. Müller-Karpe, Handbuch der Vorgeschichte, op. cit., plate 135, fig. 1.
44 Source unknown.
45 Photo: M. Hirmer, Munich.
46 Photo: M. Hirmer, Munich.
47 Photo: Zweites Deutsches Fernsehen (TV channel ZDF), Mainz.
48 Photo: I. Decopoulos.
49 From: H. G. Wunderlich, Wohin der Stier Europa trug. Kretas Geheimnis und das Erwachen des Abendlandes. © 1972 by Rowohlt Verlag GmbH, Reinbek/Hamburg.
50 From: H. G. Wunderlich, Wohin der Stier Europa trug, op. cit.
51 From: H. G. Wunderlich, Wohin der Stier Europa trug, op. cit.
52 Photo: National Geographic Society, Washington.
53 Photo: Photographic archives Kösel-Verlag.